C Day-Lewis

C Day-Lewis
A Life

PETER STANFORD

continuum

CONTINUUM

The Tower Building   80 Maiden Lane
11 York Road   Suite 704
London   New York
SE1 7NX   NY 10038

www.continuumbooks.com

Credits for plate section:
Page one: Jill Day-Lewis
Page two: Jill Day-Lewis/Sean Day-Lewis
Page three: Sean Day-Lewis
Page four: Sean Day-Lewis/Jonathan Fenby
Page five: Sean Day-Lewis
Page six: Sean Day-Lewis
Page seven: Natasha, Lady Spender/Jill Day-Lewis/ Estate of Janet Stone/ PA Photos
Page eight: Estate of Janet Stone/Jill Day-Lewis

First published 2007

British Library Cataloguing-in-Publication Data
A catalogue record for this book is available from the British Library.

ISBN–10 0 8264 8603 7
ISBN–13 978 08264 8603 5

Typeset by YHT Ltd, London
Printed and bound by MPG Books Ltd, Bodmin

To Lilla I. M. Birtwistle,
lyric poet, gallery owner and all round inspiration
(1918–2006)

Contents

Prologue

'I have just been appointed Poet Laureate', C Day-Lewis wrote to his American academic friend, Al Gelpi, on January 1, 1968, the day the news was formally announced.[1] The revelation came halfway through his letter. Day-Lewis was not one by nature to boast. The role, he explained to Gelpi, was often seen as 'being put out to grass, or receiving the Kiss of Death'. The wife of John Betjeman, one of his rivals for the job, had taken much the same line a few weeks earlier in a newspaper interview. 'If John gets it,' she said, 'he'll never write a decent line of poetry again.'[2] She was to be proved wrong when Betjeman later succeeded Day-Lewis.

The role of Poet Laureate can be both a blessing and a curse. It is an honour in a poet's lifetime to be singled out. It offers a way of drawing attention to their poetry, a mark of achievement in a career which usually offers few tangible rewards, and the guarantee of a certain kind of immortality by being included in a list that includes Dryden, Wordsworth, Tennyson – as well as the now forgotten Laurence Eusden, Nahum Tate, Thomas Shadwell. 'There were no decent Poets Laureate between Tennyson and Ted Hughes' is a proposition that has of late found its way onto more than one student examination paper.

To be Poet Laureate is also to lay yourself open to ridicule for being too establishment, too close to the royal family in an age where such proximity is taken as a disadvantage, and too ready to pop up with platitudes in verse to mark national events. Only Kipling, Day-Lewis was warned by his old friend W. H. Auden at the time of his appointment, 'was crazy enough to believe that, in recording his personal highly idiosyncratic reactions to public events, he was speaking with the Voice of England'.[3] For Stephen Spender, being Laureate meant that 'fellow poets, like fieldsmen standing round a batsman, wait for their egregious colleague to hit up a poem celebrating a royal birth or other such public event, which provides them with the chance to catch him out'.[4]

As a claim to any kind of enduring significance, then, to have been Laureate is not the first quality a biographer would want to quote to recommend his subject. Yet when I have mentioned the name of C Day-Lewis over the several years I have been researching and writing this book, it has been one of three details about him that appear to have lodged ever after in the public consciousness. Top of the list by a long way is the identity of his son. 'Ah, he's the father of Daniel Day-Lewis.' And indeed he is, though he did not live, as any father would have wanted, to see his youngest son achieve acclaim as a film and stage actor. The other two known attributes are quoted in roughly equal measure – the laureateship and Day-Lewis's role, with Auden and Spender, as one of the celebrated poets of the 'thirties.

All three feature in this biography, but the last of them takes up significantly more space. The laureateship came at the end of a long life when Day-Lewis was already ailing. This book is about what happened before. By Day-Lewis's own description he had been many men before he was Poet Laureate.

> *Suppose, they asked,*
> *You are on your death-bed (this is just the game*
> *For a man of words),*
> *With what definitive sentence will you sum*
> *And end your being? ... Last words: but which of me*
> *Shall utter them?*

'Last Words': *Pegasus and Other Poems* (1957)

PART ONE

Youth

Chapter 1

Never of a Land Rightfully Ours

We Anglo-Irish and the memory of us
Are thinning out. Bad landlords some, some good,
But never of a land rightfully ours.
We hunted, fished, swore by our ancestors,
Till we were ripped like parasite growth from native wood
'The Whispering Roots': *The Whispering Roots* (1970)[1]

Blink and you miss Ballintubbert – three or four houses, a long-redundant school, a small church and an abandoned general store whose promise above a red front door to stay open eight till late is betrayed as hollow by the rusting petrol pumps on the forecourt and the peeling yellow paper blanking out the main window. It hardly counts as a place, more just another meeting of country lanes in rural Ireland, this time plumb on the border between County Kildare and County Laois. The latter begins as the biggest of the roads that run into each other at Ballintubbert climbs gently westwards through the Oughaval Woods towards the small town of Stradbelly and the Slieve Bloom Hills beyond.

Appropriately for such a non-place, St Brigid's Church is a non-descript ecclesiastical building – an oblong nave covered by a low-pitched roof and beige-brown render. All that distinguishes it from a bungalow is the small bell on the gable end nearest to the road and the double doors of the entrance porch which protects new arrivals against the wind as it whips across the fields. On the gatepost, though, there is a modest black plaque that sets out Ballintubbert's own small claim to a place in history. 'C Day-Lewis, Poet Laureate. Born Ballintubbert, April 27, 1904. Died May 22, 1972. These limes planted in his honour by local writers, April 27, 1985.' And in the graveyard six fragile lime trees do indeed stand to attention in Day-Lewis's memory.

It was to St Brigid's in the early months of 1902 that the newly-wed 24-year-old Reverend Frank Day-Lewis brought his bride Kathleen Squires, a year his junior. They had come from Dublin to take up his first incumbency after being ordained as an Anglican clergyman. He was the curate-in-charge at Ballintubbert, on a modest but adequate stipend of £150 a year, ultimately answerable to Canon Robert Armstrong, Rector of the nearby town of Stradbelly, but in practice pretty much his own man of God.

The church – named after St Brigid's Well in its graveyard (Ballintubbert in Gaelic is Baile an Tobair, or the town of the well) – did not serve the majority Catholic population of Ireland, but instead the Protestant Anglo-Irish minority who, until 1921, ran the country as a colony of Britain. It was a rural outpost of the Church of Ireland, united in faith since 1800 with the Church of England, and therefore the established church throughout Ireland.

Many in this ruling class – sometimes also called the Ascendancy – could trace their family lines back to the Cromwellian settlement of a conquered Ireland in the seventeenth century, and beyond, and so felt themselves as Irish as the next man. But they also regarded themselves as British, and so were British-Irish, subject to dual loyalties. That is what set the Anglo-Irish apart in the land of their birth from their compatriots for whom they would never be anything other than interlopers.

Writing just at the time the Day-Lewises arrived in Ballintubbert, Daisy, Countess of Fingal, surveyed her own Anglo-Irish class, with an unflinching eye. 'The Irish landlords continued to be colonists. The very building of their houses, the planting of trees, the making of walls around their estates ... declared their intention ... They lived within their demesnes, making a world of their own, with Ireland outside the gates.'[2]

An essential part of that British-Irish identity – and hence part too of that closed-in world – was membership of the Anglican established Church. By contrast the Catholic Church, when it wasn't subject to penal restrictions, was the refuge and champion of those who worked on the Anglo-Irish families' estates and in their factories and homes, and who were excluded from any political or economic power.

The Anglo-Irish had grand taste when it came to building homes. Thanks to them the Irish countryside still runs to impossibly romantic and often impossibly uneconomic castles. And, as befitted their status as the religious backbone of the same elite, Church of Ireland vicars, however small their congregations, often benefitted from disproportionately large rectories. Like Ballintubbert House. Hidden behind trees, the only hint from the road today that it is there at all is that tell-tale Anglo-Irish sign of a stout boundary wall with a gate giving on to an avenue of trees. From the graveyard of St Brigid's, however, the rear of this handsome Georgian house and its large formal gardens can be clearly seen and admired. It dwarfs the church it once served.

Frank Day-Lewis would walk purposefully through these gardens and graveyard on a Sunday to the lean-to sacristy where he would prepare for the 11.30 morning service, the only one on the Sabbath day at St Brigid's. The wooden pews would be full, for the Anglo-Irish were unusually thick on the ground in these parts, making up as much as 10 per cent of the local population according to some estimates. Hence the need for a resident curate-in-charge.

The Midlands of Ireland was amongst the heartlands of the Ascendancy, even down to the given names of its counties. What is now Laois was then Queen's County, and neighbouring Offaly, King's County. Forming a rich, largely flat agricultural plain, the land with its natural drainage and open, fertile soil was intensively farmed by the Anglo-Irish landowning class. Some of their monuments can still be seen in St Brigid's churchyard – the Butlers, the Kellys of

Kellavil (one of whose number produced the definitive Church of Ireland hymnal), the Walsh-Kemisses and the Merediths.

It was amongst such folk that the Day-Lewises settled into what would have been a comfortable life. Expectations of the curate were clear, contained and never arduous. Day-Lewis was a diligent, unimaginative man, eager to please his leading parishioners and, though intelligent, had few fixed opinions. He was always smart and traditional in his ecclesiastical dress and conscious of his dignity as a clergyman. High Churchmanship was frowned upon in the Church of Ireland as being uncomfortably close to Catholicism and so his theology was at the Low or Protestant end of Anglicanism and decidedly unadventurous. Indeed enthusiasm of any type was regarded with distaste and dissent was tantamount to heresy. There was no call then for Frank, even if he had the inclination, to use the Bible to question the prevailing economic and political inequalities of Ireland. The unpopularity with some local leading families suffered by Canon Armstrong from Stradbelly on account of his 'modernist' leanings was sufficient warning.

Ballintubbert House is typically Anglo-Irish in that it looks grander than it is. Flat-fronted with a slate roof, it has two Georgian sash windows on the raised ground floor to either side of a wide hall and elegant stairwell. Here in twin formal rooms the couple would entertain leading members of their congregation. The five front-facing first floor windows give on to just two bedrooms. It was in what was then the shabbier wing at the back, and the basement floor below, that the real domestic business of the house would be done, largely by servants, away from the eyes and concern of the visitors.

The stiff but undeniably handsome new curate and his young, pretty and vivacious wife soon found themselves swept up in the afternoon teas, tennis parties and picnics of the Anglo-Irish families of the area. As a graduate of Trinity College, Dublin, Day-Lewis would have earned immediate respect. His kinship through his mother with the highborn Butler clan also served him well in such circles around Ballintubbert for the Anglo-Irish were great ones for show and snobbery. The link may indeed have had a role in landing him the job in the first place. For it was Caroline Butler of Ballyadams who played the organ in the church on Sunday and Rosie Butler who ran the Sunday school.

Both Frank and Kathleen were newcomers to the countryside. They had both grown up in Dublin where they had met through the church. Both came from the devout, hard-working, middle-class layer of Anglo-Irish society, the officials, shopkeepers and small businessmen who kept the country ticking over and endured for their trouble the occasional condescension of the Ascendancy grandees.

Frank's father was a wholesale chemist in the city, one step up from a shopkeeper. His membership of the Anglo-Irish merchant class was recent. He had been born into modest circumstances in Hertfordshire, one of ten children of a railway station-master, but had been adopted by a prosperous, childless maternal uncle from Dublin. Day-Lewis was the result of running together the surnames of his natural and adopted fathers.[3]

Frank's mother, Elizabeth, had died when he was just three and so a step-mother had brought him up. It was through Elizabeth, though, that he could claim a link with both the extended Butler clan, headed by the Dukes of Ormonde, and, distantly, with the poet W. B. Yeats.[4]

A bright pupil at school in Dublin, Frank Day-Lewis had felt himself called by God to ministry. There was little tradition of going into the church in his family so his vocation did not spring from parental expectation. Indeed while studying divinity at Trinity, alma mater of the cream of Anglo-Irish society, a family friend offered to make him his heir in a thriving business, but Frank declined. His ambitions lay somewhere less worldly. He was ordained in 1901 at the Anglican cathedral in Tuam, Co. Galway where he had served out his diaconate.

The offer of a stipend and a house in Ballintubbert convinced him that he was now in a position to support a wife. His sweetheart, Kathleen Blake Squires, was then working as a nurse at a tuberculosis hospital. On January 2, 1902 at Christ Church, Leeson Park in Dublin they married. She was the last of ten children of William Squires, a senior Dublin civil servant and his wife Annie Goldsmith, who descended from an uncle of Oliver Goldsmith, the eighteenth-century Irish writer and playwright best remembered today for *She Stoops To Conquer*.[5] It was a remote connection but such links were badges of honour in Anglo-Irish circles.

Where Frank could appear pompous and self-conscious, Kathleen had the high spirits of a much-loved youngest child. In her family she was known as 'the Angel'. She was not conventionally beautiful but her tumbling auburn hair set off her striking eyes and strong cheekbones. They must have seemed to their new parishioners the perfect couple. To complete the happy picture, in the summer of 1903 Kathleen discovered she was pregnant. 'On the whole they had a pretty good life,' one parishioner, a Mrs Jeffares, recalled of the Day-Lewises 70 years later. 'It always seemed such a warm, cosy little place down there behind the hill.'[6]

Cecil was born in Ballintubbert House on Wednesday April 27, 1904. In hurrying in his pony and trap to Maryborough (now Port Laois), the nearest big town, to summon the doctor, Frank collided with an ass which was asleep in the middle of the road. But mother, child and even father thrived. Cecil was Frank's middle name. The Anglo-Irish preferred as a rule distinctly English names and it was a popular one of the times. Cecil himself as an adult grew to dislike it and outlawed its use by his publishers. Like his friend W. H. Auden,[7] he preferred his initials and so was always C Day-Lewis (and for much of his life he also omitted the hyphen, lest it make him sound grand, he later acknowledged, though he started using it again at the end of his life).[8]

He had no memory of Ballintubbert House, save for a vague and unplaced recollection of the smell of bacon and breadcrumbs, and a glimpse of a white china cup in a green wood. 'Because [they] seem to speak the world-without-end language of infancy, I can believe them to be memories from my first two years,' he wrote in his autobiography.[9] That cup was the starting point for 'Passage from Childhood', written in the third person as if to express how hazy such memories were.

His earliest memory, the mood
Fingered and frail as maidenhair,
Was this – a china cup somewhere
In a green, deep wood.
He lives to find again somewhere
That wood, that homely cup; to taste all
Its chill, imagined dews; to dare
The dangerous crystal

'Passage from Childhood': *Overtures to Death* (1938)

Day-Lewis was not quite two when his parents left Ballintubbert and Ireland forever, though ever after he always defined himself, when asked, as Irish. In late 1905 the family set off for England. Frank had been appointed curate at Malvern Priory in Worcestershire. It was by any standards a radical change, but for all the ease of life at Ballintubbert, Frank was ambitious for ecclesiastical preferment and could see that going through the motions in a rural Irish parish was not going to catch the eye of the hierarchy on whom such matters depended.

By contrast Malvern Priory, which dated back to the Norman times, was a prestigious appointment for a young cleric. The large and busy Priory Church, with its medieval stained glass, had been restored under the direction of Sir George Gilbert Scott, the leading light of the Gothic revival in Victorian England and creator of London's St Pancras Station and the Albert Memorial.[10] Here Frank was sure he would find more and more varied pastoral work than in St Brigid's and an opportunity to shine.

But why go to England? Why not look for a post in one of the Church of Ireland cathedrals where he could equally make his mark? However apolitical Frank Day-Lewis was, he could see that the way of life he was enjoying at Ballintubbert could not go on much longer. The Church of Ireland itself was changing. William Gladstone had removed its status as the established Church in 1869 as part of his commitment to bring Home Rule to Ireland. And by 1905 the fall-out of that disestablishment was plain. The tithe that every Irishman had hitherto been obliged to pay to the established Church – whether they were Protestant or Catholic – had gone, and so parishes and dioceses were struggling to raise their own costs from small congregations.

The Day-Lewises may have enjoyed Ballintubbert House, but Frank knew that the well-heeled life of a rural curate that its Georgian elegance represented was no longer sustainable financially for the Church of Ireland. Parishes would have to amalgamate, properties be sold off and stipends cut. And although St Brigid's was well attended, all over the country Church of Ireland parishes were reporting a steep drop in numbers after disestablishment. One apocryphal story had it that the Duke of Leinster, a leading Anglo-Irish grandee, was travelling back to his seat at Maynooth in his carriage when he came across his curate walking home. 'Why aren't you in church for the evening service?' the Duke asked him. 'Our one parishioner is ill', he was told.[11]

The story may be exaggerated but is an illustration of how the spirit of the age was running against the Anglo-Irish. Since 1800 the ineffective Anglo-Irish run parliament in Dublin had been replaced with direct rule from Westminster. At a stroke that took away one of the key props for continued domination by the Protestant overlords of Ireland, leaving the British Parliament in 1829 to give some Irish Catholics the vote and in 1872 the right to a secret ballot. No longer could landlords arrange seats for their own kind in the House of Commons as a way of maintaining the status quo in Ireland. Now representatives at Westminster of the Catholic majority in Ireland pressed for an enhancement of the rights of Irish tenants at the inevitable expense of those whose principal function had been to keep them down and destitute.

As revenue from rents fell and clamours for Home Rule or even independence grew ever louder, many Anglo-Irish saw their estates as more of a burden than the prize they had once been for loyalty to the British crown. Changing times caused them to reassess where their true allegiances lay and when the Wyndham Act of 1903 offered them subsidies to sell out to their tenants many took them, costing the British Treasury some £12 million. The Anglo-Irish began to decamp to Britain.

The Day-Lewises joined the exodus. They left behind large families in Dublin but, if their son is to be believed, Frank at least did so with few regrets. 'He was little interested in the past,' Cecil wrote of his father, 'and inclined to separate himself from the hordes of relations, his own and my mother's, which littered Dublin and overflowed into England.'[12]

It was to be a new start, a rejection of the past, a move to seize a glittering future. There may also have been another reason for heading for Malvern which the couple kept secret even from those around them. The town stood on the steep slopes of the Malvern Hills and its many wells had made it a popular spa town. Princess Victoria, soon to be Queen, had visited in 1830 for the sake of her health, prompting many imitators and beginning a fashion. Since Cecil's birth Kathleen's health had been giving the couple cause for worry. She was struggling to regain her energy and appetite. In Malvern, they hoped, by taking the waters and breathing its reputedly life-enhancing air, her condition would improve.

Once more the Day-Lewises found themselves in a welcoming, well-heeled, theologically conventional parish. Their accommodation was again spacious, if not so romantic, a large redbrick Victorian villa called Jesmond, one of the many that had risen up in Malvern as its popularity as a spa town had increased. Frank continued to be a hard-working, eager if unremarkable curate. He undertook additional theological qualifications and wore his new knowledge with a certain pride. Parishioners from the time recalled him though mainly as delicate in health. Once he fainted in the middle of conducting a service and had to be revived on the altar by the Priory's aristocratic vicar, Canon Raymond Percy Pelly.[13]

However, it wasn't Frank but Kathleen who was seriously ill. It was probably during their time at Malvern that the maladies that had plagued her since her son's birth were finally diagnosed. The news was devastating. She had lymphoma, cancer of the white blood cells. Medicine at the time offered little hope of a cure, but by living a careful life, she was told, there was a chance that she might see her son grow up.

Whatever their private fears, the Day-Lewises gave the outward appearance of being a happy family. If Kathleen had any doubts about the man she had married she confided them in a scrapbook which contained stories and sketches she had written for various parish magazines. Included in it were some of her own poems which, her son later reported when he stumbled across the album, had 'no poetic merit, but one or two of them hint at a man's failure to understand a woman'.[14]

Cecil's own recollections of Malvern were slight and fleeting. He left before he was four and the few things that he recalled may have come down to him via stories he was told by relatives or from photographs he had seen. There was the hole in the garden hedge through which he would crawl to play with the children next door. Then, a less precise but more haunting image, there was the impression of going in his pram with his mother to feed swans, something that later appeared as a stanza in his poem 'The Innocent', again told in the distancing third person.

> *The bells that chimed above the lake,*
> *The swans asleep in evening's eye,*
> *Bright transfers pressed on memory*
> *From him their gloss and anguish take.*

'The Innocent': *Word Over All* (1943)

Kathleen's condition continued to deteriorate and she spent long periods resting. In what was by standards of the time an unusual decision and clear evidence of his loving devotion, Frank Day-Lewis gave up work in the summer of 1908 to nurse her for whatever time she had left. They moved out of Malvern and settled in Ealing, west London. Church House in Warwick Road was an Anglican property but it came with no strings attached. Frank had no regular parish responsibilities.

Such an offer may have been what drew them to London. Or it could have been the ready availability of more advanced treatment for Kathleen at one of its teaching hospitals. It was at the city's Guy's Hospital, in the middle years of the nineteenth century, that Thomas Hodgkin[15] had discovered the particular strain of lymphoma which carries his name to this day. By the turn of the century the first experiments in treating patients with an early form of chemotherapy had been undertaken there.

Cecil never knew which form of lymphoma his mother had, nor how it was treated, for as he detailed in *The Buried Day*, her illness was never spoken about. Kathleen celebrated her thirtieth birthday that summer. She was still able to get out and about, as her son had two memories of the family's time in Ealing – the first a walk with both his parents in a paddock behind their house, and the second of going to a shop with his mother to buy pink sweets.

Two days before Christmas, Kathleen died at home. Her death certificate names lymphadenoma – now called lymphoma. It also mentions effusions –

collections of fluids — in her pleural cavity in the chest which would have compressed her lung and caused breathing difficulties. It would most likely have been an agonizing death and, as she struggled for breath, one that would have been hard to hide from a four-year-old in a small house.

Cecil's only precise memory, though, he wrote, was of being taken to his mother's bedroom for a last farewell. His description carries an air of detachment from what was happening around him. 'My mother is lying in bed. I notice a smell like fish-paste. I am put into her arms and she kisses me ... I can remember no pain, no perturbation, no sense of parting. I was brought away to a neighbour's house, ignorant of what was happening at home, and all I can remember of it is that there was a fire in my bedroom and a too heavy eiderdown'.[16]

Chapter 2

A Hostile Land to Spy

Life was a hostile land to spy
Full of questions he dared not ask
Lest the answer in mockery
Or worse unmask
'Passage from Childhood': *Overtures to Death* (1938)

In the late 1930s, when publishers were competing to get the celebrated new wave poet C Day-Lewis to sign up for their imprint, he was persuaded by the influential publisher and man of letters Rupert Hart-Davis[1] to write a series of three literary novels for Jonathan Cape. They were not a great success, either critically or commercially, but in the first, *The Friendly Tree*, published in 1936, the heroine Anna Charteris grows up with a benign but overbearing lone father. 'Nothing of her mother remained now', Day-Lewis writes of Anna, 'except the tarnished silver-framed photograph on the study desk and the constrained visit every Christmas-tide to a suburban cemetery.'

Kathleen Day-Lewis was buried in suburban South Ealing Cemetery on Boxing Day, 1908. Her husband and son moved out of the house in Ealing soon afterwards but remained nearby at another church property in Maxilla Gardens in Notting Hill. Frank Day-Lewis slowly eased himself back into the active ministry and from 1910 onwards was curate at Christ Church, Lancaster Gate. He had chosen another prosperous, theologically mainstream parish with a grand 1850s asymmetrical Gothic church topped by a tall needle spire. It stood in the centre of a square lined with large stucco-fronted town houses, with classical porticos and colonnades, and faced out onto Kensington Gardens.[2]

Congregations were large. Frank Day-Lewis was one of two curates, assisting the vicar. With the post came a maisonette above an estate agent's office at 1a Craven Terrace, a narrow street of brick-fronted shops in a dip between the church and Paddington Station. Shabby and cramped in comparison with the houses that surrounded Christ Church, it had no garden save for a small curved first floor balcony outside the French windows of the pink-carpeted drawing room on which Cecil would play alone with his toy cars.

The restrained Christmas pilgrimage to the grave described in *The Friendly Tree* has the ring of experience to it, a trek father and son would make each year, while the rest of the world was celebrating. It was a rare acknowledgement of a death that was seldom spoken of otherwise. Frank's reaction to losing his wife was to try to seal off what had happened and hence his pain and any guilt he

11

may have felt about his own failures as a husband, hinted at in Kathleen's scrapbooks. So there was no question of returning to Ireland where his anxious relatives and in-laws would have been keen to take him in along with his child. Only a photograph of Ballintubbert House, simply framed in passe-partout, was allowed to suggest there had been something before, in another country, but it was hidden away on a dark corridor wall.

Frank did not – or could not – mourn his wife openly. 'About my mother he rarely talked with me,' Day-Lewis wrote in his autobiography. 'Having that strange Anglo-Irish blend of reticence and emotionalism – tears would come into his eyes and his voice would choke at an affecting passage in one of his own sermons – he would have found such intimate revelations doubly hard, while on my part I instinctively shrank, as any child does, from the touch of grown-up distress.'[3]

Frank Day-Lewis's faith should have been a support. Yet even for a religious man like him there might have been the inevitable question as to why God had let this happen to a young woman with everything to live for. There is no evidence that he ever found a satisfactory answer. Certainly his son does not record in his autobiography or elsewhere his father ever offering one, and Frank's ministry thereafter has a dutiful, at times almost mechanical, feel to it. The once keen interest in theology that had seen him undertake further studies at Malvern now evaporated.

It may simply have been a question of lack of time for further study, with a young son to bring up alone, but if his faith was indeed wounded, or destroyed, by the death of Kathleen, Frank Day-Lewis did not let it interfere with his career. To renounce the road he had chosen would perhaps have been a step too far for such a naturally cautious man. His attachment to the incidentals of ordained life, however, became ever more marked, the outward signs compensating potentially for a loss of inner grace. If his sermons did not win him the ecclesiastical advancement he had until so recently craved, there was the compensation every Sunday of catching the eye of Christ Church's fashionable congregation with his elaborate top hat and tail coat. His clerical suits were all from Vanheem and Wheeler, ecclesiastical outfitters of choice for prelates but rarely for humble curates living on a modest stipend. He even had for a while in their small maisonette his own valet, Baxter, who, Cecil recalled, 'gave off the faint greasy smell of bone-collar studs'.[4]

For all his love of show on a Sunday, Day-Lewis's appetite for the weekday round of parish tea parties with his wealthy congregation was small. His son noted in his father an irritation with the demands of the hostesses who courted this handsome, lone father, the unmarried among them occasionally metaphorically casting wedding rings into the collection plate, and some trying to woo him by offering his young son rides in their carriages round Kensington Gardens. Their efforts were all to no avail. 'The faces of these gentlewomen are all lost on me,' Cecil later wrote, 'but a faint, diffused impression of luxury lingers in my mind: the touch of furs, silk, a bearskin carriage rug: smells of violets and warm leather: a silver box containing wafer-thin gelatine sweets which one lady always offered me, and the delicious short-cake biscuits of another: the shopkeepers hurrying out of shops and bowing beside the carriage to take orders.'[5]

Cecil took his cue from his father in dealing with his own grief. He cut himself off from any memories he had of his mother's death throes, save for that single distanced picture of her deathbed scene. There is only one hint of a recollection elsewhere in his writings of having listened to his mother gasp for breath through the bedroom wall of the Ealing vicarage. In a meditation on mortality where he recalls how distant death seems to children, he indicates that occasionally it would encroach:

> And often lying safe
> In bed we thought of you, hearing the indrawn
> Breath of the outcast surf.
>
> 'Overtures to Death': *Overtures to Death* (1938)

There is a temptation with any poet, novelist and playwright of reading autobiography into every line in their published work. This tendency leaves no room for imagination, flights of fancy or the author's including fragments from his or her past into a wider fictional picture. Day-Lewis was undoubtedly and unashamedly often a strongly autobiographical poet, writing about details and events in his own and his family's life, and reflecting at length on his own roots and upbringing. He wrote, as he put it on more than one occasion, 'to understand, not to be understood'. Yet part of this endeavour involved putting his memories through a refining process – not least the demands of verse form, of metre and rhyme. The further away he was from what he was recalling, inevitably the less reliable was his account, mitigated as it was by more recent influences on his adult self. So he wrote, for instance, a great deal about his childhood relationship with his father only when he himself had become a father.

Such a background must be borne in mind in examining any evidence about his childhood found in both his prose and his verse, even in such apparently straightforwardly autobiographical poems as 'Passage from Childhood'. Here he described his younger self as 'this hermit and contorted shell' and hints that suppressing his mother's memory came at a price, but one that he felt worth paying.

> Self-pity like a thin rain fell,
> Fouling the view:
> Then tree-trunks seemed wet roots of hell,
> Wren or catkin might turn vicious,
> The dandelion clock could tell
> Nothing auspicious.
>
> 'Passage from Childhood': *Overtures to Death* (1938)

The Buried Day, his prose autobiography, offers by contrast little clue as to how he dealt with losing his mother so young. There is a certain note of bravado when he writes of the capacity of children to 'ride such disaster with extra-ordinary buoyancy: at the mercy of their environment, preoccupied with exploring the world through their senses, feeling no distinction between their tiny tragedies – a rained-off picnic, a broken toy – and the greater ones which may press indirectly upon them, the small fatalists accept more easily than most philosophers the knowledge that what is, is, and seem to bear a charmed life because they know so little of any life but their own'.[6]

In thereby disclaiming any long-term damage, he raises more questions than he answers. For instance his horizon may not have stretched as a child much beyond the narrow confines of his daily life, but even there, once at school, he would have mixed with other children who had two parents. This could easily have prompted questions about his own lost mother.

Later in the same chapter he apparently contradicts that earlier, breezy disclaimer when he stresses the importance of two, often contrasting, parents in allowing a child to develop his or her own personality. Because he had only one, Day-Lewis suggests, there was an imbalance in his childhood and he was thrown back on himself. 'As a boy,' he wrote, 'I was often staring into looking-glasses ... it was not from vanity – for I thought my face weak and rather absurd – nor straight narcissism, but in a spirit of inquiry: "are you real?" "who are you?" and later, more teasing still, "which of you is you?" '[7]

It is a reaction that finds an echo in his poetry.

> Who can say what misfeatured elf
> First led him into that lifelong
> Passage of mirrors where, so young,
> He saw himself
> Balanced as Blondin, more headstrong
> Than baby Hercules, rare as a one-
> Cent British Guiana, above the wrong
> And common run?

> 'Passage from Childhood': *Overtures to Death* (1938)

That interior life that was so much a feature of his work seems on this evidence to have begun early. Being an only child left him to make up his own games. Having a parent who would not talk about crucial emotional issues left Day-Lewis to muse alone, to stand back and look at himself in the mirror.

Quite when he realized that his childhood was unusual is hard to pin down but as an adult it was something freely explored in his writing. In *Child of Misfortune*, the last of the three late 1930s novels he wrote for Rupert Hart-Davis, Arthur Green, one of the two brothers at the centre of the narrative, reflects back on his Anglo-Irish father who had died when he was just a small child. 'Dan Green was scarcely even a memory now in his son's mind. He had remained there for longer than his footprints in the dew upon this grassy terrace, but that was all; he was fading fast now, and soon would be all but obliterated. The phantasies Arthur had built around him in his life had steadily been encroaching upon his memory, choking, distorting and obscuring it, just as in this garden the flower beds and ornamental shrubberies, so lovingly planted, had run riot, outgrown, then overgrown the pattern of their design.'

Kathleen's loss and its effect on him became a subject for Day-Lewis of almost academic speculation. Towards the end of his life he was asked in an interview what he believed had made him a poet. 'I would think that probably it was being an only child, therefore having a pretty lonely childhood ... What else would there be? My mother dying when I was four ... all deprived children do go a bit queer and my form of going queer [was to] become an incipient poet.'[8]

Prominent in his later poetry, as he began to reflect more and more on his own origins, is a question that he could neither avoid nor answer satisfactorily. What is the effect of not knowing a parent? It is there, for example, when he seeks the childhood sources for his adult behavioural patterns in 'Sketches for a Self-Portrait':

> I am one who peered
> In every stranger's face for my identity,
> In every mirror for a family likeness,
> In lakes and dewdrops for the antiself.
> I stunned myself upon their shallow eyes
> Like a chaffinch slamming against a windowpane.
>
> 'Sketches for a Self Portrait': Poems 1943–1947 (1948)

And the pain of that unending search is movingly there too in 'The House Where I was Born', a reflection on the framed photograph of Ballintubbert House that was always hidden away. (The title recalls the second line of Thomas Hood's poem, sometimes called 'Past and Present', but popularly known as 'I remember, I remember', a favourite of Day-Lewis's.)

> No one is alive to tell me
> In which of those rooms I was born,
> Or what my mother could see, looking out one April
> Morning, her agony done,
> Or if there were pigeons to answer my cooings
> From that tree to the left of the lawn.
>
> Elegant house, how well you speak
> For the one who fathered me there,
> With your sanguine face, your moody provincial charm,
> And that Anglo-Irish air
> Of living beyond one's means to keep up
> An era beyond repair.
>
> Reticent house in the far Queen's County,
> How much you leave unsaid.
> Not a ghost of a hint appears at your placid windows
> That she, so youthfully wed,
> Who bore me, would move elsewhere very soon
> And in four years be dead.

I know that we left you before my seedling
Memory could root and twine
Within you. Perhaps that is why so often I gaze
At your picture, and try to divine
Through it the buried treasure, the lost life –
Reclaim what was yours, and mine.

I put up the curtains for them again
And light a fire in their grate:
I bring the young father and mother to lean above me,
Ignorant, loving, complete:
I ask the questions I never could ask them
Until it was too late.

'The House Where I Was Born': *Pegasus and Other Poems* (1957)

The young Cecil did, however, still have his father and, despite Frank's reticence on the subject of his mother, the bond between them following Kathleen's death was unusually close. 'I was a receptacle for the love which he had given my mother,' his son reflected, 'the basket in which he would henceforth put all his eggs.'[9] This resulted in what was not an altogether healthy love between father and son. It meant, in simple terms, that Cecil was spoilt – bought expensive presents beyond a curate's pocket. More significantly, however, it also meant that Cecil was drawn in to Frank Day-Lewis's inability to mourn openly. By refusing to mention Kathleen in conversation or to allow pictures of her around the house, his father made Cecil complicit in the almost ritualized denial of the past. And because Frank could not let himself grieve openly, his capacity to be truly intimate with his son was compromised. A part of him was always shut off.

In practical terms, this resulted in Day-Lewis growing up amid a series of contradictions. The first surrounded intimacy. In the house at Maxilla Gardens, Day-Lewis remembered a box room filled with trunks 'which my father and I used to dispose in the shape of a boat, and using a plank for gangway, walk up over the trunk bulwarks, settle down inside and sail the Seven Seas'.[10] Frank was not then a conventional distant Edwardian father. He could crawl around on the floor and make up games with his son or tempt him into eating by pretending to be a bear. When he was in a good mood, he would delve enthusiastically into the toy cupboard halfway up the Craven Terrace flat's first flight of steps to find something with which to entertain his son. He was capable of displaying affection, had pillow fights with him like an older brother would, and, when he was ill, would tenderly rub camphorated oil into his chest.

All fathers tire of playing games at some stage, or have to attend to their work. But when Frank retreated into his study with its oak prie-dieu and glass fronted bookcases, Cecil seems to have been over-sensitive to what he read as rejection. There is a stanza in 'The Innocent' which describes the sudden and inexplicable withdrawal of intimacy and the guilt and alienation that resulted.

When I was desolate, he came
A wizard way to charm my toys:

16

But when he heard a stranger's voice
He broke the toys, I bore the shame.

'The Innocent': *Word Over All (1943)*

It is not a direct reference to his father, but the unpredictable and therefore unsettling unnamed figure in the poem makes the child believe it was he who was doing something wrong. Such a sentiment chimes with how Day-Lewis elsewhere describes his childhood.

Certainly when Frank was relaxed and uninhibited, he could be young Cecil's hero and playmate. On holidays at popular Edwardian seaside resorts like Sheringham (1911), the two would play tennis together and befriend craggy fishermen. A photograph from that trip shows a stern but good-looking Frank, his hair carefully parted in the centre and oiled down, wearing a well-cut civilian tweed suit but unmistakably still a clergyman, with his arm round a bare-legged blond boy in a sailor's suit, their hands entwined.[11]

Both of them are, though, slightly frowning. It may just be the sun or the flash of the camera's bulb, but even on holiday the threat of a dark mood descending on Frank would have been present. 'My father's moodiness was still a natural thing to me,' Day-Lewis wrote, 'accepted like changes of weather and not a source of much disquiet or grievance.'[12]

At home Frank was alternately loving and short-tempered. 'He was my judgement and my joy', Day-Lewis writes of the same unnamed subject in 'The Innocent'. His father would react at the smallest thing – tiny infringements by his son against his strict code of manners and deference – but take calmly in his stride what seem like greater misdemeanours. So when Cecil accidently shot a furious passer-by with his toy bow and arrow from the balcony at Craven Terrace, his father angrily rejected the man's demand that the boy be punished. And when he stole the contents of the Church Missionary Society box from the back of the church to indulge his sweet tooth, spent the money on chocolate, coconut ice and butter toffee and was discovered in the toy cupboard eating it, he was let off with hardly a cross word.

'When the discovery came, the atmosphere in the house was hushed, as if I had contracted a fatal disease or stolen the Crown Jewels. With the small boy's natural optimism, I of course "owned up like a man".'[13] His father did not punish him. Instead he called in his fellow-curate to give the youngster a talking-to. Cecil was never beaten by his father in an age when corporal punishment was routine. In some ways, he later felt, it would have been easier to handle if he had been. '[My father] would at the slightest provocation lower his eyelids rebukingly and put on a hurt expression which for years succeeded in piercing me with guilt'.[14] The message was clear. He had let Frank down. He had driven him away. He had forfeited intimacy.

The loss of his wife made Frank want to protect their child but this became what Day-Lewis later called 'smother-love' and led to still more contradictions.[15] So when the boy suffered a number of childhood illnesses, he was immediately labelled delicate and directed away from rougher games – for which he later showed an aptitude – towards gentler (and solitary) pursuits like sailing his prize blue cutter in the nearby Round Pond in Kensington Gardens.

Faced by these contradictions, Cecil's chosen method of navigation was to retreat into himself. Dreamy was a word often used of him as a child. He seemed detached from the life going on around him – one way of coping with his father's unpredictability. And he was, he later admitted, slow to grow up. After a bout of diphtheria, when he was eight, he was taken to Bournemouth for a rest cure by the sea. As he walked along the beach, he would pull behind him a wooden engine. He remembered later 'being torn between pleasure in my toy and mortification that I, a schoolboy now, should be seen by others to be enjoying so childish a pleasure'.[16]

> *You will forgive him that he played*
> *Bumble-puppy on the small mossed lawn*
> *All by himself for hours, afraid*
> *Of being born.*
>
> 'Passage from Childhood': *Overtures to Death* (1938)

His clearest memories of childhood were solitary ones, of often melancholy, disturbing sounds and smells rather than other people, children and events. Like the railway noises from Paddington Station he could hear when tucked up in bed which resurface in his meditation on ageing and death 'Last Words'.

> *The child, who in London's infinite, intimate darkness*
> *Out of time's reach,*
> *Heard nightly an engine whistle, remote and pure*
> *As a call from the edge*
> *Of nothing, and soon in the music of departure*
> *Had perfect pitch?*
>
> 'Last Words': *Pegasus and Other Poems* (1957)

Or the German band playing in the night-time streets below his bedroom window – sounds, he wrote, 'like intimations of cosmic sadness'[17] – which is described in 'Cornet Solo'.

> *That was the music for such an hour –*
> *A deciduous hour*
> *Of leaf-wan drizzle, of solitude*
> *And gaslight bronzing the gloom like an autumn flower –*
> *The time and music for a boy imbrued*
> *With the pensive mood.*
>
> *I could have lain for hours together,*
> *Sweet hours together,*
> *Listening to the cornet's cry*
> *Down wet streets gleaming like patent leather*
> *Where beauties jaunted in cabs to their revelry,*
> *Jewelled and spry.*

Plaintive its melody rose or waned
Like an autumn wind
Blowing the rain on beds of aster,
On man's last bed: mournful and proud it complained
As a woman who dreams of the charms that graced her,
In young days graced her.

Strange how those yearning airs could sweeten
And still enlighten
The hours when solitude gave me her breast.
Strange they could tell a mere child how hearts may beat in
The self-same tune for the once-possessed
And the unpossessed.

'Cornet Solo': *Word Over All* (1943)

His mother, he suggests, was replaced by solitude – 'the hours when solitude gave me her breast' – and the once-possessed child became unpossessed, set apart from everything around him.

Like his father he grew adept at locking away inside him the things that troubled him, storing them in compartments, always present and casting a shadow over life, but rarely opened for fear of causing upset. It was only as he grew into adulthood that Cecil found that in poetry he had a way of seeking understanding.

Frank Day-Lewis appears to have tried for well over a year to bring up his son on his own following his wife's death. There may have been some domestic help but nothing to come between father and son. However, he began to see that it was impossible, especially when he returned to full-time ministry. Soon after they left Maxilla Gardens and settled in Craven Terrace in 1910 they were joined from Ireland by Kathleen's older sister, Agnes Squires, always known in the family as Knos, an affectionate corruption of her Christian name.

Thirty four when she arrived in London, and a trained (at the Royal Irish Academy of Music) musician, Knos gave up her own life and any remaining chances of marriage to look after her nephew and his bereaved father. It was, Day-Lewis later came to believe, a heroic and saintly action.

. . . her sister dying, took on the four-year
Child, and the chance that now she would never make
A child of her own; who, mothering me, flowered in
The clover-soft authority of the meek.

'My Mother's Sister': *The Room* (1965)

Some of his happiest, most carefree memories of childhood were of times spent away from his father with Knos – visits to the zoo, to have tea at Gunters in Bond Street, or wandering along the Bayswater Road with her Irish spinster friend, Miss Monsell, windowshopping because it was all their purses could afford. Knos had a childlike quality that attracted Cecil's devotion, though occasionally he hints in *The Buried Day* (which he dedicated to her) that this was rooted in her simple, if not simplistic, view of the world.

He describes her as mothering and elsewhere as a second mother, but she was not his mother and Frank most definitely did not treat her as he might a wife. Her luxuriant, waist-length hair gathered and pinned up neatly behind her head, Knos set about being her brother-in-law's housekeeper. He set the tone of the household. He made decisions for his son. She followed.

Theirs was never an easy relationship. Despite his extravagances on his own clothes, and the expensive toys he would buy to indulge his son, Frank Day-Lewis kept other household costs to a minimum. The flat could be a cramped and joyless place. He didn't allow, for example, a Christmas tree and took the privations traditionally undertaken by religious folk at Lent very seriously indeed.

A curate's stipend could only stretch so far after all and he had no other source of money. Knos was allowed a cook-general to make meals and clean – and employed in the role a series of Irish girls – but was forced by her budget to serve up the cheapest cuts of meat. Stews and hashed-up concoctions of un-identifiable origins were the order of the day during the week, with meat and two veg on Sunday after service.

With Knos all Frank's suppressed anger at the loss of her sister seemed to come pouring out. Each Friday the two would go through the household accounts. 'He questioned every item of her modest expenditure,' Day-Lewis remembered, 'in a nagging, cold, unreasonable voice which made him seem a stranger to me, and the inquisition sometimes reduced Knos to tears.'[18] Witnessing such recurrent scenes was, he came to believe, part of Day-Lewis's lifelong antipathy for personal conflict. He would do anything to avoid a row.

> *He knew the secrecy of squirrels,*
> *The foolish doves' antiphony,*
> *And what wrens fear. He was gun-shy,*
> *Hating all quarrels.*
>
> 'Passage from Childhood': *Overtures to Death* (1938)

If not a substitute for his mother, Knos was nevertheless for Cecil a Godsend, someone to soften the pain of the unmentionable loss of Kathleen, someone moreover who in contrast to his father was always constant in her love, never reticent about the past, a vital link, as she read to him the long letters she received from her family, back to the child's Anglo-Irish roots that later would become such a part of him. And it was Knos – rather than his father – who finally took him back to the land of his birth.

Chapter 3

A Land of Milk and Honey

There was a land of milk and honey.
Year by year the rectory garden grew
Like a prize bloom my height of summer.
Time was still as the lily ponds. I foreknew
No chance or change to stop me running
Barefoot for ever on the clover's dew.

'Golden Age, Monart, Co. Wexford':
The Whispering Roots (1970)

In his autobiography Day-Lewis devotes most of one of its ten chapters to the summer holidays he spent as a child in Ireland with his Aunt Knos.[1] They would travel over from London by train and boat to Rosslare, and then take another train to the small town of Enniscorthy in County Wexford in the south-east. There they would be met in his pony and trap by Knos and Kathleen's eccentric older brother, The Revd William Squires, who in 1908 at the age of 40 had been appointed as Rector of Monart, a small rural Church of Ireland parish in an overwhelmingly Catholic area.

The gaunt Uncle Willie loomed disproportionately large in Day-Lewis's recollections of childhood, 'a full-blown eccentric' as he described him, 'with eyebrows black and thick as Groucho Marx's moustache, lantern jaw, mouth trembling on the brink of some profound and inaccessible humour, huge teeth stained by pipe-smoking'.[2] His significance to the young Cecil, though, was not so much how he looked as what he represented. Compared to Day-Lewis's sparse description in his autobiography of home life in Craven Terrace, with its ever-present contradictions, his lyrical account of the six summers between 1908 and 1914 that he spent at Monart with Willie and Knos Squires, and their talkative sister Alice who was the rector's housekeeper, show him as a child utterly at ease. It was a place where he felt he belonged and where that early unresolved loss of his mother could somehow be soothed and even partially unlocked by the proximity of her family. Full in detail and full of joy, his memories of those times were strong, constant, engaged and uncomplicated, although inevitably somewhat idealized, written as they were in 1960 when he was focusing more strongly than before on his own Anglo-Irish roots.

In the 'shabby, queer-shaped'[3] one-storey whitewashed rural rectory, worlds apart from both the elegant Georgian proportions of Ballintubbert House in the Anglo-Irish agricultural heartlands or the urban constraints of a flat above a

21

shop in Craven Terrace, the young Cecil found a rare freedom. In the large garden bordered by meadows, chestnut trees, a lily pond and, in the distance, the Blackstairs Mountains, all the physical and emotional restrictions imposed on him in London were at once removed. His father never accompanied them, having an antipathy to all things Irish, and so Knos could let her long hair down, literally and figuratively, and for once mother her nephew unimpeded and unchallenged.

'Smother-love' gave way each summer to a far looser rein, with the otherwise timid Cecil confident enough to wander and explore unhindered and without fuss amid the clumps of red-hot pokers, the paddock and the raspberry canes, plum trees and gooseberries as big as ping pong balls. Instead of tours in the grand carriages of wealthy spinsters of the parish in Bayswater, Cecil was allowed in Monart to take the reins of the churchwarden's dog-cart as they careered round the sharp bends on the road into Enniscorthy with an almost casual disregard for danger.

Cecil would pass the long summer days helping out the Squires' gardener, Johnny Keyes, while listening to his extravagant stories of fairies and magic goings-on and learning patriotic songs about an independent Ireland. Keyes was later the model for Charlie Connor, the Republican gardener in Day-Lewis's 1939 novel *Child of Misfortune*, while the memory of clearing a spring in the paddock at Monart with Keyes occurs in his poetry as a metaphor for the arousal of childhood curiosity.

> Children look down upon the morning-grey
> Tissue of mist that veils a valley's lap:
> Their fingers itch to tear it and unwrap
> The flags, the roundabouts, the gala day.
> They watch the spring rise inexhaustibly –
> A breathing thread out of the eddied sand,
> Sufficient to their day.

'O Dreams, O Destinations': *Word Over All* (1943)

The two Squires sisters would sit out each morning in the yard where nettles were free to grow, shelling peas, gossiping about their large extended family and laughing out loud. And the domestic economies of the Craven Terrace dining table were replaced by a continual round of eating the fruit of the garden and drinking the water from the rectory's own well or buttermilk 'in cool earthen crocks' from the local cows.[4]

The life the young Day-Lewis sampled in Monart was timeless, calm and without anxiety. It was, he believed – and here hindsight may be shaping his memories – a formative time. 'At Monart,' he wrote, 'I enjoyed the repetitive rhythm which children and poets thrive on. After breakfast, I went out with Aunt Alice to feed the hens. Her hens were never so happy as when laying eggs in out-of-way places ... Aunt Alice I remember as a kindly, comfortable, clucking woman, with blue eyes, a red face and an incipient white moustache. She, like Knos, was a chatterbox – the more so for living most of the year with the almost Trappist silences of Uncle Willie.'[5]

Though he subsequently rose in 1936 to be chancellor of the local Church of Ireland diocese of Ferns, sitting as part of the chapter of the cathedral, Willie Squires shared neither Frank Day-Lewis's love of clerical dressing up or the ecclesiastical ambition that had caused the latter to turn his back on the dwindling congregations of the Church of Ireland. Uncle Willie was a natural but amateur scholar, precise about time but otherwise genial, disorganized, untidily dressed and decidedly unconventional in manner. On rail journeys up to Dublin, for instance, he would get out of the carriage at every stop and only reappear moments before the train pulled out for reasons which no-one ever uncovered.[6]

The rector quickly befriended his motherless nephew. Cecil, for his part, was drawn to an adult who was so very different from his father. Uncle Willie would emerge each day from his study, piled high with the second-hand books he loved to buy and sell, and join his sisters for lunch where he champed like a horse through soda bread and home-made jam. He would speak at table only to his nephew – a slight long since ignored by his sisters – and afterwards would happily play rough and tumble games with him in the garden or go ghost-hunting in the rectory outhouses. Later when Uncle Willie had returned from doing the parish rounds (which, given the size of the congregation wouldn't have detained him long) he would give Cecil a penny to push his bike up the path from the gate, money that could later be spent at the sweet shop on the road to Enniscorthy.

In his autobiography Day-Lewis rhapsodized: 'The routine of our days at Monart I see now, looking back, as a positive thing, a trellis on which my young life could climb and spread.' His memories of the place were once again of sounds and smells which he would experience alone, such as 'the hoarse clanking of the [water] pump, like the braying of asses which it resembled a little in rhythm and even in timbre'.[7]

There were more traditionally idyllic vignettes – of lying in bed in the candle-lit room he shared with Knos and listening to her singing in another room. '[It] lent still greater enchantment, like music over water, when I heard it from the distance between our bedroom and the living room. After I had gone to bed, I lay awake to her pure, rather doleful voice, which made everything she sang sound like religious music, rising up through the floor and flooding the night'.[8]

A particular and unlikely favourite of Knos was Tom Moore, the eighteenth century Protestant poet who had lived in a dissolute exile most of his life and whose settings of traditional folk tunes like 'The Last Rose of Summer' were popular with Irish nationalists and with Cecil ever after (*Child of Misfortune* being a quotation from a Moore song).[9]

At Monart, music, which became a lifelong love, was for the first time part of Day-Lewis's everyday life. It was unlikely that his father would have allowed Knos to perform Moore songs in Craven Terrace, but in the evenings in her brother's rectory, lit by oil lamps, she did so 'at the funereal tempo with which the Irish so often devitalize his airs'.[10] She accompanied herself on the harmonium and Cecil would stand next to her manipulating the stops.

'I have to thank them,' he wrote, 'for a certain fund of calm in myself, which Monart surely did much to create and which I am able to draw upon in emergency – a sense, even when I am out of my depth, lost and struggling desperately, that there is firm ground not far away.'[11] Implicit in this passage is a damning verdict on home life at Craven Terrace.

Back in London, though, his horizons were finally beginning to expand. Day-Lewis's earliest education was at home with his aunt. She started him on arithmetic and reading. The newly published Beatrix Potter[12] stories were a particular favourite, but by 1912, he was already eight and even his over-protective father could see that his son needed to go to school.

So at the start of September, he set off in his blue and pink blazer and cap for Wilkie's Preparatory, a fifteen-minute walk up the Bayswater Road. At his father's insistence he also wore heavy leather leggings to protect him from the cold and rain but these ungainly encumbrances made him stand out from the crowd and he lobbied successfully to have them discarded.

Initially Cecil found the whole experience of school disorientating. He was a solitary boy, used to his own company, inventing his own games. He had little experience of being around other children. In his early days at Wilkie's he wet himself because he was too timid to ask permission to go to the toilet. On another occasion he came home with a black eye having been bullied by an older boy called Woolmer. He was keen, though, to fit in and so quickly adapted to the new regime, enjoying in particular the three choices of pudding available at lunch each day. He also belatedly made friends of his own age.

Among the other pupils at Wilkie's was Nicholas 'Nico' Llewellyn Davies, two years older than Cecil, who lived following the death in quick succession of his parents with his guardian, J. M. Barrie.[13] The last of five brothers on whom Barrie based *Peter Pan*, Nico started at the school in the same term as Day-Lewis and was immediately hero-worshipped by the younger boy. 'He seemed to me an altogether superior kind of being,' Day-Lewis wrote. Part of that attraction may have been that Llewellyn Davies also knew what it was to have lost a parent. 'My first bid for his attention, while we were walking in a crocodile to the gymnasium, was a mortifying failure: he asked me if I was going on to Eton: I had never heard of Eton, strange as this may seem, and my ignorance con-founded me.'[14]

Despite this inauspicious start, the two became firm friends, their mutual liking for ice-cream soda drinks after games' lessons helping along their friendship. There were trips to the cinema at Marble Arch (to see, among others, a film on the Carthaginian war) and other joint expeditions but Day-Lewis was invited back to the Barrie house at 23 Campden Hill Square just once. It bore little resemblance to Never Never Land. 'I remember a large dark room,' he wrote, 'and a small man sitting in it; he was not smoking a pipe, nor did he receive us little boys with any perceptible enthusiasm – indeed I don't think he uttered a single word ... After this negative encounter we went up to the attic and fired with an air-gun at pedestrians in the Square.'[15]

Compared with the odd figure of Barrie, his new headteacher at Wilkie's was much more congenial (Barrie is said to have used some of his characteristics in the character of Captain Hook). Herbert Wilkinson appeared stern with his greying moustache and had his quota of eccentric gestures – blowing his nose like 'a ship's steam-whistle' to announce the end of break.[16] But, by Day-Lewis's account and that of others, there was a warmth and energy about him. Sir Max Beerbohm, the writer and Wilkie's old boy, used to have lunch with his old headteacher at the Savile Club and noted in the 1920s that Wilkinson retained an extraordinary capacity to 'sympathize with the mind of a small boy' as well as remaining 'as boyish as ever, making me feel always like a nonagenarian'.[17]

The school in St Petersburg Place, next to Orme Square, was small. There were no more than 30 pupils. It was also a home. Mrs Wilkinson, who taught drawing, and their son, Geoffrey, lived alongside what was by the standards of the time a progressive establishment. The usual stand-bys of prayer, the playing field and fagging were eschewed in favour of genuine intellectual curiosity and nurturing.

That is not to suggest there was no sport but it was simply another part of the curriculum. Twice a week the boys would be taken up to Wormwood Scrubs for football or cricket – Herbert Wilkinson's particular favourite. Day-Lewis, freed from his father's watchful eye, revealed himself as athletic, rising to captain the school at soccer, an achievement somewhat undermined when the team went down to a 14–nil defeat. With no other children at home, opportunities to practise were limited, but he used to move the table aside in the dining room, make goal posts with two chairs and play against himself, left foot against right.

Wilkie's was an odd choice of school for Frank Day-Lewis who was by temperament conservative and suspicious of innovation. What attracted him to it? It was certainly near to their home and highly regarded. Wilkinson was a first rate classicist and had a distinguished record in getting boys into Eton. But it was also expensive. Cecil's classmates all came from much more prosperous homes. One, Dawson, was the son of a wealthy professional billiards player and used to take his school friends back to his very large house in Cleveland Square.

It may simply have been that his father was projecting his own social ambitions on to his son and so scraped together out of his stipend the money to pay the fees so Cecil could be part of a world of privilege from the start. If that was Frank Day-Lewis's straightforward ambition, then Wilkie's still remained a peculiar option for the son of a clergyman. There were routine prayers at the start of each day but none of the religious observances then standard in many other more traditional prep schools. Indeed the absence of too much overt muscular Christianity made the Wilkie's a particular favourite with Jewish parents from the nearby synagogue in St Petersburg Place.

'My father,' Day-Lewis later recalled, 'did not overstress my religious duties.'[18] There were few demands in regard of regular church attendance, beyond the bare minimum, little encouragement for choir membership and complete absolution from Sunday school. Such behaviour again suggests a certain loss of faith (albeit unacknowledged) on Frank Day-Lewis's part, leaving Cecil balancing being in public the son of a vicar who in private seems to have made little effort to pass on the faith.

A recurring childhood dream had, Day-Lewis later recalled vividly, undermined the claims of Christianity and in particular its belief in an eternal reward. In it he had seen himself as 'an infinitesimal point upon which vast and indefinable entities pressed swiftly in from all sides, and the next moment these vague figures had dwindled to microscopic dimensions while I expanded horribly, filling the universe. This night the images were not vague. I saw something like a glacier – the "glassy floor" of the hymn, perhaps – cold, shining, and extending illimitably beyond me, empty save for one object in the midst of it – the head of a pin. Waking, I knew the pin was me and the glacier was the life eternal'.[19] The troubled child would, he recounted, sit up in bed sobbing and have to be comforted by Knos.

As well as his success at sport, Day-Lewis generally thrived in his lessons, though there were occasionally troughs of under-achievement. He was by nature competitive in the classroom and on the games field. In particular he enjoyed writing and, in *The Buried Day*, reproduced his first attempt at poetry:

Avatory, avatory, avatory
Baby fell down the lavatory

He was also, admittedly by his own account, precocious in his attraction to word patterns. An advertisement he spied in a newspaper about 'How to Develop a Beautiful Bust' so seduced him because of its 'alliteration and smooth undulating run of the line ending in explosion' that he chanted it rhythmically out loud on a bus journey, much to Knos's horror.[20]

However, if he was developing a taste for writing verse, it was to be some time yet before he started to appreciate the poetic canon. Sitting in his classroom at Wilkie's, one hot summer afternoon, trying to learn by heart the first two stanzas from the early nineteenth century Poet Laureate Robert Southey's 'After Blenheim'[21] – *It was a summer's evening/Old Kaspar's work was done* – Day-Lewis sought every excuse possible to avoid making the necessary effort. 'How I envied Old Kaspar – whoever he was. I couldn't see the point of learning it, or the point of the poem at all. The page grew blacker and blacker with my sweaty fingermarks.'[22]

The detached, lonely oddball youngster slowly became a conformist during his five years at Wilkie's. 'The state of being an Outsider,' he reflected in *The Buried Day*, 'does not strike me as a source of gratification, let alone a cause for self-congratulation. My disposition has always been to conform; and though, time and again, I have been at odds with the smaller or larger social units to which I belonged, the struggle has gone against my own grain too, and beneath the romantic rebel there has always been the man who longed to come to terms with society or wanted a society with which he could be reconciled.'

His daily walks to school along the Bayswater Road allowed him a glimpse at a changing world. Horse-drawn buses, for instance, began to give way to solid-tyred steam-driven public transport. Towards the end of his time at Wilkie's,

Frank was even persuaded to allow his son to ride to school on the black bike he had been given on his birthday in 1916 as a reward for good work in class. It was while he was cycling home one afternoon that he witnessed in 1917 his first daytime air raid by the Germans on London. He looked on in awe as if at a spectacle, though the attack left 158 people dead.

Although a teenager by the time it ended, the events of the First World War did not make any profound impact on Day-Lewis. The evidence was all around him but it left few abiding memories. At the outbreak of hostilities in 1914 while Cecil and Knos were at Monart, Frank Day-Lewis had made a rare trip to Ireland to escort them home across an Irish Sea made dangerous by German submarines. His son's only recollection of this perilous journey was of seeing dead small animals in sacks, washed up on the beach south of Dublin. They had been drowned, he was told, by departing sailors on troop ships who couldn't take their pets with them into conflict.

Back at home in London, Day-Lewis helped Knos knit khaki scarves and acted as dummy for her bandaging practice as she trained to work as a volunteer nursing auxiliary. At Wilkie's, a map of the front line appeared on the wall, with the snaking line of Allied flags almost imperceptibly pushing their German counterparts back, but Herbert Wilkinson avoided the jingoism of the time. 'We were not encouraged to think along the lines of "the only good German is a dead German",' Day-Lewis recalled, 'nor were we affected by the adult hysteria which looted ships with German names above them and banned Beethoven from the concert halls.'[23]

Frank Day-Lewis was still a young man of 37 and therefore eligible for military service. In 1915 he volunteered as a chaplain to the Forces. It may have represented an escape for him – from his small, dark flat in Bayswater and the social round of Christ Church parish life.

At first Cecil and Knos were left alone in Craven Terrace while Frank undertook basic training. Without his father's nagging and exacting presence this was a happy interlude, Day-Lewis remembered. Eventually, though, the flat was let and aunt and nephew took up residence in a hotel in the square of the parish church.

In the school summer holidays of 1916, he was reunited with his father. They took a cottage at Witley in Surrey, near the army camp where Frank Day-Lewis was based with the East Lancashire Regiment. His father – and his batman – would come over to the cottage to stay.

Army life suited Frank. He liked the ceremonial aspect and took great care over his uniform. He easily adapted his parochial air of authority to the role of military chaplain. 'His explosions were rare these days,' his son wrote, 'for he was living a life new to him, a healthy outdoors life amongst men which must in some ways have suited him much better than the rather woman-ridden milieu of a fashionable parish.'[24]

Frank Day-Lewis was never sent to the front and the following summer found him at Wetherby in Yorkshire with the Royal Fleet Auxiliary. Knos and Cecil again joined him in rented accommodation and with his father's encouragement

Cecil successfully learnt how to ride a horse, as is recounted in detail in *The Buried Day*. There is no hint, though, of the horror of battle touching Cecil, even indirectly. He remained young for his years and self-absorbed with narrow horizons.

Looming large in that summer of 1917 was the scholarship examination for Sherborne, a public school in Dorset with close links with Wilkie's and more modest fees than Herbert Wilkinson's other favoured option, Eton. With his headteacher's careful tutoring – and, he subsequently liked to believe, a stanza of poetry he wrote for the English paper – Day-Lewis was placed third on the final list and given an award.

Chapter 4

Black Frost of my Youth

Oh, black frost of my youth, recalcitrant time
When love's seed was benighted and gave no ear
To others' need, you were seasonable, you were
In nature: but were you as well my nature's blight?
'Son and Father': *Pegasus and Other Poems* (1957)

The Sherborne that C Day-Lewis described so lyrically in *The Buried Day* has changed little in the intervening decades. 'The strong, slow, golden boom of the Abbey clock striking' still sends ripple after ripple through the Dorset air, and there remains that charm which he defined as 'blended of its mellow physical beauties and the sense of generations of young life which, passing through court and cloister, have left something of themselves behind to form an invisible compost'.[1]

The school itself, founded in 1550 in the reign of Edward VI in the buildings of an abbey dissolved by his father, Henry VIII, continues to be at the heart of this small town, rather as the university colleges fill every corner of the centre of the city of Oxford. And it was the Oxbridge colleges that the Victorian governors of Sherborne had in mind as a model when they effectively relaunched their establishment in the 1860s to profit from the boom in public schools that came with the expansion of empire and the arrival of the railways. The Courts, the central space lined largely by Victorian buildings on its four sides (albeit some of then specifically designed to hark back to earlier times and styles) differs only from any number of similar quads at Oxford or Cambridge in the stone used. Sherborne has its own distinctive honey-coloured local variety.

Growth had continued unchallenged in the early years of the twentieth century, with more and more boarders arriving by train and schoolhouses spreading throughout the narrow streets of the town. However, Sherborne School was in the midst of a great crisis when Day-Lewis arrived in September of 1917. One of its recent old boys, Alec Waugh,[2] had that July published an openly autobiographical novel, *The Loom of Youth*, which caused a public scandal by breaking the taboo on portraying the homosexual passions and activity between schoolboys – 'the inevitable emotional consequence,' Waugh claimed, 'of a monastic herding together for eight months of the year of 13-year-old children and 18-year-old adolescents'.[3]

Written with humour and the iconoclasm of a 17-year-old, anxious, in his own words, to 'expose the myth of the ideal Public School boy',[4] and so

29

challenge the whole public school ethos, *The Loom of Youth* had successfully caught the mood of the times. Here was a challenge to the existing order from a young author, now serving on the front line of a war in France that had become bogged down because, many felt, of mismanagement by a public school educated military and political establishment.

As the novel quickly went into many reprints, the school authorities at Sherborne indulged in a frenzy of denial. Waugh and his father, Arthur, a well-known critic and publisher,[5] were expelled from the old boys' society. Alec's younger brother Evelyn was redirected, as a result, for his education to Lancing College.[6] And concerned parents were told that, whatever was claimed of *The Loom of Youth*, no part of the description of sexual practices at the fictional Fernhurst bore any relation at all to Sherborne. Nevertheless, housemasters added reassuringly, staff henceforward would be vigilant and stamp out any hint of adolescent eroticism between pupils in their care. Any boy found in possession of a copy of *The Loom of Youth* would be expelled.

The storm would have passed Day-Lewis by. His sexual development, as with other aspects of his childhood, was not precocious. So when his worried father tried, prior to delivering him to the school, to have a frank conversation about the facts of life in the garden of Sherborne's Digby Hotel (now a school house), they simply merged, in Day-Lewis's dreamy young head with 'a general diffused bewilderment that hung low above these hours on the edge of my new life'.[7]

The change, for any boy going away at 13 from the family home to boarding school, is considerable, but for Cecil it meant partial liberation from the 'smother-love' of his father, with all its attendant anxieties. In place of a small flat in a dingy part of London with no outside space, he found himself in a pretty, old town in the middle of the countryside. In this constant world he learned – by design and by default – to conform, to fit in with a crowd but still to have confidence in himself. It became inevitably as important as home in his development, but also a necessary counterbalance to a world dominated by his unpredictable father.

He was put in Harper House, a large Georgian building on the opposite side of the main street from the Courts. Named after the Victorian headmaster who had revived the school, it had just 25 boarders when he arrived, though it grew over his six years there to around 40. It was an intimate environment, presided over as housemaster first by Kenneth Tindall and later Armine Fox, with meals taken together in house and games in the large garden.

Just as he began to find his feet in this new world, the fears excited by *The Loom of Youth* returned. At the start of his second term, the head of his dormitory, another ex-Wilkie's pupil, was expelled for what the housemaster called 'immorality' with another pupil. The younger boys got off with a stern warning since they were considered too immature to indulge willingly in any such behaviour. *The Buried Day* suggested, however, that such absolution was misplaced. 'My own disposition to join the herd,' Day-Lewis wrote, 'together with a natural sensuousness which was ripe to become sensuality, and my total ignorance of the "facts of life" made me a predestined victim.' What his father and his masters labelled 'vice' – solitary and mutual masturbation – was something, he recalled that 'I had taken to like a duck to water, but it ran off me like water from a duck's back, in the sense that it was not to warp my hetero-sexual responses later'.[8]

Much more affecting in the long term, however, was an epistle he received from his father in the early months of 1918 when he was in the sick room with measles. The furore surrounding the expulsion of the head of Cecil's dormitory had just been unleashed and Frank Day-Lewis, under the guise of offering moral guidance, was writing to castigate his son for any part he might have had in the affair. It doesn't seem to have occurred to him to doubt Cecil's complicity. The letter set out on paper all the contradictions that had been a part of Cecil's childhood.

' "You have broken my heart", ' Frank Day-Lewis began melodramatically in 'lines laden with reproach and self-pity, as if they had been written in blood from his own wounded pride ... He had said this to me before, said it more than once; but this time, seeing it written down, I was for a while entirely convinced of its truth and stood convicted in my own heart for the crime of having broken his ... Then a light appeared on the horizon, a saving scepticism moved closer. I had not been so irredeemably wicked; and even if I had, my father would survive it, and he should have thought less about his own feelings than about the ordeal I had been going through. Something tough, buoyant, resentful and realistic in me – a self I had hardly met before – came to my rescue.'[9]

These lines in *The Buried Day* present the episode as a kind of epiphany. In retrospect it may have seemed so. What was certainly true was that after just a few short months of separation, an unbearable weight began to lift from Cecil's shoulders. To grow, he realized (probably instinctively and as all teenagers do, albeit in his case with a peculiar force given the nature of his upbringing so far) he had to start to distance himself emotionally from his father. Sherborne allowed him to do so.

The long-serving head, Nowell Smith, a small man with a gold pince-nez, was in principle enlightened but some, including Waugh who dubbed him 'the Chief' regarded him as ineffective in curbing the more brutal tendencies of some of his staff. The rugby field, rather than the classroom or chapel, Day-Lewis recalled, was the real centre of the school. Success at sport was highly prized. Those who disdained it were bullied.

Day-Lewis had already discovered at Wilkie's a certain aptitude at games and coming third in the Sherborne junior steeplechase and playing as scrum half for his house gave him some protection from the rougher elements at the school. He eventually rose to claim his colours in the second XV at rugby and once played for the first XV. Inevitably, given the ethos of the school, he would have liked to do better, but those around him judged him to have acquitted himself more than adequately.

However, it was his more enduring interests that marked him out: performing in the chapel choir and listening to the distinguished musicians invited down to lift the philistine gloom by Nowell Smith; acting in plays where his Clytaemnestra in a February 1922 production of *Agamemnon* was praised in the school magazine for 'managing to convey a cold fierce tone very cleverly'[10]; debating as part of the Sophists; reading papers to the literary society, the Duffers; and above all writing poetry.

Having a foot in both worlds – on the sporting field and in drama soc. – did occasionally cause him to trip up. Once he was rushing from a rehearsal as Clytaemnestra to cricket practice when he was stopped by a master. 'I say Day-Lewis,' he asked, 'are you taking care of yourself?' On closer examination Cecil realized that as well as his cricket whites he was still wearing full stage make-up.[11]

This double life eventually came to the attention of the sports field elite. In his autobiography Day-Lewis presented being forced by a group of 'half-savage' bullies to swallow a concoction of 'ink and bad cheese', crawl through a burning tunnel, be whipped with wet towels and then thrown fully clothed into a cold bath as partly badge of honour, partly rite of passage. 'I seem to remember that, when it was over, D [the principal bully whom he did not name] shook my hand and said, "you took it very well"; to which I replied, "I deserved it".' It was, he wrote, 'the nadir of my time at Sherborne' but also another landmark on his road away from his cosseted, anxious childhood towards self-reliance and resilience.[12]

Despite this warning shot, it remained in the more cultural pursuits at Sherborne that Day-Lewis thrived. He was, however, careful publicly to embrace all aspects of the curriculum so as to avoid standing out too much from the crowd

Our youthtime passes down a colonnade
Shafted with alternating light and shade.
All's dark or dazzle there. Half in a dream
Rapturously we move, yet half afraid
Never to wake.

'O Dreams O Destinations': *Word Over All* (1943)

He was fortunate to be at a school where, amongst some of the teaching staff at least, his enthusiasm for poetry was shared. Nowell Smith was a distinguished Wordsworth[13] scholar and Day-Lewis's English master, The Revd Henry Robinson King – 'a gentle, moody, often distrait man with white hair and a drooping white moustache, who looked like a minor Victorian celebrity' – had a more general passion for the poets of the nineteenth century, often declaiming Tennyson[14] to the class. Every schoolchild, it is often said, has one teacher who influences and inspires them above all others. If this is true, then for Day-Lewis it was King.

Other past pupils continued to regard him with gratitude and awe. John Cowper Powys, poet, novelist and old Shirburnian, wrote in his autobiography: 'he was one of those men who by some massive instinct of their whole being gather up as they go about the world the lasting essences of life and savour them with a calm and constant satisfaction'.[15]

Day-Lewis collected his own juvenile attempts at verse in an exercise book ambitiously headed 'Early Poems – First Series' and prefaced by a quotation from his distant relative, W. B. Yeats.[16] He took as his prototype the Celtic Twilight period of Yeats's poetry, centred on the collection of the same name of 1893, and full of romantic lushness and celebrations of nature that is endowed with a mythical, mystical power.

King encouraged him in such pursuits. One early effort appeared in *The Shirburnian* magazine in May 1921. 'Reverie' was signed not with Cecil's own initials, but with those of his dead mother.

> *A gentle breeze, stirring the tree tops;*
> *A faint whisper, a rippling stream:*
> *The sun-splashed shadows in the green copse –*
> *A cuckoo calls – the woodlands dream.*
>
> *Nature a'drowse, scent-laden visions*
> *Before my eyes, and mem'ries dear,*
> *Born of stillness; gentle-eyed slumber*
> *Soothing my heart – sings sweetly clear*

By the summer term of 1922 Day-Lewis had grown confident enough to use his own name (already rendered as C Day-Lewis) on 'St Ambrose', a 150-line paean of praise to the fourth century saint which won the school's Barnes Elocution Prize. 'The lives of holy men are beacon-flares/On heights above the vale of mortal cares'.[17]

Day-Lewis would have struggled to remain anonymous for part of the prize was to read aloud the winning entry to staff, pupils and parents at speech day. The link between performing and writing poetry was made early in his life.

In the following year, his last at Sherborne, he won the school's English Verse Award with 'The Power of Music' a poem whose debt to Yeats's 'He Wishes For The Cloths of Heaven' is plain in lines such as 'And wove it with the stars and the moon's beams/To mesh the diaphanous carpet of man's dreams ...'

Although his tribute to St Ambrose might have suggested that the muscular Christianity of Sherborne's chapel had brought Day-Lewis closer to God, the opposite was true. It appeared that it was more tales of Ambrose's supernatural healing powers that attracted the young poet to his subject than the details of his faith. Certainly Day-Lewis's account, in *The Buried Day*, suggested that he was left unmoved by regular attendance at services, for much of his time at Sherborne held in the Abbey church, with its celebrated Perpendicular architecture, because the school chapel was closed as part of rebuilding works.

He found, in particular, that long sermons from the headmaster about the sinfulness of self-abuse were an exercise in hypocrisy since everyone knew it was going on all the time amongst the boys. Great statements from the pulpit on the subject 'by those elders who proclaimed such things could not happen in Sherborne ... devalued in our eyes the religion of which they were spokesmen'.[18]

Nevertheless, he was confirmed when at the school. It was not an automatic part of the curriculum, but an option. Whatever his motives, it proved a disappointment. 'I had expected,' Day-Lewis wrote, 'that the laying-on of hands would reveal some truth or put me closer in touch with a Source of Power that should enable me to overcome my weakness. During the service in the school chapel, I tried hard to feel that I was undergoing a religious experience, but without effect. I had not lost my faith, for I had nothing so positive as a faith to lose – only a tradition and a habit of Christianity.'[19]

If Christianity passed him by while at Sherborne, so too did any great sense of the county in which he was living. Later he was to grow passionate about Dorset, and especially about Thomas Hardy[20] who so celebrated it in his work, but as a schoolboy Day-Lewis rarely ventured outside the town, save for compulsory countryside exercises with the Officer Training Corps. He was, he later admitted ashamedly, as ignorant as a schoolboy of Hardy, who lived nearby and called Sherborne Sherton Abbas in his 1887 novel *The Woodlanders*, as he was of William Barnes, the nineteenth century Dorset poet whose verse prize he won.[21] Even a visit to the town in July 1923 by the Prince of Wales which included a lunch with Thomas Hardy at his home near Sherborne, failed to alert Day-Lewis to the presence of the man who was to become his literary hero.

Later, though, he hinted that the backdrop of his schooldays had indeed impressed itself upon him, albeit subconsciously.

> ... the mellow South West town
> That spoke to him words unheeded but unforgotten
> > 'Sketches for a Self-Portrait': *Poems 1943–1947* (1948)

In the same poem, he described adolescence as a kind of chaos – 'even in the haunts where he was most himself/If a chaos can be a self'. Teenage years can be times of changing horizons and hormones. Day-Lewis had the added problem of a claustrophobic relationship with his father to escape. But chaos? The description seems to be overstating what he described in *The Buried Day* and what contemporaries recalled of him later.

Perhaps what he meant is revealed by another line in the same poem where he wrote of being 'trained to climb my own thread'. He learnt at Sherborne – in reaction not only to his father but also to school rules, moral injunctions and pressures to conform by doing well on the sports field – to be his own person. Not naturally a rebellious leader, his own revolt was an already familiar retreat into solitude, present but also detached, wrapped up in his own thoughts while seeming to conform. He was head of house, a school prefect, and appears to have been popular. 'He never bullied those under him,' recalled his contemporary Ronald St Vincent, 'and was universally liked.'[22]

Yet there is no close school friend, no co-conspirator or fellow aspiring poet referred to in *The Buried Day*. There is little reference to going to visit other boys at home in the holidays. Or of them coming to see him. Instead Day-Lewis's youthful heroes and companions were teachers like H. R. King, dead saints like Ambrose or the poet W. B. Yeats.

34

He had already learnt at Craven Terrace, by observing and reacting to the example of his father, to inhabit his own world, compartmentalize life, internalize experiences both negative and positive, and so appear to be one thing when he was in reality feeling another. At Sherborne, he put such knowledge to good effect. He stared out, handsome but aloof, from annual house photographs, taken outside the housemaster's study on the lawn at Harper. The removal of a large sebaceous cyst from his chin – 'the visible badge of immoral practices' he suggested in *The Buried Day* – left him with a scar for life but did nothing to dent his burgeoning good looks.

Some perceived that air of solitude and took it as evidence of being self-important. Day-Lewis himself wrote of how in his final days at Sherborne he adopted a 'superficial perverseness – the simple arrogant desire to be different'.[23] Self-centred is adjective used of him by his contemporary at school, The Revd T. C. Teape-Fugard.[24] But soon-to-leave schoolboys are fond of posing and seldom astute in judging others.

> *Solitude then was my métier. I wore it*
> *As an invisible cloak, or a glass cloche*
> *To save from nibbling teeth and clodhopper boots*
> *And focus the sun's eye on my sullen growth.*
> *I kept my solitude as a young girl guards*
> *Virginity yet wishes it away.*
> *Impatient of the blossom cloud that endears her.*
> 'Sketches for a Self-Portrait': *Poems 1943–1947* (1948)

Underneath that air of self-confidence lay its opposite. Failure to make the school first XI and XV niggled away at him. Worse was his inability at maths, the first time he had tried and failed to master a school subject. And then there was his failure, first time round, to get a scholarship to Oxford in classics. Without the financial support such an award brought, the cost of four years studying for a degree would be beyond Frank Day-Lewis's clergyman's pay. So Cecil had to stay on for another year, expressing his dissatisfaction at being a 19-year-old schoolboy by penning editorials in *The Shirburnian* which were mildly critical of the masters but which stopped well short of any open incitement to rebellion.

Even though he was later in the 1930s to cultivate an air of revolting against an establishment which included the public school – 'with its false heroics, its facile religiosity and distorted values'[25] – Day-Lewis showed little sign of any discomfort while at Sherborne. If the public school ethos of serving country and empire sparked anything in him as an adolescent, it was not disgust but a much more conventional strong sense of social and public responsibility. As head of house he took a paternalistic and kindly interest in youngsters who had just started, and in Sophists' debates he spoke up for 'the tiller of the soil' and 'the inmate of the slum', though his experience of either was at this stage non-existent.[26]

At his second attempt, he was awarded an exhibition to read classics at Wadham College, Oxford. His tutor, Maurice Bowra[27], later surprised him by telling him it had been granted not only on the strength of his English essay in his examination paper but also his reputation as rugby footballer.

His last month at Sherborne saw little study and much celebration. At one such event, he met the daughter of H. R. King, the teacher who had so inspired him. Mary King was two years older than Cecil and had recently returned from London where she had been studying mime and dance at the fashionable Ginner-Mawer School. 'She had an air of independence,' he recalled, 'for which, in my role as the-cat-that-walked-by-itself, I felt a strong affinity.'

Chapter 5

Rip Van Winkle Forest

Consider the boy that you were, although you would hardly
Recognize him if you met him, even in his old haunts –
The well-shaved lawn or the Rip Van Winkle forest,
With the slag-tip reek acrid as youth's resentments
Tainting their green
'Sketches for a Self-Portrait': *Poems 1943–1947* (1948)

On November 11, 1918, Cecil Day-Lewis had joined the school community in Sherborne's central Courts to hear the headteacher, Nowell Smith, announce the armistice that brought an end to the First World War. There was, one of those present recalled, no celebration, just an overwhelming sense of relief.[1]

For Frank Day-Lewis, it meant an end to the all-male life of a military chaplain which he had so enjoyed and a necessary return to parish work that didn't have quite the same allure. Reluctant as he approached 40 to go back to being a curate in London, he applied to be and was appointed as vicar of Edwinstowe in Nottinghamshire on a stipend of £600 a year, twice his pre-war income at Christ Church, Lancaster Gate. It could hardly be counted a prized ecclesiastical job, more of a solid but obscure backwater, but with the job went a stout, red brick Edwardian rectory, a large garden where he grew tomatoes, and a parish church with a colourful history. Surrounded by Sherwood Forest, the tall-spired St Mary's is, according to local legend, the place where Robin Hood married Maid Marian.

Edwinstowe itself in 1918 was a small, sleepy, country village, isolated from larger conurbations at Nottingham and Mansfield by the encircling forest and by the relatively late arrival of the railways there in 1890. Named after the seventh-century King Edwin of Northumbria who died in battle nearby, it boasted in 1918 only two paved streets and a population of under 1000, made up mainly of farm workers.[2] The vicar's responsibilities also covered outlying rural churches at Clipstone and Carburton in the adjoining agricultural area of north west Nottinghamshire known as the Dukeries.

If Day-Lewis had in mind a comfortable posting with few challenges for his fragile faith and plenty of agreeable perks, then he was to be disappointed. His living was in the gift of the local landowner, Earl Manvers, whose Thoresby estate included Edwinstowe. Soon after the new vicar's arrival, Manvers, pleading financial hardship brought on by the post-war slump, took a decision which was to change Edwinstowe for ever. He agreed to lease the mineral rights to the part of his estate that adjoined the village to the Bolsover Colliery Company. Underneath the Dukeries lay thick seams of coal and profitable pits had already been sunk in towns across what was to become the North Nottinghamshire coalfield.

As a result of Manvers' decision, Thoresby Colliery opened just to the north of Edwinstowe. By the 1940s it was producing a million tonnes of coal a year.[3] A small industrial revolution was unfolding all around the vicarage. On his vacation visits from Sherborne, Day-Lewis witnessed the rapid transformation of village into town. In a ten-year period from 1921 the population tripled. Houses were built on what had been fields of oats and barley to accommodate families drawn by the promise of work, however tough the conditions underground might be. 'When we first went there, the black-faced miners cycling home were outnumbered by the farm labourers whom they passed in the village street, exchanging a curt Midland "How-do". Twenty years later, almost every man would be working in the pits.'[4]

Already in 1918 collieries around Mansfield to the east had begun to give the prevailing wind a whiff of their slag heaps, while the long coal trains that trundled from pit to pit would clank along the embankment that was visible from the rectory windows. And when Thoresby came into operation, the whole town languished under a thin layer of black coal dust.

The influx of pit workers caused social tensions in Edwinstowe between long-established farm hands and the incomers. The agricultural community tended to associate with the parish church, while the miners often headed for worship to two Nonconformist chapels in the town. Though the distinction was not absolute, it may account for some of the unfavourable memories of The Revd Day-Lewis among mining families still living to this day in Edwinstowe.

Jack Bramley, who arrived there as a small child with his miner father at the same time as the Day-Lewises, described the vicar as 'toffee-nosed'. Dorothy Dean, who used to deliver milk to the vicarage, concurred. 'It was the general opinion that the vicar was hoity-toity, one of the social elite.' Cyril Beardsley, a pupil at the newly-built council school that adjoined St Mary's added: 'I remember Day-Lewis as a man who hated and despised the miners like the plague. He only looked after the farmer and farm hands of that day.'[5]

John Manning, whose mother Annie Parnell used to play tennis with Cecil on the courts laid out by the colliery company at Forest Green, had more mixed memories. The vicar was 'known to villagers as that nasty-tempered Irishman. He was autocratic and considered himself a cut above his parishioners [but] on hearing of illness or a mine accident would lose no time in visiting the sick person's home, or hospital, and showing Christian concern.' In this, as in other things, it seems Frank Day-Lewis sent out mixed messages. Some recalled that he would go to the local Miners' Institute (or working men's club) to listen to complaints about conditions in the pits. Others, though, maintained that he was more interested in currying favour with Manvers and the local landowners.[6]

For Cecil, returning from Sherborne where he had begun to assert his independence, the mixed feelings of local people towards his father mirrored his own ambiguous responses.

> Love I desired, but the father I loved and hated
> Lived too much in me, and his images of me
> Fretted a frame always outgrowing them:
> I went into a wilderness bearing all
> My faults and his ambitions on my head
>
> 'Sketches for a Self-Portrait': *Poems 1943–1947* (1948)

His way of breaking through this emotional roadblock was to steer the conversation towards arguments with his father that would only emphasize the growing distance between them. There would still be occasional moments of warm companionship. There was, for instance, a visit to Trent Bridge in Nottingham to watch Harold Larwood bowling. And, although he had little taste for it himself, Frank encouraged his son's interest in poetry by giving him as presents collections of verse that Cecil kept ever after on his bookshelves, the title page inscribed simply 'from Dad'.

Once Cecil could drive, he would act as his father's chauffeur at the wheel of, first, his back-firing, two-cylinder Humberette and, later, a two-seater Renault with a dickey seat in the back, as the vicar made his house calls (in full clerical dress) and conducted services in the far flung churches of the parish. As they drove and later at home over meals, though, there would be a series of debates – over books, or politics, or the social changes happening on their doorsteps, or even the most trivial matters – where Cecil would strain to cause offence and his father would eventually respond with violent explosions and cut short the conversation with 'when you have had my experience of life, you will see that I am right'.[7]

Such rows accompany most teenagers spreading their wings, but here they were overlaid by the old cycle of contradictory signals and urges that had been so much part of life in Craven Terrace. So Frank Day-Lewis was keen to have his only child around as much as possible in the vacations. A return to the pre-war habit of going to Monart each summer would be out of the question now that Cecil was away at school for so much of the year.

Yet once he had a surly teenager under his roof, he quickly got angry with him. It was as if there was not one but two teenagers in the house. 'Recoiling from the inordinate love I obscurely felt as a menace,' Day-Lewis wrote, 'hardening myself against the scenes which so unnerved me, I had little by little built up within myself a resistance to emotional pressure – built it all too effectually, for a time came when it seemed that my own capacity for feeling was atrophied.'[8]

There were few outlets for the tension. Edwinstowe boasted no boys of Cecil's age and background to mix with. There would be occasional invitations to tennis parties at the local big houses – Thoresby, Welbeck, Clumber, Rufford – but in such an aristocratic world the vicar's son felt out of place, attending 'always with a sense of de bas en haut'.[9] And the teenage sons of miners and farmers would, at his age, already be busy earning their living. He existed in Edwinstowe between one extreme and the other.

John Parnell's evidence would suggest that the handsome son of the vicar was more successful with local girls. Aged fifteen, Day-Lewis reported that he had his first love affair with a girl he called only E, the daughter of a private chaplain to one of the local nobility, 'sweet-natured, shy, with a rose-petal complexion'.[10] They played tennis, went for walks and bicycle rides and exchanged letters when he was away at school. Eventually they got as far as holding hands and Cecil even put his arm round her while sitting on the sofa. He subsequently made a passing reference to their chaste friendship in verse:

> Later, after each dream of beauty ethereal,
> Bicycling against the wind to see the vicar's daughter,
> Be disappointed.

'Poem 21': *From Feathers to Iron* (1931)

Then his over-protective and judgemental father intervened. One evening Cecil had to walk the four miles home from E's house because the fog made it impossible to ride his bike. Her father telephoned ahead to say Cecil would be late, but when he finally reached the rectory, Frank was in a rage. 'I heard him bellowing from the top of the drive. He was beside himself. He shouted at me all the way up the drive, followed me into the house and up to my room, shouting down my attempts to explain why I was late.'[11]

The anxiety of a father that his one and only son might be lost in the fog was natural enough. Contributing too may have been a suspicion that Cecil had been delayed by indulging in something 'immoral' with E, an assumption that had already surfaced in outraged letters Frank Day-Lewis had written to his son at Sherborne. But it is hard not also to see the suppressed anger that had long hovered near to the surface in Frank over his wife's untimely death, and also his related 'smother-love' for their son.

The solitary streak in Cecil grew at Edwinstowe with each holiday. To the parish he was the vicar's polite but aloof son of whom he was inordinately proud. But inside the vicarage, he felt trapped and bored. While his school friends at Sherborne would have adventures in the long vacation, he would hang around at home with a father who was unable or unwilling to pay for him to travel. The only place to escape was within himself.

Geographically the farthest afield he ventured was when he would take long walks or rides into the public parts of Sherwood Forest (most of it remained fenced off, the preserve of families like the Manvers). The sounds remained ever after imprinted on his imagination -'the hooters from the mines and the distant rattle of the pit-head winding gear as the cages went up and down'.[12]

Despite the background noises, however, he found among the trees something approximating to the kind of inner and outer peace that the nature-loving Yeats would have appreciated, a heady somnolence and timeless apartness from events reshaping Edwinstowe and his relationship with his father. Later, in his decidedly autobiographical poem, 'Sketches for a Self-Portrait', he was to label

Sherwood a 'Rip Van Winkle Forest' after the story, told memorably by Washington Irving, of a wastrel who gets so seduced by the calm of a forest that he sleeps through the American Revolution.

Back at the vicarage there was some respite to be had from the tension with his father in the shape of Knos, but, bullied as ever by her brother-in-law and accepting of his ways, she could not provide the necessary escape valve for Cecil. The childlike qualities in her that had so attracted her nephew as a youngster no longer appealed to a discontented teenager. Mostly he preferred to be on his own. Mrs Lawrence, who worked as the Day-Lewises' cook, used to call him 'Cuckoo' because she had often seen him climbing a tree in the garden, sitting there and imitating the call of the cuckoo.[13]

There was a perhaps unintended irony here for he was to become, at least in the eyes of his stepmother, the unwanted one in the family nest when Frank Day-Lewis, after much procrastination, decided in 1921 to remarry. It was thirteen years since his wife had died. Still in his early 40s, he could have chosen as his bride a woman young enough to give him more children. He was still a handsome man as shown by the expensive photographic portraits he had taken of himself in 1920 at London society's favourite studio, Bassano on Piccadily.[14] There had certainly been plenty of unattached female parishioners at Christ Church in London who would gladly have answered the call to go north to assist their one-time curate.

Instead, though, he chose from among their number a woman five years his senior. Margaret Kathleen Maud Wilkinson, always known as Mamie, had met Frank Day-Lewis several years earlier because her family had lived in Cleveland Square in his old parish. She had made it plain to him that she was available for marriage early on in their relationship, but he had dithered for a long time. In her favour in Frank's eyes was the fact that her social credentials were good. She had titled cousins and her father, who came to live briefly at the Edwinstowe vicarage, had been a major in the Durham Light Infantry during the Crimean War. Moreover she was well-off, with a substantial private income that would have appealed to a vicar who was struggling to maintain on £600 a year the household staff of a gardener and two maids that he felt a man in his position required.

It was not Mamie's looks that attracted him. Plump, with a small mouth and a beak of a nose, she was matronly and prudish. Though no intellectual, she would nevertheless have shone in Frank Day-Lewis's eyes on account of her compliant manner, their shared social pretensions and a natural tendency to defer to her future husband's views and needs.

Included in Frank's deliberations on whether to marry her were his local bishop and his 17-year-old son. One concern was appearing disloyal to Kathleen's memory. Frank's unhappiness at her death was still in evidence. He was known locally for drinking heavily at the Royal Oak on the High Street and for failing to pay his bills.[15]

Another factor was Knos. Mamie would not want her in the vicarage. Yet Knos had devoted the prime of her life to her dead sister's husband and son and, despite his harsh treatment of her, may even have developed a genuine affection for Frank, though the two would have been prevented from marrying by law at the time.[16] There was never any credible suggestion that their relationship might have become more intimate, though some malicious gossips in Edwinstowe had questioned the propriety of a vicar sharing his home with his late wife's sister.[17]

In the end it was Cecil's enthusiasm for the idea of a second marriage that convinced his father to proceed. It can only be presumed that at this stage he had little knowledge of Mamie since most of the consultation was done by letter when he was away at school. There was, as ever, an emotional burden placed on the teenager's shoulders by his father. 'I remember my father saying to me,' he wrote, 'that, if he did remarry, it would be partly for my sake, and I should always be the first person in his life ... It is strange to me now that I should have welcomed the prospect and anticipated with such equanimity the supplanting of Knos.'[18] This willingness to see her discarded adds weight to the suggestion that he did not truly regard her as a second mother.

Any pangs of guilt, however, were 'quickly deadened by the prospect, always enticing to a temperament like mine, of a radical change in my life, and by the expectation that a stepmother would at least do something to relieve the grinding boredom of holidays in Edwinstowe'.[19]

On June 1, 1921 he was best man at the marriage, in Christ Church, Lancaster Gate, of Frank Day-Lewis and Mamie Wilkinson. For all his scruples about Kathleen's memory, choosing Cecil as his best man did not apparently strike Frank as odd.

Knos was swiftly sent back to Ireland. If Cecil hadn't considered sufficiently before what the effect of his father remarrying would be on her, he did now. For Knos, it was like a bereavement. Some 30 years later there were still tears in her eyes when she spoke of being parted from Cecil by the arrival of Mamie.[20]

> Exiled again, after ten years, my father
> Remarrying, she faced the bitter test
> Of charity – to abdicate in love's name
> From love's contentful duties. A distressed
>
> Gentle woman housekeeping for strangers;
> Later, companion to a droll recluse
> Clergyman brother in rough-pastured Wexford,
> She lived for all she was worth – to be of use.
>
> She bottled plums, she visited parishioners.
> A plain habit of innocence, a faith
> Mildly forbearing, made her one of those
> Who, we were promised, shall inherit the earth.
>
> 'My Mother's Sister': The Room and Other Poems (1965)

Nowhere in Day-Lewis's poetry is there any obvious mention of Mamie, much less a tribute. With Knos gone, she quickly turned the vicarage into a shrine to her own Victorian values. There was her large, heavy furniture, her collection of china figurines and stuffed animals under glass domes, her oil paintings of hunts, hounds and dismembered foxes, and her sporting memorabilia. One relative had once owned a Derby winner. The maids were given frilly aprons and anything of any value (and many things without) were locked away, with access only granted on applying to the new Mrs Day-Lewis for the key. It made the whole house seem ever more to Cecil like a prison.

Mealtimes were regular and often. Mamie liked rich food. Her wealth meant that lobster started to feature on the vicarage menu on Fridays. Her once-athletic husband blossomed and sagged under her care. She was devoted to her dogs but it was as nothing compared to her devotion to Frank. She was meek, applauding his prejudices and smoothing over any ruffled feathers he caused among parishioners. All who remembered her later in Edwinstowe had nothing but good to say about her.[21]

With her stepson, she set off on the wrong foot, probably unintentionally, by asking him to call her mother. He refused and behind her back referred to her as the 'step-dragon' or 'step-d'.[22] She did not bring out the best in him. Her interest and even her language irritated him. She would, for instance, describe a beautiful countryside view as a 'pretty peep'.[23] Already prickly, tense and bored, Cecil found in Mamie and the world she created in the vicarage an easy target on which to aim all his resentments. 'Outside our house were the League of Nations, the Bright Young Things, Birth Control, the rise of Labour, the "Trouble" in Ireland . . . within, the habits and values of the Victorian age largely held sway – a provincial Victorianism of which my stepmother, with her closed mind, was the chief source.'[24]

Just as his father would end all arguments with his son with a variation of the line that when he grew up, he would come to agree, Cecil always felt he ran aground in the quarrels he provoked with Mamie on her blanket condemnation of anything new or different. 'I argued with her, of course; but it was like arguing with a glacier – a transparent and infrangible surface beneath which the prejudices lay safely forever embedded.'[25]

In such a setting, each holiday the young Day-Lewis would stew and withdraw ever more into himself. 'My adolescence smoldered away, acrid as the reek of the slag-tips which tainted the air, an odour of harsh sterility.'[26] As the fight was drained out of him by his father, stepmother and boredom, he would sink ever more into detachment and solitude and later experienced for the first time depression – what he called his 'black moods'.[27]

Amid his boredom and resignation, he began to take some notice – initially no doubt to be difficult – of the national, international, political and social issues that Frank and Mamie tried so hard to shut out of their lives. Out of pure provocation something more started to grow. Cecil realized that his own observations of a fast-changing Edwinstowe gave him an insight rare in the cosseted corridors of Sherborne. As well as the inspiration he found in Sherwood Forest for the Yeats-esque mythical nature poetry that he was then writing in his notebooks, there were also the images of industrialization that he registered and stored away in a compartment, opened later, to such acclaim, in *The Magnetic Mountain*.

Men are wanted who will volunteer
To go aloft and cut away tangled gear;
Break through to blocked galleries below pit-head,
Get in touch with living and raise from the dead:

'Poem 10': *The Magnetic Mountain* (1933)

More immediate, though, was the knowledge, admittedly at least second-hand, that he gained in Edwinstowe of the often brutal nature for many of the world of work. 'Remote though the miners' lives were from me, it is at Edwinstowe that my social conscience was born.'[28] It was not that he was overnight radicalized. By his own admission 'accidents had occurred deep down below my very feet as I sat in a sunny rock garden reading Swinburne or the early Yeats',[29] but the blinkered view of the world that was shared by home and school was being challenged.

Chapter 6

The Sunless Stream

Ennui of youth! – thin air above the clouds,
Vain divination of the sunless stream
Mirror that impotence, till we redeem
Our birthright, and the shadowplay concludes.
Ah, not in dreams, but when our souls engage
With the common mesh and moil, we come of age.
'O Dreams O Destinations': *Word Over All* (1943)

Cecil Day-Lewis arrived at Wadham College in October of 1923. Oxford was enjoying one of its periodic 'golden ages', though it did not feel that way to a fresher like Day-Lewis without money or social connections. The dominant figure on the university scene was Harold Acton,[1] self-styled aesthete, often to be glimpsed, Day-Lewis later recalled, 'tittupping along the High his Oxford bags [loose, wide-cuffed trousers] flapping, his big head rolling and nodding like a toy mandarin's as he chattered vivaciously with the group that trailed beside him'.[2] The hedonistic goal of this group was to dispel by their dress, their manner and their studied interest in artistic matters the shadow of the First World War (the last ex-servicemen students had just left Oxford when Day-Lewis arrived). And they succeeded. The age of the aesthetes saw Oxford experiencing a self-indulgent kind of freedom from anxiety and outside events that was all too soon to be overtaken by the political and economic upheavals that built towards a second world conflict.

Overlapping with the aesthetes were the 'Bright Young Things' who were busy reacting with a constant round of partying against their parents' Edwardian attitudes. Day-Lewis may have spotted – or heard – the drunken excesses of these wealthy aristocrats after the high jinx arranged by the university's Bullingdon Club (immortalized soon afterwards as the Bollinger in Evelyn Waugh's *Decline and Fall*[3]) but his exhibition at Wadham, plus a leaving award from Sherborne, covered less than half his basic expenses. It was a world beyond his wallet. His allowance, he later used to remark, hardly stretched to an ice cream on a Sunday.[4]

John Betjeman,[5] his contemporary at Oxford but from a more prosperous, better-connected background, described university life at this time as essentially a clash between two camps, Acton's aesthetes and 'hearties'. These, he wrote, 'were good college men who rowed in the college boat, ate in the college hall, and drank beer and shouted. Their regulation uniform was college tie, college pullover, tweed coat and grey flannel trousers.'[6]

He was, of course, exaggerating. There were few undergraduates who would have fitted the aesthete or heartie stereotype exactly. Many, though, would have existed on the fringes of the two camps, some of them connected to both simultaneously. There were also many more who stuck to their studies and their college dining hall. They had little connection with any of the headline- and history-grabbing antics going on around them. It was in such company that Day-Lewis initially felt most comfortable.

Wadham, though ancient and venerable, was not one of the smarter colleges. Its undergraduates were deliberately drawn from a wider (though still by modern standards narrow) range of essentially middle class backgrounds and included a larger than average number of Jews and Americans. In an atmosphere where there was little overt snobbery and a strong inclination towards tolerance, Day-Lewis found he could comfortably retreat into himself in those first weeks there, declining invitations when he could and dressing up as aloofness his shyness and the inadequacy he felt at his provincial roots.

Subsequently he was to write of himself in this period as 'lonely, inexperienced, with mildly gregarious tendencies and a keen desire to be liked' and therefore 'a predestined victim' for a group he labelled 'learner-bores' – 'young men who ingratiated themselves by showing me the ropes ... they were already in training to be the terror of their common rooms, clubs and closes ... [and] would one day haunt Old Boys' Dinners and College Gaudies'.[7]

He quickly tired of these learner-bores and, having found his feet, began to widen his horizons. Going up to university where there is almost no one who knows anything about you affords, Day-Lewis soon realized, the opportunity to remodel yourself, to become whatever you wanted to be. His firm ambition already was to be a poet. And so that was how he sought to appear – by, for example, sitting in the copper beech in Wadham garden with a lock of hair falling over one eye, reading Homer. He even describes in *The Buried Day* how he gave himself a new walk – to match the image he wanted to convey.

One of his first role models was Robert Graves,[8] the poet, classicist and novelist, nine years Day-Lewis's senior, who was then living south of Oxford at Boar's Hill. 'I remember meeting Graves at the bus stop and deciding instantly that this was what a poet should look like: blunt-featured, shock-headed, with a butcher-blue shirt, a knapsack and a manner withdrawn yet agreeably arrogant.'[9]

If the fledgling dandy in him – a shared trait with his father – struggled with such a rough, romantic way of dressing, Day-Lewis did, according to some of those who went up to Wadham at the same time, seem either instinctively or by design to have managed more easily to capture the withdrawn and arrogant manner. Charles Fenby[10] remarked that his first take on Day-Lewis was as 'haughty and aloof ... My earliest impression of him is of a tall and good-looking undergraduate, extremely well-dressed in the clothes affected in those days and known as plus fours ... He seemed to me reserved in manner, even rather icy, and I regarded his general bearing and the expression of his mouth as supercilious and perhaps "stuck-up".'[11]

It took Fenby a while in that first term to get behind the projection but once he did the two became great friends. Pale, bespectacled, already balding and plagued by boils, Fenby had come up to read history at Wadham from his Darlington grammar school. His family was well-to-do and Nonconformist, with his uncle, Sir Charles Starmer, a pillar of the Liberal Party and a newspaper publisher. Fenby was kept on a tight allowance and like Day-Lewis initially felt an outsider in the Oxford of aesthetes and hearties, though he found his confidence sooner and became a leading light in OUDS, the university drama society, and the Union, its debating forum. 'The accepted wisdom in the family', said his son Jonathan, 'was that Oxford was my father's liberation, the seminal event in his life, and that once there he never wanted to go back to Darlington.'[12]

Among Day-Lewis's classics set at Wadham was another fresher, Rex Warner,[13] who was also in revolt against his background – this time one more closely akin to Day-Lewis's than Fenby's. Warner's father was an impecunious Anglican vicar – albeit of a more modern and eccentric disposition than Frank – and he had arrived in Oxford with a passion for poetry via a minor public school where the strong emphasis was on games. Tall, pale-faced and black-haired, Warner had striking good looks, dressed fashionably and was something of an intellectual show-off.

The three became in the course of that first term a trio, with Warner the brains, boisterously spouting radical ideas, Fenby the ballast, offering a calming voice of reason, and Day-Lewis once again the dreamer, slower than those around him to adapt to the new freedoms and challenges of university life, and slightly in awe of his two new friends who seemed brighter and more able in every way than him.

The bond that developed between the three young men in those student days was a first for Day-Lewis. There had been friends at Sherborne, but no one close. Getting to know others intimately – and letting them get to know him – was part of his journey away from his father and the constraints of the Edwinstowe vicarage. All three young men shared a restlessness with their lives as they were and had been. It came out at first as anxiety but gradually, with mutual encouragement and long debates into the early hours, enabled them to move from the margins to the mainstream of Oxford life.

In those first weeks and months, Day-Lewis recalled, life was all 'intellectual ferment: the impact of a mature society upon the more or less unsophisticated freshman, the intoxication of larger intercourse with brilliant minds, living and dead, the heady, home-brewed ideas to which we treated one another, all made for a certain insobriety of outlook and an erratic course – a process often aggravated, for those of us who had had authority in our public schools, by outbreaks of wild nonsense and high spirits, as though our recent responsibilities must be compensated now by a period of pure irresponsibility, a regression to the boyhood which had been curtailed before we could fully experience it'.[14]

With Warner and Fenby he would walk around college and the streets of Oxford, making sure to spend as little as possible from the meagre allowances, but drunk nonetheless on ideas and debate. These three tall young men would be so wrapped up in 'one of the three-cornered arguments, half-serious, half

47

frivolous, in which we exercised our brains like sophists by inconstantly changing sides' that they hardly would have noticed Acton's flamboyant followers or the antics of the Bullingdon.[15]

What they did share with those more confident undergraduates was a need to discard old conventions and manners. It was the prevailing sentiment at Oxford in the mid-1920s according to one of their contemporaries, the future Labour Party leader, Hugh Gaitskell. 'Oxford was gay, frivolous, stimulating and tremendously alive ... it was a brief, blessed interval ... Most of us weren't sufficiently bitter or perhaps sufficiently serious to be angry young men ... [in] the heavenly freedom of Oxford revolt took the form of an outburst of scepticism, a mistrust of dogma, a dislike of sentimentality and of over-emotional prejudices or violent crusades'.[16]

Among the debating topics bounced round between Day-Lewis, Fenby and Warner was politics. Warner was the most openly rebellious, though much of his sympathy for the working classes and their lot was theoretical. The centre of Oxford was then almost hermetically sealed off from the motor works and factories on its outskirts at Cowley. Fenby was more moderate, detached and eventually cynical. Day-Lewis, his conscience already troubled by what he had seen happening when the mines came to north Nottinghamshire, was the novice who listened and learnt from his friends. By the time he returned to his old school during the Christmas vacation, he took with him a copy of the left-wing publication, *Lansbury's Weekly*. On the back cover were the words of 'The Red Flag' which he mischievously delighted in teaching some of the Sherborne pupils to sing.

The trio's talk also stretched to discussing more intimate concerns. Day-Lewis had learned as a small child to bottle up emotions and worries. Confiding in others did not come easily. With Fenby and Warner he felt sufficiently confident to reveal himself. Warner in particular recalled Day-Lewis 'getting in a great state after a letter from his Dad'[17] and occasionally lapsing into melancholy or depression.

Part of the intensity of the friendship between the three can be explained by the absence in their lives of girlfriends. Rare was the female undergraduate who ventured out of the world of the all-women's colleges on the outskirts of Oxford to mix freely with men. Elizabeth Harman, later Lady Longford,[18] became in 1930 the first woman student ever to feature as an 'Isis Idol' in the university magazine of the same name on account of her boldness in demanding that male undergraduates treated her as an intellectual equal.

'I am sure that fewer than 10 per cent of my contemporaries had ... "girl friends",' Evelyn Waugh later wrote of these times at Oxford. 'Some had made a single, pleasureless adventure with a prostitute abroad. Few had any serious interest in women.'[19] Many who later went on to marry had homosexual relationships. Waugh was, for example, observed by Tom Driberg[20] at the all-male Hypocrites' Club 'rolling on a sofa' with another man, their 'tongues licking each other's tonsils'.[21]

Fenby, Day-Lewis and Warner had, however, already outgrown the adolescent same-sex experiments that kept other undergraduates satisfied, particularly in the fashionable world of the aesthetes. Warner in particular was openly homophobic. They craved female company and encounters, but had little idea how to make it happen.

In this area Day-Lewis could for once steal a march on his otherwise more worldly friends. Since their first meeting in his final days at Sherborne, his attachment to Mary King had grown ever closer. It was 'her beautifully cool voice and the grace of her movements' that had, he recalled, first attracted him.[22] Dark-haired, with a smile that lit up her face, her training as a dancer and her almost pagan interest in nature, legends and nymphs and fairies gave her an exoticism that drew him in. Yet her show of free-thinking and confidence was only skin-deep. The only daughter among the five children of his old school-teacher, H. R. King, she was used to being around boys but like many who had grown up as tomboys was unsure how to act with men who were courting her.

At the outset this was a bonus for the equally inhibited Day-Lewis. Mary, he wrote, 'had certain acquired traits of boyishness that made it easy for me to approach her – a frankness of address, a mind both idealistic and satirical, a lack of feminine subtlety and disingenuousness which at this time I would have found an insuperable barrier'.[23]

For her part after that first meeting in July 1923, Mary had written in her diary: 'Met Day-Lewis, he gave me his paper on W. B. Yeats to read. Irish eyes which see dreams.'[24] They had corresponded over the summer and Mary had visited Edwinstowe in the September before Cecil went up to Wadham. Her presence inevitably sent Frank and Mamie into a fluster as to how to chaperone the young couple. They grew alarmed when Cecil and Mary sat up talking late into the night, while the step-dragon insisted on accompanying them on walks into Sherwood Forest.

She needn't have worried. Both were innocent and fearful, promiscuous only in the verbal declarations of love they made, once they had shaken off Mamie, as they sat amongst the trees of the forest. They would spend, Day-Lewis later remembered, hours trying to commune with beech trees and reading to each other Yeats's early period poetry and two prose works – *The Education of Uncle Paul* and *A Prisoner in Fairy Land* by Algernon Blackwood – that held a mystical glamour for them. Though 19 and 21, they were both children in emotional matters.

Part of Mary's attraction for Day-Lewis was her family. That summer visit to Edwinstowe led to love letters and return trips to Sherborne and the King family home in the vacations of his first year at Oxford. The contrast with Edwinstowe struck him immediately. 'Never before had I lived in a household that was civilized, relaxed, various, yet a close network of relationships. Here consanguinity seemed a bond, not a fetter ... Talk leapt madly about like a fire-cracker, from nonsense to high seriousness. There was good music in the house, and more books than I had ever seen; and there were HRK [Mary's father, his ex-teacher]'s incomparable readings aloud from Jane Austen, Thackeray, Dickens or the poets.'[25]

On one visit to Sherborne Mary took Day-Lewis to her favourite place – a hill above the town where an oak tree had acquired a spiritual significance for her. (It featured later in his 1936 novel, *The Friendly Tree*.) She christened him her 'piper'. Yet that night in her diary she wrote: 'I miss the human element in CDL – the piper talks as sprite to sprite, as artist to artist, but not as friend to friend.'[26] Later in March of 1924, after another meeting, she penned an entry which gives some clue about her inhibition. 'I believe I am half a boy in thought and feeling.'[27] The combination of her lack of confidence in her femininity and his dreamy self-absorption would make this a long and chaste courtship.

Neither had strong religious or moral objections to sex before marriage, but equally neither would easily take the lead in consummating their relationship. Day-Lewis wanted to but was too shy and nervous of getting it wrong to act on his feelings. He was also too self-absorbed either to make Mary believe that something lay behind his protestations of love or to give him insight into the inhibitions that were holding her back. Seduced by his poetry and by his good looks, she was struggling to move beyond feeling towards him as a sister might.

They were apart at the start of the summer vacation of 1924. Day-Lewis returned for the first time since 1914 to Monart to see Uncle Willie and Knos who had taken the place of her recently deceased sister Alice as the rector's housekeeper. On his first visit to what was now the Irish Free State, he enjoyed once more the 'hand-to-mouth life at the top of the morning!'[28] and wrote of its joys to the more adventurous Warner who was travelling round France on a miniscule budget. Day-Lewis used the teasing banter they had developed, accusing him of 'hob-knobbing with a lot of damned dagoes in some God-forsaken part of the globe'.[29]

Later in August Day-Lewis joined a King family holiday to Loch Linnhe in Argyllshire and delighted in the long walks and bicycle rides, followed by evenings of declaiming poetry and highly competitive games of poker and patience. He tried not to neglect his girlfriend in favour of her brothers, but increasingly found time alone with her an agony. 'All day I had been with him,' Mary wrote in her diary, 'and at night we talked by the river. Always we hammer away at the same question in the same old way. I cannot love and he cannot leave me'.[30]

In September, she went again to Edwinstowe. Even allowing for the frustration Day-Lewis felt when entombed in the vicarage, Mary's diary suggests that the emotional and sexual tension caused by their differing reactions to the relationship was building. 'Days of tearing depression – my knight is sad because I cannot give him more and I know not the way of mine own heart.'[31]

When Mary came to Oxford in the May of Day-Lewis's second year, it did little to improve matters. She felt shut out of his new world and patronized by his new friends. 'It does not seem possible in Oxford', she told her diary, 'to make a simple remark, everything is twisted into an epigram.'[32]

Such a verdict suggests that in academic matters as in others the trio of friends was adjusting to the Oxford world. Warner and Day-Lewis were taught by Maurice Bowra. Brisk, short, witty, camp, outrageous and older than his 30 years, Bowra was one of the brightest lights at Wadham and indeed the whole university. He had been a hero in the First World War and both his intellect and his delight in displaying it were already assuming the proportions of local legend. Tutorial room and salon merged seamlessly in his world. As well as encouraging and directing Day-Lewis and Warner towards what became for both a life-long passion for ancient Greece, Bowra introduced them to a gossipy set where the merciless edge in their tutor's conversation was geared, Bowra claimed, to drawing out intellect. 'Cecil,' he once rebuked his pupil, 'conversation should be a vehicle of, not a substitute for, thought.'[33]

Though never entirely at ease with Bowra, Day-Lewis accepted his invitations to lunch in rooms full of Etruscan and Greek figurines where he met glamorous university figures like Lord David Cecil[34] and John Betjeman who might otherwise never have come into his orbit. It achieved what Bowra clearly had in mind – to bring the handsome young man he was teaching out of himself. There was, though, recalled Anthony Powell,[35] another habitué of the Bowra salons in this period, often an uncomfortable edge to the gatherings, with the host throwing out sexual and personal innuendo about those present. Bowra always, Powell wrote in *Infants of the Spring*, 'talked as if homosexuality was the natural condition of an intelligent man'.[36]

In their discussions, then, tutor and pupil strayed far beyond the set texts of the classics. They shared an admiration for Yeats and Bowra introduced Day-Lewis to T. S. Eliot's recently published *The Waste Land*.[37]

Bowra had high expectations for both Day-Lewis and Warner in Mods at the end of the summer term of 1925. The latter lived up to them and was awarded an outstanding first with 13 alphas in 15 papers, though the effort so exhausted him that he afterwards had a nervous breakdown and returned the following year to gain an undistinguished but unstressful English degree.

Day-Lewis managed only a sound second. He had struggled with ancient history and philosophy but had worked hard, competing with Warner, and so was disappointed. He treated suggestions that he was simply no good at handling the pressure of a public examination with disdain. He took his poor result to heart and had, he believed, been caught out once more as the intellectual fraud he had known himself to be since he struggled with maths at Sherborne.[38] He carried with him thereafter at Oxford a view of himself as hopeless academically and began to withdraw more and more from his studies to concentrate on his poetry.

In the summer of 1925, Day-Lewis once again turned down all suggestions from his friends that he should go with them to Europe. Travel to foreign parts as yet held little attraction for him. It wasn't so much the inevitable roughing it on the leftovers of an already stretched student budget that put him off. 'I didn't go abroad because I was afraid of making a fool of myself speaking a foreign language and people laughing at me', he later confessed.[39]

Instead he headed for Monart. Mary King joined him there. In *The Buried Day*, Day-Lewis presents the place where he was happiest as a child as the key to unlocking their blocked relationship. 'At Monart, that summer, the knot that held me powerless was cut. We went out one night, and by the gate into the meadow we kissed for the first time. When at last I went to bed, in the shabby little room I had shared with Knos as a child – it smelt now of the apples that had been stored there through the winter, and was swimming with moonlight – I was in a daze of glory, flooded with incredulous joy like a prisoner miraculously released after years of solitary confinement.'[40]

If this breathless account of their first kiss was written thirty-five years later and should necessarily be read with caution, then Day-Lewis also offered another similarly romantic description just three years after the event.

> In a windless garden
> At the time of plum-gathering
> When the hedge is plumy
> With Traveller's Joy,
> Beautiful gay candid
> My love came to me.
>
> Autumn closed around her,
> But her breath was all daffodils
> And her face all springtime:
> And now she has laid
> On my heart perennial
> Spring to renew me.
>
> In a windless garden
> At the time of plum-gathering
> My love came to me.

'My Love Came to Me': *Country Comets* (1928)

In the journals where he worked on his poems, an early draft of 'My Love Came to Me' is called instead 'An Irish Rhapsody'. Pressed in the page is a flower, perhaps picked in the Monart rectory garden.[41]

In her diary Mary was no less ecstatic. 'We were beneath the laburnum by the gate with the stars shining on us steadily ... Monart was magic in her ways. There was no passionate entreaty in our kiss, only starlight and lightness, warmth and happiness.'[42]

Beneath these accounts lay a certain amount of relief. 'He could not dream there how one kiss/Cancels a century of pain' continues 'My Love Came to Me'. Day-Lewis's inhibitions around the relationship were slowly breaking down. For Mary, all her self-doubt appeared to have been consigned to the past.

Yet looming in the background too is the shadowy figure of Margaret Marshall, the wife of the local doctor in Edwinstowe and someone who had in Day-Lewis's description 'trained as a psychiatrist'. He had met her at a tennis party just before he went up to Oxford. Four years his senior, she stood out from the daughters and wives of the local gentry who frequented such events on account of her 'lewd giggle', 'sensual mouth' and her reputation locally for being unconventional.[43] She noticed Day-Lewis, she told him, because he was hitting the ball so aggressively. 'He would throw his racket at the net when things went wrong,' she recalled in old age of the incident. 'He really loved to win, he would even play Monopoly with a wicked gleam in his eye.'[44]

Two misfits in the mining town, they were attracted and became friends. Marshall wrote poetry and they shared their verse with each other. Her disrespect for authority and occasionally colourful language appealed to the rebel in Day-Lewis. Soon afterwards, though, she left her husband and moved to Surrey where she set up home with another man, causing a stir in Edwinstowe. But she kept up contact with Day-Lewis and in his first summer vacation from Oxford invited him to stay at her new home near Guildford. Frank and Mamie put up no more than token objections despite the stigma that surrounded divorcees.

Margaret's second husband, Douglas, a singer, was already seriously ill as a result of tuberculosis but he too struck up a friendship with the young student based on their shared interest in music. In his autobiography, Day-Lewis describes Margaret Marshall as 'the elder sister I never had'.[45] Despite his usual reserve, he was encouraged by her frank talk, her unshockable manner and psychological insights to pour out to her all the self-doubts and worries he had been storing up about his life, his struggle to free himself from his father and his becalmed relationship with Mary. 'If in my late adolescence I had become a haunted house,' he wrote, 'it was Margaret more than anyone else who exorcised my ghosts and made it possible for me to live in myself.'[46]

He is vague, however, in *The Buried Day* as to how precisely Marshall helped him get over his inhibitions. They talked at length, he reports, but it 'never added up to any formal psychiatric treatment, let alone a deep analysis'.[47] This may have been because Marshall had no formal training as a psychiatrist and was simply a disciple of the then fashionable writer, Emile Coue[48] whose books included *Self-Mastery Through Conscious Auto-Suggestion*.

He continues that she gave him 'a map of the country I was lost in – a map of myself' but adds 'how far this map was objectively accurate is of no significance'.[49] Again it may be that her views – based on Coue's rather crankish mix of science and religion – were by the time he wrote this account too embarrassing to repeat.

Closer in time to their actual meeting was the tribute he paid her in *Transitional Poem* but it too suggests more than it reveals.

> She next, sorrow's familiar, who turned
> Her darkness to our light; that 'brazen leech'
> Alleviating the vain cosmic itch
> With fact coated in formulae lest it burned
> Our tongue. She shall have portion in my praise,
> And live in me, not memory, for always.

'Part II: 8': *Transitional Poem* (1929)

Whatever her methods, Margaret seems to have cajoled her impressionable guest out of solitude and self-pity and belatedly set him on the road to adulthood. One of Coue's maxims was 'every day, in every way, I grow better and better'. So Day-Lewis was encouraged to look outwards and forwards more, embrace life, seize chances, stop holding back through reticence or lack of confidence, and demand a more open and honest relationship with Mary.

He was not, he stresses in his account, in love with Marshall 'though I had felt an attraction towards her the first time we met, a sense that here was a person out of a different world from mine, but a world in which I might one day find myself and be at home'.[50] Yet that first visit to Greenlanes, her Surrey home, was recalled in a romantic early poem.

> Do you remember, Margaret, how we came
> Out on the heath our first evening
> Together? How the pines rose like a name
> Cried once by a dying man; and whirriting
> Nearby the nightjar's bell
> Rang down reluctant curtain on the day?
> Do you remember the brute smell
> Of bracken that heaved at the darkness where we lay?
>   I could hear my heart like a lupin pod
> Rattle its wizened dreams.

'At Greenlanes (An Epistle)': *Country Comets* (1928)

Day-Lewis was unambiguous later in describing Marshall as one of the most significant figures in his life but his account of their relationship is written so that it is impossible to know whether that also included being his first lover − 'alleviating the vain cosmic itch'. To seduce him would not have been out of character for Marshall. She had little time for the codes of behaviour which then surrounded sexual behaviour and had long since stopped worrying about causing scandal.

Shortly after Douglas's death she was briefly married for a third time to John Auden − brother of the poet W. H. Auden − but it ended badly when she had an affair with one of their servants. She was not a woman, W. H. Auden wrote, who wanted 'an adult love' but only 'absolute admiration and dependence'.[51] Day-Lewis was certainly naive enough to give her those in abundance when he visited her in Surrey. When he came to write *The Buried Day* Marshall was happily settled in America with her fourth husband and in a book that drew back instinctively from any potentially hurtful revelation, it makes sense that he would have spared her blushes about their past.

One clue to the nature of their relationship may have been the light-hearted suggestion he made several times in later life after visits to boys' schools, that what they really needed was what he called 'a temple of love' just by their gates where mature women could demonstrate to pent-up adolescents soon to head off for university the facts of life.[52]

Whatever went on between them, the time he spent with Margaret Marshall gave him new confidence in himself, in his desire to be a poet and in taking a lead in making a life with Mary. 'At Greenlanes' is directly followed in *Country Comets* by 'My Love Came To Me'. After their glorious first kiss at Monart, Mary and Cecil took Knos for a break to Brittas Bay, Co. Wicklow, and there they agreed, if all went well, to marry once Day-Lewis had finished his degree and got a job.

Chapter 7

Eldorados Close to Hand

The romantic youth
For whom horizons were the daily round,
Near things unbiddable and inane as dreams,
Till he had learned
Through his hoodwinked orbit of clay what Eldorados
Lie close to hand?
'Last Words': *Pegasus and Other Poems* (1958)

Day-Lewis's third year at Oxford was his happiest. He had come to an under-standing with Mary about their future together. He had decided, after his disappointment in Mods, to stop worrying so much about his academic work and devote himself to poetry. And he had moved into a student house with his great friends, Rex Warner and Charles Fenby.

22 St Giles sat right on the junction of the Woodstock and Banbury Roads at the north end of Oxford. It became the setting for his 1938 novel about four young students beginning their adult lives, *Starting Point*. As he looks out of the front window, Henry Voyce describes the view: 'droves of furiously-pedalling undergraduates; dons' wives from North Oxford in second-hand four-seaters; lorries rumbling north or south, their drivers pale for lack of sleep; the red, roaring buses, full of persons who doubtless had not received the benefits of a classical education'.[1]

The traffic noise was always there. Only at night was there peace – and then occasionally Day-Lewis, Fenby and Warner would venture out to the graveyard opposite and continue their usual discussions and debates. 'What did we discuss?' Day-Lewis asked himself when he was writing about those days in his autobiography. 'Every word of all that endless Oxford talk, in rooms, on tombs, in streets and gardens and restaurants, has gone from me into thin air, yet at the time we fed upon talk like hungry men, felt ourselves positively nourished by it, though much of it was mere chaff.'[2]

There were new distractions. Warner and Fenby had discovered the old repertory theatre just up the road and persuaded their housemate to give Chekov and Ibsen a try with mixed results. Warner, in particular, attempted to take in hand what he felt was Day-Lewis's appalling taste in literature, insisting that he exchange Michael Arlen's contemporary bestseller on 1920s high society *The Green Hat* for Henry James's *The Ambassadors* and Marcel Proust's *A La Recherche*. As with much else in his youth, Day-Lewis came to the classics later than most of his contemporaries.

Warner also lured him into the heartie bastion of the Wadham rugby team. Warner was captain of the fifteen and persuaded his housemate to turn out occasionally in inter-college fixtures, albeit to no great distinction. It did have one lasting result, however, by introducing him to W. N. Roughead, already a celebrated Scottish international player and the glamorous captain of the university team. With a tendency to be attracted to heroic figures – especially those who excelled in their chosen field – Day-Lewis soon befriended 'Roughie' in what became a longstanding association.

He even managed a few rounds of golf to fill the time when he should have been in the library – playing on more than one occasion with Frederick Lindemann,[3] Christ Church don, scientist and later as Lord Cherwell a minister in Winston Churchill's wartime coalition. He made little impact on Day-Lewis. All he could recall of him was that he was unsmiling, taciturn and drove from tees with an iron.

Day-Lewis's main preoccupation now was his poetry. In the summer of 1924 his self-confidence had grown sufficiently for him to submit some of his verse to Harold Acton who was that year editing the annual collection of student verse, *Oxford Poetry*. It was rejected – though Acton later blamed his co-editor Peter Quennell.[4] The negative response was a disappointment but not crushing, as Day-Lewis conveyed to Warner in a buoyant letter from Monart: 'One Acton of Oxford notoriety, that unsexed model for pornographists, had the astounding audacity to refuse certain poems of mine for his anaemic collection of drawing room ballads, *Oxford Poetry* ... The monumental temerity of that hairless eunuch in depriving *Oxford Poetry* of the only verse that would have raised it out of the slough of mediocrity leaves me gasping.'[5]

Behind the bravado lay the first evidence of success as a poet. Day-Lewis had a poem, 'Garden Statues', published in *Life and Letters*, and others included in *Oxford Outlook*, *Oxford Chronicle* and *Poetry of Today*. Later some of his verse was included in *Ten Singers*, an anthology of promising young poets published by Fortune and Merriman in October 1924. And in June of 1925 he used £12 out of a legacy that had come his way from a distant relative to persuade the same house to publish his first volume of poetry, *Beechen Vigil*. The deal was halfway between vanity publishing and a commercial operation, but as his copious correspondence with Fortune and Merriman makes plain,[6] it was a project in which he invested all his hopes of making a career as a poet.

The 24 short poems – including several of those from *Ten Singers* – show Day-Lewis's work at this stage firmly in the Georgian style that dominated British poetry throughout the 1910s and early 1920s. It had emerged as a label when Rupert Brooke,[7] just down from Cambridge, and Edward Marsh,[8] a civil servant and amateur enthusiast for the arts, decided in 1911 to work together on a collection of modern poems to stir up public interest and alert the world to some exciting new poets. They were reacting in part against what they saw as Victorian stuffiness and romantic sentimentality in verse. They also wanted to encourage the next generation of poets and held up as a prime example of the sought-after new note the long colloquial verse narrative, *The Everlasting Mercy*, by the already established figure of John Masefield.[9]

The anthology was called *Georgian Poetry 1911–1912*. It was Marsh who chose the label. The more rebellious Brooke regarded it as too timid and conservative but fell in for lack of a better alternative. The collection was published, its two co-editors stated in their preface, 'in the belief that English poetry is now once again putting on new strength and beauty'.[10]

There was no single outstanding figure among the Georgians. It could hardly be counted as an organized movement save that its main momentum was provided by the regular anthology of new writings which appeared in the years that followed. Between 1912 and 1922 there were five volumes, each edited by Marsh.

The First World War loomed large as a shared theme, typically in lyrical evocations of beauty and nature as a reaction against the brutality and epic loss of life of the conflict. Included under its banner – though they would each have rejected the categorization of Georgian – were W. B. Yeats, Robert Graves and D. H. Lawrence.[11]

Georgian poetry was often defined by what was excluded. Thomas Hardy and A. E. Housman[12] were left out because they were too old to be considered new. Even Masefield was used sparingly on the grounds that he had already developed a reputation. Robert Frost[13] and Ezra Pound[14] – both initially signed up for inclusion in the first volume – were jettisoned because they were not British. T. S. Eliot also fell at the same obstacle, though the Modernism of *The Waste Land*, published in 1922, was to mark the end of the Georgian ascendancy.

Of the 36 poets who appeared none, with the possible exception of Lawrence, could be called Modernist. Among the most regular names were Walter de la Mare,[15] Edward Thomas,[16] Andrew Young,[17] Siegfried Sassoon[18] and Edmund Blunden.[19]

Marsh's guiding hand was narrow and parochial but also successful, persuading large numbers to buy volumes of work by young poets. By 1922, however, he had decided to stand down, feeling that the moment for Georgian poetry was passing. Harold Acton wrote in his memoir that next to *The Waste Land* there was no place left for 'the faded pastels of the Georgians, as effete a gang of poetasters as ever won praise from a misguided public'.[20]

The Georgians, however, continued to attract a large following until the end of the 1920s when their label had become almost a term of abuse. They were Day-Lewis's point of departure as a published poet. He mixed their distinguishing features with a heavy dose of the language and romantic lushness of Yeats's Celtic twilight. So *Beechen Vigil*, for instance, includes in 'Lost' melancholy and hankering after a golden age.

> Whither is now that city vanished
> Where once I walked with innocence hand in hand?
>   O, an insidious tide hath drowned
>   Deeper than regret
>   Cupola, minaret,
> And all the street are sand.

Elsewhere there is a riot of flowers, trees, forests, weather and changing seasons. Mary's influence can be seen in two poems about fairies. And there is a romanticized celebration of their love – with no reference to the struggles they had been through – in the Yeats-homage 'He Thanks Earth for His Beloved'.

> Whence should have come this strange rebirth,
> This rose in abandoned gardens blossoming,
> Had we not long ago made Earth
> Our secret altar
> Garlanded with our worshipping?

True consummation, Day-Lewis suggests in 'Sanctuary', regarded by some as the best work in the collection on account of its use of alliteration and assonance, and the rhyme of its opening stanza, is something nobler than time allows.

> Swung in this hammock between hills
> we have dreamed a nobler quietude
> than the breathless after-hush when bells
> tire of their silver tumbling.
> Our mood
> is crystal, bright as primrose laughter
> rippling beneath the bracken, clear
> as rain's metallic plash from a rafter.

Beechen Vigil attracted no critical attention in the world outside Oxford. His efforts to persuade the *Times Literary Supplement* and *Nottingham Guardian* to review the book came to naught. Day-Lewis with considerable chutzpah took 100 copies of the book and presented himself in bookshops in Oxford and Nottingham – the nearest big town to Edwinstowe – to persuade the manager to stock the title. He placed 75 out of the 100. With total sales around 250, his own leg-work managed to get him just over £2 of his £12 investment back.

In his immediate circle, however, *Beechen Vigil* was a great success. It enhanced the image Day-Lewis had been building of himself as a poet. Tom Hopkinson, a contemporary at Oxford and later editor of the *Picture Post*, described the student Day-Lewis, for example, as 'handsome and elegant, with a fine speaking and singing voice', adding 'he had already published poetry and his intention in life was simply to be a poet'.[21]

There were approving reviews in two periodicals – *Oxford Outlook* and the *Shirburnian*. Both were penned by Mary's brother, Alec King, Day-Lewis's great friend and hardly dispassionate. But any temptation to let his praise or the mere fact of being published go to Day-Lewis's head was exploded by Rex Warner who would humorously declaim with exaggerated rhythm the opening lines of 'Rose-Pruner' – 'Meanders around the rose-beds, gnarled, clay-brown,/Old Tom the pruner, snic-snac up and down'. To which Day-Lewis would respond in the spirit of the constant sparring that went on at 22 St Giles with a line lifted from an early Warner poem – 'a touch of flesh is worth a pound of thought'.[22]

When Mamie Day-Lewis announced that 'Rose-Pruner' was 'one of the finest gems of English poetry', it convinced her step-son that Warner was right.[23] In later years he would dismiss *Beechen Vigil* as 'juvenilia' and exclude its contents from selected editions of his work. In 1925, however, it bolstered him considerably in the face of repeated rejection letters from the London magazines and publishers he approached with his poems.

He did better in the university context. Two new poems – *Sonnet* and *Autumn of the Mood* – were included by Acton's successors in *Oxford Poetry 1925*. He was encouraged enough to set up, with Warner, a literary society where students could read aloud their poems or papers and discuss others' work. They chose the name The Jawbone – in tribute to the ass jawbone with which Sampson drove back the Philistines. A trip to Selfridges in London furnished them with a piece of bone that purported to belong to an ass and which acted as their mascot.

As well as undergraduate efforts, members of The Jawbone were also treated to talks and recitals by visiting authors and poets. These included L. A. G. Strong, eight years Day-Lewis's senior, half Irish, a poet, novelist and fellow admirer of Yeats, who was subsequently to become a close friend,[24] and Humbert Wolfe, an old boy of Wadham, a senior civil servant and a poet whose war-time 'Requiem' was widely popular in its time.[25] Wolfe made a strong impression on Day-Lewis. He was, he later recalled, 'one of the wittiest men I have ever met, a figure of flamboyance and panache'.[26]

In Day-Lewis's next collection, 'Naked Woman with Kotyle', about a vase painting, was written under Wolfe's influence. When Day-Lewis read it out at a meeting The Jawbone, Tom Hopkinson was heard to exclaim 'Lucky chap, old Kotyle'.[27]

One person who enthused about *Beechen Vigil* and Day-Lewis's interest in poetry was his tutor Maurice Bowra. Such extra-curricular activities may have compensated in some measure for Day-Lewis's lack of engagement in his classical studies. Bowra invited his poet-pupil to accompany him to tea parties at Garsington Manor, outside Oxford, the Tudor home of Lady Ottoline Morrell.[28] Garsington had played host during the First World War to pacifist members of the Bloomsbury Set and Lady Ottoline was a noted patron of the arts – as well as a flamboyant if not entirely respected artist herself.

In such a setting, Day-Lewis's still fragile self-confidence ebbed. Tea, he remembered, was 'a severe ordeal'. He filled his time 'slinking gloomily amongst the peacocks' in the Italianate gardens and failed to talk to any of the great and good assembled there.[29] Instead he sought refuge with another Bowra protégé, a young Magdalen undergraduate Henry Yorke, later as Henry Green a successful novelist.[30]

At Garsington as with guest speakers at The Jawbone, Day-Lewis did not quite have the courage or inclination to push himself forward and seek to make advantageous contacts. The shy and provincial fresher at Wadham had come on a great deal at Oxford, but not that far. There was, he decided somewhat idealistically, a principle at stake. Writing was not a career to be pursued by whatever means were presented, but rather a vocation. Success, if it came, would result from talent.

Such a stance sat comfortably with his increasing political radicalization under Rex Warner's influence. A contemporary at Wadham, R. F. Bretherton, recalled that Day-Lewis took a very public stand against rough treatment meted out to a fellow student, a Jewish communist who had been beaten up. While many were prepared to look the other way, Day-Lewis wrote a letter of protest to the Junior Common Room, the main undergraduate forum.[31]

Although Oxford was insulated from the real world, occasionally seismic national or international events would impinge. In 1924 the Conservative Stanley Baldwin had succeeded the first-ever Labour government of James Ramsay MacDonald. Baldwin at once became involved in a dispute with the coal miners. Declining exports had led their employers to insist on reduced pay and longer working days. The miners refused and the two sides were at loggerheads when Baldwin intervened to give a government subsidy on wages until a Royal Commission could report on the problem. In effect the Prime Minister only managed to buy time. Eight months later the commission recommended that the subsidy be stopped. On May 4, 1926 the first ever General Strike began in support of the miners.

Day-Lewis knew about the dangerous conditions in mines and the exploitation of workers from his visits home to Edwinstowe. His sympathy lay with the miners and their Labour and trades union supporters. He was, Mary King wrote in her diary, 'thrilled with the romance of Labour's stand and will fight for them if need be'.[32]

The General Strike disturbed Oxford from its pleasures and introspection. A university strike committee was established under G. D. H. Cole, a socialist don. Students volunteered to help. How to react provoked a parting of the ways at 22 St Giles. Charles Fenby retreated to the university library and took the view that the dispute had nothing to do with him. Day-Lewis enthusiastically signed up, initially volunteering as a driver to transport the strike leaders in Oxford backwards and forwards to TUC headquarters in London. When there was not much to do in that role, he went on to work at the Hyde Park Hotel on a bulletin promoting mediation started by the Archbishop of Canterbury and run by a Balliol undergraduate. He helped bring out one number, ruining in the process his one good suit with spilt violet ink, before the strike collapsed.

Warner had, by contrast, joined the strike breakers, going to Hull to be a conductor on the trams. It was, at first glance, an odd thing for a socialist to do and it caused a row with Day-Lewis who accused him of being a blackleg. Warner's response was to describe the whole experience as a chance for an adventure. The strike could never succeed, he insisted, so it was better to get it over with quickly before too much damage was inflicted on the union movement.

They agreed to differ. Day-Lewis was moving politically out of Warner's shadow. If the First World War had passed him by as a dreamy teenager, the sight of convoys of troops passing their front door in Oxford to take the place of striking workers left a lasting impression. The General Strike, he later wrote, was 'a crisis which made our sheltered life at Oxford meaningless'.[33]

At the end of the summer term of 1926, the three young men went their separate ways. Fenby had finished his history degree and went to work as a reporter for the *Westminster Gazette*. Warner too had graduated, having changed to English after his breakdown. He stayed on intermittently in Oxford at 22 St Giles while Fenby's place was taken by Wilfred Cowley, nicknamed The Baron by his housemates on account of his fondness for dressing like Byron and his knowledge of literary and political gossip.

Finals were approaching for Day-Lewis. He viewed them, he wrote, with the 'bug-eyed frantic immobility of a rabbit confronted by a stoat'.[34] The more pressure there was to study, the less studying he did. He wanted the exams over, but he was terrified of what lay beyond them. He knew he wanted to be a poet, but he had little money, nowhere to live and little idea of what he could do to earn enough to pay the rent and allow him to write. An added pressure was his ambition to marry Mary, who had completed her studies and was working in Ipswich as a dance teacher.

One possibility was to follow Mary into teaching, but Day-Lewis rejected it out of hand as a career and sank into a depression. His one goal was to get a fourth – the next best thing, he declared to a first. In his autobiography, he claims to have succeeded. 'A fourth in Greats – and it is a mystery to me why the examiners did not fail me altogether.'[35] However, he was exaggerating for effect. Despite his lack of preparation, the official record shows that the examiners awarded him a third.

There was one glimmer of light in these dark days. Sometime in 1926 – neither of them was ever clear as to exactly when or how – he had been introduced to an undergraduate at Christ Church, three years his junior. W. H. Auden shared Day-Lewis's ambitions to be a poet and was not about to let anything deflect him.

PART TWO

The Thirties

Chapter 8

The Tow-Haired Poet

Last the tow-haired poet, never done
With cutting and planing some new gnomic prop
To jack his all too stable universe up: –
Conduct's Old Dobbin, thought's chameleon.
Single mind copes with split intelligence,
Breeding a piebald strain of truth and nonsense.
Part II, 8: *Transitional Poem* (1929)

In March 1929, after they had both left Oxford, Wystan Auden sent Cecil Day-Lewis from Berlin a note of thanks for putting him up for three days during his trip to Britain. 'Instead of a bread and butter letter', Auden wrote, he had undertaken what he described as 'a technical exercise'. The enclosed verse-letter was a celebration of the close friendship rooted above all in poetry that began with their first, undated, meeting during Day-Lewis's last undergraduate year at Oxford.

I spoke of books, and think how we have sat
Taking this poet from the shelf or that,
Read them aloud, discussed them one by one,
With praises of Middleton and then of Donne,
Of Housman, wondering which theory right
On what the excitement was which made him write,
Affairs with soldiers or attacks of 'flu,
Of Owen's iron pity, Lawrence who
Remains an invalid and worships Will,
From illness loving, and from loving ill.
We found these moderns best, though seemed to see
Conceit in Yeats, in Eliot's gravity;
While Wolfe, the typists' poet, made us sick
Whose thoughts are dapper and whose lines are slick.

I spoke of friends and now there come to mind
Associations of a different kind.
I see the features and the voices hear
Of Margaret, doctor, Christopher severe,
Of Rex who looked at much and much saw through,
And many others whom you never knew ...

I turn again to you, for we are one
In choice of calling and ambition,

To wonder if there's room for you and me
When ten tons of new prose and poetry
Is the day's normal output. Papers say
'Five masterpieces have appeared to-day'[1]

The content is revealing. From this account Auden appeared to have taken up with gusto Rex Warner's early attempts to widen Day-Lewis's reading and in the process introduced him to hitherto unknown or certainly little explored poetic influences. Day-Lewis was learning about the poetic tradition. He was learning, too, whom to like and whom to dismiss. Auden managed to end any lingering admiration he still harboured for Humbert Wolfe – 'the typists' poet' – after his visit to The Jawbone.

To range so widely over past and present poets would have been an eye-opening experience for Day-Lewis who later bemoaned the lack of ambition in his undergraduate reading.[2] It was another aspect, he said, of his slow development into adulthood. And it was over their discussions that there emerged the seeds of what was to become the distinctive approach of Auden, Day-Lewis and other leading lights of the new generation of poets of the 1930s.

There was always between the two, as Auden acknowledged in the verse-letter, a competitive edge. In June of 1927, his finals completed, Day-Lewis set off with Auden to Appletreewick in north Yorkshire, a village known and liked by Auden[3] and where, on the 29th, they hoped to see a solar eclipse. They stayed at the New Inn and worked on their introduction as joint editors of *Oxford Poetry 1927*, publisher Basil Blackwell's annual celebration of new verse in and around the university. As they talked, they went on long walks over the moors, past old mine workings, a particular interest of Auden's. He moved, Day-Lewis wrote, 'with his phenomenally long, ungainly stride, and talking incessantly, his words tumbling over one another in the hurry to get out, a lock of tow-coloured hair falling over the brow of his rather puffy but wonderfully animated white face'.[4]

In the midst of one such ramble came what Day-Lewis referred to as 'the episode of the dry-stone wall'. 'Walking the moors one day, we approached one of those dark walls which wind over the contours like strips of liquorice. A hundred yards from the wall, as if on a common impulse, we both began to walk faster; at fifty or sixty yards, we broke into a trot, and we were sprinting all out over the last thirty yards or so. Arriving simultaneously at the wall, we gave each other an amused but also sheepish look.'[5]

Writing 30 years after the event, Day-Lewis could articulate the deep-seated competition that inspired that rush to the wall. At the time, however, it was left unsaid, but noted and clearly mutual. In *The Age of Anxiety*, published in 1948, Auden too was able to reflect, albeit in more general terms, on early rivalries and 'the anxiety about himself and his future which haunts, like a bad smell, the minds of most young men ... accordingly they watch others with a covert passionate curiosity. What makes them tick? What would it feel like to be a success? Here is somebody who is nobody in particular, there even an obvious failure, yet they do not seem to mind? How is that possible?'[6]

If the edge of competition cut both ways with two young men anxious to make an impact amid 'ten tons of new prose and poetry', it did not stop the Auden–Day-Lewis friendship having its own hierarchy. This lay somewhere between Auden's good humoured depiction of them as equals in the verse-letter and the master/acolyte picture subsequently painted by critics who sidelined Day-Lewis as Auden's second-in-command.[7] Indeed Day-Lewis was in one sense the senior partner – older and already a published poet.

Yet, as Day-Lewis himself was readily to admit, initially Auden simply dazzled him on all sorts of levels. His physical presence was memorable. Blond-haired with pale skin and small yellowish eyes that had a tendency to scowl, he had stumpy fingers with bitten nails and ink and nicotine stains. Sometimes he would wear a green eye shade or carry a starting-pistol on walks where he would sport 'an extraordinary black lay-reader's type of frock coat which came half way down to his knees and had been rescued by him from one of his mother's jumble sales'.[8] On other occasions he sported a cane and monocle, or a clergyman's panama hat, or a doctor's white coat, borrowed from his father, an expert in public health.

His appeal, though, rested more on his knowledge, his reading, his technique, his iconoclasm and above all his confidence. He would pronounce definitively and iconoclastically on all manner of subjects – that cinema was doomed as an art form, that ballet ought to be forbidden, that only music-hall had any real worth. Day-Lewis already had a track record of hero-worship and Auden joined the elect. Moreover, for one with such a fragile sense of his own worth as Day-Lewis, a degree of subjugation was an almost inevitable consequence of prolonged exposure to another so convinced of his own almost God-given right to be a poet. Auden had told his tutor Nevill Coghill[9] at their first meeting that 'I mean to be a great poet'.[10] It was a conviction that bestowed upon him, Day-Lewis admitted, a tremendous vitality, 'so abundant that, overflowing into certain poses and follies and wildly unrealistic notions, it gave these an air of authority, an illusion of rightness'.[11]

It could also make him bossy and imperious, offering edicts in reply to questions. In an interview years later Day-Lewis spoke of Auden's 'wagging didactic forefinger'[12] and some reported his habit of controlling which of his circle of friends could meet others. He had to be at the centre. Yet he combined all this with an exuberance and a passion for poetry that made most who came into contact with him at this stage of his life overlook his foibles and willingly fall into line.

Stephen Spender, who was along with Day-Lewis to become one of the writers whose name was linked with Auden's in the 1930s, described the spell that Auden's certainty cast over those around him at this time in a 1968 birthday tribute.

> You – the young bow-tyed, near albino undergraduate
> With rooms on Peck Quad (blinds drawn down at midday
> To shut the sun out) – read your poems aloud

In your voice that was so clinical
I thought it held each word brilliant in forceps
Up to your lamp

'Auden aetat XX,LX'[13]

There was, as Spender wrote elsewhere, another important aspect to the Auden mystique. You felt as if you never quite knew him, but that with a little more persistence you might. 'I am very fond of my friend,' he said, 'without the least understanding of him, and I think that he is equally a mystery to his other friends . . . you feel that although he is very fond of you when you are with him, you are never quite sure of him, and that adds to the fascination'.[14]

Day-Lewis and Spender weren't the only ones among his contemporaries to be swept up by Auden. Rex Warner was so devoted that he even took to imitating Auden's style of dress – donning a cloak, though later Auden decreed that all poets should dress like stockbrokers. Day-Lewis had enough independence to eschew this rule in favour of his own more dapper dress style.

Auden's English tutor at Exeter College, Nevill Coghill, recalled of him: 'He had great intellectual prestige in the university at large; he used words . . . which nobody else knew. His sayings were widely misquoted, and would appear, in their garbled form, in the essays of my other pupils. These being cross-examined, and their nonsense laid bare, still held the trump, which they would play when nothing else would save them: "Well, anyhow, that's what Wystan says". It was the armour of God to them.'[15]

Like Day-Lewis and Warner, Auden's roots were middle class, public school and Church of England. His grandfathers on both sides were clergymen. The youngest of three boys, Auden had come up to Christ Church in 1925 to read Natural Sciences, but subsequently changed first to Modern Greats and then again to English. Eventually he graduated in 1928 with a third, but the quality of his degree was apparently the least of his concerns while at Oxford.

For the group who gathered around Auden one bond was shared homosexuality, something which excluded Day-Lewis. Spender and Auden, for instance, both wrote poems of unrequited love for a fellow, heterosexual undergraduate, Gabriel Carritt. Auden would theorize, often with another collaborator, Christopher Isherwood,[16] on the role of what were then illegal same-sex relationships in shaping personality and, by association, literary output. 'Without these prohibitive frontiers,' Auden wrote in *For The Time Being*, 'we should never know who we were or what we wanted. It is they who donate to neighbourhood all their accuracy and vehemence.'[17]

Auden did have a physical relationship with Isherwood – 'for years we fucked like rabbits every chance we got', Isherwood later claimed[18] – but his taste was mainly for young, working class men, especially if they were foreign. It was something else shared with Isherwood. 'He couldn't relax sexually,' Isherwood wrote of himself in the third person in *Christopher and His Kind*, 'with a member of his own class or nation. He needed a working-class foreigner.'[19] It was predatory and often exploitative, but Auden, Isherwood and to a lesser extent Spender were to convince themselves that such behaviour also had an element of political idealism to it, creating a kind of comradeship across class and race barriers.

There is no evidence that there was ever any sexual undertow to Day-Lewis's relationship with Auden, though there is just a hint of homoeroticism in that dash for the wall in Appletreewick. Auden did, though, appreciate Day-Lewis's good looks and teased him gently over them in a 1928 poem, dedicated to him.

Or how to Sherborne came a pretty boy
And splendid seniors bought his photograph

'Epithalamium for C Day-Lewis' (1928)[20]

But Day-Lewis's own heterosexuality was by now unwavering, if as yet narrowly explored.

Auden's darkened rooms in Christ Church were a focus for the young poets. Louis MacNeice,[21] another undergraduate contemporary whose name is forever linked along with Day-Lewis and Spender to Auden's as one of the poets of the 1930s, described how Auden would preside – 'reading very fast and very widely – psychology, ethnology, *Arabia Deserta*. He did not seem to look at anything, admitted he hated flowers and was very free with quasi-scientific jargon, but you came away from his presence always encouraged.'[22]

What gave Auden's passion for poetry a particular identity was the overt connection he encouraged those around him to make between it and the political, economic and social situation of Britain at the time. As young undergraduates they were watching the post-war hedonism of Acton's Oxford fading away. The decisive blow had been the General Strike of 1926 when they and many like them were roused from student introspection to take sides in what became for the whole country one of the defining battles of the decade.

Both Day-Lewis and Auden had worked during the strike for the TUC (Auden was disowned by some of his relatives for doing so) and had been disappointed by the collapse of the workers' resistance to their employers and the Conservative government. Their involvement left its mark. They felt that they could not in the strike's aftermath simply retreat back into the cosy and cosseted world of an Oxford that had itself, even in Day-Lewis's student house, been divided between leftist sympathy, Warner's cynicism and Fenby's more traditionalist tendencies.

For Day-Lewis, his experiences during the strike brought a new focus to his unease, on visits home to the vicarage, at the social cost of the development of coal mining in Edwinstowe.

Morning brought tears and daisies, afternoon
A tennis party. Athletic clergymen. Flannels –
The uniform of a class, of a way of thinking,
Or of not thinking: as I looked for a lost ball
In the laurels, they smirched with pit-grime.

'Sketches for a Self-Portrait': *Poems 1943–1947* (1948)

Already he realized that his own bourgeois background separated him like a laurel hedge from the working classes, but in the wake of the strike and the wider perspective he had gained at Oxford he was determined that it should not shut him off from their world. His father crossed the boundaries – albeit often clumsily and unsuccessfully – through his ministry, but already the young Day-Lewis had rejected religion, a shared characteristic with other vicars' sons and grandsons among the Auden group (MacNeice's father was a Church of Ireland bishop). Auden himself was described by the novelist, Edward Upward,[23] as being 'vehemently antagonistic' to religion at their first meeting in 1927.[24]

All were searching for another way of expressing the solidarity they felt with those working in appalling conditions on the bottom rungs of Britain's economy. The solutions they found were often idealistic and romantic – as in Auden's penchant when going for a walk in Oxford for heading not for the Meadows or its manicured parks but rather for the gas works and the municipal rubbish heap. Whether they saw it at the time, both Auden and Day-Lewis subsequently recognized their naïveté. Looking back in 1937, Auden wrote that 'good lyric poetry' depends on 'wildly taking sides, becoming in fact what Mr Yeats has described as "a foolish passionate man"'.[25] And Day-Lewis, much later, described himself in this period as 'stern-minded', 'intolerant' and a 'serious youth' still learning 'the lighter touch that is often the beginning of worldly wisdom'.[26]

But however naive and flawed – Auden would return from his walks to the privileged world of Christ Church and Day-Lewis in his coal dust blackened tennis whites to the lobster suppers at the rectory – that search did give a particular edge to their efforts to develop both a distinctive poetic style and a political purpose for poetry. The two went hand-in-hand. What was poetry and what was it for?

If Auden and Day-Lewis and the others were convinced of anything at this stage, it was that poetry could no longer stand apart from the increasingly polarized post-war world around them. A key maxim, articulated most clearly by Auden, was to look outward not inward. Outward-looking poetry, he believed, to put it at its simplest, could be an instrument of social change.

Introspection, of course, had been the mark of the Georgian poets and Day-Lewis had been among them with *Beechen Vigil*. A decade after its publication, in *A Hope for Poetry*, he was comprehensively to rubbish the movement he had so admired as an undergraduate. 'The Georgian poets, a sadly pedestrian rabble, flocked along the road their fathers had built, pointing out to each other the beauty spots and ostentatiously drinking small-beer in a desperate effort to prove their virility. The winds blew, the floods came: for a moment a few of them showed on the crest of the seventh great wave, then they were rolled under.'[27]

There was a more contemporary poetic movement that had come to prominence amid the fracture of post First World War society. 'It was left to an American,' Day-Lewis recorded in *A Hope for Poetry*, 'to pick up some of the fragments of civilization, place them end to end, and on that crazy pavement walk precariously through the waste land.'[28]

T. S. Eliot's *The Waste Land* appeared in 1922, an expression of the sense of desolation and despair which many felt in the wake of the Great War. Naturalized as British in 1927, resident since 1915 but born in the States, Eliot was a leading light among the Modernist new wave, along with Ezra Pound and William Carlos Williams.[29] Like Modernists in other fields they believed that traditional form had to be broken down, rethought and reconstructed in order to yield new insights. In the case of poetry, they sought to fracture language, as Eliot put it, into new meanings. Or as Pound later recalled: 'To break the pentameter, that was the first heave.'[30]

Though their innovation was much discussed on both sides of the Atlantic, they had no British-born disciple. Poetic Modernism was an almost exclusively American phenomenon compared with Modernism in fiction, which influenced, for example, British writers like Virginia Woolf[31] and arguably most notably, the Irishman James Joyce.[32] His *Ulysses* was published in the same year as *The Waste Land* and was its equivalent as the paradigmatic Modernist novel.

Among established British poets both Robert Graves and D. H. Lawrence rejected Modernist ideas, but to a new generation they were inspiring. Auden reported ripping up all his poems after his first reading of *The Waste Land* in 1926.[33]

Once that first rush of admiration had passed, though, and they reflected more, Auden and his circle also came to see in Modernism limitations. There was in it a sense of impotent despair at what was going on in the world and a belief that the poet could only stand back and watch. Auden, Day-Lewis and others disagreed. They had faith that the poet could be more than an observer and so they began to formulate what became the first true British response to Modernism.

They did not, it should be emphasized, set out to do down either Eliot or Modernism but rather to shape a response. Day-Lewis's own feelings at the time about Eliot mixed great admiration with reservation. And Auden was in 1930 to be published by Eliot in his Faber imprint. Spender and MacNeice joined him there. But the charge against the Modernists of being elitist and remote, often too interested in experimenting with form and therefore excluding readers and reality, was a recurring one among the poets of the 1930s. As Day-Lewis reflected in his lecture 'The Thirties in Retrospect': 'we obscurely felt the need to do more with the fragments than shoring them against our ruin. The magic word, the cant word, of the time was synthesis.'[34]

The 'synthesis' they sought was neither to escape into another world – like the Georgians' pastoral haven – nor to transcend the world around them in the manner of the Modernists. There was, they believed, another way. One possible role model for the sort of synthesis they sought was W. B. Yeats, admired by Day-Lewis since school days at Sherborne. In an introduction to a 1968 bibliography of Day-Lewis's works, Auden wrote of their youthful friendship: 'To you I owe my first introduction to the later poems of Yeats.'[35]

From romantic lushness and retreat into an idealized world of nature and myths of the Celtic twilight, Yeats's poetry had changed in the early decades of the twentieth century. In 1913 he had been sought out by Ezra Pound who claimed he was 'the only poet worthy of serious study'.[36] Yeats came under the influence of the Modernists with Pound acting as his nominal secretary for some time. Coinciding with that time with Pound, Yeats began to produce poetry that was more austere in its language and which took a more direct approach to his themes – qualities of which the Modernists would have approved.

Yet he also stuck to his traditional craftsmanship, preferring always verse forms to the free verse experiments of some of the Modernists. And his themes became more political and engaged – seen best in 'Easter 1916', his reflection on the IRA uprising of that year – though he was never a polemicist and was certainly no friend of the Left.

It was in Auden and Day-Lewis's first and only co-authored text, their preface to *Oxford Poetry 1927*, a collection that featured contributions they had selected from Louis MacNeice, Rex Warner, Tom Driberg and even an anonymous parody of T. S. Eliot, penned by Christopher Isherwood, that they set out to define precisely what they meant by synthesis. If there was a starting point for the poets of the thirties, a first statement of intent, then this introduction was it.

Up in Yorkshire that summer the two young men had hit upon the device of writing alternative paragraphs of the preface. However much Auden influenced Day-Lewis, this manifesto cannot, as it has often been, be described as one man's work. Day-Lewis took Spender (who didn't go up to Oxford until the autumn of 1927) gently to task in *The Buried Day* for having quoted chunks of the *Oxford Poetry 1927* preface in his *World Within World*[37] and ascribed them all to Auden. 'The first of the extracts which Spender quotes as showing "the abstract nature of Auden's thinking" was written by myself and embodies an idea I had thought up all by myself.'[38]

Between them what Day-Lewis and Auden suggested was that poetry could provide the 'new synthesis' that would carry individuals through 'the chaos of values which is the substance of our environment' in both the personal and the public/political spheres. Poetry functioned, they went on, 'to bring order to self-consciousness'. Trying to spell out the consequences of this elevation of poetry to an almost religious function, they highlighted its reconciling role in three key areas: in 'the psychological conflict . . . between self as subject and self as object'; in 'the ethical conflict' between ideas of a pure art and those that insisted that art operates within a social and economic context; and in 'the logical [or linguistic] context' between the classical and the romantic. It was not enough, they argued, for a poem simply to be. It must also have meaning.[39]

The introduction reads today as earnest and occasionally opaque in some paragraphs. Auden was subsequently to lampoon it as 'somewhat pompous' while Day-Lewis insisted that there was 'a note of mockery' in there. 'The editors were in deadly earnest, but they took out an insurance policy, in the form of deliberately portentous prose styles carrying pastiche to the edge of burlesque, against any risk of solemnity or self-importance.'[40]

If the preface was the theory, then there was also the actual business of writing poetry to live up to such high-minded goals. In this, Auden's influence on Day-

Lewis was to be immense. 'I willingly became his disciple where poetry was concerned', he acknowledged. 'It was only a few years before that he had switched his ambitions from marine biology to verse, but there could be no question about his devotion to the latter now, his single-mindedness, and his power of assimilation. I found his poems difficult to understand, and sometimes at first unsympathetic; but the vigour of their language, the exciting novelty (to me) of the images and ideas embodied in these early poems, and the delighted sense they gave me of a poetry which, so to say, knew its own mind – all this proved so infectious that my own verse became for a time pastiche-Auden.'[41]

Already he was working, with Auden's input, on what was to become *Transitional Poem*, his first work to excite a national audience. But first, by one of those vagueries of publishing schedules, there was to be a reminder of what he had been before Auden.

Chapter 9

Lust to Love

You, first, who ground my lust to love upon
Your gritty humorous virginity,
Then yielding to its temper suddenly
Proved what a Danube can be struck from stone:
'Part II, 8': *Transitional Poem* (1929)

In February 1928 Day-Lewis's second collection of verse, *Country Comets*, was published. On the title page he was still Cecil, but the hyphen in Day-Lewis had disappeared.[1] It contained poems written since *Beechen Vigil* in 1924 and had largely been completed by the time he graduated in the summer of 1927. It therefore all but pre-dated the influence of W. H. Auden.

Day-Lewis's reputation had developed sufficiently since *Beechen Vigil* for there no longer to be any question of him sharing the costs of production with the publishers. The new book contained poems that had already appeared in, amongst ten cited journals, *The Spectator* and the New York publication *Best Poems of 1926*. Yet he did receive rejection notes from several of the larger houses, including Jonathan Cape, before attracting the Covent Garden based firm, Martin Hopkinson. And he had to agree to cover any deficit that remained once the slim volume had been in the shops for six months. An enthusiastic review, in the *Times Literary Supplement*, however, meant that he avoided that fate.

The dedication in *Country Comets* is slightly pompous though intended as romantic – 'to her whose mind and body are a poetry I have not achieved'. Day-Lewis was writing about Mary King. The collection followed their relationship, from his inhibited pursuit, her reluctance and on to their eventual resolution. In the summer of 1925, after their first much-delayed kiss at Monart (celebrated in the collection in 'My Love Came to Me'), the couple had agreed to marry once Day-Lewis had completed his degree. Their parents had been informed, though Mary King's mother, Constance, urged her not to marry a poet.[2] Whether her objections to Day-Lewis were on moral, emotional or economic grounds was not recorded.

The prolonged courtship had continued cautiously even after the Monart kiss. 'A virginal young woman who had little or no experience of men outside her own family,' Day-Lewis wrote in his autobiography of Mary, 'she sorely needed at this stage a lover who could take the initiative, a man older than herself, possessed of physical self-confidence or some firmness of mind. In all such qualities, I was conspicuously lacking. The vein of passivity in me, my cowardice, and the inhibitions which had been stealthily building up for years, all worked together to make me follow a lead rather than take it.'[3]

He remained, in his own description, 'timid with women'[4] and took Mary's emotional reserve as natural. It may have been sexually frustrating for him, but it was also a kind of relief. She didn't demand an intimacy of him that he couldn't give – or was afraid to give. Her diary entries, moreover, suggest that she would never issue him with an ultimatum since she believed that she alone was the problem in their relationship.

In practical terms Mary remained a separate – and often distant – part of his life. He was wrapped up with Oxford and latterly with Auden. Mary had graduated and was teaching dance in Ipswich during his final year as an undergraduate. She bought her first car – a Baby Austin – but on her occasional visits to Wadham she felt herself to be apart from his world, often intimidated by it, and particularly excluded from discussions about poetry. She admired Day-Lewis's verse, was enthralled by it and was flattered to be the subject of so much of it, but she was a passive recipient of dedications and praise.

There were common interests. In the summer of 1927 the couple performed on the same bill at the Drill Hall in Sherborne in a charity concert with Day-Lewis singing songs from the Hebrides and Mary among the cast of a Victorian mime play, *While Aunt Matilda Sleeps*. Part of Day-Lewis's growing confidence was being at ease performing.

His happiness at being with the King family, so different from his own, remained a strong part of his attraction for Mary. That same summer, Day-Lewis joined the whole clan in the Lake District where the couple relaxed enough into intimacy to consummate their relationship. 'Mary began and long sustained the difficult task of weaning me from my adolescence', he wrote.[5]

There is little hint, though, of the troubles and anxieties in their courtship to be found in the high romantic drama of *Country Comets*.

> *And now each common sight*
> *Assumes a diadem*
> *Of crystalline delight,*
> *And trails a purple hem.*
> *The meadows all are paven*
> *With gold the stream along;*
> *Dangles a lark from heaven*
> *On silver threads of song.*

> *Delight floats over us*
> *Awhile, ethereally*
> *As floats the nautilus –*
> *That rare wild-rose of the sea,*
> *Sure, we have found a glass*
> *To focus mind with matter*
> *In a microcosm of bliss*
> *The tiniest mote will shatter.*

'Under the Willow'

Set against the actual details of his relationship with Mary, such verse seems to strain for effect. It is as if Day-Lewis is writing about what he thought he should feel, but didn't because of his own inhibition and Mary's reserve.

Such loud declarations of a mystical connection, endorsed by nature, give way occasionally to gloomy, almost savage reflections on love which, for all their classical allusions, must have put a chill in Mary King's heart.

> *And now the green goes out of the Spring:*
> *The lovers quarrel: one mind jolts*
> *Upon its mate. But still, it is Hera*
> *And Zeus playing at thunderbolts.*
>
> *Disgruntled fools, you would think yourselves*
> *Fortunate, did you guess how soon*
> *Love, its Olympian discords vanished,*
> *Becomes a barrel-organ tune.*

'The only Pretty-Ring-Time'

For a marriage that had not even started to become 'a barrel-organ tune' was hardly an encouraging prospect for the bride to be. Mary could have attributed it to his black moods or to the poet's imagination, putting himself outside his own experience and exploring other (in this case unhappy) scenarios. Yet there is an unmistakable and real hankering after escape in 'The Perverse', where Day-Lewis first articulates his belief in the essential transience of love. Once given, he suggests, love is no longer wanted or enough. It must have been a difficult stanza to read for the woman who had just surrendered her virginity to him.

> *His pretty came among the primroses*
> *With open breast for him. No more denied*
> *Seemed no more ideal. He was unsatisfied*
> *Till he strained her flesh to thin philosophies.*

That theme of conflict is seen only fleetingly in *Country Comets* but it links this early collection with what came after. Likewise, the arrangement of the poems as a chronological and linked sequence, rather than in *Beechen Vigil* as a collection of stand-alone poems, again points forward and makes a connection between *Country Comets* and Day-Lewis's verse of the 1930s. Day-Lewis's poetry was already taking a new direction – as he himself sought to emphasize when he sent some of the poems that make up *Country Comets* to his publishers. 'They show', he pointed out, 'rather obvious changes of style, and besides the poems enclosed have a more definite unity.'[6]

For all that, though, *Country Comets* remains as a collection largely Georgian in tone, and firmly rooted in the personal arena. Day-Lewis was not moving to embrace universal or even political themes. Indeed he was later to deny emphatically any connection between *Country Comets* and what came later. His career as a poet only truly began, according to his own account, after he met Auden. All that predated that moment was dismissed as 'juvenilia'.

So this is you
That was an I twenty-five years ago –
One I may neither disown nor renew.
Youth of the smouldering heart, the seamless brow,
What affinity between you and me?
You are a skin I have long since cast,
A ghost I carry now:
I am the form you blindly, fitfully glassed,
And the finish of your bright vow.

When I seek to peer
Through the fancy-dress words wherein you are woodenly posed
And to feel the ardours quivering there,
I am as one eavesdropping upon a captive past
Of which nothing remains but echoes and chains.

'Juvenilia': *Poems 1943–1947* (1948)

In his Foreword to *Country Comets*, Day-Lewis noted that some of his other poems, written at the same time and not in the volume, 'will be included in my next book, *Transitional Poems*' (the 's' was later dropped). As he applied himself to that new work, Day-Lewis's life was divided into a series of compartments. There was his father and Mamie in Edwinstowe, difficult, often despised and visited only under sufferance. There was his relationship with Mary, insulated from the rest of his life, troubled but moving inexorably towards marriage. And there was his poetry and the bond he had formed with Auden and the other young poets around him. The overlap between the three was slight – Auden's verse-letter suggests that he did not meet Mary until after they had married[7] – but Day-Lewis did not seem unduly worried by that. It was a state of affairs that he had grown to see as normal.

His most pressing practical need was for an income. Co-editing *Oxford Poetry* and walks by the gas works didn't pay bills. He had graduated in the summer of 1927 determined to be a poet, but with no idea as to how he could earn a living, save for a determination 'that never should I sink so low as schoolmastering'.[8]

One option was to try to write prose. In correspondence of September 1924 with the publishers of *Beechen Vigil*, he included a short story he had produced. Fortune and Merriman were not encouraging. It was 'perfectly all right', they said, but 'unlikely to get you any commissions'.[9] He had a brief stab at journalism, spending a few agonized weeks in the summer of 1927 at Charles Fenby's flat in Bayswater, west London, while trying to land a job as assistant literary editor at *The Spectator*. He failed.

Fenby then got him a commission to write a book review for his paper, the *Westminster Gazette*. Day-Lewis found such a workaday task impossible, his head full of the theories he and Auden had just committed to paper in Appletreewick. He struggled with it for several days. In the end Fenby had to write it for him.

Frank Day-Lewis, meanwhile, had suggested that his son consider something in miners' welfare. He was not so out of touch with his child's new interests as

Cecil assumed him to be. Such work had attractions – not least of being, in theory, on the front line of discontented industrial Britain and therefore awash with inspiration for the sort of politically committed poetry he had been discussing with Auden – but it would also entail returning to Edwinstowe to live in a house that still felt to him like a prison.

Such conflicting thoughts may explain why Day-Lewis turned up at the interview his father had organized for him in a dark-blue sombrero and floppy orange bow tie. He was, he recalled, striking a pose, just as he had decided to act like he believed a poet should when he first arrived at Wadham. On this occasion he was making a premeditated effort to look like W. B. Yeats. Quite how that would have helped him get a job in miners' welfare is unclear. He was rejected.

Teaching then was left as the most likely avenue of opportunity. He toyed with accepting a job in a school overseas. He could never remember subsequently if it had been in Turkey or Japan. The difference would have been lost on him since he remained uninterested in going abroad. So domestic schoolmastering it was going to have to be.

Leonard (L. A. G.) Strong was teaching at Summer Fields, a preparatory school in North Oxford. A last minute vacancy for an unmarried teacher (on account of the nature of the staff accommodation on offer) had arisen days before the start of the school term in September, he told Day-Lewis. Would he like to take it?

The £5 Day-Lewis had raised by selling his university textbooks had long since run out. And at least Summer Fields was close enough to Auden for the two to continue to meet. It wasn't exactly the real world – or at least not the sharp end of the real world he aspired to inhabit so as to grow into a better poet. But, with marriage imminent and no other prospect of employment, he reluctantly accepted. 'I took the post with the feelings of a spinster, no longer as young as she was, accepting an unattractive and socially inferior suitor to get away from home.'[10]

Summer Fields was a nursery for Eton and other leading public schools. It prided itself on its academic success but had its eccentricities. The family who owned the school was keen to live as well as possible on their earnings so kept investment down to a minimum. Buildings were cold, cramped and run-down.

Teaching was done by rote but his timetable was not, Day-Lewis was relieved to find, arduous. There would be time enough to work on the new sequence he had started in his last term. He had already shown drafts of it to Auden over the summer. Day-Lewis was given a flat in the lodge at the entrance to the school on the Banbury Road. Often he would walk in to Christ Church to see Auden. As an alternative, there were relaxed evenings of literary discussions with the irreverent Leonard Strong, sometimes followed by singing Irish songs to the accompaniment on piano of his wife, Sylvia, or excursions to Oxfordshire pubs with other members of staff for darts and drinking.

Day-Lewis had already realized that too much of Auden could stifle him. 'Auden's personality also set up in me a certain resistance, and I instinctively felt, no less than I did with Maurice Bowra, that he was perhaps best taken in smallish doses.'[11] This was written in 1960, long after the event and when he was keen to dispel the notion of himself as Auden's acolyte, but the amused detachment with which Strong would conduct their debates stood in marked contrast to Auden's didactic tendencies.

In the classroom by day, Day-Lewis immediately found himself floundering. He had no training but was expected to teach across the curriculum, he was told on his first day, and was immediately given a maths lesson to take. It was a subject for which he had long ago discovered he had no capacity at all. 'I wrote up a vulgar fraction on the blackboard,' he recalled, 'and began to work it out. Very shortly I realized that I had forgotten how to work out vulgar fractions. I saw myself publicly humiliated – my career ended as soon as it had started. Whipping round from the blackboard, I fastened upon an attentive and intelligent-looking boy, who was obviously on the point of questioning my methods, barked at him, "I see you've entirely failed to understand what I'm doing – I'd better give you something easier", rubbed out the sum and wrote up a simple addition one instead.'[12]

He saw teaching as a necessity, something to endure until he could afford to stop, and so his attitude was that of the benign amateur. 'His heart clearly wasn't in teaching,' recalled his pupil, the future Conservative politician Julian Amery.[13] Day-Lewis's detachment meant that he failed to command any sort of authority. One afternoon on the playing field, a fight got out of hand among the boys. When Day-Lewis tried to intervene, he was pelted with footballs.

Still struggling towards adulthood himself, he found some of the privileged pupils at Summer Fields challenging in their supreme confidence. At breakfast one morning he was delighted to see a very small boy reading a book of poetry. 'I leant over his shoulder to see its title. He was reading *The Land*. "Is that a good book? Do you like it?" I asked. "Of course it's a good book," he politely replied. "My mother wrote it".'[14] It was the young Nigel Nicolson,[15] with a copy of Vita Sackville-West's 1927 prize-winning long poem.[16]

His professionalism Day-Lewis saved for poetry. The extent of his reliance on Auden's guidance can be judged from a letter, dated June 19, 1927, which Auden sent to him from Berlin – 'the bugger's daydream' as he called the German capital – to the Blakeney Hotel on the north coast of Norfolk where he and Mary were guests of Arthur Morris and his wife Alison. Morris had spent three years between 1923 and 1926 as curate to Frank Day-Lewis at Edwinstowe and had struck up a friendship with his son, based in part on their shared exasperation with the vicar.

The letter, handwritten in Auden's tiny, precise script, comes as part of a longer, now lost correspondence (Day-Lewis was infuriatingly casual about keeping and dating letters). Day-Lewis was seeking Auden's opinion and he for his part was almost monitoring what was coming slowly together as *Transitional Poem*, a work in which Day-Lewis wished to leave his Georgian past behind and give expression to the beliefs he and Auden had formulated at Appletreewick.

'If I sound condescending,' Auden writes,[17] 'please forgive. It is an error in communication. What I feel about this poem and also about what I can remember of several others of *Transitional Poem* is that you are not taking enough trouble about your medium, your technique of expression. Your earlier verse was to me remarkable for its great technical accomplishment, its expressive value, even when there was paucity of conventional content. In your later work on the contrary I am intensely interested in the content of your experience which is I feel both original and valuable, but feel that you are not satisfied with your medium for expressing it, which shows itself often as verbal laziness ... Or to put it another way, you are so interested in your experience as a whole, your poetic concept, that [in] hurrying to its completion, you neglect the parts ... You sound as if you were wanting your tea.'

Form was failing to keep up with content, Auden believed, and went on to pick out specific phrases from what Day-Lewis had sent him. ' "Tormented wood" does not fit in with the Eden emotion, "semi-breves of birds" seems undescriptive. Why semi, except to fill up the line?'

Such detailed examination of Day-Lewis's work was part of the friendship. And such scrutiny was, initially at least, reciprocal. In 1929, for example, Auden sent for Day-Lewis's comment on his current work-in-progress, his chorus 'The spring unsettles sleeping partnerships ...' from what was to become the verse charade *Paid on Both Sides*.[18]

Yet Day-Lewis, having considered Auden's suggestions, rejected them. In a section of *Transitional Poem* based on the Book of Genesis, he wrote:

> And the Word was God.
> >   For him rise up the litanies of leaves
> >   From the tormented wood, and semi-breves
> >   Of birds accompany the simple dawn.

Part IV, 28: Transitional Poem (1929)

All the offending phrases were retained. In his letter, Auden then proceeds to criticize the stanza

> For there's no wonder where all things are new;
> No dream where all is sleep; no vision where
> Seer and seen are one; nor prophecy
> Where only echo waits upon the tongue.

as 'dilated and versified. The result is not poetry. The last ten lines are fine. Not sure about the "muscular stream", but it is the right sort of mistake.' 'You want to concentrate on your medium', Auden concludes, before adding a final more personal footnote about a boy he is seeing who would 'make [D. H.] Lawrence's book quite blue. He is the most elemental thing.'[19]

Yet again Day-Lewis left both the offending stanza and the 'muscular stream' unchanged in the final version of *Transitional Poem*. He may have been writing 'pastiche-Auden' but he was confident enough in his own mind to choose his own words.

Auden left Oxford after finals in the summer of 1928 and headed for Berlin. For Day-Lewis Summer Fields had only been a one-year appointment. He and

Mary were planning to marry at Christmas of 1928 and there was no accommodation available at the school for a couple. It was time to move on.

Day-Lewis applied for and was appointed to a new teaching post at Larchfield School at Helensburgh, north of Glasgow. The salary was £300 a year and there was a house available nearby. His years of living like a student had been stretched to five by his time at Summer Fields.

Chapter 10

Farewell Adolescent Moon

Farewell again to this adolescent moon;
I say it is a bottle
For papless poets to feed their fancy on.
'Part III, 24': *Transitional Poem* (1929)

On Thursday, December 28, 1928, Cecil Day-Lewis and Mary King were married by their fathers at the high altar under the ancient fan vaulting of Sherborne Abbey. Neither had any real Christian attachment left from their childhood, but neither felt strongly enough about it to rebel against family expectations and opt for a secular wedding in a register office.

Mary was 26 and Cecil 24. Rex Warner was best man. There was a reception for 250 people at Sherborne School afterwards. Then Day-Lewis changed from his traditional morning dress into something he judged more appropriate for a poet – a bright green shirt and daffodil yellow tie – and the couple set off for a night at the Royal Clarence Hotel in Exeter. It was followed by a honeymoon on the rocky (and in January bleak) north coast of Devon at the Hartland Quay Hotel which had four years earlier been visited by Day-Lewis as part of a vacation reading week with Maurice Bowra.

It was, both recalled, a happy sojourn. 'We were young for our age, idealistic, proud: a loving couple, but in public so undemonstrative to each other that few could have guessed it', Day-Lewis was to write.[1] Some years later he ascribed his own lingering emotional reticence to his Anglo-Irish roots and was fond of telling how W. B. Yeats had been taken to a railway station by his mother to watch the English kissing each other goodbye. Mrs Yeats intended it, Day-Lewis explained, 'as a dreadful warning – an object lesson in the appalling demonstrativeness of the English. This was the sort of thing the Anglo-Irish simply didn't do'.[2]

For Mary, any inhibition she was feeling towards her new husband had a more straightforward explanation. Shortly before the wedding she had met Diana Jordan, the new dance teacher at Sherborne School for Girls. There had been an attraction between the two and a flirtation. Mary was beginning to understand what lay behind her own feelings when she had written in the early days of her romance with Day-Lewis that 'I am half a boy in thought and feeling',[3] but she rejected exploring her sexual attraction for women any further with Diana Jordan. She intended to marry her 'Monkey', her new pet name for Day-Lewis, and make a life with him and in support of him.

Despite Mary's bracing taste for open windows, fresh air in bedrooms and separate beds, their sexual relationship was developing. Their only contact with their families while at Hartland, for example, was to send a note to Mary's brother, Charles, asking him to locate and destroy a used condom they had inadvertently left behind in Mary's bedroom at Greenhill, the King family home where they had been staying before the wedding, 'as HRK [Mary's father] might not understand'.[4]

Day-Lewis felt relief that their long and troubled five-year courtship had culminated in marriage. His emotional needs, as he perceived them then, were simple. 'In my younger days, a mother figure was what I wanted', he was to write,[5] and Mary immediately took to tending to his every need. He soon developed a series of minor illnesses which necessitated bed rest and her constant ministrations. Her reward would be a glimpse at his work in progress. On their honeymoon, for instance, he read aloud to her from his draft of *Transitional Poem*.

With their shared tendency towards self-analysis and self-absorption, Day-Lewis and W. H. Auden even managed to assess the consequences for their creative work of marriage. Auden summarized their thoughts in a verse letter sent to Cecil and Mary Day-Lewis in March 1929 at a time when he himself was contemplating tying the knot with Sheilah Richardson (an engagement he later broke off, remarking that heterosexual love was 'so tame').

> *Should poets marry? You have done, and I*
> *Engaged, may hope to do so presently.*
> *What do we offer wives? They can expect*
> *But disappointments, penury and neglect*
> *And kept for nothing, they will often feel,*
> *But washing dishes and to hear the bell,*
> *Pitied by relatives who only see*
> *In poetry a game for after tea,*
> *Charming in lovers, in a husband mad.*
> *Whom all think lazy, and most think a cad.*
> *At best we shall succeed. What does this mean?*
> *We're mentioned in a highbrow magazine:*
> *Schoolmistresses send photographs and quote*
> *With praise bad poems which we never wrote.*
> *Suppose we fail, we shall not be excused*
> *For chances offered now which we refused.*
> *The fools condemned us, but the fools were just.*
> *Our wives will have had nothing, yet they must*
> *Bear with our tempers when our memories are*
> *Aching in every narcissistic scar.*[6]

This painted an unappealing picture of married life for Mary and Sheilah – penury, hard work, neglect and flirtatious rivals. Auden had not travelled over from Berlin to attend the wedding at Sherborne. His subsequent letters to Day-Lewis suggest that he may not, at this stage, have even met Mary, something reinforced by the fact that the 'Epithalamium' with which he marked the event was dedicated only to C Day-Lewis – written with the hyphen that had been dropped with *Country Comets*, but the first public acknowledgement that the Cecil had now been dropped (and also a hint that Auden, who was published as W. H. not Wystan, encouraged it).

The celebratory poem nevertheless praised 'the accurate matching of a man and woman',[7] but predicted the imminent arrival of a son and evoked images of shadows, death and beasts coming out to play. This may have been pure mischief to shock the assembled vicars and schoolmasters in Sherborne – something that would have appealed to Auden – or borrowed imagery from the Icelandic epic sagas he was at that time exploring with Isherwood, but was enough to persuade the best man, Rex Warner, to decline to read it aloud to the 250 guests.

After the honeymoon, the young couple drove in Mary's car – given the pet-name Pumpkin by her – to Helensburgh. 128 West King Street was their first marital home. It was a small, modern, slate-roofed, pebble-dashed council house on a new estate looking over the Clyde estuary to Greenock on the other bank. The previous term, when Day-Lewis had taken up his new teaching post before the wedding, Mary had visited him there and set to work on decorating the place. The domestic environment, it was agreed from the start, was her responsibility.

Helensburgh itself was a stuffy, inward-looking place – the 'Wimbledon of the North' as Day-Lewis described it in a letter[8] – but its narrow-mindedness only served to give the young couple a pleasing sense of being united in youthful rebellion against a complacent world. The school, Larchfield, may have offered better wages and better accommodation than Summer Fields but it was an establishment in decline. It had in its time taught such distinguished figures as television pioneer John Logie Baird[9] and the social anthropologist Sir James Frazer[10] (whose *Golden Bough* was one of the sources T. S. Eliot drew on for *The Waste Land*), but when Day-Lewis arrived it had shrunk to just 70 pupils, 25 of them boarders, aged eight to 18, under an ageing and erratic head, T. N. N. Perkins.

It was at Perkins's behest that Day-Lewis half-heartedly penned a bland but uplifting new school song – *'Make our hearts as bright and brave/As the mountain and the wave/So Scotland may be proud of you'*. His other duties were no more satisfying. He tried valiantly to put together a Rugby XV from such a small pool of pupils of such a wide range of ages. And with Mary's help, he staged musical afternoons.

The young new master with fresh ideas didn't always endear himself to parents. Teaching gave him, he wrote, 'a lingering notion that parents are the main obstacle to the right education of their children'. Overall he found Larchfield 'uncouth and unsophisticated' in comparison to Summer Fields.[11] Auden, who was to succeed Day-Lewis as a master there, left a similarly damning but more surreal picture of the chaos and amateurism of the place in a 1931 letter written from Larchfield to his brother, John. 'The school is quite wonderful. Upstairs the headmaster, partially blinded by a recent operation, is moping over a gas stove, worried about his wife going eventually mad in a canvas shelter in the garden. The young Reptonian engaged at a moderate salary to take his work is out rock-climbing with a maiden aunt . . . I spend most of my time adjusting the flow of water to the boys' urinal with a brass turn-key.'[12]

Auden endured Larchfield for two and a half years. Less than a year after his appointment, Day-Lewis was writing to L. A. G. Strong and others looking for a means of escape. 'How do you suppose my stock stands at Summer Fields?' he enquired of Strong. 'The parents and directors at this place make life a positive misery . . . I can do nothing in this shower of bastardy; I sit about and contemplate rasping satires but nothing comes of it.'[13]

There were diversions. The economic hardships being suffered by workers on the Clyde chimed with his growing political interests. Near to his house, in the Gareloch, lines of anchored rusting steamers lay, out of commission because of the worldwide slump. In the cosseted world of a private boarding school in a genteel Scottish town, he was hardly experiencing adversity, but the reminders of a more pressing reality were inescapable.

More pleasurable were the sailing trips the Day-Lewises took with friends made in Helensburgh, Jim and Janet Allen. Still a lover of nature, if now abandoning her earlier interest in fairies, Mary organized hiking trips to Loch Lomond. She even managed to navigate her way round a visit north from Frank and Mamie Day-Lewis during which Cecil fell ill and was conveniently confined again to bed. The tension between father and son had not abated, though distance made it less urgent.

Day-Lewis had plenty of time to work on *Transitional Poem*, which he had begun over 18 months before his marriage. In February 1929 Auden came for three busy days of walks, music, discussion and examination of each other's work. Afterwards, Day-Lewis sent his own hymn to the visit and their friendship, trying initially to imitate Auden's light touch in his verse letters, but moving quickly to the more comfortable ground of a sober and stirring tone.

This was the second time that you had pulled
The rusty trigger summoning the stragglers.
Once more the bird goes packing, the skeleton
Sets teeth against a further dissolution.
And what have we to hope for who are bound,
Though we strip off the last assurance of flesh
For expedition, to lay our bones somewhere?
Say that a rescue party should see fit
To do us some honour, publish our diaries,
Send home the relics – how should we thank them?
The march is what we asked for; it is ended.
Still, let us wear the flesh away and leave
Nothing for birds, anatomy to men.

'Letter to WH Auden': Epilogue to *From Feathers to Iron* (1931)

The sense of common purpose in a great and looming battle to change the world is strong. There are phrases that could easily have been written by Auden –

'the march is what we asked for', for example, has a strongly Audenesque tone to it.

News of the first advance in that battle came soon afterwards. While he was ill in bed (again), Day-Lewis received a letter from Leonard Woolf[14] offering to publish *Transitional Poem* that autumn in the Living Poets series of the Hogarth Press, the high-brow publishing house he ran with his wife, Virginia. Book jackets were designed by her sister, Vanessa Bell.[15]

On receiving the good news, Auden was full of congratulations. He replied with a new poem of his own, 'A Free One'. In the accompanying letter, he wrote: 'It is not the bad poets who are successful that one is jealous of, but the good ones like yourself whose medium happens to be a simpler one, because then one can't be superior about it.'[16]

Another key, uniting and enduring influence for the young poets at this time was Thomas Hardy. Auden later liked to claim the credit for introducing Day-Lewis to Hardy. 'We did, of course, learn certain things from each other,' he wrote in his 1968 'Letter of Introduction' to *C Day-Lewis: A Bibliography*. 'I *think* I am right in saying that I introduced you to the poems of Thomas Hardy and Robert Frost, for both of which I had developed a passion while still at school.'[17]

Certainly as a schoolboy at Sherborne, Day-Lewis had been ignorant of Hardy, the celebrated local writer. But that note of doubt sounded by Auden was echoed by fellow undergraduates from Wadham who remember that in his years of living in college – before he met Auden – Day-Lewis already was full of enthusiasm for Hardy. 'I remember entering his room once,' G. K. Laycock recounted, 'and remarking that Hardy was well represented on his shelves. His face lit up with a glow: "He's wonderful".'[18]

What is important, though, is the enthusiastic and fertile dialogue about Hardy's poetry that developed between Auden and Day-Lewis. One key Modernist tenet was to remove the personal from poetry. In Hardy, Day-Lewis and Auden found a contemporary inspiration in the other direction. As Day-Lewis was later to highlight in a 1951 lecture, 'almost all of his [Hardy's] finest poems are nakedly personal'.[19] He mentioned in particular on that occasion Hardy's love poems – the best written after her death about his wife Emma – and his subsequent meditations on old age.

Hardy's personal subjectivity was specifically attacked in 1934 by T. S. Eliot in *After Strange Gods; A Primer of Modern Heresy*. 'He [Hardy] seems to me to have written as nearly for the sake of "self-expression" as a man well can; and the self which he had to express does not strike me as a particularly wholesome or edifying matter of communication.'[20] What Eliot saw as a flaw, though, Day-Lewis regarded as an outstanding and inspiring quality. Indeed he criticized Eliot in his turn for making his poetry 'as impersonal as he can make it; the self he has put into it has gone through such a severe screening that the very minimum of human personality emerges; or, as we might venture to put it, that he achieves poetry only by excluding large areas of personal experience'.[21]

Eliot dissociated the suffering individual from the poet, but Day-Lewis became convinced there should be no such severance. 'Hardy put everything he felt, everything he noticed, everything he was into his poetry. As a result he wrote a great many bad poems – far more than Mr Eliot ever wrote – [but] his poetry has that breadth of matter and manner which only a major poet can compass.'[22]

Day-Lewis, as he worked to find a poetry that would directly engage with the world in crisis that he saw all around him, was drawn to that lack of distancing and detachment in Hardy. It was reflected in the strongly personal tone of *Transitional Poem*, published in October of 1929. A 40-page sequence of 34 poems organized in 4 parts, dedicated to Rex Warner, it was Day-Lewis's breakthrough to critical acclaim and the first major public manifestation of the revolution headed by the poets of the 1930s.

The most obvious personal note is sounded by the stanzas in 'Poem 8' at the start of Part II. These also show a marked influence of Yeats because Day-Lewis was mythologizing, as Yeats had, his own generation and circle. Day-Lewis describes four people who:

> ... have my allegiance; they whose shining
> Convicted my false dawn of flagrant night,
> Yet ushered up the sun, as poets leaning
> Upon a straw surmise the infinite.

The quartet is not named, but the first to be praised is Mary who receives a declaration of the poet's eternal love.

> With you I ran the gauntlet for my prime,
> Then living in the moment lived for all time.

Next is Rex Warner.

> the hawk-faced man, who could praise an apple
> In terms of peach and win the argument. Quick
> Was he to trip the shambling rhetoric
> Of laws and lions:

Warner, like Day-Lewis, had married since graduating. In July 1929 Cecil was best man at the wedding of Warner and Frances Grove. Rex's vicar father performed the ceremony. And Warner too was teaching – classics to prep school pupils – while continuing to write poetry but mainly working on his novel, *Wild Goose Chase*, a tale of three brothers who set off on a bike journey to find the right way to live.[23]

Day-Lewis had the same literary and political conversations and correspondence with Warner as he did with Auden. Because they lived in the same country, Day-Lewis and Warner saw each other more often than either saw Auden. Day-Lewis read and commented on the emerging novel and ultimately championed it when publishers in the mid 1930s proved reluctant to accept it.

Though no less intense than Day-Lewis's relationship with Auden, his friendship with Warner had a lighter edge. There was more teasing of each other

– rooted in their days of sharing a student house – while the competition between the two young men found an easy and natural outlet in various games they would play.

Warner also maintained his own close relationship with Auden. He was one of the Auden group. So after the birth in 1930 of the Warners' first child, Jonathan, Auden visited the new parents at their Thames-side cottage near Reading and later sent them a poem about their baby, hailing him as the future leader who would 'rescue' society from all its ills. (The poem also condemned T. S. Eliot and Robert Graves as reactionary – an indication that Warner and Auden had been having similar discussions to Day-Lewis and Auden.)[24]

The third of *Transitional Poem*'s quartet of heroes is Margaret Marshall, described in the terms quoted earlier. The use of the phrase 'brazen leech' about her makes another link with Auden. It is a phrase he used of her – referred to only as Margaret – in his 1928 *Poems*.[25] Her inclusion highlights the sexual as well as the social tension that Day-Lewis tackles in *Transitional Poem*.

And then he pays an extravagant tribute to Auden himself, the stanza about 'the tow-haired poet' quoted earlier, before continuing of all four:

> These have I loved and chosen, once being sure
> Some spacious vision waved upon their eyes
> That troubles not the common register;
> And love them still, knowing it otherwise.
>
> Knowing they held no mastership in wisdom
> Or wit save by certificate of my love,
> I have found out a better way to praise them –
> Nestor shall die and let Patroclus live.
>
> So I declare it. These are they who have built
> My house and never a stone of it laid agley.
> So cheat I memory that works in gilt
> And stucco to restore a fallen day.

'Poem 8: Part II'

That same note of confidence, of optimism, characterizes the whole of *Transitional Poem*. Day-Lewis may have acknowledged the influence of Auden, but was no longer dazzled by him. He 'held no mastership in wisdom'.

The effects of his journey with Auden are apparent in the change of style between *Country Comets* and *Transitional Poem*. Not only do the individual poems lack a title – they are simply given numbers, a device favoured by Auden in his *Poems* of 1928 – they are written with a new brio, energy, even arrogance.

> Now I have come to reason
> And cast my schoolboy clout,
> Disorder I see is without,
> And the mind must sweat a poison
> Keener than Thessaly's brew;
> A pus that, discharged not thence,
> Gangrenes the vital sense

89

And makes disorder true.
It is certain we shall attain
No life till we stamp on all
Life the tetragonal
Pure symmetry of brain.

'Poem 1: Part I'

And early on, too, Day-Lewis makes a strikingly bold claim to be presenting something radically new when he writes of 'my scorning/Of common poet's talk'. One element of innovation was stylistic. Though some poems in the sequence hark back to the lyrical, romantic approach of his earlier work, overall *Transitional Poem* is more austere and shows Day-Lewis exercising a greater variety and mastery of form. Gone too, largely, are the melancholy and reflective stanzas of *Country Comets* and in their place is found verse brimming over with optimism, intellectual pursuit, energy and charge.

He achieves this in part with fresh, often deceptively simple metres, rhythms, half rhymes and structures – and by moving apparently effortlessly but with great calculation from one form to another. The contrasting shapes and beats of individual poems add to the sense of structural strength, and strength of purpose, throughout the sequence. Day-Lewis's technical accomplishment was one of the attributes that reviewers praised most highly.

It was his achievement to reinvigorate traditional form, rather than merely deconstructing it in imitation of the Modernists. It was an approach shared with Auden. The techniques he used echo those found in Auden's poetry of the period. So Day-Lewis offers, alongside more usual classical illusions, a contemporary imagery and subject matter, modern diction, engagement and all-too-evident passion. In Poem 18, the ancient 'city famed for talk and tolerance' is juxtaposed with 'a rubbish heap' (one of Auden's favourite destinations on walks in Oxford) which 'proclaims the pleasant norm with smouldering stenches'. In Poem 1 the image of 'fat strings of barges drawn by a tug they have never seen' suggests the view of the Clyde from his Helensburgh home, while in Poem 14 'life's pistons' are 'pounding into their secret cylinder'.

In Poem 20, the poet's journey of self-discovery takes place on a train.

The tracks of love and fear
Lead back till I disappear
Into that ample terminus
From which all trains draw out
Snorting towards an Ultima Thule.
Nothing is altered about
The place, except its gloom is newly
Lacquered by an unaccustomed eye,
Yet cannot blunt mine eyes now
To the clear finality
Of all beginnings.
Outside
In the diamond air of day

The engines simmer with delay,
Desiring a steely discipline
No less, though now quite satisfied
They travel a loop-line.

The transition of the sequence's title describes living through a conflict, both personal and social/political. Conflict of allegiance is the overall theme. In personal terms, Day-Lewis reprises his love for Mary – *My love is a tower./ Standing up in her/I parley with planets/And the casual wind* – but does so in less romantic terms than before. The tower is also earthbound, so there is the urge to wander. 'Desire is a witch/And runs against the clock./It can unstitch/The decent hem'.

And on the social/political plane, the poet is torn between his emerging left-wing beliefs, his desire to see radical economic and social change, especially for the working classes, and his own privileged position as a bourgeois school-teacher linked by a web of family and other loyalties to traditional ways of thought and behaviour. Yet he sees that to follow through his desire for change he will have to betray all he is attached to by his upbringing.

If I bricked up ambition and gave no air
To the ancestral curse that gabbles there,
*   I could leave wonder on the latch*
*   And with a whole heart watch*
The calm declension of an English year.

I would be a paedagogue – hear poplar, lime
And oak recite the seasons' paradigm.
*   Each year a dynasty would fall*
*   Within my orchard wall –*
I'd be their Tacitus, and they my time.

'Poem 11: Part II'

The sequence is then an attempt to set out and externalize the questions rather than answer them – or, in the terms of his jointly authored preface to *Oxford Poetry 1927*, to find a synthesis. The goal Day-Lewis sets himself is to reach that 'pure symmetry of the brain', that he refers to in the opening stanzas, the 'single mind' that will resolve the conflicts he feels. He believes that Auden already possesses it '[his] Single mind copes with split intelligence'. Day-Lewis himself can glimpse it:

*   I sit in a wood and stare*
Up at untroubled branches
Locked together and staunch as
Though girders of the air:
And think, the first wind rising
Will crack that intricate crown
And let the daylight down.
But there is naught surprising
Can explode the single mind: –

Let figs from thistles fall
Or stars from their pedestal,
This architecture will stand.

'Poem 1: Part I'

Transitional Poem stresses that this place in the wood is scarcely attainable within the course of one sequence, or indeed one life. The contradictions which Day-Lewis candidly acknowledges in himself are highlighted by an epigraph at the start of Part II from Walt Whitman's[26] 'Song of Myself' – *Do I contradict myself?/Very well then, I contradict myself;/I am large, I contain multitudes.* There is overall in *Transitional Poem* an optimism, shared with Auden, that synthesis can be achieved and an implicit rejection of Eliot's despair at a fallen world. Day-Lewis is, in effect, inviting the reader to join him on a journey of hope.

There are clear influences of Eliot in *Transitional Poem* – not least in the echo of *The Waste Land* in the inclusion of notes at the end (which he dropped when *Transitional Poem* was included in his *Collected Poems*). But that sense of Day-Lewis charting a new course – modern but not Modernist – is there in his pointed rejection of the Modernist detachment.

Few things can more inflame
This far too combative heart
Than the intellectual Quixotes of the age
Prattling of abstract art.

'Poem 7: Part I'

Looking back in 1960 at *Transitional Poem* Day-Lewis expressed himself surprised at its 'relentlessly highbrow' tone.[27] Certainly it is dense and contained little of the satirical wit that Auden brought to his poetry of the period. At times Day-Lewis's brave new voice slips. Some images are hackneyed – 'the first daffodil/That ever shews a spring'. And some of the imagery is confused – the Ultima Thule, the distant, mythical land of antiquity, is set alongside railway engines and loop-lines in Poem 20 to no discernible purpose. A pattern, if pattern was intended, is hard to discern. Yet for all its flaws, *Transitional Poem*'s core themes anticipated many of those pursued by other poets of the 1930s – the relationship between loyalty and belief, the cult of the hero, the poet's conflicting allegiances to the bourgeois world and to left-wing radicalism, the struggle to match thought with action.

The critical response to *Transitional Poem* was greater in the national press than for Day-Lewis's previous two collections. Some identified the influence of the seventeenth century poets, notably Donne and Marvell.[28] Publication also made Day-Lewis conspicuous among those writers and intellectuals whose response to the economic state of Britain and the rise of fascism in Europe was to move leftwards. Among the letters of praise he received was one from Naomi Mitchison.[29] A novelist, poet and campaigner for radical causes, and wife of Labour politician, Dick Mitchison, she was soliciting contributions for the journal, *Realist*, which aimed to bring art and science closer. Day-Lewis's modern, industrial imagery attracted her.

Transitional Poem was published in an edition of just 400. It was a *succès d'estime* but did not provide any means of financial support for Day-Lewis or open up the prospect of giving up teaching to concentrate on writing. His appeals to friends for a means of escape from Larchfield finally bore fruit late in 1929. His old tutor, Maurice Bowra, was a governor at Cheltenham College, and urged him to apply there.

An interview was arranged with the head H. H. Hardy. Part of it consisted of a long country walk where Day-Lewis was none too subtly quizzed about his views on D. H. Lawrence. Although he had read *Sons and Lovers*, *Women in Love* and *The Rainbow*, enjoyed them and admired their liberated sexual ethic, he realized that wasn't what Hardy – a conformist already suspicious of a young poet – wanted to hear. So he changed the subject to games and was offered the job with effect from April 1930, a decision Hardy was to come to regret.

Chapter 11

Radiance from Ashes Arises

Wherever radiance from ashes arises –
Willowherb glowing on abandoned slagheaps,
Dawn budding scarlet in a bed of darkness,
Life from exhausted womb outstriving –
There shall the spirit be lightened and gratefully
Take a whole holiday in honour of this.
'Poem 29': *From Feathers to Iron* (1931)

Soon after Day-Lewis arrived from Scotland at Cheltenham College in April of 1930 to take up his post teaching Classics, English, History and French, he was summoned to meet Bowers – first names were seldom used by boys or staff – who was his immediate superior as head of the junior school. He informed the new young master that, having read *Transitional Poem*, he wondered if Day-Lewis was an entirely suitable character to be left in charge of tender minds.

'I found the poems, some of them, very, exceedingly,' he began, but was unable to continue, Day-Lewis recalled. After much prompting, Bowers finally managed to say what was on his mind. 'Extremely, excessively, er, sexual.' 'But they're love poems,' Day-Lewis blurted out by way of reply, 'addressed to my wife.'[1]

Although Bowers wouldn't have dreamt of addressing Mrs Bowers in such terms, he was disarmed – at least for the time being. The suspicion that Day-Lewis was subversive – mainly by the simple fact that he was a poet, but also because of what he wrote about in those poems – persisted throughout his time at the school among many members of staff, parents and governors. It was just not the sort of work that this establishment hothouse for future senior civil servants, colonial administrators and military top brass regarded as gainful employment.

Shortly after the Day-Lewises arrived, they set to work whitewashing their designated quarters – a ground floor flat in Belmore House, a nondescript property in Bath Place, close to the impressive Gothic main buildings of the school. Day-Lewis put on an old green shirt for the task – perhaps the one he had worn proudly as he and Mary had set off on honeymoon two years before. The couple was interrupted as they painted by a fellow master apparently coming to welcome them aboard. He knew Mary's father and his visit seemed friendly and innocent enough, if awkwardly timed. But afterwards they learnt that he had gone straight to Hardy to report Day-Lewis's outrageous style of dress.

The head managed to keep this snippet of intelligence to himself but when a couple of weeks later Day-Lewis attended a school concert wearing a cravat, he received a 'chit' from above making plain Hardy's ruling that green shirts, cravats or any other 'bohemian' departure from convention would not be tolerated at Cheltenham. Initially Day-Lewis attempted to explain the entirely practical reasons for his choice of an old shirt when decorating, but was treated by Hardy like 'an impertinent junior officer'[2] and learned quickly to bite his lip. It was humiliating but he needed the job. Mary had just found out she was pregnant.

The couple did find kindred spirits among their colleagues – notably Lionel Hedges and his wife, Eileen.[3] He was the games master at the junior school. An Oxford Blue, a former county cricketer for Kent who still turned out occasionally for Gloucestershire, and even a sometime actor – he appeared as a batsman in Anthony Asquith's 1931 stiff-upper-lip First World War film, *Tell England* – Hedges appealed to Day-Lewis's taste for larger-than-life heroes, especially sporting ones, even if the only heroic quality that an overweight Hedges retained from his younger days was his thirst for alcohol. But in Day-Lewis's eyes, he possessed 'that rarest and most appealing of qualities – the excess of life'.[4] Moreover the two shared an amused detachment from the quasi-military regimented machine that was Cheltenham College, based on an aspiration that both of them were only there temporarily and really should be doing something else altogether more challenging and suited to their talents.

Hedges and Day-Lewis would repair regularly to the local pub, the Beehive – where inevitably they were spotted and reported to the school authorities for conduct unbecoming, as Day-Lewis described in a letter to Rex Warner. He and Hedges had been, he said, 'put on the mat for pubbing', their worst offence being 'lowering themselves by playing darts with the school sergeants'.[5]

One of their main sources of amusement during such drinking sessions was the antics of a fellow master, J. D. Parker, whose penchant for making banal remarks caused the two rebels to coin the phrase 'Parkerism' and exchange examples like 'a house is nothing without windows' or 'it is awfully depressing when it rains'. The best of the bunch were recorded in a notebook.[6]

Frank Halliday[7] was another young master who did not share the general unease at having a published poet on the staff. Later a professional writer himself, he welcomed Day-Lewis's arrival, 'a young married man,' he wrote in his autobiography *Indifferent Honest*, 'who liked Beethoven and Cesar Franck [and] ... was said to write poetry'.[8] The doubt in that last description suggests how much Day-Lewis tried to play down his other life when in school. Halliday, however, managed to get beyond both the air of suspicion that hovered around his new colleague and the Day-Lewises' own consequent tendency to keep their distance from school society. A friendship developed and he pictured Mary as possessing 'a ballet-dancer's hair and figure and a dairy-maid's complexion' and Cecil as 'reserved and almost severe, until his mouth curled into a smile and he began to speak with the trace of an Irish brogue'.[9]

Although he had only spent the first two years of his life in Ireland, the combination of an upbringing by an Irish father and aunt, plus a belief that Ireland was his natural home, nurtured during those summer vacations at Monart, meant that Day-Lewis's voice retained throughout his life the distinctive Anglo-Irish inflections and aspirated 't' alongside an otherwise standard upper middle class English pronunciation.

The sense of being continually scrutinized and spied upon at Cheltenham College made the Day-Lewises keen to move as soon as possible into their own home. Within twelve months of their arrival, they had raised a loan of £600 to purchase Box Cottage in nearby Charlton Kings, close enough for Day-Lewis to cycle to work each day. At the end of Bafford Lane, leading to open country, and named after the box hedge that surrounded it, this small but pretty house was built of mellow brick, which was exposed in its full glory when the new owners tore down the ivy that had enveloped it. With its vegetable patch and garden, the house looked over farmland towards the escarpment of Leckhampton Hill. It became both a family haven and an inspiration for Day-Lewis's poetry.

> *You have cut down the yews, say you, for a broader view? No churchyard*
> *Emblems shall bind or blind you? But see, the imperative brow*
> *Frowns of the hills, offers no compromise, means far harder*
> *Visions than valley steeples call to, a stricter vow.*
>
> *Though your wife is chaste, though your children lustily throng, though laughing*
> *Raise you a record crop, yet do you wrong your powers,*
> *Flattered no longer by isolation nor satisfied loving.*
> *Not box hedge where the birds nest, not embankments of flowers.*
>
> 'Moving In': *A Time To Dance* (1935)

Box Cottage – and the contented middle class life that it housed for Day-Lewis – became here a symbol of his own ambiguity, his unease with the conflicting loyalties that he had set out in *Transitional Poem*. It was, he commented wryly with the benefit of hindsight in *The Buried Day*, 'a sequestered, escapist kind of house for one of the new come-down-out-of-that-ivory-tower poets'.[10]

Day-Lewis had a wife, a child on the way, and a decently paid and challenging job as a schoolmaster. He had enough money to buy a house. By conventional standards, that should have been sufficient. Yet as a poet, he had committed himself to reflecting, sharing and even effecting a turbulent outside world. Box Cottage, with its rural charms, represented the antithesis of the sort of necessary if uncomfortable engagement Day-Lewis sought for his poetry. He was living another contradiction.

While the Gloucestershire countryside continued apparently undisturbed outside his window and the school went on as it had since its foundation in 1844, Britain was heading towards economic crisis. The poor overall performance of the 1920s, when the failure to regain pre-First World War markets and productivity had precipitated the painful restructuring that was the underlying cause of the 1926 General Strike, was compounded at the end of the decade by the 1929 Wall Street collapse. With unemployment levels already high and wages low, the effects of international crisis on the British economy were traumatic.

The jobless total rose from 1.5 million in 1929 to 3.4 million in 1932 – or 17 per cent of the labour force. The already cautious Labour government of Ramsay MacDonald, elected in 1929 on a promise to answer the cries of the most needy, found itself with a near bankrupt Exchequer.

To tackle a growing budget deficit and satisfy the international banks that sterling was not vulnerable, the government was forced to contemplate cutting the cause of 40 per cent of its overspend – unemployment benefits. For many in the Labour Party this was an unimaginable betrayal of its working class voters, but Ramsay MacDonald allied himself with Conservatives and Liberals in a National Government in 1931 and forced the measure through – a betrayal that may be one factor lying behind Auden's 1939 characterization of the 1930s as a 'low, dishonest decade'.[11]

The widespread hardship this move created in industrial areas – unemployment benefit ended after 26 weeks and was anyway grudgingly given – disillusioned many who had placed their trust in the Labour Party and caused them to look further left for alternatives. The launch in 1930 of its official organ, the *Daily Worker*, revealed the growing appeal of the Communist Party for workers and left-leaning intellectuals in Britain (though there was also a movement in the other direction, towards Oswald Mosley's home-grown fascist alternative which looked admiringly at the rise of Hitler in Germany).

The grinding poverty that blighted the 1930s would lead in 1936 to 200 unemployed men from the north-east industrial town of Jarrow setting out on a 300-mile 'hunger march' to London. For young idealistic men like Day-Lewis such suffering could not be ignored.

If the blight affecting much of Britain was less apparent in Cheltenham, Day-Lewis only had to travel an hour up the road to Oxford to see Charles Fenby, now installed as editor of the *Oxford Mail*, to catch sight of another world. There the Day-Lewises attended both a showing of John Grierson's pioneering 1929 documentary, *Drifters*, an account of the hardships of life in the North Sea herring fleet, and Alexander Dovzhenko's *Earth* (*Zemlya*). This 1930 epic portrayed humankind's intimate relationship with the soil and appeared to present, against lyrical scenes of life, love and death in the Russian countryside, a strong case for the communist model in the Soviet Union as the only viable way to right the current global economic wrongs and injustices. It was, Day-Lewis later wrote, 'the most real thing I had ever seen', an instinctive reaction to a film whose accuracy was later questioned. 'It gave an emotionally convincing picture of a society in which the power of every man and woman could have full exercise.'[12]

Day-Lewis was more drawn to such radical alternatives than either the pragmatic Fenby or Mary – more cautious in her politics and attracted to the Liberal Party. Auden too regarded communism with more reservation than Day-Lewis. The two continued to work closely. In the summer of 1930 they met for five days in the Lake District at the tail end of the Day-Lewises' attendance at the traditional gathering of the King clan. And by the end of 1932, Larchfield's eccentric charms had faded even for Auden. He took up a new teaching post at the more conducive liberal, Quaker-run Downs School, near Malvern, where he stayed on the staff for three years. It was close enough for regular visits with Day-Lewis in Cheltenham, Auden often bedding down in Box Cottage under piles of coats and rugs to keep him warm and eating whole bunches of bananas as the two young poets continued their intense discussions about their craft and scrutinized each other's work.[13]

Auden was particularly finicky about his domestic comforts, but even a less exacting guest would have struggled to feel at home at Box Cottage. Day-Lewis tried to find some respite from the conflict between the bourgeois reality of his life and the left-wing ideals he increasingly adopted by insisting on a spartan regime. There were few possessions – though this was just as much the result of a tight household budget and a natural distaste for clutter that associated any ornament with the Victorian ambience Mamie had imported into the Edwin-stowe rectory.

Austerity suited Mary's natural disposition. She liked the simple life, wash instead of wallpaper, though she did hanker after a radio set, banned from Box Cottage on her husband's insistence. She had to go next door to the Hopcrafts to listen to the coronation of George VI in 1936.

With the birth of the Day-Lewises' first child imminent in the summer of 1931, Rex Warner, already a father, came to Cheltenham to offer his old friend his support and the benefits of his experience. This consisted largely of competitive games of shove-halfpenny and poker patience with Lionel Hedges. Mary had the faithful Knos over from Ireland to offer more practical assistance. On Monday, August 3, 1931, at 5.20 a.m. Sean Francis was finally delivered by forceps, a week late. Day-Lewis celebrated the event in verse with exuberance and a typically modern metaphor.

> *Come out in the sun, for a man is born today!*
> *Early this morning whistle in the cutting told*
> *Train was arriving, hours overdue, delayed*
> *By snow-drifts, engine-trouble, Act of God, who cares now? –*
> *For here alights the distinguished passenger.*
> *Take a whole holiday in honour of this!*
>
> 'Poem 29': *From Feathers to Iron* (1931)

Somewhere between home and the Register Office, Day-Lewis decided against the name John – as agreed with Mary – and opted for the Irish alternative, Sean. If Mary objected, she did not mention it in her diary. But Day-Lewis's public claim to the couple's new child found its fullest expression in his new collection of poetry, *From Feathers to Iron*. Straight after completing *Transitional Poem*, he had begun work on a sequence that would eventually appear in 1933 as *The Magnetic Mountain* and address directly the questions he had posed but left unanswered in that earlier work. When Mary announced she was pregnant at Christmas 1930, however, he put that new sequence aside and started instead on what was at its most obvious level a chronological account about the hopes, fears and expectations of parents-to-be over nine months. It was, he told an interviewer in 1938, 'a step outwards for me ... a poem about a little community of three'.[14]

Day-Lewis had insisted on including in the collection a poem marking his child's birth. It threatened to throw Hogarth Press's deadlines out of kilter but nevertheless, only six weeks after Sean arrived, *From Feathers to Iron* was published. The print run was up 50 per cent from *Transitional Poem*.

The *Sunday Times'* influential poetry critic, Desmond MacCarthy, judged its title 'freakish'. Both nouns in it owed something to Auden – the iron being part of the two poets' shared attraction for more modern, more relevant imagery, and the feathers taken from a line of Auden's: 'Do thoughts grow like feathers, the dead end of life?' (Day-Lewis's letter of 1929 to Auden, quoted earlier, was also included as an epilogue in case any reader should miss the close connection between the two.) But the unusual coupling of the two images derived from Keats. 'We take but three steps from feathers to iron'. As well as creating something new, Day-Lewis was, again like Auden, conscious of being part of a poetic tradition.

The overall sense of having arrived at one of the landmarks of life is reflected in the dedication – 'To The Mother'. By not being specific, it also hinted at Day-Lewis's intention to use Mary's gestation to explore wider themes, but the dominant story in the sequence – told with the same passion, optimism and technical variety and accomplishment as *Transitional Poem* – is how physical passion between a man and a woman results in a new life which begins in dead of winter, burgeons in spring and comes to late summer fruition. This intimate subject matter was once again a rejection of the Modernist tendency to remove the poet from his poetry.

> *Twenty weeks near past*
> *Since the seed took to earth.*
> *Winter has done his worst.*
> *Let upland snow ignore;*
> *Earth wears a smile betrays*
> *What summer she has in store.*

'Poem 10'

Yet that newborn child will one day grow and so the sequence broadens its remit to embrace more political questions. What sort of world will the infant inherit? Day-Lewis's mind skips ahead.

> *It is time to think of you,*
> *Shortly will have your freedom.*
> *As anemones that renew*
> *Earth's innocence, be welcome.*
> *Out of your folded sleep*
> *Come, as the western winds come*
> *To pasture with the sheep*
> *On a weary of winter height.*
> *Lie like a pool unwrinkled*

That takes the sky to heart,
Where stars and shadows are mingled
And suns run gold with heat.
Return as the winds return,
Heir to an old estate
Of upland, flower and tarn.

But born to essential dark,
To an age that toes the line
And never o'ersteps the mark.
Take off your coat: grow lean:
Suffer humiliation:
Patrol the passes alone,
And eat your iron ration.
Else, wag as the world wags –
One more mechanical jane
Or gentleman in wax.
Is it here we shall regain
Championship? Here awakes
A white hope shall preserve
From flatterers, pimps and fakes
Integrity and nerve?

'Poem 18'

As well as the note of eager anticipation that runs throughout, there is also an undertow of looming crisis. Occasionally this is at a personal level, reflecting some of the conflicts that were emerging in his marriage. In 'Poem 15' Day-Lewis asks 'You in there, my son, my daughter,/Will You become dictator, resolve the factions?' Mostly, though, the warning cries are directed towards the situation in the outside world. Sometimes this can strike a false note when compared with the actual situation in which Day-Lewis was living.

Yes, you may know, as I do, self foreshortened,
Blocked out with blackness finally all the works of days.
O you who turn the wheel and look to both sides,
Consider Phlebas, who shall be taller and handsomer than you.

'Poem 21'

However little he enjoyed being a schoolmaster, it did not equate to daily blackness, but here Day-Lewis is transcending personal experiences and taking responsibility onto his own shoulders for the privations of the poor. There was a strong element of guilt in much of his output in this period at his comforts while witnessing others' poverty – stronger than one sees, for example, in Auden at the time. What is clear and consistent, though, is his call for good men with new solutions to stand up and be counted – *Take off your coat: grow lean:/Suffer humiliation* – against the forces of convention, 'gentleman in wax' and even those who should be grateful for such assistance but may initially feel themselves patronized and therefore be hostile.

101

Like Jesuits in jungle we journey
Deliberately bearing to brutish tribes
Christ's assurance, arts of agriculture.

'Poem 12'

There is a suggestion of vocation in this, a call to the life of the altruistic saint. That hint of religious fervour and tendency to preach, learnt in childhood, reapplied to political ends, was a shared feature of Day-Lewis, Warner and MacNeice, all of whom had rejected the faith of their clergymen fathers and were seeking a creed to replace it.

Day-Lewis's reference in 'Poem 21' to Phlebas, a mythical Phoenician sailor who sacrifices his life to save his king, shows him adapting, little altered, two lines from T. S. Eliot's *The Waste Land*.

Gentile or Jew
O you who turn the wheel and look to windward,
Consider Phlebas, who was once handsome and tall as you

'IV. Death By Water': *The Waste Land* (1922)[15]

Day-Lewis is making a literary allusion to a poem noted for its literary allusions. Indeed *The Waste Land* turned making literary allusions into a fashionable Modernist mode. Though Day-Lewis and his fellow poets had ambiguous feelings about Eliot, these lines in *From Feathers to Iron* show just how pervasive and inescapable his influence was in the 1930s. *The Waste Land* was the poem to match and respond to and here Day-Lewis is both paying his debt, but turning it towards a social and political agenda that was very different from Eliot's.

Meanwhile the strong influence of Auden – or the fruits of his co-operation with Day-Lewis – can also be seen throughout: in the numbering of the individual poems, in the overall double focus of the sequence, in the increased use of mechanical imagery (over *Transitional Poem*), in the occurrence of that distinctive Auden habit of cutting short phrases, as if composing a telegramme, and particularly in the deliberate juxtaposition of the industrial and pastoral – 'Look there, gasometer rises/And here bough swells to bud' (Poem 14).

Such lines were part of that shared drive to be modern not Modernist. The traditional images of nature found in poetry were thereby, Day-Lewis subsequently wrote, 'given fresh life and relevance. Some poems, at once explicitly sociological and deeply personal, invoke nature as a restorer, not of repose, but of strength and fecundity. What gives the best of the period's poetry it's unmistakeable quality seems to be the way in which feelings of private and communal insecurity are fused together, so that the personal lyrical anguish informs the political statement.'[16]

The poet and critic John Lehmann,[17] a contemporary and friend of both Day-Lewis and Auden, was to recall in 1955 of the publication of *From Feathers to Iron* that its striking imagery came 'unmistakeably from the bursting warehouse which Auden had thrown open'.[18] But there is a danger of overstatement. So while using a train to describe the moment of orgasm in 'Poem 4' – *the rails*

102

thrum/For night express is due – may now sound like pastiche Auden, it should be seen in the context of what was then avant-garde, the Futurist experiment in painting and prose of the 1930s. This Europe-wide movement sought to naturalize the machine, until then seen by Romantics and Georgians as at odds with the pastoral world.

Again there are strong echoes of Auden in the flippant, bossy almost messianic tone Day-Lewis uses in parts of the sequence. It made him sound more confident of his own opinions that he was – or certainly surer than his bourgeois life in Cheltenham should have allowed.

> *Today let director forget the deficit,*
> *Schoolmaster his handicap, hostess her false face:*
> *Let phantasist take charge of flesh-and-blood situation,*
> *Petty-officer be rapt in the Seventh Symphony.*

'Poem 29'

Yet to pigeonhole *From Feathers to Iron* as a pale imitation of Auden misses one essential point. Auden had by now abandoned his ambitions to marry and rejected heterosexuality. He was not going to experience mutual heterosexual love, much less conception and fatherhood – among the main themes of *From Feathers to Iron*. It was not therefore a sequence he could have written with any authority. Indeed in Day-Lewis's letter to Auden, included as an epilogue to the main sequence, he teases his friend about his sexual orientation and habit, in his poetry produced at this time, of writing laments to failed love affairs with other men.

> *You*
> *Preferred, I remember, the plump boy, the crocus.*
> *Enough of that.*

John Lehmann, for all that he could see Auden's influence in *From Feathers to Iron*, also acknowledged this point. In his 1955 autobiography, he wrote of Day-Lewis's sequence: 'the voice is consistently masculine and optimistic without that undertone of romantic despair that could still be heard in Auden's book [...] in spite of its message of break-away and renewal. And all is presented in a clear, sharply defined light, rather as in Donne's early poems, without any mists of musing and dreaming fantasy.'[19]

It was for its own qualities, rather than the influence of Auden, that reviewers in 1931 gave *From Feathers to Iron* a positive reception. Critics hailed Day-Lewis as a significant new voice and inspired enough sales for there to be a new impression in July 1932. Michael Roberts,[20] soon to collaborate with Day-Lewis and Auden, described the sequence in *Poetry Review* as 'a landmark, in the sense in which *Leaves of Grass*, *A Shropshire Lad*, *Des Imagistes* and *The Waste Land* were landmarks'. Indeed Roberts, later prime promoter of the idea of the poets of the 1930s as a unified movement, placed at this moment Day-Lewis rather than Auden in its vanguard. Referring to the ambition to incorporate images of modernity into poetry, he wrote: 'Mr Auden's *Poems* ... showed the first

103

marked advance, and now, in *Feathers to Iron*, we have the full solution: these images are used, not for their own sake, not because the poet's theory makes him choose images from contemporary life, but because they are structural: the thought requires precisely that expression'.

Much too was made of Day-Lewis's political intent, which flattered but also confused him. Later in life, he would protest that *From Feathers to Iron* was largely personal and that excessive emphasis had been placed on its political overtones. Just three years after publication, in *A Hope for Poetry*, Day-Lewis was already sounding a similar note of caution. The collection, he wrote, 'expressed simply my thoughts and feelings during the nine months before the birth of my first child: the critics, almost to a man, took it for political allegory; the simple, personal meaning evaded them'.

Less obvious to the applauding critics, but all too painfully plain for Mary, was the presence in *From Feathers to Iron* of another woman. The Day-Lewises had renewed their friendship while in Cheltenham with Arthur Morris, Frank Day-Lewis's former curate in Edwinstowe, and his wife Alison. The couple were now based in a parish at East Quantoxhead in Somerset, a couple of hours drive away. Alison Morris was dissatisfied with her marriage which ended soon afterwards and was drawn increasingly to Day-Lewis.

Mary had spotted the attraction between the two in the months before Sean's birth. If she needed confirmation that her worst fears about Alison Morris were justified, she had only to read Poems 5 and 6. The first appears to suggest that her pregnancy means that her husband inevitably has to stray, albeit temporarily. Her involvement with her unborn child is equated to Cecil's extra-marital adventures.

> We must a little part,
> And sprouting seed crack our cemented heart.
> Who would get an heir
> Initial loss must bear:
> A part of each will be elsewhere.
>
> What life may not decide
> Is past the clutch of caution, the range of pride.
> Speaking from the snow
> The crocus lets me know
> That there is life to come, and go.

And the second poem gives a clue as to who has caught his attention that summer. Alison Morris is not named but there is a description that Mary would have known was not about her.

> Now she is like the white-tree rose
> That takes a blessing from the sun:
> Summer has filled her veins with light,
> And her warm heart is washed with noon.

Day-Lewis's revelation of his betrayal was, however, in coded language that only Mary — and possibly an equally suspicious Arthur Morris — would have fully understood. His candour in print was scant reward for the friendship Morris had shown him since meeting him as a dissatisfied teenager in Edwinstowe.

For the two cuckolded spouses there was the added indignity of watching the lovers together during the second half of August when the Day-Lewises were guests in East Quantoxhead – ostensibly to help Mary recuperate after the birth of her first child and the departure back to Ireland of Knos. Their stay culminated in Sean's christening by Frank Day-Lewis on September 17.

Why did Day-Lewis betray his wife when she was at her most vulnerable? At its simplest because he could. He added an extra dimension of cruelty by depicting his infidelity in verse. In Poem 5 he puts part of the blame on Mary's pregnancy and consequent distraction. He was not at the centre of her world.

There was a deeper dissatisfaction at play. Their sex life may not have been fulfilling even before Mary was pregnant. In an undated correspondence with Rex Warner, from some time around October 1931, Day-Lewis confided he was having an affair but doesn't name Morris. Warner advised him to stop, but Day-Lewis wrote back: 'Your advice is cogent: but I must work it out myself; the body points in one way, & it will need private arguments to dissuade it.' Later he added: 'I've never deceived myself throughout ... I've pointed out often enough that she wasn't going to get further than my body'.[21]

Sex with Morris appeared to be one of the greatest attractions. The 'private arguments' he mentioned to Warner may refer to some effort to persuade Mary to reinvigorate their love life. Whenever possible the couple had separate bedrooms. While this was the norm in large middle class houses, for young newlyweds in a cramped property like Box Cottage to sleep apart may have been caused by one or other's insomnia or incompatible sleeping patterns, but also suggests a degree of physical alienation.

Mary's close link with Diana Jordan had continued. It was Jordan who bought Mary's beloved car, 'Pumpkin', when she needed to raise money to buy nursery equipment for the arrival of her baby. Though Mary had rejected taking the attraction the two women felt for each other any further, she did not allow the friendship to cool.

There was also Day-Lewis's feeling – made explicit as early as *Country Comets* – that what was 'No more denied/Seemed no more ideal', that he felt constrained by monogamy and needed to explore in other contexts the love of which he wrote so much. Alison offered that opportunity.

Mary watched as the relationship with Alison developed but kept her counsel. Confrontation was not in her nature. Their courtship had trained her to regard any problems in their relationship as her failing. Soon afterwards, as Mary had hoped it would, the relationship with Alison burned itself out. Day-Lewis, too, had never intended to leave Mary as he made plain in his correspondence with Rex Warner. 'The simplest thing,' he wrote of the affair, 'would be to let it take its course & die a natural death.'[22] Day-Lewis sent Alison as a parting gift an undated and unpublished sonnet, probably from 1933, featuring the kestrel that became a hallmark of his (and Auden's) poetry.

Dear, when at last you bow your wayward head
And like a rose to iron frosts consent,
When all your golden gallantry is spent
And little left for you but to be dead:
Remember how your cool and woodland eyes
Caught fire once from the sun and burned for me,
How at high summer stretched before the sea
Your naked breasts tore heaven by surprise.
Over the world of heather where we lay
Joy like a kestrel hovered in the wind,
He swooped, he soared, he left the wind behind
Carrying our sweet bodies worlds away.
You gathered all that grows at beauty's prime
Will have enough to warm a winter's time.[23]

Day-Lewis's motives in ending the affair may be judged from the use he made of it in his 1936 novel, *The Friendly Tree*.[24] The principal male character, Stephen Hallam, who shares many features in common with Day-Lewis himself, not least his left-wing politics and 'black moods', betrays his sick wife, the emotionally restrained schoolmaster's daughter, Anna (modelled on Mary), with Evelyn Crane, a mutual friend who bears a passing resemblance to Alison Morris. In the end, though, he rejects Evelyn and returns to Anna 'like Ulysses, chastened, from the shades'. 'Evelyn is nice, exciting, a new country,' he declares to Anna, but their infidelity was 'superficial ... You are my beloved, my counterpart, you are where I am at home forever'.[25]

Chapter 12

Make Your Choice

You'll be leaving soon and it's up to you, boys,
Which shall it be? You must make your choice.
There's a war on, you know. Will you take your stand
In obsolete forts or in no-man's land?
'Poem 10': *The Magnetic Mountain* (1933)

In February of 1932, Leonard Woolf's Hogarth Press published *New Signatures: Poems by Several Hands*. It was an anthology of 43 poems and Day-Lewis was included among the young contributors along with W. H. Auden, Julian Bell,[1] the American, Richard Eberhart,[2] William Empson,[3] John Lehmann, William Plomer,[4] Stephen Spender and A. S. J. Tessimond.[5] Though its sales were good if not outstanding – around 3,500 by 1935[6] – this slim volume had an impact way beyond the bookshop tills. For it was *New Signatures* which first firmly planted in the public mind the idea that there was a fresh, domestic, left-leaning poetic movement. There had been odd shoots visible above the ground before, but with its publication the reputation of the poets of the 1930s truly began to flower.

There were two key figures behind *New Signatures*. The first was among the contributors. John Lehmann was just down from Cambridge, brother of the already celebrated novelist Rosamond Lehmann[7] and a poet who worked at the Hogarth Press where he showed a gift for generating publicity. The second was Michael Roberts, also a poet, who earned his living as a schoolmaster. His contribution to the volume was a preface that stridently made the case for the birth of a new movement.

Two years older than Day-Lewis, and memorably described by Lehmann as 'a giraffe that had taken to the serious life of learning',[8] Roberts argued in his introduction that there was a new pattern emerging among young, mainly British poets of the period that stood in marked contrast to the American Modernists and T. S. Eliot. In part, their innovation was artistic. He highlighted in particular two shared characteristics – the use of 'imagery taken from contemporary life' and a form derived from 'the normal movement of English speech'.[9] The new grouping he was describing, Roberts continued, aimed at a truly 'popular poetry' and he picked out two recent and outstanding examples – W. H. Auden's *Poems*, commercially published in 1930, and C Day-Lewis's *From Feathers to Iron*.

Roberts' implicit attack on Eliot was crude and bordered on the caricature, but he was eager, perhaps over-eager, to make a distinction between what had

107

gone before and what was happening now. Day-Lewis, by contrast, had already acknowledged his debt by quoting *The Waste Land* in *From Feathers to Iron*, though he later tended to downplay this. 'I never thought that Eliot had much influence on me technically,' he wrote to the poet Elizabeth Jennings.[10] 'I hardly knew him in the 'thirties; but I was always much influenced by his ideas on the poet's self-discipline.'[11]

Roberts, however, was less diplomatic. The typical poet of the new movement, he wrote, was not 'contemptuous of the society around him', did not become 'aloof from ordinary affairs', or produce 'esoteric work which was frivolously decorative or elaborately erudite'. Neither was his 'keenest emotion … the delight which accompanies intellectual discovery intelligible only to an educated minority'.[12]

Whether Roberts first discussed the bold claims he was going to make on their behalf with his featured poets is not recorded. There is no surviving record of a prior personal acquaintance with either Auden or Day-Lewis beyond letters requesting permission to reproduce their poems – though Roberts did, of course, know their work and had reviewed *From Feathers to Iron*. What is striking, however, is the overlap between what he wrote in his 1932 preface and what Auden and Day-Lewis had outlined in their alternating paragraphs in the introduction to *Oxford Poetry 1927*. The clearest echo came when Roberts challenged art to develop 'an imaginative solution' to present political ills and described in overtly psychological terms 'a new harmonization such as that which may be brought about by a work of art … without recourse to any external system of religious belief'.[13]

New Signatures had such impact because it expressed a widespread mood of anxiety that was not restricted to a group of otherwise disparate poets. A whole cross-section of largely young men and women in Britain had invested considerable hope in Ramsay MacDonald's Labour government to bring about real change. Their disappointment at its failure to do so, their dismay at Ramsay MacDonald joining forces with a few Liberals and the Conservatives to form a National Government, their alarm at the growth of fascism in Europe, their fears of another war, and their distress at the unavoidable evidence of growing poverty and destitution caused at home had set them wondering if the current system of government might need a more radical overhaul than simply electing a socialist party to the House of Commons. Extraordinary times – as they perceived them – called for new courses of action.

Among the alternatives they examined were those offered in the writings of Lenin and Marx, and being put into practice in a Soviet Union of which few knew anything but the laudatory propaganda films in which 'the worker, mounted on his magnificent tractor, chugged steadily towards the dawn and the new world'.[14] The Communist Party of Great Britain, founded in 1920, enjoyed unprecedented popularity in Britain in the 1930s as middle class recruits joined forces under its banner with authentic grass roots working-class movements like Wal Hannington's National Unemployed Workers' Union which campaigned against means testing of benefits and organized the great hunger marches. In the

1935 General Election, this alliance managed to get a Communist elected to the Commons. A uniting factor between these two elements in the party, led by General Secretary Harry Pollitt, was their opposition to Mosley's British Union of Fascists which represented another approach to the political and economic crisis engulfing the country and the continent.

The critic F. R. Leavis[15] was among those who questioned the homogeneity of the poets included in *New Signatures*. Ten years older than Day-Lewis, Leavis published in 1932 his *New Bearings in English Poetry*. He and a devoted band of disciples championed the need for close reading and detailed textual analysis of poetry over and above any interest in the mind or personality of the poet, the social context of the writing and emotional response to it by the reader. Such a stance led him to look with great favour on Eliot and Pound, but to dismiss both the Bloomsbury writers and Auden, Day-Lewis and Spender. Their determination to appeal to a popular audience, their politics and their habit of referring to themselves in their poems was, Leavis believed, misconceived and to be condemned.

Even some of those included in *New Signatures* were soon to distance themselves from any suggestion of being part of a movement. Julian Bell and William Empson regarded themselves as distinct by virtue of studying at Cambridge not Oxford. Bell in particular, was openly critical of what he saw as the political naïveté of Auden and Day-Lewis. They sounded in their poems, he said, like 'enthusiastic boy scouts'.[16] However, of the eight poets featured, three in particular began individually and collectively to attract a great deal of attention – W. H. Auden, C Day-Lewis and Stephen Spender. Together with Louis MacNeice, who did not feature in *New Signatures* but had been in *Oxford Poetry 1927*, they were to become celebrated as the 1930s poets.

Both at the time and in subsequent decades a number of variations on this label have been used. A popular 1976 exhibition at London's National Portrait Gallery described the four, along with Christopher Isherwood, as 'The Young Writers of the Thirties'. An alternative is the 'Auden gang'. It acknowledges the strongest factor uniting the various writers – namely their friendship with Auden, and reflects his subsequent and enduring reputation as the most significant of the new poetic voices. It also springs from the habit of the other writers of defining themselves in terms of Auden. So in October 1932, despite the critical acclaim that had come with *From Feathers to Iron* and his equal billing in the preface of *New Signatures*, Day-Lewis was writing candidly to Rex Warner, now teaching in Egypt, that he had just read the newly-published Auden collection, *The Orators*: 'Wystan so clearly has the makings of a great poet & I can't be more than a good one ... With forty [he was 28 at the time] one ought to be first rate or drop it. That is to say drop publishing.'[17]

In a later letter to L. A. G. Strong, it is again Auden who provided the point of reference and this time there is a clue as to the real competitiveness that existed in Day-Lewis's mind about Auden and which was a significant obstacle to them ever being anything so co-ordinated as a movement. 'I feel too much time spent making final term's orders with Wystan, Stephen and myself, and so long before the term is over. It's true, I think, he's [Auden] certain to be at the top end: but I only say so out of a kind of self defence ... This perpetual playing off of one of us against the other must give a number of readers the impression that we are either cutting each other's throats in earnest, or staging a mimic battle for publicity's sake.'[18]

And in a 1932 letter to Geoffrey Grigson, Day-Lewis is explicit in seeing himself not as a follower of Auden but as a rival. 'I see from the *Bookmen* that you have now arranged us in the correct order – 1, Auden; 2, Day-Lewis – but I shall chase him home, you can rely on that, and I think we'll make the pace pretty hot between us.'[19]

Auden certainly came to see himself as the leader of the group. In a later poem on Voltaire, for example, he compared himself to his subject in his relationships with the writers around him.

> *Cajoling, scolding, screaming, cleverest of them all,*
> *He'd had the other children in a holy war*
> *Against the infamous grown-ups; and, like a child, been sly*
> *And humble, when there was occasion for*
> *The two-faced answer or the plain protective lie,*
> *But, patient like a peasant, waited for their fall*
>
> 'Voltaire at Ferney': *Another Time* (1940)

And by the time *New Verse* published an 'Auden Double Issue' in 1937 to mark his 30th birthday, few would disagree that he was the leader of the 'gang'. As effectively the house journal of the poets of the 1930s, *New Verse*, under the editorship of Grigson, another son of a clergyman, should in theory have presented the movement at its strongest. But while Grigson championed MacNeice and Auden – and initially Day-Lewis – he soon turned against the latter in a series of damning reviews.

The Auden–Day-Lewis–Spender penchant for drawing images from industrial technology gave rise to another label – 'the Pylon poets' or the 'Pylon boys' inspired by one of Spender's most celebrated stanzas:

> *Now over those small hills they built the concrete*
> *That trails black wire;*
> *Pylons those pillars*
> *Bare like nude, giant girls that have no secret*
>
> 'The Pylons': *Poems* (1933)

Another alternative tag, 'Homintern' (based on Comintern, the communist organization founded by Lenin and Trotsky in 1919), arose because three of the four were attracted to communism and two – plus their associates Isherwood, Lehmann and Plomer – were homosexual. The writer, critic and editor Cyril Connolly[20] claimed to have coined it – though some say it was Auden himself. Connolly certainly used it both of the 1930s poets and more generally of what he saw as an international network of influential, left-wing homosexuals who were, he said, 'psychological revolutionaries, people who adopt left-wing political formulas because they hate their fathers or were unhappy at their public schools or insulted at the Customs or lectured about sex'.[21]

There were other names in circulation. Most critics initially preferred to detach MacNeice and speak instead of the 'Auden–Spender–Day-Lewis triumvirate'. Day-Lewis himself at one stage described the four earnestly as 'the school of social consciousness'.[22]

The label that has endured above all others, though, did not arise until a decade later and owes something to hindsight and a lot to pure spite. MacSpaunday was a beast created in 1946 by running together the first parts of the four surnames by fellow poet Roy Campbell.[23] MacSpaunday was for Campbell a monster and one which he had long incubated along with a deep loathing for the four poets whose talent he doubted and whose success and public acclaim he resented.

Towards the end of the 1930s Campbell had found himself boycotted by other writers – including the Day-Lewis circle – because they detected pro-fascist sympathies in his work. In 1939 Spender savaged Campbell's pro-Franco Spanish Civil War collection, *Flowering Rifle*, labelling its author a 'talking bronco'.[24] The phrase must have hit home for when, after seeing active service in the Second World War, Campbell published his next collection of poetry in 1946, he used it as its title. It contained a vehement attack on those poets of the 1930s and their war records.

> joint MacSpaunday shuns the very strife
> He barked for loudest, when mere words were rife,
> When to proclaim his proletarian loyalties
> Paid well, was safe, raked in heavy royalties,
> And made the Mealy Mouth and the Bulging Purse
> The hallmarks of contemporary verse.

There was talk amongst those attacked about suing Campbell for libel. Auden, MacNeice and Spender were distressed that their own publisher, T. S. Eliot at Faber, should have chosen to allow Campbell to attack them in this way under his imprint. Eventually it was jointly decided to ignore the insult, but the name stuck.

Some have subsequently argued that, whatever its origins, MacSpaunday can be now turned into a positive celebration of four poets who defined a decade. Yet in a 1972 interview Day-Lewis reflected that there was 'very little poetic reason' for the invention of MacSpaunday[25] while on another occasion, he remarked 'we didn't know we were a movement until the critics told us we were'.[26] Auden too downplayed such talk. 'What poets of the same generation have in common is the least interesting thing about them. What really matters is the way in which they differ.'[27]

Without Auden the connections between the other three in terms of poetry and life were weak. In January 1934, long after talk of a movement had become current, Day-Lewis wrote to Grigson (with whom he was still at that stage on good terms): 'I'd be grateful if you could let me know how to come by some of

MacNeice's poems ... I don't want to write to him personally because you say he is apt to take a long time about sending things, and because it would not be very satisfactory for him if he sent me some of his work and then I wasn't able to say anything about him in the book'.[28] The book to which he refers is *A Hope for Poetry*, a prose work of 1934 which was taken as a manifesto for the poets of the 1930s. MacNeice evidently came perilously close to being excluded altogether, as he had been from *New Signatures*.

Day-Lewis was much closer to Spender, although quite when they first met is unclear. Spender's first year at Oxford coincided with Day-Lewis's last. However, Auden, Day-Lewis and Spender all later emphasized that the first time they were all in the same place at the same time was at the international conference of PEN, the writers' organization, in Venice in 1949. There may be, though, an element of wishful thinking about this claim[29] – a public slaughtering of Campbell's beast MacSpaunday – but what is true is that by 1933 Spender and Day-Lewis were in regular and intimate correspondence and friends enough for the younger man to spend Christmas at Box Cottage.

Communism was clearly high on the list of topics discussed over the turkey to judge from Day-Lewis's letter to Spender of December 30, 1933. 'I think the *Communist Manifesto* is good but I find *Das Kapital* about as heavy going as *Paradise Lost*. However, possibly Marx does more than Milton can to justify God's ways to men!'[30] This last sentence was a play on A. E. Housman, substituting Marx for malt in a line from *A Shropshire Lad*.

Although Auden influenced Day-Lewis and Spender significantly, but in different ways, in this period, his effect on MacNeice was initially slight. In his first, well-received collection of 1929, *Blind Fireworks*, for example, MacNeice showed few traces of having met Auden at Oxford as an undergraduate and was altogether more enthralled by Edith Sitwell.[31] After graduating, MacNeice moved to Birmingham where he taught at the university and concentrated mainly on writing novels. It was only in January 1933 that he re-met Auden through the intervention of Auden's father, who held a chair at the university.

If the MacSpaunday creature did ever draw breath, it did so only briefly in 1933. In the year that Adolf Hitler became German Chancellor, the four poets came closer than ever before or afterwards. There was the Auden–MacNeice reunion, the publication of Day-Lewis's most Audenesque collection, *The Magnetic Mountain*, and of Spender's similarly influenced *Poems*.

Yet even at this moment, the different interests of the four were all too apparent. While Day-Lewis and Spender were strongly and increasingly drawn to communism, Auden was already beginning to pull away and MacNeice remained sceptical. His 1933 poem 'To A Communist' expresses his reservations.

Your thoughts make shapes like snow; in one night only
The gawky earth grows breasts,
Snow's unity engrosses
Particular pettiness of stones and grasses.
But before you proclaim the millennium, my dear,

Consult the barometer –
This poise is perfect but maintained
For one day only

The slightly camp 'my dear' may well be addressed to Auden (though it was used much more in conversation in the 1930s than today). Of their first meeting that year, MacNeice wrote sceptically: 'Auden turned up and talked a good deal of communism.'[32]

The most important common thread – not enough to establish a movement but sufficient to justify the link made by many at the time – was a shared belief that literature, and for them principally poetry, had to confront the menace they saw in domestic and international events. In the face of the many challenges they would not be, as MacNeice put it, 'pedants who saw life from a corner' (a dig at Eliot).[33] They shared a determination to do something. There was a pressing question – summed up by the prize-day speaker at the start of Auden's *The Orators* who asks *'What do you think about England, this/Country of ours where nobody is well?'* And by way of reply – to use the title of a Day-Lewis pamphlet of the period that accurately sums up their collective mood – 'We Are Not Going To Do Nothing'.[34]

As well as the other similarities in their backgrounds and upbringings, three of the four came from strongly Christian homes that stressed the necessity of having a faith to make sense of the world. 'Inoculated against Roman Catholicism by the religion of my youth,' Day-Lewis wrote of his younger self in *The Buried Day*, 'I dimly felt the need for a faith which had the authority, the logic, the cut-and-driedness of the Roman church – a faith which would fill the void left by the leaking away of traditional religion, would make sense of our troubled times and make real demands on me.'[35]

They were roughly the same age – there were just five years between Day-Lewis the oldest and Spender the youngest – and had therefore lived through the Great War. Though all were too young to play any real part in it, they had come to adulthood just as the unhappy consequences of the peace that followed it were felt in what became known as the 'age of disgust'. All had experienced and been involved in the General Strike of 1926 and all had thereafter nurtured an active concern for the crisis that was engulfing their country and the world. They were young writers with consciences who were reacting to a tense decade that started with a slump and ended with a war. They wanted to respond and did so in their poetry.

Despite that shared goal, though, their experience of looming crisis in the world was very different. Where both Spender and Auden lived for periods in Berlin, Day-Lewis had yet to travel to continental Europe. Spender and Auden's alarm at the rise of fascism came from seeing it first hand in action in Germany as Hitler rose to power. Day-Lewis's knowledge was largely second hand.

They also struggled to identify or agree on the means by which they would act. They had no real programme beyond the anxiety which they expressed and which so chimed with similar concerns shared by many in the population. In a letter to his brother John in 1932, Auden wrote: 'it's difficult to know what we ought to do. It's wicked to try and keep the ship going; it's conceited to join the "we're doomed" gang, and cowardly to jump into the sea'.[36]

Another linking factor was this element of psychological doubleness – of holding two positions at once – the bourgeois figure who wants to overthrow the bourgeoisie by writing poetry that is largely read by the bourgeoisie. It was there from the start. In *Oxford Poetry 1927* Auden had written ('Prose 1') of 'the psychological conflict between self as subject and self as object'. It was crucial to the central dilemma of *Transitional Poem*. And in a characteristically revealing and memorable fashion Auden found an image for the whole dilemma in *The Orators* where near the end he depicts school as a form of guerrilla combat where the frontier is everywhere and nowhere.

It may look naive to modern eyes to assume as they did that poetry could be an instrument of social health. But that is what they came to believe under the influence of Auden. 'I sometimes think of Mr Auden's poetry', wrote Dylan Thomas,[37] then a younger admirer, in a tribute to mark his 30th birthday, 'as a hygiene, a knowledge and practice, based on a brilliantly prejudiced analysis of contemporary disorders, relating to the preservation and promotion of health, a sanitary science and a flusher of melancholies.'[38]

Day-Lewis, Spender and to a lesser extent MacNeice, as well as other writers including Lehmann, Roberts and Rex Warner, embraced this positive attitude of engagement against those who argued for a pure poetry detached from the world around it. (This wasn't just a Modernist position – Wilfred Owen had written 'All a poet can do today is warn'.)[39]

However sincere the commitment, though, Day-Lewis was a father and had to earn his living. Spender had a small private income and both he and Auden were without dependents. While they could travel to Germany, Day-Lewis remained in Cheltenham as schoolmaster at a private school and a property owner. He claimed in his poetry that he would willingly sacrifice all such trappings, but did he ever believe he was going to be asked to? He had already shown a knack for putting parts of his life in compartments: home in one, and work in one, poetry in a third. It was a capacity he had first discovered as a child as a way of coping with his father's unpredictable moods. Now it enabled him to achieve a kind of detachment from the realities of his life and so hold up the ideals in his poetry that he genuinely aspired to, but had no immediate expectation of seeing achieved.

So Day-Lewis was well aware of and indeed an observer of the ambiguity of his own position, as when he wrote to Spender in June 1935; 'I suspect I only preserve my revolutionary feeling by a kind of perpetual friction between my concrete set habits of mind and my abstract dislike of the present state of things: it is probably the "religious" conscience in me, out of work, diverted into another form of activity. It requires a constant conscious effort when one is contented within one's individual radius to keep in contact with the outside circles of discontent, and I doubt if the effort can ever be really fundamentally honest.'[40]

Such an approach enabled him to do two things. It allowed him to feel responsibility and guilt about the world around him, even when he was behaving selfishly in his own terms by teaching in a private school. And it meant that he could never be comfortable or at ease, much as he appreciated the comforts of his life.

Moreover, his developing 'abstract' attraction for communism was taking on a romantic air. It was an ideal he aspired to just as Christians aspire to love their neighbour as themselves but usually fail. And it could give him a distorted picture of the working classes. His later efforts to reproduce their speech patterns in works of prose, for example, now read as patronizing. Spender once accused him of mistaking the camaraderie he felt when having a drink in working men's pubs with true solidarity.

Auden was prey to the same romanticism. In a letter to his brother John, he described as 'the right English variant on Russia'[41] the idealistic community founded at Dartington in Devon in 1925 by Dorothy and Leonard Elmhirst where communal engagement involved agriculture, forestry, woodworking and craft along with a progressive school.

It was, as Day-Lewis argued with hindsight in his own defence in *The Buried Day*, 'an absurdly credulous' time when 'it was indeed possible for myself and many of my friends to believe that the capitalist system was obsolescent, that mass unemployment and fascism were evil things that must be crusaded against, that the nationalisation of the means of production would cure a lot of our troubles and that this would never be effectively done except under communism'.[42]

Whatever growing attraction he felt from 1932 onwards towards communism, Day-Lewis knew he could never join the party and keep his job. So he continued as a schoolmaster without any great enthusiasm but with diligence and a certain detachment that appealed to some of his pupils. He never strayed, one old-boy, David Blount, later recalled, into anything remotely political in the classroom but instead gave memorable readings of *Nicholas Nickleby*, gladly provided many hours of extra tuition to boys who wanted it, and maintained 'a certain hauteur of manner ... [he] conveyed the impression that he didn't care whether we liked him or not, or indeed what anyone else thought of him, and this was a novel experience'.[43]

Outside school, at Box Cottage, he was working on his next sequence – seeking Auden's opinion on drafts along the way when the two met. There were moments of despondency. In a letter to Rex Warner, he was full of self-pity. 'I'm full of the usual desperation & aimlessness, having finished a piece of work, with no idea what is going to happen next.'[44]

If he wanted to break away from the constraints of being a schoolmaster, he needed to earn more money from writing and in the autumn of 1932 he took on a commission from his old friend L. A. G. Strong. He was recruited – along with Warner – to write individual volumes in a series of boys' adventure tales Strong was assembling for the Oxford-based publishers Blackwell. The brief was to be simultaneously highbrow – the series was marketed as 'tales of action by men of letters' – but also to produce a page-turner. The blood-curdling *Dick*

Willoughby, a Tudor teenager with a taste for heroics, was set in Dorset, a first sign that the county had now made a more lasting impression on Day-Lewis than when he was at Sherborne. It became his first published prose work, appearing in the autumn of 1933.

Between writing and teaching, Day-Lewis had little time left to concentrate on his new son. When he was there, he was, Sean remembered, full of 'parental inhibitions about the physical display of love for a son'.[45] Neither Mary nor Cecil would put their arms round their child and hug him. In part this was simply a reflection of the standard approach of the time to fatherhood. Moreover, Mary was using the strict but popular regime advocated by Frederic Truby King, the New Zealand-born childcare guru of the 1920s and 1930s. She knew no better. So there were four-hourly feeds with nothing in between and plenty of fresh air. Picking the baby up and cuddling him were not encouraged.

'We were inhibited from fully displaying the love we bore,' Day-Lewis conceded subsequently, 'Mary because of her natural undemonstrativeness chiefly, I because I feared to repeat the pattern of my relationship with my own father and overload my children with love, and both of us in a recoil from sentiment fairly common among our generation.'[46]

There was a note of regret present too in a 1957 reflection on a photograph of Sean's early days.

> *That is the house you were born in. Around it*
> *A high old box-hedge inked out the view:*
> *And this the garden it buxomly bounded,*
> *Where salvia, syringa, tobacco plants grew*
> *Sheltered like you.*
>
> *From snapshot to snapshot you can see yourselves growing*
> *And changing like figures on a dawn-struck frieze.*
> *Ah, swift enough for my after-knowing*
> *That growth: but then you seemed to increase*
> *By mere coral degrees.*
>
> 'Father to Sons': *Pegasus and Other Poems* (1957)

The arrival of Sean had done little to ease his father's strained relationship with Frank Day-Lewis. There were brief, dutiful trips to Edwinstowe every other Christmas, in rotation with more agreeable trips to the King household in Sherborne. And in the long summer vacations, the Day-Lewises would occasionally opt for the stuffy world of the Nottinghamshire vicarage as a way of getting away from Cheltenham. There was little money for hotels or holidays elsewhere.

'After I had married,' Day-Lewis wrote in *The Buried Day*, 'the need to fight against my father and extricate myself from the toils of his love, gradually disappeared, making itself felt only in dreams. There was still a tension between us, so that I used often to react with a childish excess of violence when he showed signs of encroaching upon my life: but I could generally manage now the compromises, half-truths, evasions which were necessary if any sort of relationship between us was to continue, without feeling such compromise as a self-betrayal or a personal defeat.'[47]

Though Frank Day-Lewis would undoubtedly have been proud of the recognition Cecil had now achieved, the strident left-wing sentiments which underpinned his work were less welcome. Contentious issues were avoided, difficult subjects left untouched and father and son managed to rub along with more ease than they had managed before.

Back in Cheltenham, the publication of *New Signatures* and the interest it aroused seemed to escape the notice of the school authorities. The poems featured in that anthology had been taken from the collection Day-Lewis was still working on. When complete, it was published in March 1933 as *The Magnetic Mountain*. It was in his own phrase 'a violently revolutionary poem' yet it 'did not create the slightest ripple of outrage amongst the guardians of Cheltenham, the few who read it assuming, after the usual English manner, that since it was poetry it could have no bearing on real life'.[48] In the outside world, however, it prompted headlines in papers and made Day-Lewis's reputation.

Chapter 13

Terra Incognita

Are you sure you don't want to go somewhere?
'Is it mountain there or mirage across the sand?'
That's Terra Incognita, Bogey-Man's Land:
Why not give it a trial? You might go further
And fare much worse.
                    'Poem 4': *The Magnetic Mountain* (1933)

The omens were good for the planned publication by Hogarth Press of *The Magnetic Mountain* in March 1933. Leonard Woolf wrote to congratulate Day-Lewis in December of the previous year. It was, he said, 'the best long poem that I have read for many a long day. It has the extraordinary merit too for me that it is not only poetry but about interesting things, and so alive, whereas nearly all "poetry" today seems to me, even when you have to admit that it is poetry, to be about things and themes that no longer have the faintest interest or connection to me.'[1]

His enthusiasm for *The Magnetic Mountain* led him to take the unusual step of releasing a limited edition of 100 copies, numbered and signed by Day-Lewis just before publication of the standard edition. Such treatment was usually reserved only for well-known and well-established writers. Woolf's verdict was shared three months later by the critics. New York's *Partisan Review* hailed it as 'perhaps the most important revolutionary poem as yet written by an Englishman'. That revolutionary aspect, the appeal to action in the face of the crises of the day, was what drew most attention, though there was praise too for Day-Lewis's style. Even Geoffrey Grigson, soon to become Day-Lewis's staunchest detractor, managed kind words in *New Verse*. 'Day-Lewis cannot make himself entirely a bad artist.' It was to be the last mildly positive thing he ever wrote about him.

The Magnetic Mountain, like its two predecessors, was a numbered sequence of poems making up one long whole. Its concerns generally followed those of *Transitional Poem* and *From Feathers to Iron*. It is tempting therefore to shape these three collections into an early Day-Lewis triptych. They share a pointed use of modern imagery, an urgency dictated by the poet's perceptions of the outside world on the brink of disaster, a technical accomplishment marked by variety of form and structure, and an abiding sense of Day-Lewis's own ambiguities. Yet it is their differences rather than their similarities that are most revealing of his development as a writer and as an individual.

Where *Transitional Poem* sets out the questions that concern him, *The Magnetic Mountain* contains an answer, albeit utopian, naive and provisional. And where *From Feathers to Iron* is largely about the private sphere of Day-Lewis's life – both the arrival of his son and the strains in his marriage – *The Magnetic Mountain* is more public in its preoccupations. What distinguishes them most obviously, though, is where he places the emphasis. So *From Feathers to Iron* does have a wider message while *The Magnetic Mountain* turns to focus in its middle sections to the domestic world of the wife and mother. Yet the overall impression given by *The Magnetic Mountain* is of Day-Lewis's most openly political and polemical work yet.

This can be seen, for example, in the use of one of his favourite kinds of modern imagery – that of railways. In *From Feathers to Iron*, trains and tunnels were largely employed to describe impregnation, gestation and childbirth. In *The Magnetic Mountain*, that private, sexual and gynaecological parallel is superseded by giving railway imagery a political and ideological purpose.

> Let us be off! Our steam
> Is deafening the dome.
> The needle in the gauge
> Points to a long-banked rage,
> And trembles there to show
> What a pressure's below.
> Valve cannot vent the strain
> Nor iron ribs refrain
> That furnace in the heart.
> Come on, make haste and start
> Coupling-rod and wheel
> Welded of patient steel,
> Piston that will not stir
> Beyond the cylinder
> To take in its stride
> A teeming countryside.

'Poem 5'

Considered together, *From Feathers to Iron* and *The Magnetic Mountain* emphasize the conflict between Day-Lewis's life and his creative aspirations, and his consequent struggle to find a single focus. Indeed, the decision that he took on learning of Mary's pregnancy to set aside the draft of *The Magnetic Mountain*, with its strong political message, and concentrate instead on *From Feathers to Iron* indicates his own failure to reconcile the two. If he had been able to, he could simply have carried on writing and woven the anticipation of a new baby into a larger vision of the sort of utopian world that would answer the questions raised in *Transitional Poem*. Instead he produced, in effect, two answers – one relating largely to his own circumstances, and one an unabashed rallying cry to others.

The Magnetic Mountain charts a journey towards a new and better world, though conveys only a glimpse of the final and perfect destination.

Somewhere beyond the railheads
Of reason, south or north,
Lies a magnetic mountain
Riveting sky to earth.

No line is laid so far.
Ties rusting in a stack
And sleepers – dead men's bones –
Mark a defeated track.

Kestrel who yearly changes
His tenement of space
At the last hovering
May signify that place.

Iron in the soul,
Spirit steeled in fire,
Needle trembling on truth –
These shall draw me there.

The planets keep their course,
Blindly the bee comes home,
And I shall need no sextant
To prove I'm getting warm.

Near that miraculous mountain
Compass and clock must fail,
For space stands on its head there
And time chases its tail.

There's iron for the asking
Will keep all winds at bay,
Girders to take the leaden
Strain of a sagging sky.

Oh there's a mine of metal,
Enough to make me rich
And build right over chaos
A cantilever bridge.

'Poem 3'

The image of sky riveted to earth, as if heavens were drawn down to the ground, is typical of the missionary tone of the whole sequence. Day-Lewis is describing a search for a new secularized form of religion, a fresh kind of belief. Its goal is an earthly paradise beyond even the reach of technology in a land where clocks and compasses fail.

This utopia has a pastoral as well as industrial dimension.

Break from your trance: start dancing now in town,
And, fences down, the ploughing match with mate.
This is your day: so turn, my comrades, turn
Like infants' eyes like sunflowers to the light.

'Poem 36'

121

This continuing use of pastoral imagery by Day-Lewis – to a greater extent than either Auden or Spender – traces a line back to his own Georgian roots. His achievement is to marry traditional lyrical preoccupations with a strong political message. 'Day-Lewis was a more traditional writer [than his two colleagues]' Spender wrote in his 1951 autobiography, *World Within World*, 'a writer steeped in the work of his immediate predecessors, the "Georgians", much as Yeats had, when a young man, been steeped in the *fin de siècle*. Day-Lewis to some extent corrected the blurred quality of the Georgians by introducing images drawn from factories and slums and machinery into his poetry ... He had a metrical strictness and an intellectual sternness which were impressive and refreshing.'[2]

Accordingly only the use of the word 'comrade' in the stanza above gives away that this pastoral land is touched by communism, a community of equals toiling like the figures Day-Lewis had seen in Alexander Dovzhenko's *Earth*. Yet alongside this willingness to countenance the communist influence – seen by many at the time in Britain as a form of betrayal of the national interest – Day-Lewis also invokes patriotism.

> You that love England, who have an ear for her music,
> The slow movement of clouds in benediction,
> Clear arias of light thrilling over her uplands,
> Over the chords of summer sustained peacefully;
> Ceaseless the leaves' counterpoint in a west wind lively,
> Blossom and river rippling loveliest allegro,
> And the storms of wood strings brass at year's finale:
> Listen. Can you not hear the entrance of a new theme?

'Poem 32'

The guiding figure in the whole journey is the kestrel – an image Day-Lewis and Auden both employed. Auden and the kestrel share a single line at the start of Part Three.

> Look west, Wystan, lone flyer, birdman, my bully boy!
> Plague of locusts, creeping barrage, has left earth bare:
> Suckling and centenarian are up in the air,
> No wing-room for Wystan, no joke for kestrel joy.

'Poem 16'

Auden's shadow falls over the whole of *The Magnetic Mountain*. In a letter to Grigson in September of 1932 when he was working on his draft, Day-Lewis admitted 'I am stealing some of Auden's thunder for it'.[3] More intriguing is his remark to Naomi Mitchison, made during the early stages of the composition of *The Magnetic Mountain*, that 'I am engaged on a satire at present'.[4]

Satire and scorn were tools skilfully and often memorably used by Auden and in *The Magnetic Mountain* Day-Lewis tries to emulate him. There is sometimes a bold and brutal almost playground scorn in his tone, especially when referring to his own middle class ('Terence the toff') and more generally in other images of 'chorus girls surely past their prime' or damning attacks on those who have '*made yourself cheap with your itch for power/Infecting all comers, a hopeless*

122

whore'. They give a harder, more caustic edge to the sequence than any previous Day-Lewis work.

The section where his efforts at satire are most obvious is Part Two when the poet savages four defenders of the status quo. This quartet includes most of the people in Day-Lewis's everyday life. There is a pummelling for the schoolmaster – '*White hopes of England here/Are taught to rule by learning to obey*'; and for the clergyman – '*Promising the bread of heaven to the hungry of the earth,/Shunting the spirit into grassy sidings,/I have served the temporal princes*'.

Another defender is 'the mother'. Although taken as an archetype with no specific reference to Mary, here Day-Lewis blunts his sharp tongue.

> *I that was two am one,*
> *We that were one are two.*
> *Warm in my walled garden the flower grew first,*
> *Transplanted it ran wild on the estate.*
> *Why should it ever need a new sun?*
> *Not a navel-string in the cold dawn cut,*
> *Nor a weaned appetite, nor going to school*
> *That autumn did it. Simply, one day*
> *He crossed the frontier and I did not follow:*
> *Returning, spoke another language.*

'Poem 7'

For Mary this ambiguous image of a mother left behind could perhaps have been dismissed as rhetoric, but in Part Three, among the four enemies of the revolution, Day-Lewis includes 'the demanding woman'. Such an image would have given Mary reason to pause and may have reinforced her natural inclinations to make few demands on her husband.

Turning to other enemies of the revolution, Day-Lewis issues violent threats against newspaper owners:

> *Scavenger barons and your jackal vassals,*
> *Your pimping press-gang, your unclean vessels,*
> *We'll make you swallow your words at a gulp*
> *And turn you back to your element, pulp.*
> *Don't bluster, Bimbo, it won't do you any good;*
> *We can be much ruder and we're learning to shoot.*
> *Closet Napoleon, you'd better abdicate,*
> *You'd better quit the country before it's too late.*

'Poem 20'

Scientists fare little better with their 'glib equations' and finally the otherworldly poet is given his marching orders.

> *Drug nor isolation will cure this cancer:*
> *It is now or never, the hour of the knife,*
> *The break with the past, the major operation.*

'Poem 25'

123

This tone is a new departure. Often shrill and uneven, it sits uneasily with the daily reality of Day-Lewis riding on his bike from his pretty cottage with its vegetable garden to teach in a private school. He didn't feel any real violence towards any of the individuals he indicts, save in terms of the ideological and political rhetoric of the class struggle which he was adopting, but his language conspired to suggest otherwise. It was mostly down to straining for a certainty he did not feel deep down in which opponents were not seen as individuals but as an almost impersonal enemy to be defeated.

Another element – and short-coming – was technical ambition. He was trying to follow Auden's lead and Auden could skilfully carry off such scornful, violent assaults in verse with a satirical edge. In August 1932 in *Twentieth Century Magazine*, he had published his poem 'A Communist to Others' (later included in *New Country*). Addressing himself to 'oppressors' – namely the middle classes, Christians and university dons – Auden was unsparing:

> *Let fever sweat them till they tremble,*
> *Cramp rack their limbs till they resemble*
> * Cartoons by Goya:*
> *Their daughters sterile be in rut,*
> *May cancer rot their herring gut,*
> *The circular madness on them shut,*
> * Of paranoia*

Day-Lewis's efforts paled by comparison. 'You aren't depraved enough to write like this,' Spender was to tell him bluntly in a letter. 'You haven't got a developed and sophisticated enough sense of humour.'[5]

Because of the obvious debt to Auden in *The Magnetic Mountain*, some critics were inclined to describe the sequence as if it were something that Auden might have written on an off-day. Dilys Powell, for instance, at the time of publication, felt that Day-Lewis 'had completely surrendered' to his friend's spell.[6] Yet such a view is too narrow. Day-Lewis's reference in verse to Auden as his 'bully boy' suggests that such influence could be at least resented if not resisted, as has already been seen in their correspondence over *Transitional Poem*. And the accompanying description of Auden as a 'lone flyer' challenges the notion that Day-Lewis or anyone else was his number two, following through his prescriptions.

More significantly, the tendency to write off Day-Lewis as, in his own words, 'pastiche Auden'[7] overlooks much of the evidence to be found in *The Magnetic Mountain*. It was because readers saw in Day-Lewis's individual reaction to the world around him an echo of their own that they were drawn to *The Magnetic Mountain*. He was inviting them to join a brotherhood of the disaffected, promising them revolution. It is clear from the text that he knew what price they may have to pay because he was struggling with the cost himself.

> *You who would come with us,*
> *Think what you stand to lose –*
> *An assured income, the will*

In your favour and the feel
Of firmness underfoot.

'Poem 30'

Where Auden brought ironic ambiguity and subtle psychology to play in his poetry – Spender later remarked 'Auden arrived at politics by way of psychology'[8] – Day-Lewis was more the enthusiast, his missionary spirit overwhelming any attempts at irony.

In this context, Day-Lewis's September 1932 letter to Grigson, where he acknowledged that he was stealing some of Auden's thunder, continues: 'but I don't believe either of us will be the worse for it'.[9] He thought there were clear differences between the two poets' technique and approach and that both were learning from the other. The directness and simplicity of *The Magnetic Mountain*, for instance, can be set against the hectic obscurity that even Auden's ardent admirers acknowledge in *The Orators*, his roughly simultaneous publication. Sections of this parable-like work have been described by the novelist, Edward Upward, Auden's friend, as containing 'some of the obscurest lines Auden ever wrote'.[10] The in-references to his colleagues, the allusions to former and hoped-for lovers, and the boarding-school imagery Auden employed would have defeated that wider public which Day-Lewis was trying to engage.

The Magnetic Mountain was deliberately accessible. Day-Lewis was staking his own distinctive claim for a direct and public role for poetry amid a political and economic crisis. That was part of its propaganda element. Day-Lewis was deluding himself, on the evidence of the sales of *The Magnetic Mountain*, which were under 2,000 copies, that his poetry was suddenly going to become the reading matter and rallying cry of the working classes. The ambition, however, was not so unreasonable. Less than two years after his book had come out the publisher Allen Lane[11] started a revolution in his industry by producing the first ten sixpenny paperback Penguins, aimed at that same wider readership and his venture was a landmark success.

The propaganda element in *The Magnetic Mountain* was calculated. In June 1932, Day-Lewis had replied to a fan letter from the older poet, E. H. W. Meyerstein:[12] 'I value your good opinion of my book [*From Feathers to Iron*] and hope the next book will not disappoint you. There is a certain amount of (deliberate) doggerel in it; propaganda: I feel the present poisonous state of England more & more strongly & cannot refrain at times from coming off my perch – as the *Daily Mail* would put it – & loading into the poisoners to the best of my ability.'[13] Six months later he wrote of his work in progress to Rex Warner in similar terms, saying it was 'at least half propaganda' but added 'the more the better, I suppose. God knows what anyone else can do it for now, except that. It's all very well to say that one writes because one wants to make something: but it's not as simple as all that: when you have made a chair somebody can sit in it – & who is going to sit down on a piece of poetry in 1932 – a few bloody juveniles in Bloomsbury – they'd be better sitting on the floor.'[14]

And in another 1932 letter to Grigson, Day-Lewis wrote: 'I am for anything that will help to throw open the park to the public: it makes one despair to think that one is preserved for an aesthetic aristocracy ... As you know, our writing is half propaganda: we can't help it: nobody else seems to be doing anything about "this England of ours where nobody is well". And it's so silly to be spilling propaganda only into the mouths of a few incurable neurasthenics. I feel somehow that it is really quite a practical matter, the purveying of our brand of salvation – a matter of distribution and advertisement and business methods.'[15]

Among the letters of congratulation for *The Magnetic Mountain* was one from Naomi Mitchison. Day-Lewis's reply shows him in more self-assured mood, the praise being heaped on him by critics bolstering his confidence. 'It is comforting to have one's views fairly definite at last; though in another way distinctly uncomfortable – the views being of a type likely to lose me my job here, where one can't expect the authorities to read between the lines and realize how salutary and pro-British it all is really. I am quite certain that Wystan and you and myself and the rest of us have in our various ways got hold of the right end of the stick; and that does give me an amazingly peaceful feeling in my centre, though with the rest of me I am frightened to death with the sense of personal and public insecurity.'[16]

The Woolfs later used to recall that they had piled up in their office copies of *The Magnetic Mountain* – only 356 of the original print-run of 500 had sold despite its critical acclaim – and covered them with a chintz cloth so as to use the stacks as seating when suddenly, over a year after publication, a wave of demand for the collection and its two predecessors caught them quite unawares. The catalyst was T. E. Lawrence, 'Lawrence of Arabia', then one of the most celebrated, if enigmatic, men in the country.[17]

On August 15, 1934, the London *Evening Standard* reported in its diary under the headline 'England's Great Man' that Winston Churchill, then a former senior cabinet minister on the backbenches but still a vivid figure on the national landscape, had met T. E. Lawrence at a country house party. They had bemoaned the state of the country and talked about the dearth of great men in the post-war period – 'present company excepted'. Lawrence, though, the report went on, 'claimed that he had discovered one great man in these lands. His name is Cecil Day-Lewis. He was, of course, unknown to the other guests'. There followed a brief resume of Day-Lewis's life, mention of his work as a poet and a decidedly apolitical quotation – mistranscribed – from *Transitional Poem*.

This gossip item started a run on Day-Lewis volumes at Hogarth Press. It also inaugurated a friendship between Lawrence and Day-Lewis. Most importantly, though, it planted the name Day-Lewis in the public consciousness in a way that it had never been hitherto. Such an accolade in the mainstream of national life pushed Day-Lewis to the front of a literary movement that had hitherto largely been characterized in specialist publications as consisting of Auden and his followers.

There was also something in the image reports of Lawrence's remark about Day-Lewis conjured up. 'When he is not writing poetry, Mr Lewis is a schoolmaster', as the *Evening Standard* put it. Day-Lewis was made to appear, at a time when Europe's political and economic future was seen by many as in the balance, unthreatening and rather wholesome. This, of course, completely ignored the revolutionary message of his poetry – but the *Standard* hadn't quoted from it. The good-looking public schoolmaster with his wife and small child seemed an altogether more acceptable image for the leader of a new literary movement, a 'great Englishman' to prevent the country going to the dogs, than either Auden or Spender, both of whom still spent time in Berlin and delighted in discarding convention.

Those newspaper readers attracted to such reports of Day-Lewis would have been forced to reconsider if they had studied *The Magnetic Mountain* in detail. Or Day-Lewis's contribution to a new Michael Roberts anthology, *New Country*, published at the same time.[18] It included Day-Lewis's latest work – 'Letter to a Young Revolutionary', a prose offering based on a correspondence he had been having with Jonathan Smith, a 25-year-old university student thinking of joining the Communist Party and seeking the poet's guidance. The theme of impending revolution was the dominant note of *New Country*. In contrast to *New Signatures*, Roberts as editor adopted a more militant tone in his introduction. 'It is time,' he wrote, 'that those who would conserve something which is still valuable in England began to see that only a revolution can save their standards.'[19]

While issuing his call to arms, Day-Lewis also revealed in *New Country* his ambivalence about taking the step Smith was contemplating. 'If you must join yourself to this body [the Communist Party],' he wrote, 'then let it be without reservations, a submission of your entire self; you'll not be there to make revised versions of the faith or minister to your private salvation.'[20] So far Day-Lewis was unable to set self aside sufficiently to make such a commitment, though its appeal to him was plain.

His life and his poetry were at odds. One factor was fear for his job at Cheltenham and he now needed his wage more than ever. On February 17, 1934 (not 1932 as he carelessly wrote in *The Buried Day*), his second son Nicholas Charles was born at Box Cottage – 'all rather bloody', he reported to Spender.[21] Like many parents with their second child, the Day-Lewises were more relaxed in their attitude to the new arrival than they had been with his older brother. Truby King's regime was again followed but without the rigour that marked Sean's early days. They had a nurse to help Mary with Nicholas and a local girl, Rosemary Whitlock, as nanny to Sean.

Life in Gloucestershire had fallen into a superficially agreeable pattern. Day-Lewis's literary interests and widening circle of contacts saw him, in the summer of 1934, establish a literary society with local bookseller, John Kay. Day-Lewis was chairman and managed to recruit Auden and Naomi Mitchison as the first speakers that autumn. He had also discovered sailing. As a child one of his favourite outings with Knos had been to sail his boat on the Round Pond of Kensington Gardens in London. Now, thanks to the encouragement of John Moore,[22] a Tewkesbury-born writer and journalist who in the 1940s was acclaimed for his *Brensham* trilogy, celebrating rural life, Day-Lewis took up dinghy sailing on the River Severn. Moore was even to tempt him into a light aircraft. It was Day-Lewis's first time in the air.

Among friends, he lost much of the reserve he maintained in the staff room and with his pupils, though the principles he espoused in his poetry were always present. Eileen Hedges later remembered being at a large dinner with him during this period at a smart restaurant 'when in came a very old, very dirty, very drunk woman who sat herself down at a table and began shouting and swearing. Most of the party started to laugh, all except Cecil, who really lost his temper with us and made us feel ashamed of ourselves.'[23]

There may have been other witnesses noting down the incident. In May 1933 Day-Lewis – along with Auden and Spender – had come to the attention of MI5 when they put their names to an anti-war manifesto. Sir Vernon Kell, the head of MI5, wrote to Major Stanley Clarke, the Chief Constable of Gloucestershire, to request 'particulars' on Day-Lewis. As a result, for several weeks, mail to Box Cottage was intercepted. Aside from a £5 donation to the Communist Party's election fund which Day-Lewis made, this turned up little evidence of any subversive efforts at revolution beyond his already public activities of writing and speaking.[24]

Major Clarke detailed one of his detective sergeants to follow Day-Lewis round Cheltenham in November 1933 and compile a report for Sir Vernon. The subject, the report notes, was a teacher at 'Cheltenham Gentleman's College' and was 'usually dressed in a grey jacket, grey flannel trousers very wide, and dark overcoat. Seldom wears a hat and not altogether smart appearance in dress. He was described to me as a "hale fellow well met" type and is a good singer.' With very little, beyond the cut of his trousers, to arouse suspicion, Sir Vernon seems to have decided not to alert the school authorities to the 'extremist sympathizer' in their ranks, but the Day-Lewis file was kept open.[25]

Despite his predictions to Rex Warner in October 1932 that *The Magnetic Mountain* would be 'sufficiently lively to get [me] chucked out of here',[26] Day-Lewis's latest publication seemed to go unnoticed – or certainly unremarked upon at his workplace. There was much more fuss generated by his first, tame radio broadcast soon after Nicholas's birth. The subject, for BBC Midland region, was 'Spring in the Cotswolds'. Day-Lewis provided a suitably pastoral celebration, avoiding polemics and concentrating instead on the theme of new birth. An angry parent, however, telephoned the school to accuse his son's master of insulting the King. There was a full investigation at the head's behest and some anxious times for Day-Lewis before it was discovered that the real offence had been caused by reports from son to parent of his teacher's disparaging remarks about Henry VIII in a history lesson which somehow 'in the addled wits of some colonel or Mem-Sahib'[27] had got conflated with his radio talk and turned into a slight on George V.

T. E. Lawrence's description that summer of Day-Lewis as a great Englishman also registered at Cheltenham. Rather than being a cause of pride for the school, it was yet another black mark. 'Lawrence apparently told Winston Churchill that I was the one great man in England, which was rather hard on poor WC,' Day-

Lewis wrote to Spender, '& in consequence my name is as much mud to the common room as it is to *New Verse.*'[28]

At the start of 1935 Day-Lewis published his first detective novel, *A Question of Proof*. He was called in to see the headmaster, Canadian Dick Roseveare, who had succeeded Hardy three years earlier. There had been concern raised, Roseveare told Day-Lewis, by the chairman of the governors, Lord Lee, that the book, set in a preparatory school, saw the hero, a young schoolmaster, having an affair with the head's wife. Lord Lee was worried, Roseveare continued, that Day-Lewis wanted to have or was having an affair with Mrs Roseveare. 'Fortunately,' Day-Lewis remarked in *The Buried Day*, the Roseveares 'were friends of ours and had a keen sense of humour'.[29]

The new head, a distinct improvement from Day-Lewis's point of view on his predecessor, laughed the whole episode off, but Arthur Lee, diplomat, politician and owner of Chequers, the Buckinghamshire estate he gave to the nation for the use of the Prime Minister, was not convinced that this particular member of staff was an asset to the school.

The confusion over *A Question of Proof* might have been avoided if Day-Lewis had kept to his plan to write detective fiction under a pseudonym, Nicholas Blake – a combination of his second son's Christian name and his mother's middle name. Collins, the publishers who brought it out in their Crime Club imprint, home to such big names as Agatha Christie, stuck to their side of the bargain, informing readers simply that the author was a 'well-known writer' using a pen-name. However, in correspondence with friends like L. A. G. Strong, Day-Lewis was less discreet and he also told his close colleagues at Cheltenham.

In going for a pen-name, Day-Lewis's main concern was that writing detective books might harm his growing reputation as a serious-minded poet. And vice versa. As he told a newspaper reporter later: 'I have a feeling that people who read detective novels don't like the detective novelist to be anything like a serious poet.'[30]

In September 1934 he had confided in Spender: 'This has been a boring holidays. I've not been anywhere or seen anyone. I've been trying to write commercial prose as I may get chucked out of my job any time now for my political opinions ... I am horrified but secretly fascinated at the ease with which I can write good, window-box, bloody awful entertainment stuff'.[31]

So why do it at all? The idea of writing detective fiction had been in Day-Lewis's mind since completing *Dick Willoughby* for children. He was also a keen reader of the genre. In the 1940s he justified his detective novels to a hostile interviewer by pointing out that they were bought by a popular audience, whereas poetry was elitist, and he was a writer interested in reaching the widest possible readership. Nicholas Blake might, though, never have appeared in print if the roof on Box Cottage had not needed £100 of repairs. The Day-Lewises didn't have the money to pay. A two-guinea commission to pen a short story for BBC Radio, Day-Lewis reported to Spender, was not enough. Detective novels, he later said, allowed him 'to put butter on the bread provided by poetry'.[32]

As with many novelists, Day-Lewis lifted situations and characters out of his own life and used them in his book. The backdrop to the murder is Sudeley Hall, a prep. school that combines features of Summer Fields, Larchfield and Cheltenham. The hero, Michael Evans is a games master with more than a passing resemblance to Lionel Hedges. And the detective, Nigel Strangeways, is heavily based on W. H. Auden – an accolade that even four decades later delighted his old friend.[33] Strangeways, like Auden, sleeps under a great weight of blankets and carpets, walks 'with ostrich-strides', is blond, shortsighted, didactic and fussy. However, Day-Lewis was sufficiently subtle to realize the need to develop his sources beyond biography by using his imagination. So Strangeways, like Auden, may boast an inglorious examination record at Oxford but was sent down after Mods for answering the questions in limericks.

The outing of his alter ego Blake did, as Day-Lewis had feared, raise doubt about his commitment to poetry. Geoffrey Grigson, already sceptical, was soon accusing him in *New Verse* of 'hiding his threepenny self in Nicholas Blake, a thriller writer on the literary make'. In straight commercial terms, though, *A Question of Proof* was a great success, selling almost 200,000 copies in various editions in Britain. It more than covered the repairs to the roof and relieved some of the economic pressure on Day-Lewis by indicating one economically viable way out of schoolmastering.

Once the true identity of Nicholas Blake was revealed, the book also drew the attention of publishers who had not hitherto suspected Day-Lewis of having a talent for prose as well as poetry. Rupert Hart-Davis of Jonathan Cape, publishers of T. E. Lawrence's *Seven Pillars of Wisdom*, wrote in March 1935 to offer him a three-book contract for works of highbrow fiction. That was a step too far for Day-Lewis. 'Actually, my seriousness at present runs into verse', he replied.[34]

Chapter 14

On a Tilting Deck

I sang as one
Who on a tilting deck sings
To keep men's courage up, though the wave hangs
That shall cut off their sun
　　　'The Conflict': *A Time To Dance* (1935)

All new movements, especially those with an overt political purpose, are fond of issuing manifestos and several poets of the 1930s produced prose works showing their individual vision of poetry's role in meeting the world crisis. There was, inevitably, much self-justification in this writing. There was also an element of giving a public airing to the private discussions they had been having amongst themselves for several years, and therefore a good deal of overlap in what was proposed, contributing to the impression, not wholly borne out by the facts, of being truly a coherent group.

In February 1934 C Day-Lewis published *A Hope for Poetry*, the most enduring of the various manifestos issued by the Auden group. (Spender had published an essay in 1933 entitled 'Revolution and Literature' in *New Country*, and MacNeice in 1938 was to issue *Modern Poetry: A Personal Essay*.) Day-Lewis's short book ran to six editions within the decade, three more during the Second World War, and was reprinted in the United States in the mid-1970s. It has been hailed, as recently as 2005 in the poetry journal, *PN Review*, by Bernard O'Donoghue, Irish poet and Oxford don, as 'one of the most influential and admired works in its own time' and as 'taking over' from *New Bearings in English Poetry*, published two years earlier by F. R. Leavis.[1]

The immediate origins of *A Hope for Poetry* lay in a talk Day-Lewis had given to the Cheltenham College Masters' Essay Society in 1933. Under Dick Roseveare's more enlightened regime, Day-Lewis had felt able to blur the strict demarcation he had maintained when H. H. Hardy was in post between his day job and his poetry. He then set about working up that talk into a book for Basil Blackwell that he hoped would, as he wrote to Spender, 'discover a basis for writing from a Marxist standpoint' as well as justifying his optimism that 'impure poetry' which descends to the everyday and the public could be an instrument of social change.[2]

He embarked on the challenge with a certain trepidation despite the fact that the arguments he was developing were largely ones he had already outlined in the joint introduction he had penned with Auden to *Oxford Poetry 1927* and afterwards in conversations with Auden, Spender, Warner and other fellow travellers. Where he felt most tentative was in writing, in the early chapters of *A Hope for Poetry*, about great poets of the past such as Gerard Manley Hopkins[3] and the inspiration they had offered. His knowledge of such writers was of relatively recent vintage and, as he admitted in a pre-publication letter to Lady Ottoline Morrell, the book 'has given me a shocking inferiority feeling, when I compare it with criticism by Eliot or Edmund Wilson,[4] but there may be some value in it that I can't detect'.[5]

In his introduction, Day-Lewis begins by trumpeting the link between himself, Spender and Auden. The three were, he writes, 'true poets having more in common than mere contemporaneousness'. He was choosing his words carefully. In an undated communication of 1933, he describes *A Hope for Poetry* to Spender as 'a good opportunity to boost the old firm & at the same time explain to our gaping public that we are not triplets'.[6]

The gossipy tone of such letters stands in marked contrast to the rather pompous tone of the introduction. As befits a manifesto, *A Hope for Poetry* is not, he stresses, 'for the expert or the converted'. Yet neither is it 'another of those cheap excursions for the idle curious'. The missionary is asking for commitment to the search.

Day-Lewis mounts a vigorous defence of the use of modern imagery in his poetry – and that of Auden and Spender. 'Ideas are not material for the poetic mind until they have become commonplaces for the practical mind.' For commonplace, read widely understood and so Day-Lewis rejects the notion of the poet separating himself from the wider world. This leads him on to what is his principal argument in *A Hope for Poetry*, namely to reject the view that poetry is an end in itself or that it is impotent to take on a campaigning role because it is elitist. Such an approach is not new, he admits, and has been adopted by some poets and opposed by others down the centuries. After giving an overview of such efforts, Day-Lewis builds an argument that social engagement comes in poetry via 'a perpetual interplay of private and public meaning: the inner circle of communication – the poet's conversation with his own arbitrarily isolated social group – is perpetually widening into and becoming identified with the outer circles of his environment; and conversely, the specifically modern data of his environment – the political situation, the psychological states, the scientific creations of twentieth century man – are again and again used to reflect the inner activities of the poet.' So the personal becomes public and the public personal, when experienced deeply enough and felt with sufficient passion. The two, for Day-Lewis, cannot be separated and this interplay results in 'impure' poetry – or 'propaganda' – conditioned by the poet's life as well as his interaction with the world around him.

Reactions to the publication of *A Hope for Poetry* were mixed. Fellow poet, William Plomer, also featured in *New Signatures* as among the new wave and therefore not wholly disinterested, praised Day-Lewis for saying 'what a number of people have only been able to feel'.[7] The two had been introduced in 1933 by Spender, and Plomer subsequently came to stay at Box Cottage.

T. E. Lawrence was more equivocal. He wrote to Day-Lewis from the Ozone Hotel in Bridlington to compliment him on what he had read but complained that it was 'only half an effort'. He bemoaned the concentration on 'those few thought-ridden poets' like Donne and pronounced himself 'glad' when Day-Lewis instead 'concentrated on Auden, Spender and yourself'.[8] Lawrence was trying to decouple the new generation from any link with their past – thereby rejecting a central claim of A Hope for Poetry.

Lawrence may have been an invaluable public promoter of Day-Lewis but his predictions for the future of poetry – while revealing of perceptions at the time – were of variable quality. 'Auden', he pronounced, 'makes me fear that he will not write much more. Spender might, on the other hand, write too much. You have given numbers of us the greatest pleasure – though for me The Magnetic Mountain was a qualified pleasure.' He ended with a warning note. 'Poets hope too much, and their politics, like their sciences, usually stink after 20 years.'[9] That said, he was looking forward to reading Day-Lewis's next collection. It was not to be. Shortly after writing the letter he was killed in a motorcycle accident in Dorset.

One critic unimpressed by A Hope for Poetry was Geoffrey Grigson. Relations between him and Day-Lewis had collapsed since the publication of The Magnetic Mountain. In New Verse Grigson rejected Day-Lewis's attempt in A Hope for Poetry to draw a wider audience to the new poets. 'Instead of writing for his equals or his betters, has written to persuade others to read himself, Mr Spender and Mr Auden . . . [in a] prose style as cheaply poetical as Mr Humbert Wolfe . . . or any other Sunday journal buffoon'.

Grigson had embarked on a vendetta. Day-Lewis's principal crime appeared to have been his refusal, in the summer of 1934, to answer a questionnaire Grigson sent from New Verse to poets about their political affiliations. Auden, Spender and Day-Lewis did not reply. For Day-Lewis there was a reluctance to nail his colours to the mast as a communist for fear of how it would play with his employers at the school. The questionnaire demanded a short and blunt answer. He preferred to confine himself to the longer and more nuanced presentation of A Hope for Poetry. He wrote back: 'One or two of the questions I felt quite incapable of answering, and some of the others seemed to me unanswerable in any brief space. Actually several are dealt with indirectly in my book.'[10]

That breezy, slightly dismissive tone, characteristic of much of his private correspondence with people he considered friends at this time, counted against him on this occasion. Grigson was a self-important and vindictive man who had decided that Day-Lewis was a light-weight Auden camp follower. Day-Lewis, not realizing his crime, then compounded it in October 1934 when he agreed to appear in a new journal, Left Review, an organ of the British section of the communist-run Writers International (which he joined in June 1935) and, in Grigson's eyes, a rival to New Verse. Spender too was involved in this and both poets managed to provoke particular scorn in Grigson.

Beyond this, it may simply have been that Grigson judged Day-Lewis to be a not particularly good poet. Yet his bullying criticism went beyond the professional and hinted at a more personal agenda. In his review of *A Hope for Poetry*, for instance, Grigson concluded: 'There is a nasty resemblance between *A Hope for Poetry* and a romance for boys written not long ago by the same writer.'

Day-Lewis's high profile, especially following the T. E. Lawrence remark, may have irked Grigson. He felt such praise undeserved. Grigson also wrote poetry that attracted very little attention compared to Day-Lewis's. Though they shared a passion for verse, Grigson's was often better expressed in his criticism than in his own poems. 'Grigson's does seem to me the worst kind of success-worship and success-envy-combined,' Day-Lewis wrote to Spender. 'He takes up a young writer, gets some reflected glory, gets a laugh or two when he drops the writer with a bump in the mud, but is remarkably cautious about attacking anyone like Wystan who is really secure.'[11]

The poet and critic, Al Alvarez,[12] described Grigson as 'mean-minded, malicious and not a very good poet'. He added: 'As Robert Frost once remarked, the trouble with poetry, is that there is no money in it. It is all about reputation. And that can make people involved in it vicious and back-biting.'[13]

Growing success as a writer was broadening Day-Lewis's horizons and ambitions. *The Magnetic Mountain* had been published in America to some acclaim. 'I'm entering the American donkey race,' Day-Lewis wrote to Spender in November of 1934.[14] There were trips to London for lunch with grandees like Ottoline Morrell and E. M. Forster.[15] There were also meetings with his agent. Curtis Brown tried to recruit him around the time of *The Magnetic Mountain's* publication, but at the start of 1934 – at the suggestion of L. A. G. Strong – Day-Lewis opted instead for A. D. 'Peter' Peters whose clients included some of the great names of English literature – J. B. Priestley,[16] Rebecca West,[17] C. S. Forester[18] – plus emerging stars such as Evelyn Waugh and V. S. Pritchett,[19] and a sprinkling of Day-Lewis's friends such as Strong and, on the agency's staff, W. N. 'Roughie' Roughead.

In January 1933, while he was in Oxford visiting Charles Fenby, news had come through in the *Oxford Mail* offices that his great Cheltenham friend, Lionel Hedges, had died suddenly. 'I felt as if all the blood was running out of me,' Day-Lewis recalled.[20] His tribute to Hedges was the title poem of *A Time To Dance*, his new collection of poetry, published by Hogarth Press in March 1935. Leonard Woolf also brought out at the same time in a single volume Day-Lewis's three previous collections under the title *Collected Poems 1929–33*.

A Time To Dance saw Day-Lewis move away from numbered poems making up a single book-long sequence to short and medium length poems grouped around and highlighting one longer work, the poem which was also the whole collection's title. Among these short poems are pieces which illustrate well that private–public interchange discussed in *A Hope for Poetry*. 'Learning to Talk' is, at one level, an affectionate father's account of one-year-old Nicholas Day-Lewis grappling with language.

Dawn's dew is on his tongue –
No word for what's behind the sky,

Naming all that meets the eye,
Pleased with sunlight over a lawn.

But as the poem continues Nicholas's linguistic development becomes that of the proletariat.

Yes, we shall learn to speak for all
Whose hearts here are not at home,
All who march to a better time
And breed the world for which they burn.

The leap from domestic life with the infant Nicholas to the sufferings of the children of destitute parents is swift in 'A Carol' where Day-Lewis more successfully than previously manages to satirize a familiar scene to make his political and anti-religious point.

Oh hush thee, my baby,
Thy cradle's in pawn:
No blankets to cover thee
Cold and forlorn.
The stars in the bright sky
Look down and are dumb
At the heir of the ages
Asleep in a slum.

Yet alongside such 'impure' poetry are moments of greater purity and technical mastery without overt political connotations – like 'The Ecstatic', recalling most obviously Shelley's 'To A Skylark' and 'The Windhover' by Gerard Manley Hopkins.

Lark, skylark, spilling your rubbed and round
Pebbles of sound in air's still lake,
Whose widening circles fill the noon; yet none
Is known so small beside the sun:

Be strong your fervent soaring, your skyward air!
Tremble there, a nerve of song!
Float up there where voice and wing are one,
A singing star, a note of light!

Buoyed, embayed in heaven's noon-wide reaches –
For soon light's tide will turn – Oh stay!
Cease not till day streams to the west, then down
That estuary drop down to peace.

Other by now familiar personal themes are also aired alongside revolutionary tracts like the longer 'Johnny Head-In-Air' where the masses move across the land 'to a better time'. 'Poem for An Anniversary' reveals once more Day-Lewis's uneasy resignation to the routine of his marriage to Mary.

Remember, not regret
Those cloudy dreams that trod on air

How distantly reflecting fire below:
The mating in air, the mute
Shuddering electric storms, the foul or fair
Love was used to know

And there is eloquent expression of his own internal conflict between his beliefs and the realities of his life in 'In Me Two Worlds'.

In me two worlds at war
Trample the patient flesh,
This lighted ring of sense where clinch
Heir and ancestor.

This moving point of dust
Where past and future meet
Traces their battle-line and shows
Each thrust and counterthrust.

All build to the final long poem. Subtitled 'A Symphonic Poem in Memory of LP Hedges', 'A Time To Dance' attempts to mirror the shape of a symphony, with poems differing in metre and mood, all owing their origin to a single source, building like movements to a climax. '*Let us sing then for my friend not a dirge, not a funeral anthem,/But words to match his mirth, a theme with a happy end.*'

Marrying elegy with epic, Hedges's own heroism is in the first movement set alongside that of two lieutenants, Parer and M'Intosh, T. E. Lawrence-like figures who in 1920 had captured the public's imagination by flying in an aged and primitive aircraft all the way to Australia. Their journey in all its heroic twists and turns is recounted in a sustained narrative, carefully crafted to rise to a crescendo. It reads like a verse novel and shows Day-Lewis for the first time truly mastering what was to be one of his hallmarks – the narrative poem.

Baghdad renewed a propeller damaged in desert. Arid
Baluchistan spared them that brought down and spoilt with thirst
Armies of Alexander. To Karachi they were carried
On cloud-back: fragile as tinder their plane, but the winds were tender
Now to their needs, and nursed
Them along till teeming India made room for them to alight.
Wilting her wings, the sweltering suns had moulted her bright
Plumage, rotten with rain
The fabric: but they packed her with iron washers and tacked her
Together, good for an hour, and took the air again.

The two airmen are superficially improbable role models for a left-leaning poet anticipating a communist revolution. Their courage, grit and endurance were precisely the 'English' qualities that were celebrated and inculcated in their pupils by the public schools that Day-Lewis in theory rejected. It was principally the spirit of those 'who obeyed no average law' and their 'courage steadfast and luminous' that inspire Day-Lewis. Here are popular heroes for the masses to emulate in navigating the obstacles on a collective journey towards renewing society. The following year the Marxist writer and poet Christopher Caudwell[21] was also to pick on Parer and M'intosh in his book *Great Flights*.

There follows an elegy to Hedges that conveys the shock that the death of a young contemporary had on Day-Lewis. The traditional formulas of the Christianity of his upbringing are rejected explicitly.

> *The friend I had lost sprang*
> *To life again and showed me a mystery:*
> *For I knew, at last wholly accepting death,*
> *Though earth had taken his body and air his breath,*
> *He was not in heaven or earth: he was in me.*

Day-Lewis finds a characteristically pastoral resolution for the mystery.

> *Today the land that knew him shall do him honour,*
> *Sun be a spendthrift, fields come out with gold,*
> *Severn and Windrush be Madrigal and Flowing,*
> *Woodlarks flash up like rockets and unfold*
> *In showers of song, cloud-shadows pace the flying*
> *Wind, the champion runner.*
> *Joy has a flying start, our hopes like flames*
> *Lengthen their stride over a kindled earth,*
> *And noon cheers all, upstanding in the south.*
> *Sirs, be merry: these are his funeral games.*

Though these stanzas make for a natural end to the poem, Day-Lewis feels he must move beyond this note of individual survival and renewal and so continues with a polemical third movement (most of which he later omitted from a volume of *Collected Poems* in 1954). Here the voices of the masses tell the poet of their woes and aspirations as 'our land grows cold as clay'. These conclude with Marxist slogans but not before a celebrated and successful pastiche on Christopher Marlowe's[22] 'The Passionate Shepherd To His Love' which Day-Lewis translates to an urban slum setting and adapts to the subject of living on the dole.

> *Come live with me and be my love,*
> *And we will all the pleasures prove*
> *Of peace and plenty, bed and board,*
> *That chance employment may afford*
>
> *I'll handle dainties on the docks*
> *And thou shalt read of summer frocks:*
> *At evening by the sour canals*
> *We'll hope to hear some madrigals*

'A Time To Dance' ends, however, on a much heavier note with unashamed pro-Soviet propaganda borrowed from images on Russian posters and in films that Day-Lewis had seen.

> *Yes, why do we all, seeing a Red, feel small? That small*
> *Catspaw ruffles our calm – how comes it? That touch of storm*

> Brewing, shivers the torches even in this vault? And the shame
> Unsettles a high esteem? Here it is. There fall
> From him shadows of what he is building: bold and tall –
> For his sun has barely mastered the misted horizon – they seem.
> Indeed he casts a shadow, as among the dead will some
> Living one. It is the future walking to meet us all.

Despite this naked evangelizing, *A Time To Dance* was well received. Day-Lewis's admiration (from a distance) for the Soviet Union struck a chord with many readers who, like him, were at this stage prepared to overlook the first reports reaching the West about forced-labour camps and the failure of collectivization of the countryside in the 1933 Russian famine. This was the dawn of the brief pre-war era of enthusiasm for a Popular Front, uniting all left-wing parties in alliance with Stalin against the rise of fascism on the continent, which was to culminate in 1938 with the Oxford by-election at which a Popular Front candidate came close to defeating the Conservative Quentin Hogg.

For the first time in Day-Lewis's career, there were major reviews of his new book by the leading critics in the broadsheets. Desmond MacCarthy in the *Sunday Times* hailed him as 'a poet of exceptional impetus and directness'. He registered in his verse 'something of Gerard Hopkins, T. S. Eliot and [Wilfred] Owen, but spiritually his work is an escape from the extreme subjectivity of their other followers, away too from *"The Waste Land"*'. Basil de Selincourt in the *Observer* was also full of praise, especially for 'The Ecstatic' where, he wrote, 'Mr Lewis hovers with the kestrel, he even soars with the lark, and, wind-borne in those ecstatic heights, sees a new world coming – this is our chief need.' But he suggested that 'the grimness is overdone'.

Another prominent literary critic, Lord David Cecil (married to MacCarthy's daughter) had been a tutor at Wadham when Day-Lewis was an undergraduate. He wrote to congratulate him. The new collection, he said, 'seems a large advance of anything you have done as yet, and places you at a bound far ahead of all other poets of your particular generation'. Shortly afterwards David Cecil came to speak to the Cheltenham Literary Society.

And Spender too detected a new maturity in his friend's verse. 'In all your early work I find that there is a slight stiffness, something not quite free and unashamed of itself, too much emphasis on the stiff upper lip and the deliberate love, which puts me off a good deal and even annoys me occasionally,' he wrote, 'but *A Time To Dance* contains the most beautiful poetry you have written. You have begun to write poetry which is quite uninhibited.'[23]

Sales reflected the critics' enthusiasm. The initial 750 printed by Hogarth Press soon sold out, and a further three editions followed. The *Collected Poems* too went into several impressions. Such details meant little to Day-Lewis's most determined detractor. In answer to Spender's letter of praise Day-Lewis conveyed the news that 'Griggie' (they had developed a nickname for their nemesis as a way of laughing off the damage this malicious but influential critic was inflicting on them) had had 'a field day in the *Morning Post*. Among other insults he called me one of Wystan's "private moons".'[24]

Chapter 15

Dreams Dared Imagine

Delight shall Noah have, as a man returning from exile
Beholds a land greener, more great with growth and ease
Than dreams dared imagine
'Prologue': *Noah and The Waters* (1936)

Emboldened by his literary success, Day-Lewis agreed in the spring of 1935 to give a talk to the local branch of Friends of the Soviet Union (FSU) on collective farming. The FSU, originally set up in the 1920s as a fund-raising body to channel money to help tackle the effects of a 1921 famine in Russia, was closely linked with the Communist Party of Great Britain and worked to spread favourable propaganda about the Soviet Union.

Soviet agriculture was not a subject Day-Lewis knew anything about at first hand. Instead he gave an eloquent résumé of the films he had seen and books he had read, all of them bearing the official Soviet stamp. No doubt his audience were familiar with the same works. The Cheltenham governors, however, were not, and when news of Day-Lewis's appearance reached them they sent their chairman Lord Lee to convey their displeasure personally to the moonlighting teacher.

'I had been extremely nervous at the start: but the manner of this bantam tycoon quickly got my back up,' Day-Lewis recalled of their interview, 'so I ceased to be afraid of him. At the end of his remarks, which I heard out in silence, he again referred to my addressing the FSU and continued, "d'you realize what would have happened to you if you'd done that sort of thing in the Regiment?" I shook my head, dumbfounded by this extraordinary question ... "The Colonel" he went on, "would have handed you over to the subalterns' mess; and when they'd finished with you, you'd have been asked to join some other regiment".'[1]

It was a glimpse of precisely the England that Day-Lewis wanted swept away by revolution. He was to use this encounter in his 1937 novel, *Starting Point*, where John Henderson, a socialist and a scientist, is forced to bury his beliefs during a confrontation with his firm's head, Lord Lewin. Like Day-Lewis, Henderson had a wife and children to support so could afford no grand gesture of resignation.

Starting Point also gives a clue to Day-Lewis's attitude to the daily routine of schoolmastering at Cheltenham in 1935. Another of the central characters, Anthony Neale, a left-wing schoolmaster, is struggling to choose between 'the good he could do in this school – the fight against the distortion of historical and social fact, against false values and incipient snobbery – and the good he could do if he left and worked actively with the Communist Party'.[2]

Neale had no dependents so decides to leave. Day-Lewis had Mary and two sons to support, but finally was to follow the same course. With the money from his detective novel, and the promise of more, plus renewed negotiations undertaken on his behalf by A. D. Peters with Rupert Hart-Davis regarding a contract to write highbrow fiction, he decided he could afford to resign. He told the head soon after his clash with Lord Lee. One tension in Day-Lewis's life was heading for resolution.

'My position at the school has been getting more and more intolerable,' he wrote to Spender, 'so I've decided to be a literary hack – at least it gives one freedom from the institution.'[3] His leaving date was set for Christmas 1935.

The autumn term of 1935 saw Day-Lewis increasingly free to follow his heart outside school hours. It was a foretaste of what was to come. However, he did not rush to join the Communist Party. Partly it was because, modestly, he saw membership as a dramatic but futile gesture. 'I'm afraid I shall never be much use to them', he wrote to Spender.[4] This private line, of course, was not what he had been promoting in his public pronouncements about the place of poets in the front line of revolution.

Day-Lewis's contradictions, however, meant that his reservations went deeper than concerns about his usefulness to the Communist Party. Despite the overt pro-Soviet rhetoric of *A Time To Dance* and the political theories he had expressed to such applause in *A Hope for Poetry*, he worried that to be part of a political party was a compromise too far even for a writer dedicated to revolution. In a letter of October 27, 1935, to Naomi Mitchison, he explained: 'I don't call myself a communist at all, nor ever should unless I was a working member of the party.' There was a clear distinction for him between writing polemical poetry and being a communist. 'It's just that I believe that dialectical materialism is much nearer the truth than any other philosophy I have come up against: and that communism appeals to my prophetic (or self-hallucinatory) faculty as being the inevitable next mode of life ... Going all out to the left, at the very sober pace I have gone, does not give me a particularly nice feeling: I was quite happy before in my innocence, and am now full of self-reproachings for my own inactivity.'[5]

In a letter to Spender he debated the essential difference between 'the artistic conscience' and 'the Party Conscience'. 'I do think that a Party Conscience – loyalty to a Party – is not necessarily incompatible with the artistic conscience; but the only way to find out whether, in one's own case, the two can be reconciled is through a certain amount of practical Party work, probably not among writers. Here ... then is the danger of being split into a half-time communist and a half-time bourgeois–nostalgic writer. It has to be mixed though, I believe. Because the essence of communism for us is that one goes over to the working class.'[6]

Day-Lewis was clearly in two minds about joining the Party. One part of him held back, the other told him to go forward. He therefore played little role in the November 1935 General Election where in Cheltenham a left-wing Labour candidate, Elizabeth Pakenham, stood uneasily on a platform that stuck to the official party line against a Popular Front. She managed to cut the majority of the Conservative incumbent, Sir Walter Preston.

Auden visited Cheltenham several times in the summer and autumn of 1935. He brought with him new collaborators to Box Cottage. There was Rupert Doone,[7] a trained ballet dancer who had worked under Diaghilev. Doone had created the Group Theatre which had in 1934 performed Auden's *The Dance of Death* (a piece of theatre and dance about the moribund middle classes) and was the following January to stage the Auden/Isherwood collaboration, *The Dog Beneath The Skin*. The first was criticized by the *Times'* reviewer as 'predetermined', predictable and having 'the desolating air of schoolboy brilliance'. The second, on the subject of all three, was dismissed by the *Observer* as reminiscent of Noel Coward.[8]

His meeting with Doone unearthed in Day-Lewis either admiration, that only just buried sense of competition with Auden, or simply the desire to emulate – or possibly a little bit of both – and set him thinking about writing his own verse-play.

Auden also brought to Box Cottage Erika Mann, the eldest daughter of Thomas Mann[9] and a refugee from Nazis. The two of them were to marry shortly afterwards, an arrangement of convenience so that Erika could get a British passport. Staying with the Day-Lewises at the same time was Basil Wright, a fellow old Shirburnian, now working with the pioneering documentary maker, John Grierson at the GPO Film Unit. Wright and Auden hit it off and soon afterwards Auden was to join the Film Unit as writer and assistant director.

Another visitor in the autumn of 1935 was the publisher Rupert Hart-Davis who admired Day-Lewis for his writing and his principles. The two became such good friends that on one occasion the young Sean and Nicholas Day-Lewis were left with Rupert and Comfort Hart-Davis for several days while their parents were away. Day-Lewis had by now decided that his earlier rejection of Hart-Davis's offer of an advance to write serious novels had been an error. He could, he believed, produce both fiction and poetry once the distraction of the schoolroom was removed from his daily life. Moreover the £300 a year to produce three books agreed in a contract with Hart-Davis's publishing house, Jonathan Cape, would provide some financial security now he had thrown in his day job.

One attraction was that Hart-Davis did not insist, as A. D. Peters had suggested he might, that Day-Lewis relocate to London. That came as a relief, Day-Lewis had confided to L. A. G. Strong, because it was 'a prospect I do not altogether care for'.[10] Despite his growing reputation and the well-known authors who came to stay at Box Cottage when they addressed the Cheltenham Literary Society (among them Elizabeth Bowen[11] and Rosamond Lehmann), a still diffident and un-self-confident Day-Lewis continued to regard himself as a provincial schoolteacher and had little appetite for anything more than short and sweet samplings of the London literary scene.

Box Cottage and the world about it felt secure and he had no wish to leave it. As if further to reassure himself with so much change going on about him, in September Day-Lewis returned to familiar ground with the publication of *Revolution in Writing*, a short polemical pamphlet in the Hogarth Press's 'Day to Day' series. It contained three pieces including a transcript of a BBC broadcast he had made in March of 1935. 'Youth Looks Ahead' had caused some disquiet among the BBC producers because of what they had seen as its communist bias. Day-Lewis had refused, though, to soften his line. 'The only point on which I am bound to stand firm is that some adequate reference to the relation between politics – the science of living together – and literature should be made.'[12] The BBC capitulated but by sticking to his guns Day-Lewis contributed to a growing perception of him among broadcasters and literary journalists as 'Red Cecil', despite the fact that he was not a member of the Communist Party.

Also included in *Revolution in Writing* was a new essay, 'Writing and Morals', inspired by the situation in which Day-Lewis found himself, namely worrying how to support his family by working in a capitalist system where 'the very air I breathe is the air of a society I believe to be rotten'. He also wrote again of the difficulty the middle classes experienced in getting 'real contact' with the working classes.[13]

Such remarks were noted in his MI5 file,[14] but the truth of *Revolution in Writing* was that it was more an eloquent exposé of the dilemma facing bourgeois radicals than a programme of actions to be taken. The pamphlet attracted some unflattering reviews. Julian Bell, one of the poets championed by *New Signatures*, accused Day-Lewis of sentimentalizing the proletariat and confusing the personal with the public.[15]

After a muted Christmas with the King clan in Sherborne, the family's first since the death of Mary's father in September, Day-Lewis returned to his bedroom study at Box Cottage to begin in earnest the task of being a full-time writer. Aside from the single bed there was just his desk and an uncomfortable small rocking chair for company. It felt like a reminder of his boarding school accommodation. In an effort to dispel the impression he painted it all orange – 'a disastrous impulse'.[16] Like the rest of the house it was cold. The single fire in the living room provided little warmth upstairs and only an oil stove took the chill off a January morning but its fumes gave him a headache.

There was the distraction in January of the publication of his second Nicholas Blake, *Thou Shell of Death*. In line with his revolutionary fervour Day-Lewis had included in it a gentle attack on materialism – in this case the giving of unwanted Christmas presents at a time of economic hardship – but was too conscious of his audience and the need to ensure the book matched the commercial success of its predecessor to labour the point. Nigel Strangeways, solving a murder by poisoned walnut, is still showing a range of Audenesque affectations and meets in the course of his investigation his future wife, Georgia Cavendish, a free-spirit and explorer with a hint of Margaret Marshall about her.

Finally in February, Day-Lewis found himself where he thought he wanted to be – alone in his study to concentrate exclusively on writing. His closest confidant was increasingly Stephen Spender rather than Auden who was in June 1936 to head for Iceland with MacNeice and work on more theatrical collaborations with Isherwood. It was principally with Spender that Day-Lewis was to exchange drafts of new work over the next decade. Occasionally, too, he would offer constructive criticism, writing in an undated letter of the period of a new piece Spender had sent him: 'it's a bit too like Wystan and Eliot – I particularly dislike that kind of Athenaeum wise-crack Eliot is always using'.[17]

Mainly, though, he was encouraging in his remarks, as in an April 1935 letter to Spender on receipt of an early copy of Spender's new poem, 'The Exiles'. '[It] is damned good – I like it all now, except the last stanza which you were going to alter & feel I understand it. I feel it is a complete poem and that is rare. Most of us are capable of writing a number of lines of genuine poetic value, but they seldom add up to a poem.'[18]

Aside from his correspondence there were other attractions to compete with writing. Mary danced and he sang traditional ballads in a performance to raise money for the local Tewkesbury Abbey Appeal. They went out together to the cinema. He was encouraged by Rex Warner to take up birdwatching. Then there were his children. Although he was now working at home, he remained a distant, detached, distracted figure. 'As far as I can remember,' wrote his son, Sean, 'I was never admitted to my father's bedroom/study at Box Cottage. My brother and I knew that if the door was shut and he was at home, then it was out of bounds.'[19]

With few other role models to inform his behaviour with his sons, Day-Lewis could occasionally, despite his best intentions to do the opposite, slip back into behaviour that had an echo of Frank Day-Lewis's earlier attitude towards him. 'Sometimes if we were lucky, he'd play,' recalled Sean Day-Lewis. 'He'd rag us – his word for tickling and rough and tumble. There would be terrific bursts of fun. He liked games but he also liked to win. But then he could turn suddenly severe.'[20]

Day-Lewis's attachment to Mary remained strong. She was fundamentally, though never openly, out of sympathy with him on communism, while he judged that she knew too little about poetry to merit being shown drafts of work-in-progress. She later remembered trying to bridge this gap that was opening up between them and asking him about what he was writing. 'You know nothing about it,' he cut her off.[21] Her own youthful flirtations with fairies and nature worship had given way to practical good household sense and an interest in gardening. She was hospitable to his friends and other writers who came to stay, proud of her husband's success, but excluded from much of his professional life now. Where once they had been able to share staff room gossip when he returned home from school, now there was too often silence.

After his affair with Alison Morris, Day-Lewis's eye continued to wander and there was for some time a fairly open flirtation with Eileen Hedges, widow of Lionel, whom he called 'Jinnie' for reasons that are now forgotten. Eileen Hedges was not averse to his advances, Mary Day-Lewis later recalled, but she was a better friend of Mary than her husband and so rebuffed him out of loyalty. She was to remarry soon afterwards.[22]

The transition from parcelling out his life between home, school and writing to being a full-time 'literary hack' was not, for Day-Lewis, an easy one. In February 1936 he confided his disillusion to Spender: 'I shall be writing hard the rest of my life to fulfil my three-year contract with Cape.'[23] There would be, he feared, no time left for poetry. The depth of his despair – and particularly his unease at having to spend time on the Blake books – was captured in a poem he wrote at this time, entitled simply 'February 1936'.

Infirm and grey
This leaden-hearted day
Drags its lank hours, wishing itself away.

Grey as the skin
Of long-imprisoned men
The sky, and holds a poisoned thought within.

Whether to die,
Or live beneath fear's eye –
Heavily hangs the sentence of this sky.

The unshed tears
Of frost on boughs and briers
Gathering wait discharge like our swollen fears.

Servant and host
Of this fog-bitter frost,
A carrion-crow flaps, shadowing the lost.

Now to the fire
From killing fells we bear
This new-born lamb, our premature desire.

We cannot meet
Our children's mirth, at night
Who dream their blood upon a darkening street.

Stay away, Spring!
Since death is on the wing
To blast our seed and poison every thing.

'February 1936': *Overtures to Death* (1936)

Another source of despondency was the reaction to the publication in that month by Hogarth Press of *Noah and The Waters*, his morality play in verse. After his recent experience of an ever-rising tide of critical acclaim – save for Grigson – this new work saw the first ebb. It was almost universally panned. This reversal in his fortunes, at a time when he was already feeling distracted from his poetry, hit Day-Lewis's self-confidence hard.

Noah and The Waters was, Day-Lewis wrote in his foreword, 'a mixture of poetry, doggerel and rhetoric'.[24] One inspiration was Auden's collaborations with Rupert Doone. The two had talked with him on visits to Box Cottage about writing a choral ballet. Day-Lewis, though, changed course halfway through and instead produced a modern variation on a medieval morality play. Behind this volte-face seems to lie the huge success of T. S. Eliot's *Murder in the Cathedral,* a poetic drama in two parts, with a prose sermon interlude, about the martyrdom of Thomas Becket, twelfth-century Archbishop of Canterbury. It was first performed at Canterbury Cathedral in 1935 and published in the same year.

Noah and The Waters was Day-Lewis's response, taking another revered biblical figure as its subject, imitating Eliot's structure, but rejecting his Christian morality in favour of Marxism. Dedicated to his theatre-loving friend, Charles Fenby, but unlikely to be much to this political pragmatist's taste, it gets its prose sermon in early, beginning with a quotation about class war from *The Communist Manifesto.* 'Finally, when the class war is about to be fought to a finish, disintegration of the ruling class and the old order of society becomes so active, so acute, that a small part of the ruling class breaks away to make common cause with the revolutionary class, the class which holds the future in its hands ...'[25]

Set in such a context Noah is portrayed as a bourgeois idealist whose dilemma is whether to cling to his old life or entrust himself to the flood, not knowing where he will wash up, and with whom. Noah is described as 'the figure of your fate' and his indecision mirrors Day-Lewis's own. Should he, for all his doubts as to whether it would work and what damage it would cause in his own comfortable life, plunge into the tide of communism and join the Party, or dither on the shores of the old, flawed but familiar world?

The verse-play opens with a lengthy prologue, evoking the British countryside in utopian terms.

> *This curve of ploughland, one clean stroke*
> *Defining earth's nature constant to four seasons,*
> *Fixes too for ever her simple relationship*
> *With the sky and all systems imaginable there.*

This was, the critics suggested, its only successful section. When Noah is transformed into a contemporary Everyman figure, in urban setting, he faces up to a character called Flood, who personifies the revolutionary class and assails him with the worst points of the capitalist system. Noah, as befits his indecision, speaks with two voices – his 'life-will' which pushes him to embrace revolution, and his 'death-will' which clings to the status quo. In the struggle to choose Noah is addressed by a chorus which urges him forward and three antagonists, the capitalist Burgesses, who cajole, bribe and threaten him into staying put. The use of such a chorus owes something to classical Greece, but more to Eliot's poor women of Canterbury who nervously await Becket's return from his seven-year exile, fretting over his volatile relationship with King Henry II.

Where in life Day-Lewis was in two minds, in his writing he found it easier to come down firmly on the side of revolution. Noah is persuaded by the chorus.

He says good-bye
To much, but not to love. For loving now shall be
The close handclasp of the waters about his trusting keel,
Buoyant they make his home and lift his heart high;
Among their marching multitude he never shall feel lonely.

The utopia he arrives at, having left behind cities engaged in 'unremitting war', is pastoral – 'radiant valleys' where happy folk live in classless harmony, 'wearing the sun on their wide shoulders'. It was too much for many critics – including that of the communist *Daily Worker* – who accused him of reaching backwards to a pre-industrial age rather than forward, in tune with his recent taste for modern, industrial imagery, to embrace a new twentieth-century world.

Moreover, the play was utterly without the necessary drama to make it suitable for performance. To be fair, Day-Lewis acknowledges this in his foreword. 'Like that of morality plays, its drama derives largely from the weight and imminence of the issue it represents and little from any conscious dramatic construction.'[26] It is a defensive remark which suggests that he may even have anticipated the critics' reaction. And it shows a willingness, as he had been preaching, to sacrifice the pure art of writing a decent play in favour of the impure purpose of getting over an urgent political message. Indeed *Noah and The Waters* shows Day-Lewis taking this commitment to its furthest extreme, to a point when it began to damage his credibility as a writer.

Yet, for all his caveats in his foreword, he still harboured hopes of seeing *Noah* staged. Doone made no move to put it on, but there was later a brief attempt by others, with Day-Lewis's approval, to mount a London production in the early 1940s. The novelist Elizabeth Jane Howard,[27] then a struggling young actress, remembered being called to a first rehearsal in Wembley only for the whole project soon afterwards to be abandoned. 'We all found that it was too full of incomprehensible jargon to make any sense out of it,' she recalled.[28]

It was a humiliation for Day-Lewis. In years to come *Noah and The Waters* was the one piece of work from the 1930s that he tried hardest to forget, omitting all but the prologue from his *Collected Poems* of 1954 and everything from his *Selected Poems* of 1967. In 1936 its failure highlighted the gap that existed between reality and his wish to join the proletariat in a revolution that would transform their lives. Geoffrey Grigson, vicious as ever, touched a nerve when he scoffed at Day-Lewis's 'patronizing' depiction of the working classes as 'an undifferentiated mass of H_2O'. Sales held up well – 600 in the first six months – but Hogarth Press, encouraged by Day-Lewis's high profile, had printed 2000.[29]

The review which stuck in his mind, however, was by Edwin Muir[30] in *The Spectator*. Muir, an older poet Day-Lewis admired, had grown up in a poor family, first in the Orkneys and later in Glasgow where he had a series of menial jobs before making his name. He was politically to the left and had previously expressed his admiration for Day-Lewis, Auden, Spender and their colleagues. However, he wrote in March 1936, Day-Lewis, while 'a man of talent', had allowed in his new 'Marxian' work his gift for verse to 'deteriorate' and 'become facile and careless'. His political attachments and his revolutionary aspirations were, Muir suggested, in danger of destroying Day-Lewis as a poet. 'The choice was,' Day-Lewis wrote after reading Muir's verdict, '[between] being an amateurish political worker or trying to make myself a better poet'.[31]

Chapter 16

No Man's Land

Move then with new desires,
For where we used to build and love
Is no man's land, and only ghosts can live
Between two fires.
        'The Conflict': *A Time To Dance* (1935)

The more Day-Lewis dwelt on Edwin Muir's suggestion that his inclusion of political propaganda was damaging his poetry, the more he came to see it was true. And Muir was not the only erstwhile admirer who felt that he had lost his way. In *The Leaning Tower*, his publisher, Virginia Woolf, once so enthusiastic about *The Magnetic Mountain*, attacked him. 'Everything is a duty – even love. Listen to Mr Day-Lewis ingeminating love ... We listen to oratory, not poetry.'[1]

By the time this was published Day-Lewis had left the Woolfs' Hogarth Press, but her complaint went deeper than any personal disagreement, and deeper than a particular dislike of his verse. She believed that the mixture of idealism, didacticism and poetry that had characterized and made celebrated the poets of the 1930s had failed because it had ended up in 'confusion and compromise'.[2]

It was a view that Day-Lewis himself began to entertain as he reflected on *Noah and The Waters*. The questions he was asking himself were shared in a lengthy and occasionally acrimonious exchange of letters with Stephen Spender. 'I do entirely agree that ... the poet has to think about what is the best kind of life to live to give himself the best chance as a poet. This seems to me so important that, if you show me a worsening of my poetry and establish a cause and effect between that and my present [political] activities, I will drop them: and I am not in the least assuming that you couldn't show me both of these.'[3]

Day-Lewis sought increasingly to retreat from polemics and concentrate on poetry. Yet events in the outside world conspired to give him little opportunity to follow that through. Instead they produced ever more demands on him that as a by now well-known writer – Spender once called him 'the Left-Wing Laureate', a description Day-Lewis said was 'as laughable to me as it is depressing to you'[4] – he should live up to and indeed amplify what he had previously so evangelically preached.

In March 1936 Hitler's invasion of the Rhineland caused new fears throughout Europe about the German Chancellor's ultimate territorial ambitions. At home, the abdication crisis, with Edward VIII renouncing his throne to marry Wallis Simpson, seemed to many on the left to be evidence that a disintegrating British establishment was ripe to be overthrown. Day-Lewis wrote in the *Daily Worker* of George VI's coronation that it had the air of the 'frantic window-dressing of a shop on the verge of bankruptcy'. And in July 1936, while the Day-Lewises were holidaying at Lyme Regis in Dorset, the Spanish Civil War broke out after a group of right-wing military figures staged a coup against the republic, pitting the left-wing government against fascists in a struggle that came to symbolize the wider clash of ideologies in a tense Europe.

All could only harden the political resolve that Day-Lewis had been feeling since the start of the decade. Yet at home in his Cheltenham study he was daily juggling the need to pay the household bills by taking on well-paid but apolitical commissions with his urge to work towards redefining himself as a poet in the face of the flaws shown up by *Noah*. The task was not eased by the countless invitations from left-leaning groups to contribute an essay here, an introduction there and a rousing poem to further the causes with which he was by now so publicly associated.

His output was almost unceasing between the publication of *Noah and The Waters* in February 1936 and his next collection, *Overtures to Death* in October 1938. There were two new detective novels (*There's Trouble Brewing* and *The Beast Must Die*); two of his three contracted novels for Rupert Hart-Davis; a polemical pamphlet to rally support for a Popular Front; another less controversial tract on 'Imagination and Thinking' for the British Institute of Adult Education; introductions to two collections of poetry, the first by Julius Lipton,[5] and the second a selection by the much admired American, Robert Frost;[6] and a host of credits as editor or co-editor ranging from memorial volumes to celebrate the lives of writers Ralph Fox[7] and Julian Bell, both killed in the Spanish Civil War, through *The Mind in Chains*, essays on socialism and cultural revolution which lavished praise on the Soviet model, and on to *The Echoing Green*, an anthology of verse for children, and *Anatomy of Oxford*, a light-hearted compilation of local folklore put together with Charles Fenby.

Some paid well. Many paid nothing. Some caused headlines, others went largely unnoticed. Often it was guilt that prompted him to offer his services for nothing. So when Spender announced late in 1936 that he was going to Spain to join Auden and others in supporting the Republican cause, Day-Lewis could hardly refuse his invitation to do his bit back home by writing an unpaid monthly political column in *Left Review*.

He was in demand, but without the first-hand experience of Spain of Auden and Spender felt himself to have nothing new to say. Moreover he was questioning whether he had said too much already. Where he succeeded in this period it was often when his writing touched least on the ambiguities he felt. So Nicholas Blake's *The Beast Must Die*, the tale of a father's determination to avenge his son's death at the hands of a reckless driver, prompted by a similar near-miss incident with Sean, was one of his best. Its moral message was a good deal subtler than that of *Noah and The Waters* and in the United States, it was his most commercial book, selling over 300,000 copies. In Britain it notched up 135,000 and later the French director, Claude Chabrol, made it into a film.[8]

In detective fiction Day-Lewis could escape. Elsewhere it was harder. Ideologically, he responded to extraordinary times by setting to one side his long-harboured doubts about membership of the Communist Party. It was not an unusual story in this period. The spectacle of Hitler marching around Europe and Oswald Mosley and his black shirts recruiting to the fascist cause turned more than one left-leaning doubter into a staunch socialist or communist.

So ironically, just when the critical reception to *Noah and The Waters* was confirming the importance of maintaining the distinction between being a communist and being a communist-influenced writer, Day-Lewis joined the party. One element was simple weakness. There was a concerted campaign to recruit him by Communist Party officials, including Harry Pollitt's wife, Marjorie, who all beat a path to Box Cottage. Day-Lewis found he ran out of reasons to say no. He took his own advice and followed the example of his Noah. '*So shall you fold your fears and be/The alert equal of necessity*'.

The local party branch in Cheltenham, he reported back to Spender (who was also briefly to join) was of a 'good-size: the comrades are all very respectful & call one "sir" – it's like being back at school again'.[9] There were workers from the local aircraft factory, waiters and farm hands amongst his new comrades as well as a smattering of schoolteachers. Day-Lewis was keener on singing at the social events than declaiming at public meetings or selling copies of the *Daily Worker* on street corners. Local people he knew in Cheltenham, he wrote, regarded the sight of Day-Lewis leafleting for the Communist Party as 'harmless eccentricity'.[10] With fellow party members, as in an undated letter to William Ismay from this period, he was scrupulous in his manner of address – 'Dear Comrade' – and farewell – 'Yours fraternally'.[11]

There were inhibitions, though, from the very start. When one speaker from headquarters cancelled an open-air lecture he was scheduled to give in the centre of Cheltenham, Day-Lewis, who had been drafted in to chair the rally, admitted 'my shame at the feeling of relief was almost as great as the relief I felt'.[12] His allotted task in the branch was political education which appeared to consist of distilling the core message from official tracts and sharing it with the rest of the comrades. There was, he recalled, an air of amateurism to the whole thing, an 'impression more of a combined study-group and nonconformist chapel than of a revolutionary body'.[13]

For all his willingness to do things he fundamentally regarded as futile, some comrades, he told Spender, remain 'very suspicious of us' by which he meant middle class radicals.[14] At party headquarters, there was also disillusionment. Having finally wooed the famous Day-Lewis into the fold, officials were dismayed he was not contributing more. In the file that MI5 was keeping on him, there is a note, based on a conversation with senior Communist Party officials, that states 'Harry Pollitt incidentally thinks less than nothing of their [Day-Lewis and Spender] value to the Party'. They are, it adds, 'communists of a highly idealistic and literary brand'.[15]

Otherwise a natural performer, Day-Lewis struggled on various political platforms. Louis MacNeice, in his autobiography, described watching Day-Lewis at an anti-fascist meeting where he was speaking alongside the Welsh Marxist writer, academic and firebrand, Goronwy Rees.[16] 'Day-Lewis spoke first,' MacNeice reported, 'in his tired Oxford accent, qualifying everything, nonplussed, questioning.'[17]

It was a weakness Day-Lewis recognized in himself. In reply to a September 1937 invitation from a Mr J. Crump of the Birmingham branch of the Communist Party to address the comrades, Day-Lewis declined on the grounds of workload but added: 'I am a writer and no speaker. I can lecture, take part in discussions, that kind of thing, but I've no experience of straight propaganda-speaking, nor the voice for open-air work.'[18]

He did, however, agree to represent the Cheltenham branch at the 1937 National Party Congress. His attendance was duly noted by MI5 in their file – alongside his attendance in November of the same year at a conference for Communist Professional Workers at the Royal Hotel in London.[19]

Even in his own sphere of the world of books Day-Lewis was a less than successful agitator. In 1936 he tried to persuade the Society of Authors to affiliate to the Trades Union Congress. Having managed to get himself a seat on the main committee, he set about recruiting what he took to be kindred spirits to vote with him. 'I should have liked to be associated with you,' E. M. Forster replied by letter to his advances, 'and should have thought it an honour', but nevertheless he cried off from the July vote, citing his involvement in a libel case.[20] The motion was defeated.

If the MI5 watchers had been taking notes of Day-Lewis's efforts to radicalize the Society of Authors, they might have done well to balance their accounts with other more reassuring details of his life. In 1936, for instance, he agreed to become a regular reviewer of novels for the *Daily Telegraph*, owned by Lord Camrose, a Conservative supporter of Winston Churchill, later a member of his wartime cabinet and just the sort of 'scavenger baron' that Day-Lewis had been threatening to shoot in *The Magnetic Mountain*. It was a well-paid role and quickly allowed him shamelessly to plug his friend L. A. G. Strong's new novel, a small return for the support Strong had given him over the years.

And as if consorting with the Tory press wasn't enough, Day-Lewis in February 1937 took up an offer from the popular novelist Hugh Walpole[21] of a place on the selection panel of the Book Society. Started by the novelist Arnold Bennett[22] in 1929, the society appointed five distinguished literary figures as judges. This quintet would select each month a 'Book Society Choice' for the benefits of members, as well as listing six other titles that they might consider reading. Nomination could transform the fortunes of a novel. When *Stamboul Train* by Graham Greene[23] was chosen in 1932, its sales went up from 2,000 to 20,000.

Day-Lewis's instinct was to accept. The fee was good; he considered the offer an honour; he was flattered by the invitation to join such established writers; and the role offered another opportunity to pursue his conviction that the printed word, if put into the hands of sufficient people, could bring about social change. However, before going to his first monthly selection meeting with the other judges – who included the poet Edmund Blunden – at Walpole's flat overlooking Green Park in Piccadilly, Day-Lewis decided he ought to consult the Communist Party as to whether the Book Society was a fitting organization with which to be associated. Walpole was scorned in left-wing literary circles as middlebrow and old-fashioned. The Book Society was, by the same judgement, part of the system that needed overthrowing and replacing by the more radical Left Book Club, set up by the publisher Victor Gollancz (which Day-Lewis also supported by giving talks at its local branches).

The Party encouraged him to join and so he put his qualms to one side. He was proud of his achievements during his tenure in getting Auden and Mac-Neice's *Letters for Iceland*, a Christopher Isherwood short story and even a collection of Lenin's letters on the list of recommended titles. Others, though, took a dim view of his 'betrayal'. Grigson as ever was soon lambasting him in *New Verse*. Day-Lewis's membership of the panel, he wrote, 'establishes him as the Thriller Writer, the Underworld Man, the yesterday's newspaper, the grease in the sink-pipe of letters who has posed for ten years as spring water'.

Such a reaction was to be expected, but in 1938 Spender wrote in the autumn issue of *New Verse*, attacking as a sell-out Auden's acceptance of the King's Gold Medal for Poetry and Day-Lewis's position on the Book Society. Both his old friends might see their decisions as tactics, Spender acknowledged, but they were 'part of the process by which the English writer, who has a good heart at the age of twenty and is therefore a socialist, develops a good brain at 40 and becomes a Conservative'.

Day-Lewis was particularly offended by his friend Spender's suggestion that he was being 'dishonest' by his Book Society membership which had led to him 'writing in a style and developing an attitude adapted to the quotations printed on the publishers' advertisements'. The fact that the article had appeared in Grigson's journal rubbed salt into the wound. He sent Spender an eight-page letter of protest about his 'malicious tongue'. 'You & I being friends is ... no reason for our being a mutual admiration society: but it is, I think, a good reason for attacking each other – when we feel it necessary – in private rather than in public; or at any rate not coming into the open with our differences until private expostulation has failed.'[24]

Day-Lewis defended his involvement with the Book Society, pledged never to write for Grigson himself, but ended on a conciliatory note. 'This competition in unrespectability is going to become like that Comic Writers' Association meeting with its manual labour snobbism: Wystan is surely much better known, much more of a success than I am, isn't he? But seriously we can make as false an *idée fixe* or cult of unsuccess as the bourgeois do of respectability. Let us look at the writer's work first, last and all the time.' He added in pencil, 'It's too late to be romantic rebels.'[25]

Spender was equally anxious to avoid a rift in his reply of November 26, and invited Day-Lewis to stay at his Brook Green flat. 'We'll get some Irish whiskey, if that's what you really like, and have a talk.' He continued: 'I didn't intend any personal attack on you and ... apologise if my article could be so interpreted'.[26]

But Spender stood his ground on the principle behind his article in *New Verse*. 'I wanted to raise the question,' he wrote, 'whether you were paying any price as an artist for what I take to be a concession. Personally I think we all pay a price; I think that to some extent we are the creatures of the public that reads our reviews when they are quoted on the blurbs of advertisements. I should have thought that the very mention of reviewing would have shown you that I was deliberately introducing something that I did myself, in order not to seem superior in discussing the problem.'[27]

Spender went on: 'It isn't just that I have a puritan's fear of success, it's that I feel the task of being a poet is an immensely difficult one, one which is attacked both from the Left and the Right. It may be that I am only stating my own problem, but I can't help feeling that it is absolutely essential for a poet to reserve a kind of continuum in the part of his mind which is *always* being exercised at a poetic level. Poetry isn't a kind of bath which one can plunge into when one's actually writing a poem; it is a continual stream, a continual conscious dream, if you like, which demands that every external preoccupation be sacrificed to its own internal development.'[28]

While the immediate matter of the Book Society was comparatively unimportant when the world was teetering on the brink of war, what lay behind Spender's objection had a greater significance. For his words amplified the doubts that Day-Lewis was already experiencing about his own public and political role, the commercial writing projects he was involved in and the damage both were causing him.

'My own feeling,' Spender had added, 'is that the Party hasn't the slightest interest in poets as poets; they are just interested in anyone who can transfer his reputation to them. They simply want to use your reputation.'[29] Spender's disillusionment with Communist Party membership came sooner than Day-Lewis's, but he was making arguments that Day-Lewis found increasingly impossible to counter.

By the time of this exchange of letters, Spender had returned from the Spanish Civil War. He hadn't experienced front-line action but what he had seen had not inspired him. For all who looked to the Soviet Union to save Europe from fascism, the late 1930s were a time of disillusionment. Eyewitness accounts were trickling out of Stalin's purges of opponents and his callous displacement of whole peoples as part of his grand plans to remodel his country. The Moscow Show Trials of Gregory Zinoviev and fifteen other Trotskyites which culminated in their execution in August 1936 exposed the authoritarian nature of the Soviet regime to the world. Day-Lewis, in a September 1936 article for the *Manchester Guardian*, tried to distract attention from Stalin's excesses by finding fault with the way 'biased' British newspapers had reported events in Moscow. Spender in his 1937 book *Forward from Liberalism*, sought to maintain his admiration for Russia by arguing that a planned new Soviet constitution would remove the all-too-obvious barriers to true liberty. But the new religion was beginning to ring hollow.

Reflecting back in *The Buried Day*, Day-Lewis wrote that his own communism had been inspired by a kind of 'romantic humanism, a bent of mind quite incompatible, I would discover, with the materialism and rigidity of communist doctrines'.[30] A similar judgement was made in the late 1930s in Day-Lewis's MI5 file. 'As an intellectual,' wrote Colonel P. R. Chambers of the poet's membership of the Communist Party, 'he was probably actuated by his hatred of social inequality rather than by revolutionary desires.'[31]

Day-Lewis had agonized briefly about heading for Spain. The logic of what he had been writing was that he should go. Others followed it through. In the autumn of 1937, having devoted a series of issues to the war, the magazine *Contemporary Poetry and Prose* closed 'as the editor is going abroad for some time' to join the Republican side.

'The International Brigade was formed,' Day-Lewis recalled, 'and I believed I ought to volunteer for it, but I lacked the courage to do so.'[32] He was writing 25 years after the event. A more contemporary flavour of his qualms can be found at the end of his 1937 novel, *Starting Point*. Anthony Neale, an unattached young communist and teacher, does join the International Brigade. 'The point is,' he explains to his friend John Henderson, 'that we've been talking for some time about how valuable democracy is, and the general bloodiness of fascism, so it's only logical for us to fight for the one and against the other ... it's a simple matter of self-preservation.' Henderson applauds such words. Neale's courage, he says, 'will guide a new world struggling out of the womb' but, after his wife's tearful intercession to remind him of his responsibilities towards her and their children, decides he cannot follow suit.[33]

Mary would have been unlikely to place such open pressure on Day-Lewis, but his situation was essentially the same as Henderson's. So he made do with fine words to encourage those who fought the fascists in Spain, and moving tributes to those like his old detractor Julian Bell who were killed there. In November 1936 he exorcised some of his guilt when he wrote a pamphlet which emphatically rebutted Aldous Huxley's[34] pacifist 'What Are You Going To Do About It?: The Case For A Constructive Peace'. That had suggested that there was no public appetite to take on Hitler and Mussolini and that a peace deal should therefore be brokered. Day-Lewis's 'We're Not Going To Do Nothing' was published by the *Left Review* and its 32 pages were wrapped in a puce cover appropriate for the angry sentiments they enclosed.

The main argument was to commend the idea of a Popular Front of Labour, Liberals and Communists as a practical and realistic way to face down the fascists. 'We must act at once', Day-Lewis insisted, even though back in Cheltenham his efforts to arrange just such a coalition had been received, he later admitted, 'with the embarrassment a bishop might show if publicly asked by a tart to contribute money to a good cause'.[35]

The gap between fine words and reality was exposed when the pamphlet made headlines and thrust Day-Lewis once more into a leadership role on the left. The truth, however, was that a substantial part of it was written by Rex Warner who went uncredited.[36] It may have been that Day-Lewis was just too busy with other, better-paid jobs. Or that he wanted to encourage Warner who was still seeking a publisher for his early 1930s Marxist novel, *Wild Goose Chase*. Day-Lewis at one stage offered Faber a subsidy of £100 out of his earnings from commercial fiction if they would take it, but they declined. When it finally was published in 1936 he was a generous patron in making sure it was a recommended title by the Book Society.

However, if the aim had been to boost Warner's career, why not include his name on the jacket of 'We're Not Going To Do Nothing'? The reason seems to be that Day-Lewis did not quite have the heart to write the reply that was being urged on him by colleagues and party officials. He was losing faith in his own arguments, but was not quite ready candidly to acknowledge the chasm that had opened up between his public persona and his private thoughts. Drafting in a ghost – and one so sure of his views as Warner – may have been a shabby compromise but it got him round the dilemma. Fortunately Grigson never found out and so laid into the pamphlet as vintage Day-Lewis with a full complement of insults.

By Day-Lewis's own account much more influential on him at the time than Warner, though, was Charles Fenby. Day-Lewis made regular trips in late 1937 and early 1938 to stay in Oxford with his old housemate. Fenby didn't marry until 1941 and, left to their own devices, the two men could continue the intense discussions of their undergraduate days. In theory they were working together on *Anatomy of Oxford*, but in reality Fenby did most of the work and Day-Lewis allowed his better-known name to appear on the jacket to pull in readers. With Fenby who had never espoused communism, Day-Lewis was able to be open about his own doubts. 'Charles' independence of mind, so different from Rex's logical yet violent unorthodoxy, had a calming, stabilizing effect upon me,' Day-Lewis wrote. 'I admired his sober questioning of many of my own flightier opinions, both political and literary; and in his company I entered an Oxford I had known nothing of during my undergraduate days – the Oxford of pubs and factories and trade union and local politics . . . I envied him this participation in a community, for it made me feel that my own political activities were only on the fringe of things'.[37] For Day-Lewis one part of the appeal of left-wing opinions was the chance to feel he was close to the proletariat. Fenby showed him you could achieve that without signing up to Marx.

Day-Lewis's core despondency during all this frantic activity was only increased by his sense that the poetic momentum, which he had briefly held with Auden and Spender, was moving on and leaving them behind. There was the disappointment of *Noah and The Waters*. There were Auden's growing doubts as to the power of poetry to usher in social change, hastened by his renewed interest in Christianity and by his disquiet about some of what he had seen on the Republican side when in Spain.[38] And there was Day-Lewis's perception, expressed in a new postscript to the 1936 reissue of *A Hope for Poetry*, that the moment for 'impure poetry' may have passed.

Listing the publications that had come along since *A Hope for Poetry* first appeared two years earlier, he makes special reference to Louis MacNeice's *Poems* of 1935. In a detailed critique of the volume, Day-Lewis is anxious to praise, but cannot help noticing MacNeice's 'armed neutrality' and return to 'artistic individualism'. 'Like all the present-day young writers, he feels the need to withdraw on to some *terra firma* from the bewildering flux of modern life: unlike most of them, he does not intend or believe this vantage point to be also a starting point toward any new continent of thought or action.'[39] For Day-Lewis one without the other was still untenable, but there is doubt in his tone about whether that long-held goal of synthesis is any more possible.

He also notes in the postscript 'the appearance of a new generation of poets, 'not so much influenced by the *New Country* school as reacting away from it: among these – George Barker,[40] Dylan Thomas, Clifford Dyment,[41] David Gascoyne[42] – the most promising seems to be Barker'. There has been, Day-Lewis goes on, with just a hint of *mea culpa* 'a reaction from the recent pre-occupation of poets with social justice, their possibly over-mechanized vocabulary, and often slapdash technique: a return to the ideals of poetic integrity and artistic individualism; a setting-out-again in the direction of "pure" poetry'. This Day-Lewis laments, calling with something short of conviction for a new fusion between social justice and artistic integrity, revolution and poetic tradition, the twin pillars of 'the society some of us hope for and are fighting for'.[43]

While poetry was developing in ways that unsettled him, Day-Lewis was spending much of his time in his study earning his £300 a year from Rupert Hart-Davis. The three novels he produced were neither critical nor commercial successes. The first, *The Friendly Tree*, came out in October 1936. It was a slight romance in three parts, charting the meeting between Anna Charteris, a young woman with an overbearing lone father, and Stephen Hallam, a radical who woos her with talk of Soviet collective farms. They fall in love and marry but Hallam then betrays her with a friend before finally returning to her arms.

It was followed in September 1937 by *Starting Point*, a much more ambitious novel structurally, which takes four undergraduate housemates from Oxford and pitches then into the crises of the 1930s. It has melodramatic moments – as when Theodore, one of the four, shoots his actress mother in a fit of rage and then turns the gun on himself – and attracted an admiring letter soon after publication from the novelist and critic Edward Sackville-West.[44] 'Not being a communist,' he wrote, 'I took the book up with suspicion, expecting to find that you had made the usual propagandist's mistake of describing only the worst examples of the types he dislikes. But you seem, on the contrary, to have succeeded in being wonderfully fair: your characters are alive and drawn in the round.'[45]

Finally in June 1939, *Child of Misfortune* appeared, again set against the backdrop of contemporary politics, but this time focusing in on a single family and adding an Anglo-Irish element. Monart makes an appearance as do Uncle Willie Squires and Knos. The novelist Elizabeth Bowen, who had become a good friend since addressing the Cheltenham Literary Society, wrote to Day-Lewis full of reassurance after he had sent her a copy with a note of warning attached. 'My own view is that it starts very well and gets tired about halfway through.' Bowen rejected such self-criticism and was full of enthusiasm. 'It's got such tremendous density and life.'[46]

In all three novels, Day-Lewis took situations and characters out of his own life and adapted them to fiction, but he did so subtly. Nothing was lifted wholesale. In building a character, there would be the arms of one friend, the legs of another and the head of a third. It is impossible, for example, to label any of the four young men in the student house in *Starting Point* as Warner, Fenby or Day-Lewis. Features of all three are attributed to different characters. And though there are inevitable echoes of Auden — in political cartoonist Arthur Green, who likes paintings of industrial canals in *Child of Misfortune* and in the didactic and outrageous Theodore Follett in *Starting Point* — they are only echoes.

What the books lack is dramatic impact and a clear message. There are too many interior monologues — essential to the work of a poet, but potentially an obstacle in a novel — for them truly to engage the reader. And there is a strong sense that Day-Lewis was holding back from delivering any definite political points. Even when he begins with a point to make — attempting to justify Marxism in *Starting Point* — he seems to lose his way. So there are often his own political observations scattered about — in Hallam's descriptions of the tough life of coal miners or the various challenges that Anthony Neale and John Henderson face when reacting to outside events in the 1930s — but no coherent philosophy ultimately emerges to satisfy the expectations of readers who would have picked up the novel knowing Day-Lewis's position from his poetry and pamphlets. If anything, the novels taken together were a public escape valve for the doubts that hitherto he had kept private.

He also felt that he was out of his depth with literary fiction, however much the idea of experimenting in other genres appealed to him, as it also did to Auden, MacNeice and Spender. Sending a draft of the second of the three, *Starting Point*, to Leonard Strong, to whom it was dedicated, Day-Lewis included a note: 'the general feeling about it (shared by myself) is that there are some good things in it but it doesn't hang together: you and Sylvia will have to take the good parts as your own, and grin and bear the rest'.[47]

The Day-Lewises had just returned from a holiday in Dorset with Knos, who was over from Ireland, when, on July 29, 1937, Mamie telephoned from Edwinstowe to tell Cecil that his father had died in the night from a coronary thrombosis. He drove straight to Nottinghamshire where he was shown his father's dead body, lying on his bed, lilies beside him and a crucifix in his folded hands.

'I had never seen a dead person before,' he wrote, 'and had not known how small the dead look: my father's head seemed to have shrunk, and his face was the face, almost, of a stranger — a waxwork face which looked so remote from the living, the human, that it made death all the more impenetrable a mystery. I held the back of my hand against his cheek for a few moments, then I left him.'[48]

He felt only numb, and let Mamie organize the funeral at the church in Edwinstowe as she wished. Afterwards she insisted that the hearse transport the coffin halfway across England to Bath so that her husband could be placed in her family tomb. Day-Lewis followed with his stepmother in his father's car on a boiling hot day. Soon afterwards she retired to Bournemouth where Day-Lewis would pay dutiful visits to a woman he never liked in an attempt to make good the guilt he felt about his long emotional estrangement from his father.

Without any religious belief that offered the comforting promise of an afterlife, Day-Lewis was left with only memories and regrets. Some were recent. Four months earlier his father and Mamie had come to Box Cottage. Frank had spoken of a warning from his doctor to take things easy but his son had dismissed it as another attempt to attract his attention. No mention was made of the unflattering portrait of the lone father in *The Friendly Tree*.

Day-Lewis had felt forced, as a young man, to make a stranger out of his father to escape him, but once a father himself he had begun to understand Frank better and rue his actions. Now it was too late to act on those insights. Subsequently Frank would come back to him in dreams. 'In one, I pick a quarrel with him and begin to belabour his head with my fists: he does not hit back, and my fists are as huge and innocuous as pillows.'[49] In the other Day-Lewis would discover that his father wasn't dead but old and infirm. He goes to visit him but his father is indifferent.

Day-Lewis's search in his poetry to understand his father, and his own background, only began with Frank's death. 'I can pray now,' he wrote in 1960, 'that, when alive, he did not know how much both he and I had to forgive each other for.'[50] In 1938, when it was all so much more recent and raw, he wrote:

A hand came out of August
And flicked his life away:
We had not time to bargain, mope,
Moralize or pray.

Where he had been, was only
An effigy on a bed
To ask us searching questions or
Hear what we'd left unsaid.

Only that stained parchment
Set out what he had been –
A face we might have learned better,
But now must read unseen.

Thus he resigned his interest
And claims, all in a breath,
Leaving us the long office work
And winding-up of death:

The ordinary anguish,
The stairs, the awkward turn,
The bearers' hats like black mushrooms
Placed upon the lawn.

As a migrant remembers
The sting and warmth of home,
As the fruit bears out the blossom's word,
We remember him.

'Overtures to Death': *Overtures to Death* (1938)

Chapter 17

Earth Shakes Beneath Us

Gallant or woebegone, alike unlucky –
Earth shakes beneath us: we imagine loss.
'Bombers': *Overtures to Death* (1938)

From the floor of the Axe valley, it looks like a white dot. Halfway up the eastern slope, almost hidden by trees and hedgerows and standing just inside the Devon border with Dorset, is Brimclose, the cottage Cecil Day-Lewis and his wife Mary bought for £1,600 in the Easter of 1938. On a then unnamed country lane, the house seems to float above the world and offered to Day-Lewis a perfect place to retreat from all the personal, professional and political pressures that had been building up.

The view from Brimclose's large garden remains one over a timeless landscape. Rising behind it is the Iron Age hill fort of Musbury Castle and spread out in front, as the land falls away steeply over the roofs of the small village of Musbury and its church tower, is Beer Head, the most westerly chalk cliff on the south coast of England, framing the point where the River Axe meets the English Channel.

When the Day-Lewises came to look at the house, during another family holiday at Lyme Regis, it was called Woodlands and the garden was a wilderness, full of old cars. Its main focus was a large kennel the owner, R. A. Deacon, used for breeding dogs. The remnant of a grass tennis court was pasture for a handful of goats. There was no electricity; the water came from a spring; and the whole place smelt of damp. But for Day-Lewis it was ideal. With his earnings from Nicholas Blake and his recent venture into novel writing, plus some capital of Mary's, they bought the house on first viewing. In August, they finally moved in and Day-Lewis, as he put it, 'noiselessly slipped the painter' of the public life that had so consumed him throughout the 1930s.[1]

Originally two cottages, Brimclose dated back around 400 years. It had been used by the local Drake estate to house gamekeepers. Long and low, its thick stone walls, faced in uneven white render, were topped by a thatched roof with iron guttering sticking out beyond as if to underline the cottage's top-of-a-chocolate-box good looks. The Day-Lewises added a kitchen extension in 1939 and were connected to the mains for power. A telephone was installed (Colyton 126) but water continued to come from a spring in the garden. They kept the house simple and true to its origins.

Upstairs, with a bedroom for Sean and Nicholas, another for the nanny they brought with them from Cheltenham, and a third (above the new kitchen) for visitors, there was only one left for husband and wife. So they broke the habits of their marriage so far and shared, albeit with one single bed in one corner and the other opposite, as far away as space allowed. Downstairs the stone-floored living room, with beams so low that Day-Lewis at six foot had to duck his head to get past, was filled by a grand piano and warmed by a large open fire. Next door was the study, with a desk for both parents, plus an old bread oven. Behind the bookshelves there was damp in the walls, but to the back it looked out onto the garden – from Day-Lewis's desk – and occasionally doubled as a table-tennis room.

Mary set to work at once on the overgrown three and a half acre garden – occasionally with Day-Lewis's help. The physical exercise, he wrote in *The Buried Day*, was a relief after the cerebral strains of recent years. The disused tennis court played host to aggressively competitive cricket matches with a visiting Rex Warner. A marrow patch was planted and the old cider apple orchard tamed. 'We are living a wonderfully escapist life here', Day-Lewis boasted to his old schoolteacher friend, Frank Halliday, on September 24.[2] Husband and wife, engaged on making a new home, were drawn together once more.

Mary made friends in the village, frequenting its bakery (now closed) and post office. She would occasionally attend evensong at St Michael's parish church, though more for the social side than out of any religious conviction. She struck up a friendship with Barbara Cameron who lived in the village. The newly-arrived couple, Cameron remembered, initially gave every appearance of being happy. 'There were some lovely summers back then. Brimclose was very peaceful. A lot of the time I think Mary kidded herself that she had the perfect marriage. She cooked for him [Cecil], she liked watching him cut the grass, and she was happy to see him sitting in the porch writing ... A lot of the time Mary and Cecil were very close. Mary's eyes always shone when she was happy and Cecil knew only too well that a smile from him would make her so.'[3]

Day-Lewis preferred on religious high days and holidays to stay in his study, his chosen devotional reading Thomas Hardy whose hallowed Dorset lay so close at hand and was regularly explored. When he ventured down into Musbury, there were a few who recognized his face from the newspapers. Mrs Hawker, whose cottage stood on the main road out of Musbury, would always 'genuflect' when she saw his father, Sean Day-Lewis remembered.[4]

Sean was sent off as a day boy (later a boarder) to the prep. department of Allhallows, a local public school housed in a large Victorian mansion on the cliffs between Musbury and Lyme Regis. The plan was for both Sean and Nicholas eventually to follow their father to Sherborne, but Sean fluffed the entrance exam and so stayed on at Allhallows. There was, he recalled, apparently no question of his left-wing father sending his children to the nearby village school. 'I used to ask him about it later on. "We weren't liberals," he'd tell me, half in jest, "we were communists. We wanted to get as close to the establishment as possible".'[5]

By contrast, Day-Lewis wanted to get as far away from his own class as possible and so preferred the Red Lion in the centre of the village to the more refined New Inn on the outskirts on the main road to Axminster. Now a pink-fronted cottage, the Red Lion in 1938 was the pub where the farm workers congregated. 'The local pub is excellent,' Day-Lewis told Halliday, 'full of Shropshire Lads and foul-mouthed veteran rose-pruners: my form at darts has been quite electrifying, and every now and then I put in a dirty crack at [Neville] Chamberlain, which is received very well for this sort of pocket of Liberalism.'[6]

He thought he had found the sort of enjoyable classless camaraderie that he had long sought without any of the political overtones that had weighed him down in the Cheltenham branch of the Communist Party. There was no local party branch near Musbury. It was part of the appeal of Brimclose. It wasn't so much that Day-Lewis wanted to resign from the Party, just take a step back from activism that he could no longer justify intellectually. His future as a member was a question that he left open.

He was, he wrote to Spender, still giving talks to local Workers' Education Authority branches – where bright, young university graduates with a social conscience would offer lessons to local labourers under the motto 'learn as you teach'. 'I came to live here,' he continued, 'because I felt too much political activity was drawing off energy that ought to go into verse ... I still believe that working for the CP may be able to provide me with the synthesis that, as you and I agree, I need; and might it not do the same for you? I wish I could influence you at least to stay in the Writers' Association.'[7]

Spender had left the Communist Party soon after he joined. Day-Lewis's continuing attachment, once he had moved to Musbury, was something he downplayed in *The Buried Day*. There, he suggested that he was so unimportant to the Party that it hardly noticed his leave of absence from the ranks. No effort was made to pursue him, he recounted.[8] In a memo in his MI5 file, however, an undercover agent reported back on a conversation he had in 1942 with Emile Burns, a leading member of the Executive Committee of the Communist Party of Great Britain. Burns reported that with his move to Musbury Day-Lewis had 'disappeared ... because he felt that the party was taking an anti-cultural line and he was rushing about speaking and doing this, that and the other and not being allowed to write poetry'. But Burns also told how he personally had tried 'every conceivable method when I heard that he [Day-Lewis] was drifting away to get him to meet either me or Harry [Pollitt] and never got an answer out of him ... He just deliberately refused to meet leading Party people who were wanting to make an effort to talk it over with him'.[9]

It wasn't only the opportunity it offered of escaping for the time being from the Party and the conflicts it threw up in him that drew Day-Lewis to making a new life in the countryside. Though he had spent most of his life in cities or towns, he had retained from those early visits to Monart a romanticized picture of rural life. Box Cottage stood on the edge of a town, looking over fields, but was part of the life of Cheltenham. At Musbury he was delighted to find a genuine and thriving rural community.

The search for a new house had begun in earnest the previous year when Charles Fenby had taken Day-Lewis to sample rural pubs in Oxfordshire. 'Imperceptibly, a longing for the countryside, for some more rooted life, began to grow within me', he wrote of those excursions.[10] At first he had looked around Oxfordshire and then the Thames Valley, close enough to get to London easily, but increasingly he saw the capital as bound up with activities that were nothing but a burden. So the search moved to Devon and Dorset, already a favourite holiday destination, the area where Mary had grown up and where her mother, Constance, still maintained the family home, Greenhill, in Sherborne.

Day-Lewis had continued in these months, in spite of his growing misgivings, to accept Party invitations to speak in favour of a Popular Front. In March 1938 he addressed 1,000 delegates at a Communist rally at St Pancras Town Hall in London. Some who ran into him on such occasions were convinced of his sincerity. V. S. Pritchett, critic and short story writer, noted in 1938 encountering Day-Lewis and Warner 'starry-eyed and very exalted' by communism, but in Day-Lewis's case Pritchett was being taken in by a public face.[11]

Day-Lewis still believed that poetry should have a public and indeed political role, but was trying to redefine how to live that out. The fundamental commitment, though, left him vulnerable to those who wanted to enlist his services as a speaker. For his part he saw saying yes as the only small contribution he could make in anxious times while others were risking their lives in Spain. 'I look upon it quite simply as a battle between light and darkness, of which only a blind man could be unaware,' he wrote in the *Left Review*'s 1937 survey 'Authors Take Sides on the Spanish Civil War'. He was one of 127 out of 148 writers who replied. T. S. Eliot was in the minority when he said that he chose to 'take no part'. Evelyn Waugh refused to condemn Franco, but Spender, Day-Lewis and even the normally sceptical MacNeice all threw their lot in with the Republicans. 'Both as a writer and as a member of the Communist Party,' Day-Lewis said, 'I am bound to help in the fight against Fascism, which means certain destruction or living death for humanity'.

Faced by such a choice, he could not remain silent when asked to speak, but if he could identify the problem confronting the world, he no longer was clear about the answer. His faith in a revolution to establish a Soviet-style republic in Britain had always been more theoretical than real, but even that had now all but deserted him. He was mouthing empty words. He wanted them to be true but knew they could never be. His rhetoric as a result grew strained, shrill and hollow.

In early 1938, for example, he felt he couldn't refuse to contribute a new poem to E. A. Osborne's anthology, *In Letters of Red*. 'On the Twentieth Anniversary of Soviet Power' saw Day-Lewis saluting Lenin as a hero 'loved by the people' but avoiding praising Stalin in similar terms. He was now aware of the reality of Stalin's brutal regime, whatever denials Harry Pollitt and Party officials continued to issue of detailed reports of atrocities. Though there was still a stated, almost by-rote belief in the poem in Soviet power, that '*wherever/Man cries against the oppressors "they shall not pass",/Your frontiers stand*', it lacked any sort of conviction. The whole piece was flat and clichéd and Day-Lewis saw to it subsequently that it was never reprinted again.

The decision to move to Musbury had already been made when Day-Lewis went on the evening of June 8, 1938, to the Queen's Hall in London to join on stage 50 other writers to protest at the rise of the fascism in Europe and Britain's failure to respond. However, events that night convinced him that taking a step back by moving to the countryside was not sufficient to ease his divided mind. He needed to withdraw from all public support of the Communist Party.

There were suspected Mosleyites in the audience and so police had been posted at the doors to stop any trouble. 'I was nervous, keyed-up, but confident that I should speak effectively,' he wrote. 'My own subject was to be the warping of children's minds in Germany and Italy. When I got up to speak, I at once felt myself possessed of a spirit and a fluency greater than I had ever before, on such occasions, experienced. My speech, I was told afterwards by friends and the long applause it evoked, had been one of considerable power. But these congratulations were meaningless to me; for, half way through the speech, I seemed to detach myself from the man who was so eloquently holding forth, to hover above my own shoulder and with X-ray eyes to look penetratingly down. I heard myself speaking: I saw myself enjoying the exercise of power over an audience: it was in a good cause, and I could approve every word I was saying, yet to my detached self up there it was as though reality had evaporated out of the performance. When I sat down, all in one piece again, I distinctly heard above the applause a small voice saying three or four times inside my head, "It won't do. It just won't do".'[12]

He had finally arrived at the position Auden summed up in May 1937, on his return from the Spanish Civil war, in his poem 'Spain' where he questioned whether there was any real value in the political process with its twin standbys of 'the flat ephemeral pamphlet and the boring meeting'. In contrast to Auden's scornful irony, Day-Lewis gives the Queen's Hall incident the sound almost of a religious revelation. It was the point at which he acknowledged to himself that he must relinquish the political activism – including pamphlets and meetings – that had been his bedrock throughout much of the decade. This realization was a traumatic one but Day-Lewis, watching himself, knew that while the cause may in theory be right, he was the wrong person to be advancing it.

Yet there was also a sense in his description of having made some sort of breakthrough. He left Queen's Hall that night determined to follow through what he had finally accepted about the need to make a radical change. Courteous by nature, he didn't cancel any existing engagements he had already accepted on behalf of the Party or the cause, but he refused to take on any new ones. Slowly and dutifully he saw out those remaining dates, even making his first-ever overseas trip in July 1938 to Paris as chairman of the British branch of the International Association of Writers for the Defence of Culture to a weekend rally in support of the Popular Front.

MI5 faithfully recorded his attendance and highlighted his meeting with the German Communist, Egon Kisch, who planned to open a string of cultural centres around Europe to disseminate Soviet propaganda.[13] But Day-Lewis wanted nothing to do with the scheme or with anything else planned or promoted in Paris that weekend. He remained largely silent throughout. His companion, Rex Warner, put it down to his old friend's reputed nervousness around foreigners and foreign languages, but it is more likely that Day-Lewis simply had a strong sense of the futility of the whole event, or at least of his own participation in it.

Shortly after his return the Day-Lewises said their farewells to Cheltenham, packed their last few possessions and their two sons into the Hillman Minx Coupé that had been bought with money left to him by Frank Day-Lewis, and set off to take possession of Brimclose. There Day-Lewis intended to turn his back on politics and concentrate his attention on rediscovering his poetic voice.

Auden was by 1938 touring China and then the United States with Christopher Isherwood. In America he decided to remove himself from the battle in Europe and settled there. His loss of faith in 'impure poetry' was complete when in 1939 he wrote in a tribute to W. B. Yeats:

> For poetry makes nothing happen: it survives
> In the valley of its making where executives
> Would never want to tamper, flows on south
> From ranches of isolation and the busy griefs,
> Raw towns that we believe and die in; it survives,
> A way of happening, a mouth.[14]

Day-Lewis's farewell to all that had gone before in the decade came in much less emphatic form in October 1938 with the publication of his new collection of poems, *Overtures to Death,* by Jonathan Cape. Having moved to Rupert Hart-Davis's house for his apprenticeship as a novelist, Day-Lewis now took his verse there too, another break with the recent past. His reasons were pragmatic, as he had told Leonard Woolf in an affectionate December 1935 letter. He felt he had to go to a publisher with a larger sales department because he had a family to support through his writing, but added: 'your encouragement of my earlier work has meant an enormous amount to me'.[15]

The publication of *Overtures to Death* came within a month of the visit by the British Prime Minister, Neville Chamberlain, to Munich to meet the German Chancellor, Adolf Hitler, to settle the future of the Sudetenland. By agreeing to Hitler's demand to cede this German-speaking region of Czechoslovakia, Chamberlain believed he had bought 'peace in our time', but many felt he had at best postponed the inevitable war. Six months later, Hitler marched into the rump of Czechoslovakia. Meanwhile in Spain, by October 1938 the Republican cause looked doomed as Franco's Fascists made advances against beleaguered government forces.

Overtures to Death successfully caught the pessimism of the time both in its title and in its opening poem, 'Maple and Sumach', which follows the autumn glory of trees through to the sterility and death of winter.

but no such blaze
Briefly can cheer man's ashen, harsh decline;
His fall is short of pride, he bleeds within
And paler creeps to the dead end of his days.
O light's abandon and the fire-crest sky
Speak in me now for all who are to die!

Day-Lewis establishes himself at the outset as a kind of everyman, speaking through his own reflections on death in his political ambitions, and in his family with the loss of his father, to a broader concern at the lives that would be lost in the European conflict that was looming. No longer writing a single, linked sequence of poems, he groups his collection around distinct themes.

So *Overtures to Death* opens with poems whose theme is death, decay and destruction. It then searches for meaning and symbolism in such loss before retreating at the end into a series of intensely personal pieces about doubt and desire. The overall impression is of the poet – and his audience – being lost in a no man's land between the shattered idealism of the past and a dismal future.

Day-Lewis's own conviction that the time had passed for the sort of decisive, revolutionary action he had previously preached dominates the early poems like 'February 1936', 'Bombers', 'A Parting Shot' and, 'Newsreel', which takes a personal nightmare of sleepwalking into war and gives it a universal echo.

See the big guns, rising, groping, erected
To plant death in your world's soft womb.
Fire-bud, smoke-blossom, iron seed projected –
Are these exotics? They will grow nearer home.

Grow nearer home – and out of the dream-house stumbling
One night into a strangling air and the flung
Rags of children and thunder of stone niagaras tumbling,
You'll know you slept too long.

The political observation is still there, but Day-Lewis no longer offers idealistic or dogmatic solutions. He is simply resigned. Nor does he yet attribute blame, save perhaps in 'When They Have Lost' where he laments his own naïveté, and that of the 'Pylon Poets', in imagining that mechanization would overturn the European social order. He employs the same industrial imagery as before but now sees it as in ruins, leaving only a besieged human spirit to endure.

Then shall the mounting stages of oppression
Like mazed and makeshift scaffolding torn down
Reveal his unexampled, best creation –
The shape of man's necessity full-grown.
Built from their bone, I see a power-house stand
To warm men's hearts again and light the land

There are a few reminders of the upbeat style of earlier collections, as, for example, in 'Sonnet for a Political Worker' but even its 'message' is muted and reflective.

Do you not see that history's high tension
Must so be broken down to each man's need

If the world he had inhabited and sought to animate as a poet is dying, then Day-Lewis turns to the loss of his father in 'Overtures to Death' and addresses, in the manner that once he addressed enemies of the revolution or defenders of the status quo, death itself as variously an enemy, a counsellor and a friend. He seeks no comfort in the Christian beliefs of after-life of his upbringing, but in 'The Bells that Signed' grasps at something transcendent in humankind's hankering after immortality.

Broods the stone-lipped conqueror still
Abject upon his iron hill,
And lovers in the naked beds
Cry for more than maidenheads.

He offers no definition of that transcendence until he returns to it again in 'In The Heart of Contemplation' where he espouses in the face of death the philosophy of living for the moment.

You and I with lilac, lark and oak-leafed
Valley are bound together
As in the astounded clarity before death.
Nothing is innocent now but to act for life's sake.

The poem that dominates the collection, however, sees Day-Lewis in more upbeat mood. 'The Nabara' takes an episode from the Spanish Civil War, reported by the journalist G. L. Steer in his 1938 study of modern warfare, *The Tree of Gernika*, and fashions it into the most powerful narrative poem he wrote. Its epic qualities – crafted by Day-Lewis using heavy stresses, strong rhythms and alliterations, and metrical and rhetorical stratagems that recall Hopkins's 'The Wreck of The Deutschland', Tennyson's 'Charge of the Light Brigade' and behind them the alliterative, stress-based verse of Anglo-Saxon epics like 'Beowulf' and 'the Seafarer', both of which Pound had recently translated – show him reprising his success in 'A Time To Dance' as a master story-teller. The poetic tradition is invoked to promote a contemporary cause. With that developing narrative element in Day-Lewis verse, came also a purifying element in his language that took him beyond the propaganda and self-consciously modern imagery of earlier collections and towards a mature style of his own.

'The Nabara' tells of four Spanish government trawlers, manned by Basque fishermen, helping a ship full of refugees and nickel to break the Francoist forces' naval blockade. Though the odds are hopelessly stacked against them, the fishermen take on their enemies' cruiser which pounds them out of the water with its guns until only the 'Nabara' is still afloat, fighting on, though

Of the fifty-two that had sailed
In her, all were dead but fourteen – and each of these half-killed
With wounds

Such heroism against the odds inspired Day-Lewis, perhaps because it stood in marked contrast to his own failure to follow the logic of his own earlier fine words and go to fight in Spain.

> *For these I have told of, freedom was flesh and blood – a mortal*
> *Body, the gun-breech hot to its touch: yet the battle's height*
> *Raised it to love's meridian and held it awhile immortal;*

The fishermen are then his heroes, celebrated each time the poem returns to its refrain 'Men of the Basque country, the Mar Cantabrico'. Their fate is, Day-Lewis suggests without ever saying it, the fate of the Republican cause in Spain and so 'The Nabara' is both epic tragedy and elegy for the cause that so inspired so many young men and women of Day-Lewis's generation.

Its real sting, though, comes in two stanzas included at the end as a coda so their political message doesn't interfere with the poetic achievement of the narrative. Here Day-Lewis contrasts his fishermen with the politicians who vacillate in the face of the fascist threat.

> *Freedom was more than a word, more than the base coinage*
> *Of politicians who hiding behind the skirts of peace*
> *They had defiled, gave up that country to rack and carnage:*

The fishermen's example also draws from Day-Lewis in another poem, 'The Volunteer', a fierce patriotism about the battle which, for all his campaigns for a Popular Front to face down Hitler, he now appears to accept lies ahead for Europe.

> *Tell them in England, if they ask*
> *What brought us to these wars,*
> *To this plateau beneath the night's*
> *Grave manifold of stars –*
>
> *It was not fraud or foolishness,*
> *Glory, revenge, or pay:*
> *We came because our open eyes*
> *Could see no other way.*

Critical reaction to *Overtures to Death* was positive – a relief after the reception given to *Noah and The Waters*. Edwin Muir, who had sounded a warning note back then, wrote in *The Listener*: 'These poems probably contain Mr Day-Lewis's most serious work thus as a poet [showing] a preoccupation with deeper problems than Mr Day-Lewis has yet treated; the vocabulary is more natural and unforced, the intonation more immediately moving.' The *Manchester Guardian* too remarked on the absence of 'shrill hysteria' and its replacement by 'an authentic emotion controlled by an assured art'.

The collection proved Day-Lewis's most popular of the decade with the public, selling almost 1,800 copies and going into several reprints into the 1940s. It was dedicated to E. M. Forster who wrote in gratitude but despair. 'I can see no way out of our dilemma. Either we yield to the Nazis and they subdue us. Or we stand up to them, come to resemble them in the process, and are subdued to them that way. Your poems, particularly the long one ['The Nabara'] offer the possibility of heroic action, and many will be satisfied by this.'[16]

Overtures to Death ends with a series of poems first lamenting lost innocence in 'The Three Cloud-Maidens' and then in 'Spring Song', 'Night Piece' and 'Song' acknowledging frankly and occasionally saucily Day-Lewis's sexual frustration. 'Spring Song' concludes:

> *Now the bee finds the pollen,*
> *The pale boy a cure:*
> *Who care if in the sequel*
> *Cocky shall be crestfallen?*

The honeymoon period of pulling together to start a new life at Brimclose did not endure long for the Day-Lewises. In The Red Lion, Day-Lewis had met farmer John Currall whose land was on the other side of Musbury Castle mound to Brimclose. Currall and his wife, Edna Elizabeth, known to everyone as Billie, only arrived in Musbury in October 1938. They had bought the small and uneconomic Bullmore Farm with money from John's parents who had sent them away to escape censure in their native Warwickshire after Billie had become pregnant before they married.

Billie Currall was a free spirit who could not be constrained by conventional rules and sexuality morality, or by her decent but dull husband. At 33 she retained a childlike enthusiasm and adventure that drew Day-Lewis to her. He later described her as 'Harry' in his Nicholas Blake novel, *The Private Wound*. 'I see again the hour glass figure, the sloping shoulders, the rather short legs, that disturbing groove of the spine halfway hidden by her dark red hair which the moonlight has turned black ... Her lips were on the thin side; she had used a lot of lipstick on them, not too skilfully. Her eyes were greenish hazel. I realized, with a shock, that she was something of a beauty.'[17]

To reach Musbury from her farm Billie Currall had to walk past Brimclose. A friendship with Day-Lewis quickly turned into a joyous and intense affair.

> *That winter love spoke and we raised no objection, at*
> *Easter 'twas daisies all light and affectionate,*
> *June sent us crazy for natural selection – not*
> *Four traction engines could tear us apart.*
> *Autumn then coloured the map of our land,*
> *Oaks shuddered and apples came ripe to the hand,*
> *In the gap of the hills we played happily, happily,*
> *Even the moon couldn't tell us apart.*
>
> *Grave winter drew near and said, 'This will not do at all –*
> *If you continue, I fear you will rue it all.'*
> *So at the New Year we vowed to eschew it*
> *Although we both knew it would break our heart.*
> *But spring made hay of our good resolutions –*
> *Lovers, you may be as wise as Confucians,*

Yet once love betrays you he plays you and plays you
Life fishes for ever, so take it to heart.

'Jig': *Word Over All* (1943)

Day-Lewis had, in *Overtures to Death*, once more alluded to his frustration with Mary's maternal attitude towards him. When they had first met it had appealed to him, the motherless child. He still liked her to take care of him. He took for granted her unconditional love, but after a decade together he was eager for the sort of sexual excitement that Mary could not provide. Musbury was a small place and soon enough she learned of her husband's affair with their neighbour. Her hopes of a revival in their marriage with the move to Devon dashed, she steeled herself to sit out another affair, supported this time by her friend Barbara Cameron. 'Mary learned to accept Billie Currall,' Cameron later reflected. 'She knew Cecil would never be happy with the same woman for long and she was afraid of smothering him. If Cecil went for a walk she was afraid he was with Mrs Currall, if he was later than usual at the pub, she would begin to worry. She covered up so much.'[18]

Cameron's support brought her ever closer to Mary. The two took to dressing alike – on rare excursions to Cornwall or when tending their gardens together. Day-Lewis noticed the growing but platonic bond between his wife and their neighbour who was married with three children. 'Barbara and my father strongly disapproved of each other,' Sean Day-Lewis remembered. 'They had nothing in common, but I think my Pa was actually quite jealous of the Mary and Barbara attachment.'[19] He could hardly raise an objection though when he had taken to trysting with Billie at 'their tree' in a small copse on the way from Brimclose to Bullmore Farm, or on nights away in London and Oxford, stays at local inns and on at least one occasion in his single bed in the marital bedroom at Brimclose when Mary was absent.

For Day-Lewis, the affair, though longer lived than his attachment to Alison Morris, and given an added frisson by Billie Currall's working class background, was essentially the same in nature – an escape, from Mary, from his worries, and on this occasion from the shadow of war. He was taking his own advice in 'In The Heart of Contemplation' 'to act for life's sake'. Rising to the surface in him was a basic conflict about loyalty which no change of address could resolve. He craved domesticity, a throw back to his own unsettling childhood, but once he had it – in Brimclose – he couldn't bear its limitations. Moreover he experienced equal and opposite pulls to the rootedness of fidelity to, and the cosseting of, Mary, and to the thrill of new emotional and sexual experiences. Once he had one he wanted the other. The tension between the two flowed into his poetry.

Switch love, move house – you will soon be back where you started,
On the same ground,
With a replica of the old romantic phantom
That will confound
Your need for roots with a craving to be unrooted

'Ideal Home': *The Gate and Other Poems* (1962)

Billie Currall was an experienced lover and had no inhibitions about betraying her husband. Indeed she began to talk about abandoning him. Day-Lewis, though, had no intention of leaving Mary. Billie, who nicknamed her poet lover 'Po', was taking the affair more seriously. She later wrote: 'I flatter myself that I had his greatest love. No one could have had a greater or more wonderful [time] together.'[20]

In his autobiography, Day-Lewis made a brief reference, without naming Currall, to their 'shameless, half-savage, inordinate affair which taught me a great deal about women, and about myself, that I had never known'. He described the affair, half apologetically, as 'sowing my first wild oats at the age of thirty-five', thereby overlooking Alison Morris. And looking back, he condemned himself for his 'desperate irresponsibility' but put it down to the 'fatalism which had been in the air since Munich, infecting everything one did or thought with a quality of make-believe'.[21]

It was certainly part of the truth, and he did throughout the first half of 1939 aimlessly tread water, now that his political commitments had evaporated, all the time awaiting the conflict ahead. There was sailing at Lyme Regis in the small dinghy, the Avocet, that he had bought; poaching with Rex Warner; and a cricket tour around Bath with a bunch of enthusiastic amateurs assembled by the dramatist, Clifford Bax.[22] The new Nicholas Blake, The Smiler With the Knife, was serialized in the News Chronicle in the summer. Its tale of a pro-Fascist cell, the 'English Banner', led by Oswald Mosley look-alike Chilton Canteloe, and its plans to betray the whole nation to Hitler captured the public's imagination.

In April, Day-Lewis and Rex Warner followed once more in Auden's footsteps and collaborated with documentary maker Basil Wright on a film. The subject was the boat that brought coal from the north-east to London's gasworks and the two writers decided to experience their subject and its crew at first hand. It was not a success – not least because of the absence of alcohol on board to relieve the boredom. Proximity with the realities of working class life once again was a disappointment to Day-Lewis. With Wright's help, though, he worked on a script but The Colliers was overtaken by the declaration of war.

If he needed any further confirmation that he had been right to abandon his support for Stalin's Russia as a bulwark against fascism, it came on August 23, 1939 with the announcement of the Molotov-Ribbentrop Pact, joining the Soviet Union and Hitler in a non-aggression pact. Two days later the Day-Lewises were given their allocation of gas masks as Britain prepared for war. Knos had come over from Ireland but cut short her trip for fear that the Irish Sea would soon be uncrossable.

Day-Lewis was sitting on the terrace at the back of Brimclose with Mary and Sean, looking out to Beer Head, on Sunday September 3. It was, Mary recorded in her diary, a fine and sunny day. They were listening to the radio – now allowed in the house – when at 11.15 Neville Chamberlain broadcast his announcement that Britain was at war with Germany. 'Listened to Prime Minister,' Mary wrote. 'Picnic in garden. Evacuees arrive.'[23]

PART THREE

At War

Chapter 18

Where are the War Poets?

Where are the war poets? the fools inquire.
We were the prophets of a changeable morning
Who hoped for much but saw the clouds forewarning:
We were at war, while still they played with fire
And rigged the market for the ruin of man:
Spain was a death to us, Munich a mourning
'Dedicatory Stanzas': *The Georgics of Virgil*
translated by C Day-Lewis (1940)

Despite Mary Day-Lewis's fears of imminent upheaval, the first autumn and winter of the Second World War saw few changes to the routine at Musbury. 'We picked our apples,' Day-Lewis remembered, 'the rough touch of the branches as we climbed the fruit trees was reassuring in this ghostly time when war distantly oppressed us like a premonitory haunting of the mind'.[1]

Day-Lewis had an opportunity to escape the conflict and follow Auden and Isherwood to the United States. The University of Iowa offered him a teaching role with the prospect, as he described it to Stephen Spender, 'to do some pro-Ally propaganda on the side'. Day-Lewis reported he had turned it down. 'I cannot write in an unfamiliar place & feel that a close contact with the war must be good for my poetry.'[2]

He filled his time instead completing his next Nicholas Blake, *Malice in Wonderland*, the tale of a deranged murderer running riot in a holiday camp, published in the summer of 1940. He was persuaded by the BBC to try his hand once more at writing drama after the disappointment of *Noah and The Waters*. This time, though, it was a less ambitious project with no obvious political overtones. *Calling Nicholas Braithwaite*, a play for radio, featuring Nicholas Blake's private investigator, Nigel Strangeways, was broadcast in two instalments in the 'Detection Club' series in July 1940.

Day-Lewis continued to work away at his poetry in his study overlooking Brimclose's garden, but was struggling for perspective in changed circumstances. While the unchanging rural landscape of Devon was a potent source of lyrical inspiration, he also felt its whole way of life was under threat as its young men went off to fight and preparations were put in place to repel a feared German invasion on the beach at nearby Seaton. Moreover, after his public campaigning for a Popular Front to defeat the fascist threat, and his urgings of a domestic revolution to overturn an economic and political system in Britain that he continued to regard with profound distrust, Day-Lewis found himself unsure how to react to the advent of a war he had never wanted. He could not manage the jingoistic outpourings or declarations of bravery of some. It would be hypocritical given what he had written before. There was a profound disillusionment in him at how events had turned out. Yet there was also patriotism, always there in his poetry, rising to the surface in the face of an external threat.

An added pressure was that the 1930s poets were now being scrutinized for their public attitudes to the conflict. J. B. Priestley, for instance, was scathing in a BBC broadcast, early in the war, about the decision of Auden and Isherwood to stay in America when war broke out. He also criticized Day-Lewis, as a 'fire-eating poet' who was now showing himself in time of conflict as a lamb. The outburst prompted Day-Lewis to write a private letter of protest to Priestley at his use of 'the white-feather technique'. Priestley, though, replied eager to make peace, assuring Day-Lewis that the offending phrase had not been his own and that 'the little I have seen of you I have liked'.[3]

As Day-Lewis pondered on the right response to the new circumstances in which the world found itself, there were plenty of distractions in Musbury during the months of the 'Phoney War', the lull between the declaration of hostilities and the Nazi push in the spring of 1940 into first Denmark and Norway, and then France, via Holland and Belgium. He was able to spend, for example, more time than ever before with his sons. Nicholas Day-Lewis recalled that his sailing lessons at Lyme Regis ended when his father's dinghy was mothballed for the duration of the war, but not before a last trip one hot late summer afternoon. 'The wind had dropped to a whisper. He had a quick look round, just to check there weren't any other boats close by, then stripped naked and dived overboard. "Come on" he called when he'd surfaced some distance from the dinghy. I was terrified, never having swum out of my depth before, and still suffering from a certain modesty. And I was a little unsettled; I'd never seen a naked man before, not even my own father. However, I dived in too, eventually, leaving the boat to drift.'[4]

At other times Day-Lewis helped out on local farms with haymaking and indulged his anti-establishment feelings with 'a little mild poaching' with some of his new friends from the Red Lion.[5] This mainly consisted of shooting rabbits in the fields around Brimclose, sometimes with Nicholas at his side. And he continued with his passionate and very public affair with Billie Currall.

He was still travelling up occasionally by train from Axminster to London on business – mainly attending Book Society meetings, seeing his publisher and friends such as Stephen Spender. The train also brought friends down to Devon to visit. Frank Halliday was drawn by Day-Lewis's reports of a rural idyll and brought his easel and paints with him to capture the countryside. Rex Warner's arrival prompted another highly competitive game of cricket on the overgrown tennis court with his host. 'They looked to me,' Sean Day-Lewis said, 'like two bulls disputing mastery of a herd, and I became rooted where I stood, until I was noticed and told to retire to safety.'[6] Another visitor, John Garrett, a head-teacher, had to rescue a fully clothed Billie Currall from the waves on Seaton beach after she had had too much to drink while in the local pub with Day-Lewis.

When Mary's brother, Francis King, now a master at Winchester College, came to stay, he brought with him a short passage from Virgil's *Georgics*, which had recently been set in a school examination, and challenged Day-Lewis, as a classics graduate, to make a decent translation of it in verse. 'The passage excited me,' Day-Lewis later wrote, 'particularly the line about the bees holding little stones to ballast them when they flew in a gusty wind. I felt I would like to translate the whole of the *Georgics*; and soon I began work, my imagination quickened and enriched by all that I had come to love here [Musbury] ... and by a sense that this work might be a valediction to them [Musbury's working men]'.[7]

It was an undertaking well suited to his current mood and circumstances. Written in 29 BC, the four books of the *Georgics* examine in hexametric verse farming in all its aspects, from crops and trees through to cattle breeding and beekeeping. The broader theme of the work is a celebration of the countryside and of time-honoured agricultural patterns. The pastoral utopia it described had an obvious appeal to Day-Lewis who had imagined such a place before, albeit in Marxist terms. Virgil's original had also had, when written, a political dimension. His patron, Maecenas, was an adviser to Caesar Augustus and wanted the *Georgics* to support and applaud the Roman Emperor's efforts to build up farms again after a period of civil war. His celebration of the countryside became in Day-Lewis's translation a rousing hymn of classless patriotism at a time of national emergency. It was a distinct change of emphasis from his 'political' work of the 1930s. Now he was about preserving something priceless rather than overthrowing the whole system, but the *Georgics* allowed him to extricate himself from the class struggle while still using poetry publicly to identify himself sincerely with his fellow countrymen and their aspirations at a time of crisis.

Translating the *Georgics* increased in Day-Lewis that sense of rootedness in a landscape that had come with the move to Devon, and which he had never known before in his adult life. In wartime he experienced that rootedness as patriotism. 'I felt more and more,' he remembered in a lecture, *On Translating Poetry*, 'the kind of patriotism which I imagine was Virgil's – the natural piety, the heightened sense of the genius of place, the passion to praise and protect one's roots, or to put down roots somewhere while there is still time, which it takes a seismic event such as a war to reveal to most of us rootless moderns. More and more I was buoyed by a feeling that England was speaking to me through Virgil, and that the Virgil of the *Georgics* was speaking to me through the English farmers and labourers with whom I was consorting.'[8]

As Day-Lewis worked on the *Georgics*, news was arriving at Brimclose from old friends telling of their plans in the battle ahead. W. N. 'Roughie' Roughead joined the Royal Navy, Rupert Hart-Davis the Coldstream Guards. Stephen Spender's health was judged too poor to fight and so he enlisted in the volunteer fire service. Louis MacNeice worked at the BBC keeping up the nation's morale.

Day-Lewis, as was his habit, found himself in two minds as to what his own 'war work' should be, as he described on the eve of the conflict in a letter to Hugh Walpole. 'I am exercised about this war-service business. When I was last in London, Alan Ross suggested that I should ask you about the kind of jobs that writers could do best and would be asked to do. Do you know of anything particular I could apply for in this line? I am no good at languages, which I imagine puts me out of the running for a good many jobs, and for this reason I am inclined to join up in one of the ordinary war-services.'[9] Many men were coming forward to volunteer in just such a fashion, but Day-Lewis didn't. Instead he decided to seek to do his bit for the war effort at the recently established Ministry of Information.

To those, like Priestley, who remembered Day-Lewis's belligerent rhetoric of the mid-1930s, his desire to work behind a desk at the Ministry of Information may have seemed a cop-out, inspired less by a genuine concern for the country to make the best use of his talents than a wish to avoid front-line service. He had not, it was recalled, gone to Spain to follow the logic of his poetry and take up arms for the Republican cause. The same domestic responsibilities that had held him back then still existed, but now the future of Britain was at stake and many men who were signing up were leaving behind families to join the fight.

The charge of cowardice is, however, misplaced. While not as dangerous as front-line service, working at the ministry meant that Day-Lewis would be based in the capital where air raids were expected and where German bombers appeared in the skies in September 1940. Moreover, of all the 1930s poets, he had shown the greatest capacity for producing propaganda and propaganda was the business of the ministry. His talents might indeed be useful in the national cause.

However, writers and artists who had in the past been linked with communism were in the early months of the war being shunned by the ministry. In its film division, for example, the head, Joseph Ball, refused to use the talents of acclaimed pre-war documentary makers because he was suspicious of their leftist political allegiances. Day-Lewis encountered the same doubts. MI5 was still keeping a file on him as a potential communist subversive, though it by now had come round to the view that he was a naive idealist rather than a dangerous activist. They responded to an enquiry regarding Day-Lewis from the ministry in late 1940: 'while we raise no objection to his employment, we advise that the ministry should keep a close watch on him'.[10]

Initially, though, Day-Lewis seemed in no great hurry to press his services on a reluctant ministry. When his offers to work there, usually made through friends with contacts on the inside, produced no rush to welcome him with open arms, he simply carried on with life in Musbury. If he resented the fact that his past was being held against him, he turned it into a joke. In a letter to a colleague in America about the *Georgics*, he added a note: 'what I am really aiming at is being appointed Official Poet to the Royal Navy, with the rank of Rear Admiral (at least) but I doubt if the authorities will see their way to it'.[11]

He channelled his commitment to defending Britain against fascism into his translation, into his poetry, and into the local Home Guard. Launched by Anthony Eden, Secretary of State for War, in May 1940 as Local Defence Volunteers, just as the Dunkirk evacuation was getting underway, the Home Guard owed its name to Winston Churchill, who had replaced the discredited Chamberlain as Prime Minister. Local Defence Volunteers, he judged, would be 'uninspiring'. Home Guard, by contrast, was a title that attracted 1.8 million men, including Day-Lewis. 'If we were playing at soldiers', he wrote, 'I have never enjoyed a game more.'[12]

Day-Lewis enlisted at the end of May 1940 as a private in the Musbury platoon, but for all his egalitarian beliefs quickly emerged as the natural candidate for the post of company commander. It had initially gone to an aged local dignitary, Sir George Pickering. There was a bloodless coup, with Day-Lewis installed and Pickering given instead some honorary title.

Day-Lewis particularly relished the camaraderie of the platoon. It was a natural extension of the world of the pub, where he felt most comfortable, and fitted neatly with the vision of the classless rural Britain that he was committed to defending from attack.

A hill flank overlooking the Axe valley.
Among the stubble a farmer and I keep watch
For whatever may come injure our countryside –
Light-signals, parachutes, bombs or sea-invaders.
The moon looks over the hill's shoulder, and hope
Mans the old ramparts of an English night.

... The farmer and I talk for a while of invaders:
But soon we turn to crops – the annual hope,
Making of cider, prizes for ewes. Tonight
How many hearts along this war-mazed valley
Dream of a day when at peace they may work and watch
The small sufficient wonders of the countryside.

'Watching Post': *Poems in Wartime* (1941)

There was in the Musbury platoon an element of the comic amateurism later well-captured in the television series, *Dad's Army*. Day-Lewis would use his car to carry his men on night patrols in the Devon/Dorset lanes. There was a near miss when they were supplied with an old American gun, assembled it in the garden of Brimclose and sprayed bullets by accident all over the nearest field. By good fortune, no one was hurt. The same was true on New Year's Eve, 1940, when a combination of snow on the ground and mild inebriation almost led to the entire platoon marching over a cliff at Seaton Golf Links and into the English Channel. One key requirement of the commander, Day-Lewis liked to recall, was to wind up operations 15 minutes before the Red Lion closed. On the command 'Dismiss', the men and their leader would turn smartly to the right and march into the pub.

There were more serious moments too, though. On September 6 and 7, 1940, the Musbury Platoon was on 'stand-to' for 36 hours expecting a German landing on Seaton beach and a push up the Axe valley. 'We were scared that day, and if the Germans had landed, I daresay we should have scattered like chaff', Day-Lewis wrote.[13]

The Home Guard took up a great deal of his time, even if he continued to regard it with a detached amusement. 'My own writing,' he reported to Spender, 'is at a temporary standstill as I was put in command of the local Home Guard and find it a distracting business. My order of the day is "Musbury fights to the last man but one".'[14]

One person who didn't join the Musbury platoon was John Currall, Billie's husband. He had opted for the Home Guard company in nearby Uplyme. His willingness to turn a blind eye to his wife's infidelity with Day-Lewis was tested to the extreme when in September 1940, Billie gave birth to Day-Lewis's son, William. There was a crisis meeting summoned at Bullmore Farm. Mary Day-Lewis took Barbara Cameron with her for moral support. John Currall agreed to treat the child as his own. William, it was decided, was never to be told who his real father was.

Day-Lewis was let off the hook by all concerned. Mary's stoicism prevented her, even when provoked beyond normal human endurance, from confronting her husband about his flagrant infidelity. She saw it instead as one more slight to be endured in silence, blaming herself as she had grown accustomed to doing for failing to meet his wants, aware too that her own sexual orientation may lie towards women but unable, by upbringing or inclination, to follow that through into anything more than close friendship.

Billie Currall meanwhile was so enamoured of her 'Po' that she made no demands that might mean she would lose him, no doubt sensing already that he was tiring of her as he sidestepped her suggestions that they should set up home together with William. She was happy to brazen out being cold-shouldered by some of the women in the village, who sided instinctively with Mary, if it meant that their affair might continue. Even John Currall made it easy for Day-Lewis. He didn't ask for any financial support in raising the child. The only hint of his anger came when his older son, Peter, one day confronted his contemporary, Sean Day-Lewis, with the taunt that his poet father was lily-livered and was sitting out the war.[15]

The indulgence Day-Lewis was shown, however, seemed only to provoke him. At Billie's suggestion he would go walking through the country lanes with her and William, in the pram that he had bought as his contribution to the child's upbringing. One afternoon, as an act of defiance against those in the village who knew of his conduct and disapproved of it, he ostentatiously pushed the pram up the main street of Musbury. If he was staking his claim as William's father, it was to be a passing enthusiasm. There was little or no contact between natural father and son thereafter and John Currall's wish that he be left to raise the boy as his own was honoured to the letter.

Day-Lewis's remorse came, eventually, in his poetry, but his words were as much an elegy for his love for Billie, now fading fast, as they were an acknowledgement of his unspecified deceit.

Now the peak of summer's past, the sky is overcast
And the love we swore would last an age seems deceit:
Paler is the guelder since the day we first beheld her
In blush beside the elder drifting sweet, drifting sweet.

Oh quickly they fade – the sunny esplanade,
Speed-boats, wooden spades, and the dunes where we've lain:
Others will be lying amid the sea-pinks sighing
For love to be undying, and they'll sigh in vain.

'Hornpipe': *Word Over All* (1943)

One month after William's birth, Day-Lewis's *The Georgics of Virgil* was published by Jonathan Cape. It was a line for line translation, he wrote in the foreword, 'literal except where a heightening of intensity in the original seemed to justify a certain freedom of interpretation'. There was a hint of the old Day-Lewis in the evangelical political tone to some of the foreword. 'It may, indeed, happen that this war, together with the spread of electrical power, will result in a decentralization of industry and the establishment of a new rural-urban civilization working through smaller social units. The factory in the fields need not remain a dream of poets and planners.' But Day-Lewis's main concern, he wrote, had been 'to steer between the twin vulgarities of flashy colloquialism and perfunctory grandiloquence'.

Oh, too lucky for words, if only he knew his luck,
Is the countryman who far from the clash of armaments
Lives, and rewarding earth is lavish of all he needs!
No foreign dyes may stain his white fleeces, nor exotic
Spice like cinnamon spoil his olive oil for use:
But calm security and a life that will not cheat you,
Rich in its own rewards, are here: the broad ease of the farmlands,
Caves, living lakes, and combes that are cool even at midsummer,
Mooing of herds, and slumber mild in the trees' shade.

Book 2: *The Georgics of Virgil*

The help of Maurice Bowra, his old classics tutor at Wadham, was acknowledged, and the volume also contained seven dedicatory stanzas, addressed to Stephen Spender. 'If you don't like it,' he had written to Spender enclosing a draft, 'I will tear it up and try again.'[16] These stanzas give the clearest insight into Day-Lewis's developing attitude to the war. They were his first attempt to salvage something from their shared 1930s idealism once outside events had discredited it. They reflect on the sense both Day-Lewis and Spender shared of having gone from being men of the moment to outcasts.

Poets are not much in demand these days –
We're red, it seems, or cracked, or bribed, or hearty
And, if invited, apt to spoil the party
With the oblique reproach of émigrés:

The jaunty air does not disguise the angst. Where should they turn now?

181

No wonder then if, like the pelican,
We have turned inward for our iron ration,
Tapping the vein and sole reserve of passion,
Drawing from poetry's capital what we can.

Part explanation for his decision to translate the *Georgics* and part signpost for the more personal, less political poetry, in the collection he was now working on, these opening stanzas are both defiant and determined, but suggest someone still feeling his way towards a new voice. 'Poetry's capital' draws attention to Day-Lewis's growing interest in a pastoral, lyrical tradition in English poetry, which brought together his patriotism, his need to feel rooted in a landscape and his dislike of the prevailing class-based economic and social system. That tradition was best exemplified, to his mind, by the down-to-earth, scenes-from-life poetry of Thomas Hardy, whose Dorset lay so close to Brimclose. His influence was to be felt ever more strongly in Day-Lewis's poetry as the decade progressed.

The Georgics of Virgil was a great success, selling 11,000 copies. Though there was an upturn in book sales generally during the war, despite the rationing of paper, the contemporary resonances which Day-Lewis saw in the *Georgics* had been successfully conveyed to a wider audience. He had made his mark on the war effort, despite the doubts of some critics about the suitability of his material. Rebecca West, writing some years later of his translation, labelled the *Georgics* 'the East Mediterranean edition of the *Farmers' Weekly* ... [and] two thousand years out of date'.[17]

The foreword to *The Georgics of Virgil* had hinted that Day-Lewis was once more at work on his own poetry and two months later a first taste emerged with the publication by Jonathan Cape of *Poems in Wartime*, eleven new poems in a limited edition 20-page booklet, with a design by John Piper[18] on the front and title page. It contained two poems charting the course of Day-Lewis's affair with Billie Currall, 'Jig' and 'Hornpipe', and his reflections on service in the Home Guard, 'The Watching Post' and 'The Stand-To'. These celebrated the profound simplicities and everyday heroism in the lives of the farm labourers in his platoon. For the first time, though, Day-Lewis was seeing them as individuals rather than as the romanticized homogenous working class featured in his earlier works – 'not quaint "characters", and still less the "toiling masses" ... of Party slogans', he reflected.[19]

I write this verse to record the men who have watched with me –
Spot who is good at darts, Squibby at repartee,
Mark and Cyril, the dead shots, Ralph with a ploughman's gait,
Gibson, Harris and Long, old hands for the barricade,
Whiller the lorry-driver, Francis and Rattlesnake,
Fred and Charl and Stan – these nights I have lain awake
And thought of my thirty men and the autumn wind that blows
The apples down too early and shatters the autumn rose.

'The Stand-To': *Poems in Wartime* (1941)

There is an almost Shakespearian tone to it, but the focus on living things and living people most obviously carried with it some true-caught echo of Thomas

The young Cecil, aged seven, with his father, the Revd Frank Day-Lewis, on holiday at Sheringham in 1911 (above), and (below), the rectory at Monart, Co. Wexford, home of his maternal uncle the Revd William Squires and for Day-Lewis 'a land of milk and honey'.

A solitary child sailing his boat on Sheringham beach (above).
(Left) Outside the vicarage at Edwinstowe in Nottinghamshire where watching an agricultural village turn into a coal-mining town encouraged the growth of his left-wing politics.

(Above) At the christening of his first son, Sean, in 1931, at East Quantoxhead Day-Lewis (far left) is joined by (from left to right) H.R. King, Charles King, Mamie Day-Lewis, Constance King, holding Sean, and Frank Day-Lewis. (Below left) Box Cottage in Cheltenham, the first home the Day-Lewises owned, 'a sequestered, escapist kind of house for one of the new come-down-out-of-that-ivory-tower poets'. (Below right) with Mary on a holiday in north Norfolk.

(Left above and below): Brimclose in Musbury, Devon, where in 1938 Day-Lewis moved his family 'noiselessly slipping the painter' of his communist involvements. (Below left) Billie Currall with Day-Lewis's son, William (1940–1983) who never knew his father. (Below right) Day-Lewis pulling his 'King Edward Potato Face' to entertain the Fenby children.

(Above) Lawrence Gowing's 1946 portrait of Day-Lewis, commissioned by Rosamond Lehmann (Below) Day-Lewis in the 1940s – 'he was like a Greek Apollo,' wrote Rebecca West. 'The effect was so splendid that other men were apt to spend time explaining that they did not know why but they could not stand him'.

(Above) With Rosamond Lehmann in 1943 (Below left) With Mary in Oxford on VE Day in 1945 (Below right) With his trademark bow-tie.

(Above) The only photograph of the 'poets of the 1930s' together – W.H. Auden, Day-Lewis and Stephen Spender in Venice in 1949.
(Left) With Jill Balcon at Dartington Hall in the 1950s. (Below left) Day-Lewis and his son, Daniel in 1963 (Below right) With Jill, Tamasin and Daniel on his appointment as Poet Laureate in 1968.

(Above) At Litton Cheney with Jill; (below) the Poet Laureate in his study at Crooms Hill.

Hardy. As well as its attitudes, the poem also recalls Hardy in its rhythms, and vocabulary. The insistent present tense of much of Day-Lewis's 1930s poetry gives way to other timescales.

Overall the collection also contains reflections, neither celebratory, nor doom-laden, but realistic, almost brutal, on the broader progress of the war. 'The Dead' guiltily contrasts the pre-war years of victims of the blitz with those of Day-Lewis. More reminiscent of his 1930s verse in seeing individuals as a mass, it does not draw back from making its political point about the powerlessness and courage of all victims of the current war.

> Still, they have made us eat
> Our knowing words, who rose and paid
> The bill for the whole party with their uncounted courage.
> And if they chose the dearer consolations
> Of living – the bar, the dog-race, the discreet
> Establishment – and let Karl Marx and Freud go hang,
> Now they are dead, who can dispute their choice?
> Not I, not even Fate.

As well as the present, Day-Lewis is also catapulted back to childhood by a combination of his change of home, the death of his father and the advent of war. Early memories and regrets resurface in 'The Innocent' and 'One and One'. And he is also straining, unsuccessfully, to look forward, in 'The Poet', staring out at the outline of the world from his garden at Brimclose at night.

> Tonight the moon's at the full.
> Full moon's the time for murder.
> But I look at the clouds that hide her –
> The bay below me is dull,
> An unreflecting glass –
> And chafe for the clouds to pass,
> And wish she suddenly might
> Blaze down at me so I shiver
> Into a twelve-branched river
> Of visionary light.

Poems in Wartime was a critical triumph, Day-Lewis's insistence that he still had something relevant to say, albeit with a changing, less rhetorical, less self-conscious, and purified voice. If readers required evidence of the change, they needed only to look by dint of contrast at a collection of Selected Poems, taken from his earlier works, brought out in the same month by John Lehmann as the second title in his New Hogarth Library series.

E. M. Forster wrote to say that Poems in Wartime 'seemed to me the best you have done ... They [the poems] were about things I could focus: particularly 'The Watching Post' and 'The Stand-To'. Those insensitive abstractions – even the Freedom I goad myself to write about occasionally – seem so dim beside the attempt of yourself and your neighbours to prevent strangers ... from coming down on top of you'.[20]

In the *New Statesman*, the novelist Rosamond Lehmann was equally enthu-siastic, claiming that Day-Lewis 'is a writer with a profound and happy experience of love'. Her words inspired Day-Lewis, who had met her several times in the 1930s, to send her a card, inviting her to dinner.

Chapter 19

The Magic Answer

You were the magic answer, the sprite fire-fingered who came
To lighten my heart, my house, my heirlooms; you are the wax
That melts at my touch and still supports my prodigal flame:
'The Lighted House': *Word Over All* (1943)

Rosamond Lehmann and C Day-Lewis had dinner sometime during May 1941. Neither recorded the date. Later Day-Lewis would claim that their first meeting had been by accident during an air raid in a shelter. It gave a romantic air to the story. Lehmann, though, was more precise and left a detailed account of the dinner and its aftermath.

However it happened, the chemistry between them was instant. Within days she had moved into a small service flat next to where he was staying during his trips up to London from Musbury. Soon afterwards they became lovers.

Lehmann was three years older than Day-Lewis. She had grown up with her mother and the MP father she adored in an affluent home, next to the Thames in Buckinghamshire. One sister, Beatrix, was a celebrated actress.[1] Her brother, John, was well known to Day-Lewis through his work at the Hogarth Press. Educated at home, Rosamond went up to Cambridge and in 1927 published her first novel, *Dusty Answer*. In the *Sunday Times* the critic Alfred Noyes wrote: 'It is the kind of novel that might have been written by Keats if Keats had been a young novelist of today.' It was a best seller, and in the 1930s *Invitation to the Waltz* and *The Weather on The Streets* increased Lehmann's critical and popular acclaim.

Her private life was less blessed. Her first marriage to old Etonian Leslie Runciman had been brief and unhappy. Her second, to the charismatic communist heir to a shipping fortune, Wogan Philipps,[2] had made her one half of a prominent couple at the heart of Bloomsbury society. They had two children but that marriage, too, had collapsed amid Philipps's infidelity and his absence fighting in the Spanish Civil War. Subsequently Lehmann had embarked on an affair with the left-wing writer and academic, Goronwy Rees. When she met Day-Lewis that relationship had also broken up, denting her self-confidence and her hitherto immoveable trust in romantic love just as she entered her forties.

Lehmann was famed for her looks. Stephen Spender, who had first met her in 1929, hailed her as 'one of the most beautiful women of her generation. Tall, and holding herself with a sense of her presence ... she had almond-shaped eyes, a firm mouth which contradicted the impression of uncontrolled spontaneity given by her cheeks, which often blushed'.[3] As she turned 40 the month before she met Day-Lewis for dinner, Lehmann's hair had started to go white, often tinted an ultra-violet colour, but with her youthful skin and carefully made-up cheeks she was, her biographer Selina Hastings wrote, 'more striking than ever. Her girlish figure had filled out to a full-bosomed shapeliness [and] ... she exerted a potent attraction'. She was used, Hastings said, to men falling at her feet, even if they had all so far ultimately disappointed her.[4]

Day-Lewis was no less striking. Tall, slender, his eyes were penetrating and Aegean-blue. With thick fair hair and an increasingly worn but ever more handsome face, attractively lined and with the scar on his chin where a large carbuncle had been removed when he was a schoolboy, he retained his dandy-ish tendencies in dress. They served to emphasize his vocation as a poet. 'He had the advantage,' Rebecca West, no great admirer of his work, wrote of him, 'of a remarkable equipment. He was like a Greek Apollo, with some irregularities set in to make him look not too bright and good for human nature's daily food. The effect was so splendid that other men were apt to spend time explaining that they did not know why, but they could not stand him.' His 'beautiful speaking voice', she said, complemented by a 'beautiful singing voice' and 'vanity but no egotism' completed a dazzling picture.[5]

Lehmann and Day-Lewis had met before 1941. In 1936 they were both at a party at Elizabeth Bowen's London home in Regent's Park. Like Bowen, Lehmann was then invited down to address the Cheltenham Literary Society and stayed the night at Box Cottage. Her main memory of the occasion was helping Mary to make the beds and feed Sean and Nicholas their breakfast the next morning, Day-Lewis having already left for school. Though in the early days of their romance, she recalled, he had told her he had been in love with her from afar for years, she had detected no sign of it on this occasion. Mary, Lehmann judged, was 'obviously terribly nice, a typical English schoolmaster's wife ... One couldn't see a sign of her ever having been even pretty'.[6]

Lehmann had been another of the speakers from the platform at the Queen's Hall in June 1938 when Day-Lewis had finally abandoned his political activities on behalf of communism. Not by instinct a political creature, she had been drawn in to left-wing circles by first Philipps and then Rees. And she had also attended soon afterwards with Rees the Paris rally in support of a Popular Front that had constituted Day-Lewis's first taste of overseas travel.

Over that initial dinner, Lehmann remembered pouring out her troubles – her failed relationships, her worries over her children (Hugo, 11 and Sally, 6), her grief over the suicide that Easter of her friend, Virginia Woolf, and the indignity of having to pack up her marital home and move back in with her widowed mother who made no attempt to disguise her distaste for a daughter who was soon to be divorced for a second time. Day-Lewis's response, Lehmann said, was like balm. 'You had better come and live with me', she reported him as saying.[7] Nothing could be more alluring to her. Within days she took him up on his offer.

Since the publication of *Poems in Wartime*, Day-Lewis had redoubled his efforts to find a role at the Ministry of Information. In January 1941 he gave a hint of why he was suddenly in a hurry in a letter to Frank Halliday. 'There is a chance I may be getting a job in London shortly: I don't know if I really want it, but it would keep me out of the army.'[8] Since the outbreak of war all men aged between 18 and 40 were liable for call-up. The initial rush of volunteers had enabled the reluctant to avoid joining up, but that first wave had now slowed. With new battlefronts opening up in early 1941 in North Africa, there was talk of extending the age limit for compulsory service to 51 (finally agreed by the end of the year). Day-Lewis, at 37, knew that his membership of the Musbury Home Guard would no longer be deemed a sufficient contribution to the war effort.

On January 10 he left a snowbound Devon to travel up to London for a job interview with the Ministry of Information's Film Division but afterwards heard nothing. Documents in his MI5 file show that his communist affiliations were the most likely stumbling block.[9]

The pressure on Day-Lewis increased in late February when he was called to Exeter for an army medical examination, the first stage of conscription. He was recommended for service in the Armoured Corps. The prospect of seeing active service in a tank did nothing for his morale. 'Do you know any one with any influence at the War Office who could get me into something I could be some good at?' he wrote in panic to Rupert Hart-Davis.[10]

Finally in March he was summoned back to the Ministry of Information and offered a temporary job in the Publications' Division at £900 a year, but no sooner had he arrived than he received call-up papers for the army. He was to join the Royal Corps of Signals in Yorkshire. Suspecting that the powers-that-be still had it in mind to punish him for his pre-war enthusiasms, he began a rearguard action at the Ministry to have his post made permanent.

If there was indeed a plot in the War Office to give Day-Lewis a nasty shock – and the MI5 file gives no hint of this – it succeeded. In early April he had to report to Catterick Barracks where, for 24 hours, he faced what to him was the disagreeable prospect of joining the ranks. The camaraderie that he had so enjoyed in the Red Lion quickly lost its appeal when he faced spending weeks and months, not a few hours, with working men.

Then equally suddenly he was granted a reprieve and sent back to London to the ministry, though his eventual fate was left hanging in the balance. The experience was recalled in his poem, 'The Misfit' where Day-Lewis distances himself from his own feelings of disorientation at Catterick by observing them instead in a farm labourer, an idealized version of one of his drinking pals from Musbury, a character from the 'deep combes', ill-at-ease in his new military surroundings.

One stood out from the maul
Who least of them all
Looked metal for killing or meat for the butchery blade.

'The Misfit': *Poems 1943–1947* (1948)

In London Day-Lewis had borrowed W. N. Roughead's flat at 78 Buckingham Gate. In between air raids as the Luftwaffe made a concerted attempt in April and May of 1941 to flatten London, he set about impressing his superiors at the ministry so much that they would keep him on permanently.

It was into the same block that Lehmann moved soon after their dinner. Her willingness to do so quickly indicates something of her powerful attraction to Day-Lewis, as well as her vulnerability and craving for love. 'You can see as much or as little of me as you want,' she reported Day-Lewis as telling her. They had dinner a couple of times. After the second encounter, she recalled, 'I stayed the night with him, and from then was the beginning of a tremendous affair . . . I was out of black despair into happiness. He was just madly, madly, madly in love with me.'[11]

Lehmann was prone, her friends describe, to believing all sorts of men were 'madly, madly, madly' in love with her. Yet while her estimation, made years after the event, should be taken with caution, the speed with which the affair was moving suggests that Day-Lewis too was swept up in it. In Musbury he had tired, as Mary trusted he would, of Billie Currall, especially after their child was born. In Lehmann, though, Day-Lewis now found a mistress who was more his social, intellectual and literary equal. In some ways she was indeed his better. While he had hitherto resolutely resisted metropolitan literary life in the capital, and retained a provincial nervousness when among his peers, or at big parties, Lehmann was at her ease at the heart of a circuit of well-known international writers and artists who held her novels in the highest esteem. She spoke French fluently, had travelled and possessed, in public at least, a core confidence in her ability (and her beauty) that Day-Lewis still lacked.

Starting an affair with her was an altogether different proposition from the dalliances with the wives of neighbours and friends. These, he always knew, had no real future. They did not pose a threat to his ongoing commitment to Mary, however frustrating he increasingly found his wife. Next to the selfless, almost maternal adoration and indulgence Mary showed him, there was something very grown-up and demanding about Lehmann's love. If Mary had, as Day-Lewis wrote, allowed him to develop slowly through a stage of delayed adolescence, even turning a blind eye and smoothing things over when he fathered a child out of wedlock, he was now embarking, with Lehmann, on the sort of adult, mutual and passionate romantic love that he had hitherto only imagined in his poetry.

In 'The Lighted House' he described the love that drew two damaged people together.

One night they saw the big house, some time untenanted
But for its hand-to-mouth recluse, room after room
Light up, as when Primavera herself has spirited
A procession of crocuses out of their winter tomb.

Revels unearthly are going forward, one did remark –
He has conjured up a thing of air or fire for his crazed delight:
Another said, It is only a traveller lost in the dark
He welcomes for mercy's sake. Each, in a way, was right.

You were the magic answer, the sprite fire-fingered who came
To lighten my heart, my house, my heirlooms; you are the wax
That melts at my touch and still supports my prodigal flame:

But you were also the dead-beat traveller out of the storm
Returned to yourself by almost obliterated tracks,
Peeling off fear after fear, revealing love's true form

'The Lighted House': *Word Over All* (1943)

The traveller was a familiar and partly autobiographical figure in Day-Lewis's poetry, appearing in both *Transitional Poem* and *The Magnetic Mountain*. Falling in love with Lehmann was the beginning of a new stage in Day-Lewis's journey. In the live-for-the-moment atmosphere engendered by the constant threat of death in the blitz, their attachment developed quickly. 'When you look at me in public with your loving look,' he wrote in an undated letter in the early stages of their romance, 'my heart swells up & I take off into the upper air.' He continued: 'I suddenly felt the soft summer air of London & it was like your hands touching me & I thought I must live with my darling this autumn, this time is so short, every day a minute without her is something lost irretrievably, *nothing* can make up for it.'[12]

His weekend trips down to Musbury became less frequent. Until the school summer holidays when Rosamond returned to her mother's house to be with her children, the couple spent as much time together as possible. Day-Lewis visited and charmed Alice Lehmann, despite her misgivings about her daughter's relationships. He also entranced six-year-old Sally, for whom he was soon to become a father substitute. Hugo, though, kept his distance.

Their mother was ecstatic. 'This time a year ago,' she wrote of her new love affair to her friend, George 'Dadie' Rylands, Dean of King's College, Cambridge and theatrical director, 'I was the unhappiest of women – now I am one of the most fortunate. And oh! I do appreciate it, savour every moment of it, and shall never get used to it & take it for granted. It is like a miracle. It is not only being given back my life – it is being given a thousand times more than I ever dreamed possible ... I don't see what the future will be – but I don't think it can go wrong through lack of love or trust and it is the calamities that come from "no love" that are the only unbearable ones.'[13]

After spending some of the summer with his wife and children in Musbury, avoiding Sunday lunches at Barbara Cameron's when both women would pool their meat coupons to provide a decent meal for their children, Day-Lewis returned to London in September and rented with Lehmann 31 Gordon Place, off Kensington Church Street, which she later described as 'the most romantic of London oases in my memory – despite the bombs'.[14]

Lehmann's range of high-powered contacts came in useful in regard of Day-Lewis's still tenuous grip on a post at the Ministry of Information. The junior minister in the department, under Duff Cooper, was Harold Nicolson, husband of the writer Vita Sackville-West and a National Labour MP. He was also a friend of Lehmann. Determined that her new love should not be taken away from her by military call-up, she met Nicolson, impressed upon him Day-Lewis's value to the nation as a writer and editor and, by her own account, left having inspired her host to send at once a letter putting an end to any suggestion that Day-Lewis should be called up to the front line.

Another to claim credit for Day-Lewis's posting at the ministry becoming permanent was E. M. Forster. Writing to Christopher Isherwood in the United States in July 1942, he recounted meeting Day-Lewis. 'He wants to remain there, doing important work and its seems just possible I might be able to pull a string over this.'[15]

Based in two new stone buildings in Bloomsbury, erected as the Senate House and the Institute of Education for London University but taken over for the duration for war use, the Ministry of Information was regarded by many as a waste of time next to the urgent business of repelling invaders from Britain's shores. J. M. Richards, the architectural critic and writer, was another editor who worked in the Publications' Division. It was, he recalled, 'in many ways agreeably amateurish in contrast to the inherited propriety of permanent government departments'[16] but full of characters. Graham Greene was there at the start of the war. John Betjeman was in the Films Division, Osbert Lancaster[17] in 'Intelligence', and the art historian Kenneth Clark[18] as Controller of Home Publicity. Even Charles Fenby was set to join when he was diverted by the offer of a senior position on the *Picture Post*. V. S. Pritchett, who did some writing for the MOI, described it as 'like a lunatic asylum, a life of taxis, telephones and everyone's office like a street corner with people coming in and out and shouting'.[19]

In charge of publications was Robert Fraser, an Australian-born journalist, brought in from Fleet Street. After the war, he went on to become the first head of the Independent Television Authority. Under him a group of editors worked away to produce booklets and pamphlets recording the progress of the war and its successes. No authors were credited and their efforts were sold by His Majesty's Stationery Office at a low cover price to satisfy the public's seemingly insatiable demand for reading matter in the war years. Unlike other publishers, the Stationery Office was not constrained by wartime rationing of paper.

Day-Lewis was responsible for titles such as *The Battle of Britain* and *Bomber Command*, both of which were accounts of history being made rather than patriotic propaganda. In total he edited around 40 ministry publications. He was, J. M. Richards remembered, 'a delightful colleague. We found that we shared the same sense of the absurdity of much that went on and of many of the people in high places in our unwieldy bureaucratic establishment ... I liked sending files on complicated journeys, inscribing queries on the margins of documents, then writing on the file-cover "Deputy Director please comment", followed by a list of people in different departments to whom it should go before it finished up in Registry. Minuting one's fellow civil servants and circulating files could, I realized, become easily and agreeably a full-time occupation. For some it was. Day-Lewis observed of one industrious department that its motto ought to be "A Minute Every Second".'[20]

Committed and hard working, Day-Lewis retained a degree of detachment. Some of his colleagues found him austere and a few nicknamed him 'the gloomy poet'.[21] Certainly the ministry did not prove a source of much inspiration for his poetry, though his first post-war Nicholas Blake adventure, *Minute for Murder*, drew on his experiences there. And poetry remained Day-Lewis's principal purpose in life. He was filling what spare time he had expanding *Poems in Wartime* into a longer collection of reflections on the changed circumstances in which he was living.

In theory the ministry gave him plenty of free time. Its routine was regular. Start at 9.30, lunch in a communal refectory, leave at six, Monday to Friday. Some nights though the air raids were so bad that he would sleep in bunk beds in the basement of the office building. Occasionally he attended a film club set up for employees. Outside the workplace, there were many distractions. Old friends would pass through London. When he and Roughie, home on leave from the Navy, had dinner at the Café Royal, 'the bombs came down like hail'.[22] In April 1941, three of the four constituent parts of MacSpaunday assembled for the marriage of Stephen Spender to the concert pianist Natasha Litvin. Only Auden was absent.

Day-Lewis had collaborated with L. A. G. Strong in editing *New Anthology of Modern Verse*, published by Methuen in July 1941. Yeats and Hardy were well represented, illustrating some of Day-Lewis's own key influences. Five Auden poems were included and five of Day-Lewis's own. In October, there was another Nicholas Blake, *The Case of the Abominable Snowman*, in which Nigel Strangeways was called in to investigate after a dead body was found hidden inside a children's snowman.

By the end of 1941, Day-Lewis was settling uneasily into his double life. Lehmann had reclaimed from her tenants Diamond Cottage in the Berkshire Downs only a few miles from her former marital home at Ipsden. When her children were at school she would join Day-Lewis in London for a couple of days each week. At weekends he would come to the cottage where, as a couple, he and Lehmann would entertain friends from London with her accompanying his renditions of the Tom Moore songs of his Monart childhood on the piano. 'I felt completely married to him,' Lehmann would later say, 'as he did to me.'[23]

She misrepresented his feelings. He was undoubtedly in love with her. 'Oh sweetie, I do wish you were here,' he wrote longingly to her during one of his rare trips to Musbury. 'We would sit in two chairs & read books, & every now & then we'd both look up at the same moment & gaze at each other as if we couldn't believe our own eyes.'[24] In another letter, he concluded: 'I bless the hour we came together. I am so utterly happy that I cannot yet begin to take the future seriously.'[25] And in a letter from the autumn of 1941, written after he had made a brief trip to Dublin to deliver a lecture, he rhapsodized. 'You have pushed out the boundaries of my life in so many directions, I feel a new man – really, reborn, like you feel.'[26]

He continued, however, in reply to a conversation: 'No my darling it isn't "better as it is". It would be better if we were married or living with each other all the time. But we can't. So we've got to make do with what we have & bear the pain of not having more.'[27] Lehmann must have been reluctant to take on board such a message, for he was soon issuing warnings to her about the limits of what he could give her. 'Rosamond, my love,' he wrote, 'don't get obsessed by me, will you? – I mean, I couldn't bear to feel that you hadn't room to move, particularly to write, because I occupied too much of you: I want you to flower as a writer because of our love.'[28] Both in fact had found renewed energy for their writing in the early days of their relationship.

Day-Lewis was anxious not to mislead Lehmann about his own character and his other responsibilities in Musbury. In the same letter as he wrote of his heart swelling up at her glance, he added: 'darling sweet, you will be patient with me, won't you, when I'm distant, awkward, churlish etc. etc. etc. It is a real agony for me sometimes, when I want to give you everything & be everything to you, to know that I can't, that to promise anything more might be a betrayal all around – & certainly would be side-stepping a difficulty which we must keep on facing squarely.'[29]

Mary was apparently unaware of Lehmann's existence in her husband's life. Day-Lewis blamed pressure of work at the ministry for only managing three weekends at Musbury in the first six months of 1942. Their principal means of communication was by letter with Day-Lewis always writing on Ministry paper and Mary addressing her newsy replies there. She would very occasionally come up to London for a day or two to see him, have dinner and see a show. She was by nature a countrywoman and was ill at ease in the city which only seemed to exaggerate the distance between them. They would stay at Charles Fenby's flat because, Day-Lewis explained, his digs were too squalid.

In his poetry of the 1930s a constant theme had been Day-Lewis's strong sense of responsibility for the inequalities of society. At the start of the 1940s, that same burden of responsibility became focused on the two women in his life. A measure of his guilt can be seen in a contemporary poem.

> Nothing so sharply reminds a man he is mortal
> As leaving a place
> In a winter morning's dark, the air on his face
> Unkind as the touch of sweating metal:
> Simple goodbyes to children or friends become
> A felon's numb
> Farewell, and love that was a warm, a meeting place –
> Love is suicide's grave under the nettles.
>
> 'Departure in The Dark': Word Over All (1943)

Lehmann had a simple solution. He should divorce Mary and marry her once her own divorce from Philipps came through. Day-Lewis, though, had already ruled out taking any such step in his letters to Lehmann. Though he recognized that in many ways he had simply outgrown Mary, he could not get beyond that sense of a continuing obligation to her. There was more to it, though. Having an adult relationship of equals with a beautiful, talented passionate woman like

Lehmann was a revelation and was inspiring poems which were to become amongst his most celebrated. Yet at the same time, a part of him remained the boy who had lost his mother at four and craved Mary's mothering. When he was ill, it was to Brimclose he unthinkingly retired for pampering and sympathy. And where Mary would give him as much freedom as he wanted, without uttering a single word of demand or reproach, Rosamond's intensity could occasionally be as suffocating as it was heady for one who had formed the habit of observing as much as participating in the domestic life around him.

In pursuit of what seemed to her the logical step of marrying Day-Lewis, Lehmann could be demanding and angry when refused. 'Darling little love,' he wrote after a row in another undated letter on Ministry notepaper, 'I shivered uncontrollably all the way to London, in a hot compartment & have only just stopped. But not stopped saying to myself – so you have failed her again, so you have failed her again, she doesn't often cry for help and whenever she does you fail her. Sweet, the reason I get so quickly infected by your despair is that I know I can do nothing to eradicate the cause: if I am angry, it is with my own helplessness, with the whole situation.'[30]

One part of him clearly wanted to make the commitment Lehmann was seeking, but he did not mislead her about his ability to do it. As well as his responsibility for Mary, there were his anxieties about the effect any formal separation from her would have on his two sons, ten and seven. 'You were obviously a "guilt figure" to a strong, perhaps morbid degree in his mind,' Lehmann later candidly told an adult Sean Day-Lewis. 'He talked a great deal about you when we were first together. Your sleepwalking was, or had been, a source of great worry to him. He took it as a sign that you were anxious or "disturbed" in early childhood.'[31]

Such concerns, Lehmann reported, could cause her lover to withdraw when under stress, either into one of his black moods of depression, or simply a form of emotional absence. Her own divorce was still some time off. It did not finally come through until December of 1943 and so for now the immediate pressure to resolve his divided life could usually be put to one side.

There were many happy times for the couple. Day-Lewis established himself on Lehmann's arm as part of the literary circuit in London. He also found himself in greater demand at events and readings. The BBC called on him a good deal as a radio presenter on subjects as diverse as the Home Guard and Madame Curie. He was a popular reader of others' poetry on *And So To Bed*, a weekly compilation of verse produced by Edward Sackville-West. The writer, James Lees-Milne,[32] who heard Day-Lewis read stanzas from *Adonais* to an audience in Belgrave Square later in the decade, praised his 'measured, rhythmical voice, emotional enough and yet so firm that I don't remember being more moved by a poetry reading in my life'.[33]

'Cecil's voice,' judged Hallam Tennyson, another radio producer who made much use of it, 'was very, very fine. He could read poets such as Hardy or Wordsworth perfectly. He had that matter-of-fact tone but infused it with poetic sensibility, which was exactly what was needed to reveal the insights and beauties of what he was reading. He read not as an actor but as a poet. He was very natural. He never put on a voice. The Irish tone was in there but a Protestant Irish tone with none of the howl of emotional suppression you often get in Celtic voices. With Cecil there was not a sense of anything suppressed, no emotional quality trying to get out. It was melodious, warm and light.'[34]

At the Ministry of Information the daily routine in the Publications' Division had been considerably enlivened by the arrival of Laurie Lee, a young writer and poet from Gloucestershire who had been in Spain during the Civil War.[35] He had met Lehmann in 1941 through her brother John and had in turn been introduced to Day-Lewis. He became the first friend the couple had made together. Everyone else they knew had a connection with their 'other' lives. Later the same year the two men were featured in a photoshoot for *Lilliput* magazine by Bill Brandt entitled 'Poets of Democracy'. It was, Lee wrote, 'a gallery of hideous morons and gargoyles. Dylan Thomas looks sick in a pub, Day-Lewis screws horrible faces at a newspaper, MacNeice scouls like a greasy witch, Spender is flayed by an overhanging lamp.'[36]

Soon Lee was a regular visitor to Diamond Cottage, his childlike antics delighting Lehmann's children and his violin playing adding another note to the musical soirées. He was going through an unhappy love affair and soon Lehmann began confiding in him. 'I was a sort of page-in-waiting,' he later remarked, 'attendant on her great romance'.[37]

Day-Lewis, too, began to talk to him about both his poetry and his own confused emotions. Often the two were as one. So when he showed him a draft he had been working on of what was to become 'O Dreams, O Destinations', Lee was made aware of the detachment which ran alongside Day-Lewis's clear and evident love for Lehmann.

> But look, the old illusion still returns,
> Walking a field-path where the succory burns
> Like a summer's eye, blue lustre-drops of noon,
> And the heart follows it and freshly yearns:
> Yearns to the sighing distances beyond
> Each height of happiness, the vista drowned
> In gold-dust haze, and dreams itself immune
> From change and night to which all else is bound.
>
> 'O Dreams, O Destinations': *Word Over All* (1943)

Chapter 20

The Maturing Field

Our words like poppies love the maturing field,
    But form no harvest:
May lighten the innocent's pang, or paint the dreams
    Where guilt is unharnessed
            'Word Over All': *Word Over All* (1943)

Though he had distanced himself from communism since his move to Musbury in 1938, Day-Lewis did not formally break with the party. Its classless ideals and its ambition to overthrow the economic system in Britain continued to appeal to his sense of social responsibility. War, however, masked many of the inequalities that had so enraged Day-Lewis during the days of high unemployment and abject poverty in the 1930s. And in May 1941, Churchill's coalition government had commissioned Sir William Beveridge, former director of the London School of Economics, to produce a report on reforming the social security system to ensure that the destitution seen in the pre-war decade was never repeated. Meanwhile, the drive for victory was uniting all sections of the population in a common and popular cause.

Day-Lewis's reluctance publicly to renounce either his Communist Party ties or to reject the communist-influenced ideals of his 1930s poetry had already interfered with his efforts to join the Ministry of Information. It was also to play havoc with his attempts later to get a visa to travel to the United States,[1] but he was not by nature inclined to grand gestures or denunciations. He did not, for instance, unlike others among the 1930s poets, try subsequently to rewrite or disown some of his best-known works from the period. There were a few poems that he judged with hindsight so ill-advised that he preferred never to see them published again, but mostly he allowed what had already appeared to stand, for better or worse. And, though he came to see the naïveté of his political enthusiasms of the 1930s, he retained an amused affection for the period, referring to it in a 1949 letter to Dadie Rylands as 'that dear old golden age'.[2]

His political views tended to develop gradually, one position being refined into another, rather than proceeding by a series of dramatic conversions and public *mea culpas* like Stephen Spender's contribution to Richard Crossman's 1949 collection of essays by writers who were once attracted to communism, *The God That Failed*.[3] Any changes of heart that Day-Lewis experienced he expressed in his poetry which was both his confidant and his sounding board.

The severing of Day-Lewis's relationship with the Communist Party seems to have taken place in 1940. Emile Burns, a senior official, reported to an MI5 informant on January 8, 1943 a conversation he had had with Beatrix Lehmann, Rosamond's sister. 'Day-Lewis has really dropped out of the party ... He was worried about the Finnish business. That was the final thing.'[4]

Stalin's treatment of Russia's small Baltic neighbour at the outset of the Second World War disillusioned many who, in spite of a growing body of evidence of its failings, had continued to defend Soviet communism, if not its leader. One such damning indictment had come from Arthur Koestler[5] in his acclaimed 1940 novel, *Darkness at Noon*, an account of the 1930s show trials. At the same time as Koestler's book was published, Stalin was busy bullying the Finnish government into ceding territory to him and allowing his forces free access to its ports and air space. The Finns rejected this virtual annexation and, against overwhelming odds, fought a rearguard campaign to frustrate the Red Army through the winter and spring of 1939–40 before finally being beaten into signing a humiliating armistice. Even the pro-Soviet *New International* despaired of Stalin's antics in a February 1940 editorial. 'By his procedure in Finland, Stalin has still further alienated the sympathy of the workers and oppressed peoples for the Soviet Union and thus further undermined its real defence.'

Day-Lewis shared the distaste. His belief in a public role for poetry remained – in contrast to Auden who had by now renounced such an ambition – but henceforth it would be pursued not through party politics but rather as a free, though left-leaning, agent. In May 1943 that ongoing commitment took on a new form when he joined forces with Spender and his wife, Natasha, Peggy Ashcroft,[6] Edith Evans[7] and John Laurie,[8] as well as Dadie Rylands and the pianist Angus Morrison, to found the Apollo Society. The aim was, according to its organizer Lucy Hoare, 'to revive the neglected art of reading poetry', often accompanied in 'sisterly union' with music. The society was, Hoare wrote, 'a modern version of the minstrel band', sending out its performers all over the country for a flat fee (£5 in London, £10 everywhere else) to entertain audiences with readings of groups of poems, interlaced with music in the rough proportions of two to one.[9] Day-Lewis's reputation as a performer of his own and other's poems was growing.

Lehmann encouraged him in this. There was a dramatic – and often self-dramatizing – streak in her that craved an audience and she convinced Day-Lewis to discard any remaining inhibitions he had about following suit. When Laurie Lee wrote to her in 1943 thanking her for her hospitality at Diamond Cottage, he recalled a musical soirée there. 'You have both – thanks to your looks, artistry and romantic air – assumed something of the character of those ballads for me always. Sentimental as I am, I'll bear the burden willingly.'[10]

Though they presented such an appealing public face, Day-Lewis and Lehmann were no closer to resolving the dilemma of their long-term future or their differing expectations of the relationship. 'If a choice must be made,' he told Lehmann after one period of intense pressure to marry him, 'I shall try to settle

down again at home ... it may not work ... I may be unhappy without you ...
M[ary], the children, everything will be infected by it & it will be proved I have
chosen wrong.'[11]

There is no trace of Lehmann's reply but her frustration at such an answer can
be imagined. Day-Lewis's pessimism about their future led him to speculate in
the same letter that he was probably jeopardizing Lehmann's chances of
remarriage with someone who was free to love her as she wanted. Lehmann, for
her part, tried everything to cajole him into action to follow his heart and choose
her, but he remained passive, refusing to look beyond the present moment
unless forced. He did, however, occasionally hit back and rebuked her in the
same letter for 'those bad hours at night when a demon seems to enter you &
makes you say cruel, stabbing things to me in a voice I can't recognise'. In the
next sentence, though, he took the blame himself: 'a demon comes into me &
makes me just as bad ... Do I fail you because my need for you is not great
enough? I suppose that is possible: though when I am thinking that I ought to
leave you & leave the field clear for someone who might need you more & love
you better, I am overwhelmed by misery at the mere thought of it.'[12]

Lehmann struggled to understand what it was he wanted. His yearning for her
was repeated time and time again. When they were apart one Christmas Day, he
wrote to her from Musbury bereft: 'Oh my darling sweet, I wish we were going
for a walk together & then having a huge tea & then going to bed & loving each
other silly.'[13] On one thing, though, he was always clear. He was not free to
marry her. She chose to direct her attention to the yearning and believe that it
would eventually, with a little pressure from her, overcome his scrupulousness
about Mary and his sons.

In April 1943 Day-Lewis took Laurie Lee down to Brimclose to accompany
him on one of his increasingly rare visits. Lehmann, who had come to resent
even these occasional trips, was angry that 'their' friend should be introduced to
the other side of Day-Lewis's life, but equally was anxious for any clues Lee
might pick up as to how Mary viewed matters. Mary gave nothing away but was,
as ever, hospitable. Sean Day-Lewis, though, was entranced. 'Laurie was the
grown-up boy who made us bows and arrows and taught me how to use a
telephone box without paying'.[14]

The pressure that was building on Day-Lewis could occasionally make him
irascible in this period, Sean remembered. 'We were playing hide and seek
around Brimclose and there was a strict rule that it was cheating to go into the
house. I was creeping around when I saw him coming out of the back door.
When I challenged him, he was furious. He chased me and threw stones at me.
Later on he came and apologised profusely.'[15]

Matters came to a head with the publication in September 1943 of Day-
Lewis's new collection, *Word Over All*. It was dedicated to Rosamond Lehmann.
Mary received her copy by post. Underneath the dedication her husband had
written 'Mary, with my love, Cecil, September 1943'.[16] When she turned to the
poems she found first 'The Lighted House', the celebration of how Day-Lewis
had found Lehmann, then 'The Album', a love poem to his new mistress. It is

one of his most admired works, later learnt by rote by generations of school children.

I see you, a child
In a garden sheltered for buds and playtime,
Listening as if beguiled
By a fancy beyond your years and the flowering maytime.
The print is faded: soon there will be
No trace of that pose enthralling,
Nor visible echo of my voice distantly calling
'Wait! Wait for me!'

Then I turn the page
To a girl who stands like a questioning iris
By the waterside, at an age
That asks every mirror to tell what the heart's desire is.
The answer she finds in the oracle stream
Only time could affirm or disprove,
Yet I wish I was there to venture a warning, 'Love
Is not what you dream.'

Next you appear
As if garlands of wild felicity crowned you –
Courted, caressed, you wear
Like immortelles the lovers and friends around you.
'They will not last you, rain or shine,
They are but straws and shadows,'
I cry: 'Give not to those charming desperadoes
What was made to be mine.'

One picture is missing –
The last. It would show me a tree stripped bare
By intemperate gales, her amazing
Noonday of blossom spoilt which promised so fair.
Yet, scanning those scenes at your heyday taken,
I tremble, as one who must view
In the crystal a doom he could never deflect – yes, I too
Am fruitlessly shaken.

I close the book;
But the past slides out its leaves to haunt me
And it seems, wherever I look,
Phantoms of irreclaimable happiness taunt me.
Then I see her, petalled in new-blown hours,
Beside me – 'All you love most there
Has blossomed again,' she murmurs, 'all that you missed there
Has grown to be yours.'

It captures successfully a sentiment many have felt when they fall in love with someone, but Mary would know that Day-Lewis was not describing her as 'made to be mine'. She may have drawn some comfort when she came, two poems later, to 'Departure in the Dark', where Day-Lewis, as already discussed, acknowledges his own divided heart. With publication, though, his affair went from the realm of suspicion to fact in Mary's mind.

As was her habit, she did not make a scene or demand an explanation. Her instinct was to remain silent and sit it out. However, in October, her husband came down to Devon, determined for once to explain himself. The impetus for this unusual candour may have arisen out of Lehmann's wish to bring matters to a head. Day-Lewis was, however, still dampening down her hopes. 'You can be sure,' he wrote to her from the train as he travelled down, 'that, when I talk to Mary, I shall not attempt to make light of the bond between you & me [arguably superfluous once Mary had read 'The Album'], any more than when I talk to you I make light of the bond between her & me. I do try very hard to be honest.'[17] He did, but it was a particular kind of honesty, which took different forms with the two women in his life. Mary was kept in the dark about his infidelity while Rosamond saw her clearly stated plans for marriage constantly frustrated.

The outcome of the meeting with Mary was that Day-Lewis continued living a double life. His wife was willing to accept his offer of a more open compromise – that he would divide his time between her and Lehmann, at least until Sean and Nicholas had left home. 'M[ary] ... is more or less content with what she has got,' he reported back. 'Her feeling for me is quite strong enough still to make it a painful thing to know how much of my love is elsewhere.' Anticipating greater objections to the arrangement from Lehmann, he reiterated that if she pushed him to make a choice, he could only select his wife and his children, however unhappy it would make him.[18]

In her diary that night Mary wrote a single word: 'Peace'.[19] The uncertainty, the suspicions of recent months, the upset at reading *Word Over All* had been transformed. Her marriage was intact and she lived in the hope that this affair, like the others, would run its course.

Day-Lewis's divided heart over his relationships and his divided mind over the war were the twin and interlocking themes of *Word Over All*. His choice of the title, from Walt Whitman's poem 'Reconciliation', in which the American poet sought the healing of divisions after his country's Civil War, suggests that Day-Lewis can see some way of his own conflicts being resolved. The collection's overall tone, though, is set by the title poem and is one of impotence in the face of greater forces, personal and geo-political.

> But now, the heart-sunderings, the real migrations –
> Millions fated to flock
> Down weeping roads to mere oblivion – strike me
> Dumb as a rooted rock.

Word Over All was one of his most popular books of poetry – selling 11,000 copies and going into five new impressions by 1946. Many critics felt it was his best. 'Mr Day-Lewis has emerged from his entanglement of ideas and political preoccupations,' wrote Richard Church in *The Listener*. 'He is now fully himself.

It is an impressive self, and likely to make a permanent mark on the history of English poetry.' 'It is because Mr Day-Lewis has matured, while his compeers, Auden and Spender, have not, that his new volume makes a more substantial appeal,' remarked G. W. Stonier in the *New Statesman*. 'He is the tortoise in that school which has produced illustrious hares: imitative, to begin with, enthusiastic, painstaking, here he comes at his own pace and with his own victories' insight. So much is *Word Over All* his own that it is astonishing to remember the pastiche of earlier years ... the industrial machinery and party flags, echoes of Auden ...'

Stonier may have been overstating the extent to which Day-Lewis trailed his colleagues in the 1930s, but the impression of *Word Over All* as signalling a distinct change from what had gone before was one the poet himself shared. 'Under a stress such as I had never known and sweet influences that for long enabled me to bear it, my life seemed to grow again,' he wrote, 'flowering into wider sympathies and a sensibility less crude, while my work was enhanced by the joy and the pain which seemed to purify vision and enlarge it.'[20]

The intense personal and emotional pain of being torn between Mary and Rosamond replaced the more abstract pain of being part of an unjust society. Naturally indecisive in emotional matters, pulled by desire on one hand and a sense of responsibility on the other, he found he had discovered a rich new vein for his poetry. It became another reason why he instinctively drew back from resolving the emotional impasse. Heart-ache, crudely put, brought out the best in him as a poet. It was what Yeats had called 'the foul rag-and-bone shop of the heart'.

> *I must lie down where all the ladders start,*
> *In the foul rag-and-bone shop of the heart.*
>
> 'The Circus Animals' Desertion' *(1939)*

Word Over All is arranged in three sections which, chronologically, should be read in reverse order. Part Three contains reflections on his past, Part Two on the continuing war, and Part One on his new love affair. It was his war poems that attracted most immediate attention. There are repeats from *Poems in Wartime*, notably his celebrations of the camaraderie of the Home Guard, 'The Watching Post' and 'The Stand-To', but Day-Lewis grapples in *Word Over All* with a broader response to what is going on around him. The closest he gets to an answer comes in 'Word Over All', which begins Part Two.

> *I watch when searchlights set the low cloud smoking*
> *Like acid on metal: I start*
> *At sirens, sweat to feel a whole town wince*
> *And thump, a terrified heart,*
> *Under the bomb-strokes. These, to look back on, are*
> *A few hours' unrepose:*
> *But the roofless old, the child beneath the debris –*
> *How can I speak for those?*

It is a rhetorical question. His answer is that, whatever his reservations and inhibitions, speak he must, even if he has little by way of comfort to offer.

> Yet words there must be, wept on the cratered present,
> To gleam beyond it:
> Never was the cup so mortal but poets with mild
> Everlastings have crowned it.
> See wavelets and wind-blown shadows of leaves on a stream
> How they ripple together,
> As life and death intermarried – you cannot tell
> One from another.

Taking up his own challenge, Day-Lewis records with a stark, horrified detachment the progress of the war and its human cost in poems like 'Reconciliation' where a soldier dies slowly beside his shattered tank. There is none of the consoling promise of eternal life that Eliot, for example, offered in 'Burnt Norton'.[21] Neither did Day-Lewis follow Auden into a rapprochement with Christianity.

His most effective retort to those who scoffed at his involvement in the war effort because of his ideological stance of the 1930s comes with 'Where Are The War Poets?' Reprising his reference to 'war poets' in the breezy 'Dedicatory Stanzas' of his translation of the *Georgics*, he resorts this time to bitterly ironic epigrams.

> They who in folly or mere greed
> Enslaved religion, markets, laws,
> Borrow our language now and bid
> Us to speak up in freedom's cause.
>
> It is the logic of our times,
> No subject for immortal verse –
> That we who lived by honest dreams
> Defend the bad against the worse.

Patriotism is defined, memorably, as defending the bad against the worse. Day-Lewis is taking his cue from W. B. Yeats, who wrote in 1919 'On Being Asked For a War Poem'. His position was 'I think it better that in times like these/A poet's mouth be silent, for in truth/We have no gift to set statesmen right'.[22] But Day-Lewis, while echoing Yeats's style, rejected his stance. He would not claim any sort of poetic exemption. Neither would he retreat from his position of the 1930s that Britain was an unequal, unjust, 'bad' society. Instead he simply acknowledges that war against Hitler – 'the worse' – gives such sentiments less urgency. If he is in the capitalist camp, it is only because of the power of external events. He remains wedded to his 'honest dreams' of the 1930s. His approach could be seen as fitting in with, and indeed predicting, the Labour landslide in the general election of 1945. Then voters turned against the wartime victor, Winston Churchill, because their memory of the deprivations under the

Conservative government of the 1930s remained acute once the immediate threat of the Nazis had been dispatched.

Though written within a specific context, however, the short two-quatrain poem is also a classical exposition of the moral problems surrounding every choice we make when there are substantial grey areas between complete right and complete wrong. And that broader resonance links 'Where Are The War Poets?' (and hence Part Two) to the sections that precede and follow it.

Parts One and Three are concerned more with the private sphere. Part Three travels back to his childhood with 'The Innocent' and 'One and One' (both of which had already appeared in *Poems in Wartime*) but also includes the more recent past in his celebrations of his affair with Billie Currall, 'Jig' and 'Hornpipe' where the music in the words and form is part of the meaning. These are followed by 'The Fault' and 'The Rebuke', by now familiar meditations on the transitory nature of love and the exhausting of desire.

Part Three is mirrored in its concerns by Part One, forming a kind of triptych. It begins with 'The Lighted House' and 'The Album', both celebrations of Lehmann, but in the poem that follows them, 'The Hunter's Game', Rosamond's love becomes a weapon used against herself, recalling Day-Lewis's letter to her worrying that their love might damage more than empower her.

> Pierced by a shaft of light are you
> The huntress, white and smiling, laid –
> The victim of your arrow.

While she may have put such lines down to her lover's passionate concern for her, Lehmann must have struggled more with 'Departure in the Dark', Day-Lewis's account of the pain of living a double life between two homes. Yet its subject was a reality in their lives which she had come, grudgingly, to accept. In 'O Dreams, O Destinations', the final poem of Part One, however, he goes further and attempts to state his own philosophy of life, something far more wide-ranging and ambitious. Its nine sonnets journey through childhood to delayed adolescence and on to adulthood.

> Ah, not in dreams, but when our souls engage
> With the common mesh and moil, we come of age.

That coming of age, Day-Lewis suggests, follows rather than precedes the first burst of political idealism when:

> Desire bred fierce abstractions on the mind,
> Then like an eagle soared beyond belief.
> Often we tried our breast against the thorn,
> Our paces on the turf: whither we flew,
> Why we should agonize, we hardly knew –
> Nor what ached in us, asking to be born.

The inference is that Day-Lewis himself is only just coming of age in the wake of the 1930s, finding maturity now in his poetry, in a more rooted, less idealistic engagement with the world, and in his relationship with Lehmann. Part of that maturity, he says, is to know there are no easy answers, no final place of comfort.

> We're glad to gain the limited objective,
> Knowing the war we fight in has no end.
> The road must needs follow each contour moulded
> By that fire in its losing fight with earth:

The resignation, though, is mitigated by the realization that there are moments of pure joy still to be had.

> Love, we have caught perfection for a day
> As succory holds a gem of halcyon ray:
> Summer burns out, its flower will tarnish soon

The acceptance of an ongoing war within himself, and the denial that love can truly endure, was yet another clear message to Lehmann that the total commitment she so desired from Day-Lewis was not achievable. He could not, the poem says, do it for her, or for anyone. What was possible for him, in so far as he could define it, is set out in the final sonnet.

> To travel like a bird, lightly to view
> Deserts where stone gods founder in the sand,
> Ocean embraced in a white sleep with land;
> To escape time, always to start anew.
> To settle like a bird, make one devoted
> Gesture of permanence upon the spray
> Of shaken stars and autumns: in a bay
> Beyond the crestfallen surges to have floated.
> Each is our wish. Alas, the bird flies blind,
> Hooded by a dark sense of destination:
> Her weight on the glass calm leaves no impression,
> Her home is soon a basketful of wind.
> Travellers, we're fabric of the road we go:
> We settle, but like feathers on time's flow.

The images from the natural landscape, the birds and the traveller are carried forward from earlier works, but here they are employed to reveal something new – the tension between settling and exploring. This is, Day-Lewis suggests, an essential powerlessness in the face of life's unpredictability. Yet there is also a commitment to seizing opportunities in the moment and enjoying them for themselves, rather than attempting to turn them into something more lasting. Again something applicable to Day-Lewis's own life is given a wider currency.

In later years, he was to say that if any of his poems were to endure he would like it to be 'O Dreams, O Destinations'.[23] Its central message of whether to put down roots or continue to journey was one that he would return to time and again. In its wry resignation and its self-exploration, carried out without falling back onto political slogans to provide an easy last line, the poem came to epitomize the uncertainty, the questions without clear answers, and the attendant melancholy, escapable briefly but always looming, that were to be recognized as the hallmark of his mature poetry.

Chapter 21

That It Should End So

That it should end so! –
Not with mingling tears
Nor one long backward look of woe
Towards a sinking trust,
A heyday's afterglow;
Not even in the lash and lightning
Cautery of rage!
But by this slow
Fissure, this blind numb grinding severance
Of floe from floe.
Merciless god, to mock your failures so!
'Ending': *Poems 1943–1947* (1948)

When letters for his father came to Brimclose in the years immediately after the publication of *Word Over All*, Sean Day-Lewis recalled, his mother would carefully readdress each one c/o The Honorable Mrs R. N. Philipps and put it back in the post box.[1] Sean and his brother Nico believed this woman to be their father's landlady in London. As both parents wished, the two boys had no idea that the marriage was in crisis.

The pressure on Day-Lewis to choose between his wife and his lover increased once more, though, when Lehmann's decree nisi from Wogan Philipps came through at the end of 1943. She was now free to marry again. 'Emotionally I want to be everything to you as you want to be everything to me,' Day-Lewis reassured her in a letter written on Ministry of Information notepaper and sent to her at Diamond Cottage. At the same time he tried once again to explain his own limitations. 'I never did think there was anything wrong with love,' he continued, 'only with the romantic conception or words of love in so far as it sets up an unattainable ideal of exclusivity and intensity & thus – exacting more from men & women than is in their nature to give, or in the nature of most of them to give, leads to disillusion, torment & the rest.'[2]

He did not describe himself as having reached that stage and was still able to detach himself from their situation, despite Lehmann's increasing efforts to force him into a decision. It was something that drove her to distraction, Laurie Lee observed. 'Cecil had the fatal quality of indifference, which was more damaging even than cruelty; but irresistible to Rosamond.'[3] It was not precisely indifference. Lehmann was closer to the truth when she spoke of Day-Lewis's 'aspen hesitation'.[4] Yet even that failed to take into account Day-Lewis's essential and guiding pessimism about the endurance of love.

Outwardly their life continued as before, with the weeks spent in London, weekends in the country, and occasional trips for Day-Lewis to Musbury where Mary provided a respite from Rosamond's unguarded neediness. She even used to send him boxes of homemade cakes by post to Diamond Cottage, fearing that Lehmann was not catering sufficiently for his sweet tooth.

His sons were growing up, as he observed when in Devon. 'Nico spends a lot of time in the woodshed now, carpenting & making various rude objects. Sean gratified me the other day by saying that his new housemaster is frightfully decent, full of jokes, just like he imagined I'd be if I was a master.'[5] Lehmann did not much appreciate such detail. 'Blast those boys!' she remarked after one such letter from Brimclose.[6] Any resolution to the triangle in which she found herself had been put off until Sean and Nico reached adulthood and she was naturally impatient.

From February of 1944 Day-Lewis and Lehmann rented a new London base at 41 Hasker Street, South Kensington, with Lee in the basement of the small terraced house. He joked that his role was that of chaperon to stop neighbours gossiping about adultery.[7] Day-Lewis would sometimes respond to Lehmann's complaints about Mary by teasing her about her attraction for Lee. 'I don't want you to think anyone more noble, brilliant or charming than myself,' he wrote.[8] He need have had no fears.

Lee and Day-Lewis developed their own bond in war-time London, especially in the summer of 1944 when the first of the flying bombs, the V1s, appeared over the city and Day-Lewis insisted that Lehmann stay in the country for her own safety. In April Day-Lewis arranged a job for Lee alongside him in the Ministry of Information Publications' Department. After work at the new offices in Russell Square House, the two men would take their turn at fire watching duty together or go to pubs where they would play on the pinball machines before heading off to a Greek restaurant.

They had poetry in common. Both had also fathered children out of wedlock, and both had complicated relationships with women. Over long, drink-fuelled conversations, 'we both', Lee wrote, 'agreed in the end that the impulse to write poetry can only really endure so long as one lives a slightly abnormal and physically unconsummated life. Marriage – ie happy marriage – is death to a poet!'[9]

It is a blunter admission than Day-Lewis might have produced, but confirms that he had absorbed the lesson of the success of *Word Over All*, namely that personal discord can produce extraordinary poetry. Lehmann too was aware of this. In a letter to Lee chastising him for getting on so well with Mary and her children, she voiced her fear that one day Day-Lewis would end their affair and 'return to the bosom of his family & relinquish me forever & write beautiful poetry about separation'.[10]

There were, however, still moments of great happiness in Day-Lewis and Lehmann's life together when both could forget their fears and celebrate the moment. One September day in 1944, after they had been talking, Lehmann remembered, Day-Lewis 'tossed' a poem over the table to her 'with a flick of the wrist and a mock-modest smile'.[11] The hand-written sheet of paper is among the papers in her archive in King's College, Cambridge.

> *Is it far to go?*
>   A step – no further.
> *Is it hard to go?*
>   Ask the melting snow,
>   The eddying feather.
>
> *What can I take there?*
>   Not a hank, not a hair.
> *What shall I leave behind?*
>   Ask the hastening wind,
>   The fainting star.
>
> *Shall I be gone long?*
>   For ever and a day.
> *To whom there belong?*
>   Ask the stone to say,
>   Ask my song.
>
> *Who will say farewell?*
>   The beating bell.
> *Will anyone miss me?*
>   That I dare not tell –
>   Quick, Rose, and kiss me.

'Is it far to go?': *Poems 1943–1947* (1948)

In this dialogue with his 'Rose', the third verse hinted that Day-Lewis was content with the balance between his two lives. Moreover, given that 'Rose' is asking her questions to prepare for her death, the resulting elegy suggested that he planned to await death's arrival at her side. And that final line celebrated the physical attraction they held for each other which could eclipse all outside concerns. Yet as ever there was ambiguity in Day-Lewis's poetry. There is a knowing irony in his suggestion that stones or songs could give any reply to the sort of questions that Day-Lewis sought to answer in his poetry – but often acknowledged were without answers. And there is, too, a more tragic undertone because the apparently comforting message could be undermined, in another reading, with the final embrace also being the kiss of death.

The good-looking couple continued to entertain and be entertained. Lee accompanied them in 1944, for example, to an evening at the home of society hostess, Lady Sibyl Colefax[12] where Day-Lewis sang for other guests who included Lady Louis Mountbatten, Kenneth Clark and Maurice Bowra.

In September 1944, Lehmann's fifth novel, *The Ballad and The Source*, dedicated 'to CDL', came out. She told William Plomer she believed it to be her finest work yet.[13] It was also her least subjective and most imaginative, casting no obvious light on the circumstances of her relationship with Day-Lewis. Sales were 'electrifying', Lehmann reported.[14] When it appeared in America, it became a bestseller and the film rights were bought for $250,000. With the proceeds, Lehmann was able, in April 1946, to purchase The Manor House, a long, low, rose-clad, bow-windowed, late eighteenth century farmhouse in the village of Little Wittenham on the Berkshire–Oxfordshire border. It became a second home to Day-Lewis and he marked their arrival there with 'The House-Warming' in which he imagines himself as a ghost, preparing the 'dove-treed house' for her arrival.

> But here may you find, for all his fretting
>   And gaunt regretting,
> Between the dove-tops and the weir's
> Undying fall, how broken years
>   Can sing to a new setting.

'The House-Warming': *Poems 1943–1947* (1948)

Again there was an edge. Picturing himself as a ghost suggested that Day-Lewis didn't really see himself as a part of the life of The Manor House, that some important part of him remained separate. This was the impression of Day-Lewis that stayed with Lehmann's son, Hugo, into adulthood. 'He [Day-Lewis] was not a spontaneous figure. He didn't put himself up as a stepfather; but he paid attention to our juvenile ploys, he was good at playing trains, specially smashes. But he certainly wasn't always there when we were at home.'[15]

Hugo resented Day-Lewis's presence in their life, but Sally's relationship with her mother's lover was much more accepting and therefore warmer. Day-Lewis did not have a daughter of his own at Brimclose and in the less inhibited environment of The Manor House he was free to become a substitute father to her.

If Lehmann's career was thriving, so too was Day-Lewis's. In February of 1944 he visited Ireland, once MI5 had been given its behind-the-scenes approval to his travel plans. He delivered a lecture at the Abbey Theatre in Dublin and read some Thomas Hardy poems to the Royal Dublin Society. Elizabeth Bowen, like Day-Lewis from an Anglo-Irish family, had been pushing him to apply to be Professor of English at Trinity College, Dublin, – 'all [the staff there] seem to me to have that Irish-Protestant-academic cagey love of the neutral second-rate,' she complained in a letter to him[16] – but the prospect of relocation did not appeal. His one real tie with Ireland, his aunt Knos, met him in Dublin and told him of her plans to retire from being Uncle Willie's housekeeper.

Later that year, in time for Christmas sales, Basil Blackwell published Day-Lewis's *Poetry For You*, an attempt to encourage teachers and pupils to make more time for poetry by sharing his enthusiasms for other writers and giving an insight into how he set about writing a poem, from the moment when a 'seed strikes the poet's imagination', to him jotting it down in a notebook, through the growth of that seed in 'the unconscious mind' over anything from a day to years, and on to the time when he 'feels an urgent desire to write' that can take the physical form of an ache in the stomach.

The book reached a wide audience. 120,000 copies were sold, a testament to Day-Lewis's reputation and his success in writing in a fashion accessible to the youthful target audience of his day. His modesty and lack of dogmatism on a subject where many poets tend to have fixed opinions added to the attraction. 'Boys and girls often ask me (particularly when their teachers are present) if I don't think it is a bad thing for them to be compelled to learn poetry by heart in school. The answer is – Yes, and No. If you've got in the way of thinking that poetry is stupid stuff, or useless, or beneath your dignity, then you certainly won't get much out of learning it by heart. But remember that it is a good thing to train your memory, and learning a poem is at least a much pleasanter way of training it than learning, say, twenty lines out of the telephone directory.'[17]

Such projects were lucrative, and satisfied Day-Lewis's acute sense of social responsibility. It was a different audience he and Lehmann had in mind in January 1945 when together as editors they launched the literary magazine *Orion*. It was a bold step for Day-Lewis and a mark of how far his confidence in his own literary pulling power had grown in his years alongside Lehmann. As editor he would be expected to persuade well-known friends to contribute articles, stories and poems for tiny fees on the basis of their respect and admiration for him.

Orion was to publish three issues a year. Its brief was, in contrast to his 1930s projects, apolitical but dedicated to the broader promotion of culture. There were many pitfalls to any such venture, the couple quickly realized, not least offending the competition in a crowded marketplace which included Rosamond's brother, John, editor of *New Writing*, and their friend Cyril Connolly at *Horizon*.

The initial idea had come from Denys Kilham Roberts, Secretary-General at the Society of Authors, who had raised the money for the venture. He had then approached Lehmann and, through her, Day-Lewis. Attached as a consultant was Edwin Muir, the poet and critic whose reviews had prompted Day-Lewis to rethink his political campaigning through poetry in the 1930s. John Lehmann warned his sister in advance that Kilham Roberts was a difficult character and that Muir would be unlikely to do much work. Though his words were ignored, he proved accurate on both counts.

Day-Lewis wanted to call the new magazine *Albion*, a suitably patriotic name, he felt, for a publication launched in wartime, but was overruled. Thereafter almost every decision was surrounded by disagreement. Kilham Roberts was not prepared to spend a great deal of time on the project. 'Have you heard any word from Kilham Roberts?' Day-Lewis wrote to Rosamond. 'If he doesn't become a bit more active, we shall either have to turn it in or push him out. We shall never produce even two issues [a year] at this rate.'[18]

Kilham Roberts laid exactly the same charge at Day-Lewis's door, especially when the latter insisted on advertising for contributions in the first edition and then refused to read through the piles of unsolicited manuscripts that arrived because he had taken to his bed with a cold. 'Under separate cover I am sending you three lots to have a look at,' Kilham Roberts wrote to Lehmann. 'Cecil himself mustn't I suppose be bothered at present, but in due course I feel that he must shoulder the major part of this burden with which he has landed me.'[19]

Lehmann was caught in the middle, and worked diligently to ensure a healthy quota of famous names inside the covers of *Orion*, as well as encouraging younger writers by careful editing of their submissions. Together with Day-Lewis, she inspired Laurie Lee to write a piece on his Gloucestershire childhood which 15 years later was to reappear as a chapter in *Cider With Rosie*. Day-Lewis, for his part, did write to friends like Elizabeth Bowen, soliciting contributions at a guinea per thousand words, but from the start his heart was not in his editorial duties.

The contents page of the first edition of *Orion* included Stephen Spender, Maurice Bowra and Leonard Woolf, as well as Day-Lewis's own new translation of Paul Valéry's[20] *Le Cimetière Marin* as 'The Graveyard by the Sea'. He had read, he later recalled, this 'great meditation upon death-in-life' during the V1 assault on London, and had found himself 'possessed' by the poem and knew he 'had to translate it'.[21] Lehmann, who had met Valéry as a young woman, encouraged Day-Lewis and used her fluent French to produce a literal transla-tion on which he then worked. The experience was, he wrote, 'a technical corrective to the strong influence of Thomas Hardy'.[22] Next to the Dorset poet's ballad-like directness, the Symbolist Valéry's work had a complex structure and unusual rhyming scheme.

Valéry's subject matter was, however, familiar. The poem describes standing in a cemetery (where he was buried after his death in 1945) and being helplessly transfixed by consciousness of his own mortality. He makes his escape, tem-porarily, by grabbing hold of life and rousing his own will to survive.

> *The wind is rising! . . . We must try to live!*
> *The huge air opens and shuts my book: the wave*
> *Dares to explode out of the rocks in reeking*
> *Spray. Fly away, my sun-bewildered pages!*
> *Break, waves! Break up with your rejoicing surges*
> *This quiet roof where sails like doves were pecking.*
>   'The Graveyard by The Sea': *Poems 1943–1947* (1948)

The translation was published in February 1947, alongside Valéry's original, in a limited edition of 500 on hand-made Italian paper by Martin Secker & Warburg and was later included in *Poems 1943–1947*.

Orion only lasted for four editions – two in 1945, and one each in the sub-sequent years. Muir detached himself after number two, and Day-Lewis and Lehmann after number three. Without them Kilham Roberts was unable to continue for long. All parties had too many other concerns to give *Orion* the concentrated attention and effort it required to succeed.

On May 7, 1945 the Germans signed a document of unconditional surrender and the war in Europe finished. Day-Lewis spent VE Day with Mary at the Randolph Hotel in Oxford, celebrating her forty-third birthday. It was to be three more months before the war in the East was ended by an atomic bomb.

Like many Day-Lewis was simply relieved and wrote an 'Ode to Victory' for broadcast on the BBC.

It had not been, however, a conflict that resolved any of the concerns about society that had pre-occupied him since the 1930s. In July he looked on as a spectator, no longer an activist, as Clement Attlee defeated Churchill by a landslide to become Labour Prime Minister. Others, too, had not forgotten.

The return of peace brought the questions about his own future back into sharp focus. Mary's mother, Constance, died of cancer in Sherborne at the end of July. He stayed for the funeral but left straightaway afterwards for London. Mary collapsed after his departure. It had been building up for some time. Just before his father's unseemly departure, Sean had overheard his mother break down. 'I had never heard her cry before,' Sean wrote. 'It was a terrible, wailing sound which drifted down through the floor-boards of their bedroom as I stood below in Cecil's study ... her cries punctuated with ineffectual mutterings of con- solation from him. The ostensible reason for the outburst was that Nick had been caught smoking, and she, who smoked forty cigarettes a day, did not want him to emulate her. Even then I realized that more than this must have upset her.'[23]

Mary's relationship with Barbara Cameron had been a strength throughout the war years. On one of his visits Day-Lewis had written to Lehmann reporting how he had been puzzling over it during a sleepless night. 'I was worrying about M's affair – thinking there must have been some grave defect in myself which turned her that way – what did I do wrong, where did I go wrong – you can imagine.'[24]

In October the two women went for a holiday to the Lake District, Mary returning via London to meet her husband and travel back to Devon with him. 'No spark' she wrote in her diary of their marriage. 'Talked to Cecil about self and Rosamond. There isn't really any way out of this trouble until we are old, nothing can cure the situation really, but it is good to talk.'[25] She was prepared to continue as before, making few demands and waiting for the time when he returned to her, as she believed he inevitably would. She would, however, have to do so increasingly alone. After Barbara Cameron's husband, Donald, returned from the war, the friendship between the two women lost something of its wartime intimacy. Cameron had two more sons in quick succession.

That summer Day-Lewis had spotted Billie Currall at Seaton beach, or at least someone who reminded him of her, and it is an indication of his unhappiness with his current life that the sight caused him to lament a lost love.

> Only my heart was shaking
> Within me, and then it stopped; as though
> You were dead and your shape had returned to haunt me
> On the very spot where, five years ago,
> You slipped from my arms and played in the breaking
> Surges to tease and enchant me.
>
> I could not call out. Had there been no more
> Than those thickets of rusty wire to pen us

Apart, I'd have gone to that girl by the shore
Hoping she might be you. But between us
Lie tangled, severing, stronger far,
Barbed relics of love's old war.

'On the Sea Wall': *Poems 1943–1947* (1948)

A clue that there was more than straight nostalgia behind the poem came in a letter Currall wrote towards the end of her life. She remembered that she met Day-Lewis in the Red Lion in Musbury the very day he wrote 'On the Sea Wall'. 'He pressed into my hand the original poem written on a scrap of paper,' she recalled.[26] Her clear implication was that their relationship enjoyed periodic revivals.

Day-Lewis's time at the Ministry of Information was coming to an end. With one household in Devon to support single-handedly, including two sets of school fees, and contributions to make to another with Lehmann, he had come to rely on his civil servant's salary to augment his now more substantial, but still modest earnings as a writer.

At The Manor House, he found little emotional comfort. John Lehmann wrote in his diary after a long conversation with his sister that he had been given the impression that 'the passion was turning sour because of the enormous tension the whole situation had put him [Day-Lewis] under for so long'.[27] Rosamond continued to aspire to marriage and Day-Lewis continued, in his letters, to spell out his unchanging reservations. 'When you use the word need, I always feel out of my depth. I just don't know how much I need you – or Mary: how essential you are to me. Probably I shall never know till I have lost you, or her ... When I think about poor Laurie [suffering another doomed love affair] I begin really to hate romantic love, to feel it should be bracketed with gunpowder as man's most disastrous invention ... what a mass of irretrievable damage, what a weight of unhappiness, neurosis, despair, crime, suicide and every kind of folly has been piled up by this conception of love.'[28]

In 1946 Day-Lewis left the Ministry of Information. It gave him more time to work on new poems and to take on well paid literary 'jobs'. Some required more effort than others for a decent advance. Day-Lewis quickly came to regret signing up to edit the ninth volume of the *Oxford Junior Encyclopaedia* whose theme was 'recreations'. *Orion* had exhausted his enthusiasm for soliciting the occasional essays, poem or short story from friends and acquaintances. Now he had to find 500 writers willing to write on subjects from accordion playing to yodelling. It took almost five years to complete the task.

It had been five years too since the last Nicholas Blake, and so Day-Lewis settled down to breathing new life into Nigel Strangeways as he investigated a killing at the Ministry of Morale, for which read Ministry of Information. In *Minute for Murder*, Strangeways had lost many of his Auden tics and became ever more Day-Lewis himself. 'Nigel S started life as a chap modelled on Auden (physically) – can he have grown to resemble me, as they say married couples tend to do with each other?' Day-Lewis was later to write.[29] One answer to the question was that Strangeways's own marriage ended abruptly in the new book. His wife, Georgia, 'was killed in the blitz of April, 1941', roughly the time that Day-Lewis had met Lehmann.

One of Lehmann's biographers, Gillian Tindall, has suggested that she disliked Day-Lewis's alter ego, or more precisely her lover's involvement with the genre of crime fiction.[30] There is little evidence for this, save the long gap between Blake books while he was with Lehmann, which could just as easily be put down to either his wartime workload or his preoccupation with his personal life. Tindall also, however, notes that in his 1949 Blake book, *Head of a Traveller*, set in a house modelled closely on The Manor House at Little Wittenham, Day-Lewis reprises a Lehmann plot device from *The Ballad and The Source*. In her novel, Lehmann has Gil, a sculptor, crafting heads that are perceived by the unhinged Ian as the real thing. In Blake's novel, a similar confusion occurs between an actual head and a modelled one. Tindall further speculates that the central female character in the Blake book, a highly powerful and amoral middle-aged woman, bears a passing resemblance both to Sibyl Jardine from *The Ballad and The Source* and to Lehmann herself.[31]

In those early months of 1946, without the distraction of the Ministry of Information, Day-Lewis began to find the strain of his double life unbearable. 'Rosamond's pressure on Cecil to marry her was constant,' recalled Laurie Lee. 'That demanded a great deal of physical, moral and emotional strength, which he was not able to maintain.'[32] Leading a double life may have given him material for his poetry, but the toll it was taking on him was, he felt, too great. Repeated periods of ill health were alternating with times when he found writing itself a struggle. His fundamental reservations about life with Mary or life with Rosamond remained, but, under siege from Lehmann, he convinced himself that the time had come to act rather than think, to discard his doubts and commit to one or the other, just as he had in the 1930s signed up for the Communist Party in heightened times despite his inner questions remaining unanswered.

With his sons now growing – Sean would soon be 16 – and there being in Mary's own words 'no spark' left in their marriage, he could see only one course of action – to be with Lehmann. She was his intellectual equal, shared his vocation as a writer and the physical bond between them was strong. Spending time at Brimclose in February with Mary, Day-Lewis raised the subject after returning from the pub. He could, she wrote in her diary, think of 'no good reason' any longer why he should not settle with Lehmann permanently. 'Whole day a mist of unreality and wondering what the result will be,' Mary continued. 'It can't end like this.'[33]

Chapter 22

Grinding Himself to Powder

Who would suppose, seeing him walk the meadows,
He walks a treadmill there, grinding himself
To powder, dust to greyer dust, or treads
An invisible causeway lipped by chuckling shadows?
'The Neurotic': *Poems 1943–1947* (1948)

Day-Lewis had not forewarned Rosamond Lehmann of his intention to tell Mary he was leaving her for good. When he arrived back from Devon to meet his lover in London for a drink at her club, the Sesame in Grosvenor Street, she was ecstatic at the news he brought with him. 'He realized overwhelmingly that he could not go back [to Mary] & face a future without me,' she reported to Laurie Lee in triumph and relief.[1] It seemed a vindication of all her hopes and therefore a final jettisoning of Day-Lewis's reservations about the possibility of romantic love.

Mary, Lehmann added, 'seems to have taken it calmly'.[2] To soften the blow, Day-Lewis had agreed to spend most of the next three months in Devon before vacating Brimclose permanently. 'He is already writing poetry about it, so his fundamental state must be healthy', Lehmann confided in her friend Kenneth Clark. 'To think I have got a future after all! – I mean the kind I want & believe in.'[3]

True to his word, Day-Lewis settled down temporarily in Musbury. Lehmann accepted his absence with good grace because it was the prelude to them being together without interruption. He made only occasional trips up to London. There were sittings for a portrait by Lawrence Gowing, commissioned by Lehmann. The result shows Day-Lewis brooding, angular, dark but fundamentally inscrutable. In mid-May, there was a grand poetry recital organized by the Society of Authors in the Wigmore Hall in the presence of Queen Elizabeth[4] and her daughters. Lehmann had already planned to attend but then Mary was sent an invitation by the organizers as the wife of one of the performers. Unusually she decided to accept. Both were therefore in the audience to see Day-Lewis share the platform with Walter de la Mare, T. S. Eliot, Louis MacNeice and the Poet Laureate, John Masefield. He read 'The Lighted House', his celebration of finding Lehmann. 'I kept my seat rigidly,' she told a friend, '& didn't dare look to left or right . . . It is all AWFUL, this position, for everybody. She [Mary] retired to Devonshire afterwards, & he and I spent the night with my brother & attended a large dinner party of Edith Sitwell's.'[5]

Day-Lewis and Lehmann continued to seem every inch the married couple when she accompanied him to Cambridge, where he had been invited to give the prestigious and long-running Clark series of annual lectures on English literature at Trinity College. In recent years lecturers had included C. S. Lewis[6] and David Cecil. The choice of Day-Lewis may have owed something to the lobbying of Dadie Rylands, prompted by Lehmann, who remained an enthusiastic promoter in public of her lover's work.

Day-Lewis took as his theme 'the Poetic Image' and tackled it in six parts, all his lectures being delivered in the first three months of 1946. His opener was to take place on January 24. Though now a confident and polished public speaker and performer, he grew increasingly nervous as the day approached, acutely aware of his own poor academic record, and worried that his audience of dons would find him third class. Lehmann did much to soothe such fears and gave him considerable support with the drafting, as he acknowledged when the lectures were later published, saluting 'the one who, from first to last, with gentle encouragement and delicate criticism helped me over the exacting course I had set myself'.[7] His dread of that first lecture, though, was so great that he was also moved to try out his text on Mary – a rare opportunity for her to be part of his professional life.

The poetic image, Day-Lewis told his audience was 'a word picture charged with emotion or passion'. He chose these two nouns with great precision, thereby rejecting the thinking of the influential critic F. R. Leavis (who taught at Cambridge's Downing College) that poetry should be approached primarily analytically rather than with emotion. The poetic image, Day-Lewis went on, 'is the human mind claiming kinship with everything that lives and has lived'. This was not, he insisted, an exclusively internal and inward-looking process, but consisted of 'looking freely outward upon the human situation', albeit passed through the filter of the poet's own experiences. He quoted approvingly from Thomas Hardy in this regard.

'Every image,' he continued, 'recreates not merely an object but an object in the context of an experience, and thus an object as part of a relationship'. It is the poet's task to seek to understand that relationship. He 'searches for connections by the light of an impassioned experience, reveals truth and makes it acceptable to us ... Beneath the pleasure we receive from the verbal music, the sensuous associations of a simile or metaphor, there lies the deeper pleasure of recognising an affinity. It has been called the perception of the similar in the dissimilar: that will do very well.'

As well as tackling Leavis head-on on his home ground, Day-Lewis was also defending what might be termed conventionality or traditionalism in poetry, the romantic view of the poet as prophet. In so doing he rejected the Modernist position that held that poetry had an integrity all of its own and did not need to have meaning in the sense of reflecting or interpreting something outside the poem itself. Poetry, Day-Lewis stated unequivocally, 'must develop its theme or develop out of its theme'. Moreover, he also questioned the Modernist tendency to seek to break the traditional form of the poem which had seen some of its proponents embrace free verse. Language, Day-Lewis told his Cambridge audience, 'cannot in fact discard sequence, cannot discard cause and effect, cannot work to a continuous present', but instead 'must have a beginning, a middle and an end'. In addition it 'must have rhythm'. By standing firm on such conventional principles, the poem, he argued, would reach a broader audience than the intellectual elite.

These were brave words given the make-up of his audience, but the positions he took were familiar ones from the 1930s when he, Auden and Spender had rejected much of Modernism in favour of political engagement as poets with the world around them. Despite his subsequent disillusionment with communism, Day-Lewis also did not retreat from his fundamental belief that poetry had a vital social and public function. The certainty of a coming Red Dawn had gone. In its place, Day-Lewis now offered only perseverance but he refused to back down from a commitment to engagement and empathy with the rest of humanity. Through poetry, he said, 'the individual is brought, however remotely, into touch with communal experience, general truths which have eternally bound mankind together'.

He continued to make of poetry itself a kind of religious creed, as he had in the 1930s. 'In the poem, you are reborn; it is a re-creation, a resurrection of the body in which your experience is given flesh and blood and bone.' It was not, he admitted in the final lecture of the series, a complete experience, as once he had imagined, but the years since the 1930s had taught him that perfection was unattainable, save fleetingly. 'Through our experience of the poem, we are reborn – not indeed complete, for perfection is the prerogative of art alone in this world – but, because poetry's illusion is a fertile one, a degree or two nearer the wholeness for which our selfhood strives.'

Day-Lewis was speaking about his subject from the inside, as a working and acclaimed poet, and therefore was revealing much about his own approach to writing poetry. To augment his arguments he quoted other poets from Chaucer to Auden. He revealed once more his acute awareness of the place of the poet within a tradition of poetry. He was also taking on the mantle of critic and theorist, a role with which he was to become increasingly familiar. That was due in part to the success of his Clark lectures – published in March of 1947 by Cape as *The Poetic Image*. The warm critical response gave him a new confidence about accepting invitations from academic bodies to talk about poetry.

In March 1947, for example, he travelled to Newcastle to deliver the Robert Spence Watson Memorial Lecture to the university's Literary and Philosophical Society. He took up again the themes he had explored in his Clark Lectures and delivered a passionate defence of 'The Colloquial Element in English Poetry'. 'The simple and the colloquial are not synonymous', he told those gathered.[8] By defending the vernacular style, a diction for poetry that is close to the spoken language, Day-Lewis once again staked his distinctive claim for a public role for poetry. He was convinced it had the potential to reach a wide audience and to make a nonsense of class barriers and distinctions between academic and lay, scholars and factory workers.

217

The essential continuity between his pre- and post-war views on this subject was emphasized in a letter from late 1946 to the younger poet Anthony Thwaite.[9] 'I don't think,' Day-Lewis wrote, 'that poetry is at a dead end just now ... The poets of my generation, at any rate, have found their own individual voices – in so far as they have any – and are concentrating more on the things to be said, and less on new ways of saying things.'[10]

Where once his commitment to that public function for poetry had found expression by taking to political platforms, now Day-Lewis was involving himself in more practical schemes. He had attended meetings at this time with the Arts Council, seeking to encourage it to join with the Publishers' Association to offer those who published verse an annual subsidy against any losses they might incur. These would apply only to published collections by poets of particular merit chosen by a panel of judges.

As Day-Lewis's confidence grew in one area, it was in sharp decline in another. As the spring turned into the summer of 1946 and three months became four then five, Lehmann began to grow concerned by the absence of any signs that he was about to take his final leave of Brimclose. There were some awkward telephone conversations. After one Day-Lewis sent her a letter of apology. 'I must keep a minimum standard of decency here in the matter of talking,' he pleaded and asked her to confine herself to letters.[11] Concerned, Lehmann commissioned their mutual friend William Plomer to raise the subject of Day-Lewis's plans on a visit to Devon. Plomer reported back confidently that his host had reiterated his intention of leaving his wife.

Her doubts quelled, Lehmann decided to tell her children that she was to remarry. Sally was delighted. Hugo received the news with less enthusiasm. Lehmann later reported that his response was 'he only wants you for your poetry'.[12]

Down in Devon, Mary was doing what she did best – looking after her husband's every need, providing a peaceful, sustaining, domestic environment for him and their sons, and making few demands for herself. By not addressing the problems in their marriage, she hoped they would go away. At this stage Day-Lewis would have been only too willing to join her in shutting himself off from anything but the present. However, the future encroached as each new letter from Lehmann arrived, or when he sat at his desk looking out towards the English Channel and found himself unable to write anything.

As Mary calculated, her selflessness only made him feel guiltier about his plans for a clean break. The desire for resolution that had led him in February to confront his wife and announce his departure (whatever his deeper misgivings) crumbled under such pressures. Unable to act, he buried himself in writing an obituary of T. S. Eliot for the *Times*, a piece commissioned in advance to be held until the great man's death.

Two things rescued Day-Lewis from sinking even deeper. The first was that Lehmann, realizing that he did not have it in him at that point to leave Mary, offered him a return to the old compromise. He resumed dividing his time between Musbury and The Manor House. 'I must try to start work & forget my private troubles', she confided in a friend. 'It isn't too difficult, when I consider his appalling predicament, & his unhappy face, & remember that he totally depends on me for comfort.'[13]

And the second, the offer of a job which would ease his financial worries. He had already talked with Lehmann's brother about working as a Reader for the publishing house John planned to establish. To be a Reader then was a more esteemed role than it is now. Most houses would employ a well-known writer as Reader – William Plomer was on the staff of Jonathan Cape – to give themselves the appearance of *gravitas*, and in the hope of attracting a better quality of manuscript.

However, John Lehmann was still struggling to raise finance for his new venture when a letter arrived at Musbury asking if Day-Lewis would be interested in a similar post at the more established house of Chatto & Windus for £1,500 a year. He wrote at once to John suggesting that he accept the Chatto offer, but only on a temporary basis until Lehmann's own house had put down firm roots. 'I am terribly keen on getting this sort of job permanently,' he told him, 'so that I can have a basic livelihood (and such a pleasant one) and pick and choose more in respect of my own writing.'[14]

Lehmann agreed to release him and Day-Lewis began work in October 1946 at Chatto's offices at 40–42 William IV Street, just north of St Martin-in-the-Fields and Trafalgar Square. They were, wrote his colleague at Chatto, Peter Calvocoressi, 'inconvenient, draughty and bedeviled by passages and odd stairways'.[15] Day-Lewis's office was at the back, on the upper floors, reached by either a trek up the stairs or an ancient, stately but unreliable lift. His window looked out over the back of the Colosseum Theatre. If he strained his neck he could see the clocktower of St Martin-in-the-Fields.

Day-Lewis took the job on a strictly part-time basis – working initially only on Tuesdays and Wednesdays, though he later modified it to one week in every two – to give himself time for his own writing. His main task (he also wrote jacket blurbs and composed advertisements) was to read his way through the thousand or so manuscripts submitted over the course of the year and write reports on them for the partners. Some would already have gone through an initial screening process – either by Peter Cochrane, a young man who had just joined the firm straight out of the army, or by one of the partners who had an established relationship with the author.

He brought to the job, recalled Peter Calvocoressi, diligence, wisdom but no great ambition. 'The job of the Reader was both crucial and peripheral – crucial because his reports decided which books we published and hence determined our reputation, but peripheral in that he did not attend partners' meetings where his reports were discussed. Cecil never saw himself as a talent spotter, though a good deal of poetry was sent to us because of his presence there. That said, he had the two important qualities for the role – he was a good critic and he had a touch of ruthlessness. If something was tosh, he would write at the bottom just one word "tosh". There was often a sardonic note to his criticism but he was never acerbic like FR Leavis. I always sensed Cecil kept his work at

Chatto at a certain distance. There were lots of other things in his life and though he was very professional, you knew some of those other things were more important – principally his writing. I never felt he thought of himself as a publisher.'[16]

Eventually Day-Lewis was elevated to the board, but that was when Chatto had become a limited company. His name looked good on the notepaper but his role remained the same. In the autumn of 1946, however, the firm was, like most of its rivals, a partnership. The senior partner, Harold Raymond, had been in post since the 1930s. His office was on the first floor, with interconnecting doors to where his two fellow partners worked. Norah Smallwood was a war widow and had once been Raymond's secretary. Ian Parsons, the other partner, was also the poetry editor. Though he had been taught by Leavis and published him at Chatto, Parsons managed to combine it with an admiration both for Day-Lewis personally and as a poet. It had been his suggestion to approach Day-Lewis about the Reader post in the first place, though Raymond, who had offered Lehmann great encouragement in the early stages of her career (Chatto had published *Invitation to the Waltz*) may also have been directed by his old friend to her lover.

Publishing houses at that time tended to be small. Chatto produced around 50 titles a year. It concentrated on high-brow fiction and poetry – authors included Lytton Strachey,[17] Aldous Huxley, Mark Twain,[18] Compton Mackenzie[19] and Sylvia Townsend Warner.[20] There was also a bit of what Day-Lewis might have deemed tosh thrown in to make a profit. The driving force behind the firm was the partners' own literary enthusiasms. Yet however much in private they might dismiss the low brow, they were also aware of the need to make money out of it to subsidize the rest.

Day-Lewis quickly fitted in. 'He had something about him,' Peter Cochrane recalled. 'He was good fun. I don't know what sort of person couldn't have liked him straightaway. He was very undogmatic. He didn't lay down the law. And he could be very informative on literary matters, but only if you asked. He didn't try to blind you with science and his opinions. He was a very gentle man. I think that word charm is horribly overused. Especially when coupled with Irish. But Cecil was charming.'[21]

Day-Lewis's life fell once more into a routine. His two days at Chatto took him to London where he lodged near Fitzroy Square with Lehmann's friend Hester Chapman and her banker husband, Ronnie Griffin. These would be followed by extended weekends at The Manor House where the dining room had become his study. And there were regular visits to Musbury to see Mary and his sons.

Returning to the old pattern, though, could not quell his disquiet. The tension of leading a double life was no longer enhancing his poetry but damaging it. As 1946 turned into 1947 he reported disconsolately to Rupert Hart-Davis that he had just scrapped 'all or nearly all' of a 600-word poem – 'the best part of a year's work wasted but it was simply not good enough'.[22] Its subject was the emotional crisis in his life. All that could be salvaged, he told Hart-Davis, was a section that became 'Married Dialogue', a 'conversation' in which the husband and wife speak what are alternating monologues without seeming to hear what the other has to say.[23]

HE: *There was a time. But time piles flake upon flake*
Lapping the traveller asleep:
And in that sleep the heart grows numb. So we awake
To severance. Oh deep
The drifts between, treacherous the frozen lake!

SHE: *Once I watched a young ocean laugh and shake*
With spillikins of aspen light.
I was your sail, your keel. Nothing could overtake
Love trimmed and stiffened aright.
But now I drown, a white reef in your wake.

'Married Dialogue': *Poems 1943–1947* (1948)

Seeing how unhappy her husband was, even Mary began to doubt that self-sacrifice and keeping quiet would be enough to save their marriage. Day-Lewis's love for Lehmann showed few signs of burning out despite all the strains placed on it. 'I'm sick of this half-life', Mary wrote in her diary after he had left Musbury for Little Wittenham once again.[24]

By February 1947, with Britain in the grips of one of the worst winters on record, Lehmann was confiding in her friend Olivia Holland that Day-Lewis was 'very far from well, with a gastric ulcer boiling up, & dreadfully thin & depressed'.[25] Two months later Day-Lewis was once more weighed down by his personal circumstances. From Devon, he wrote to John Lehmann: 'is that sum of money, which was offered to me last year to clear out of the country, still available? Rosamond & I hope to go to France in June, and perhaps to Czechoslovakia later, so it would come in useful.'[26] An inveterate sceptic about foreign travel, Day-Lewis had been one of three authors – the other two were V. S. Pritchett and William Sansom[27] – offered a £100 award by the Society of Authors in an effort to dispel his prejudices.

Quite how near to the edge he was can be judged by a poem he wrote at this time in which he is almost willing his own death as a release.

His doomsdays crawled like lava, till at length
All impulse clogged, the last green lung consumed,
Each onward step required the sweat of nightmare,
Each human act a superhuman strength

'The Neurotic': *Poems 1943–1947* (1948)

Mary recorded in her diary at the end of May: 'Cecil in state bordering on insanity, can't make up his mind between Rosamond and me.' Soon afterwards, she wrote; 'Ghastly evening with Cecil, life becoming intolerable, he can't see why he shouldn't leave me.'[28] In an effort to save himself, Day-Lewis had determined that making a choice was the only way forward. And again, in spite of the reservations he had so clearly enunciated to her, he chose Lehmann. He had once again told Mary that he was going to live permanently with Rosamond.

On June 2, Mary drove him one last time to nearby Axminster to catch the first train of the day to London. En route, she broke down and started crying uncontrollably. Day-Lewis tried to continue the journey, but faced with Mary's uncharacteristic loss of control it was impossible. They turned back, Mary still distraught and her husband by now furious. At Brimclose they retreated to their lairs to lick their wounds. In the kitchen, Mary resolved, as she later confided in Barbara Cameron, never to cry in front of her husband again.

> Take any joy – the thread leads always on
> To here and now: snow, silence, vertigo;
> His frozen face, a woman who bewails not
> Only because she fears one echoing word
> May bring the avalanche about her ears.

'The Woman Alone': *Poems 1943–1947* (1948)

Day-Lewis stayed in the study from where he telephoned Lehmann, and told her what had happened. His inability to leave Mary must finally, he said, mean that he had to end his relationship with Lehmann.

Day-Lewis and his wife spent the next six days in near silence. 'This life at present is HELL' Mary wrote in her diary.[29] Day-Lewis sent a letter to Laurie Lee. 'The hideous destined thing has happened,' he told him. 'I've had to write & tell Rosamond we must part; God knows if it is the right decision ... It has just about finished me.'[30]

222

Chapter 23

Now Comes the Zero

Now comes the zero between
Desire and resignation,
Between cast-iron past and plastic future
'New Year's Eve': *Poems 1943–1947* (1948)

On January 3, 1948 Day-Lewis appeared on BBC Radio's Home Service on the weekly poetry magazine, *Time For Verse*. It went out live at 10.38 p.m. on Sunday evenings and its producer, Patric Dickinson, liked to feature two readers. As well as Day-Lewis, he had booked a young actress, Jill Balcon, who had already established such a reputation as a reader of poetry that at the age of 21 she had been invited to join the Apollo Society. The broadcast took place on her 23rd birthday. 'He was extremely courteous,' she recalled of Day-Lewis, 'but he had a look of being light years removed from where he was. Through mutual friends, I knew a lot about the problems in his life. I left the studio sure he hadn't really noticed me.'[1]

Since his aborted attempt to leave Mary the previous June, Day-Lewis had returned to the same unsatisfactory compromise of parcelling himself out between his work in London, his wife in Devon and Rosamond Lehmann in Berkshire. The despairing letter he had sent to Laurie Lee immediately after the fated journey to Axminster railway station had brought his friend hurrying to Musbury, despite a toothache. Lee suggested an overseas trip and Day-Lewis, anxious to escape the tense atmosphere of Brimclose, for once readily accepted. 'Cecil and Laurie seem happy together,' Mary wrote despondently in her diary. 'Why can't he talk to me, I'm not always so dumb? He and Laurie have decided to go on holiday together, I wish *we* were going.'[2]

The two men sailed to Esbjerg in Denmark and stayed at the Hotel Cosmopallie in Copenhagen where good food, Lee's company and distance from his domestic preoccupations enabled Day-Lewis to return home in a more optimistic mood. Lee had kept Lehmann informed of Day-Lewis's changing moods over the course of their holiday. She responded gratefully to their mutual friend, thanking him for his trouble, and noting that his 'sweet letter' provided 'a far more vivid picture' than anything Day-Lewis had sent her. 'When he's in a bad mental state his little missives are like so many shadows falling over me: they say nothing, mean nothing.'[3]

Her despair at being rejected by Day-Lewis boiled over to reveal a deeper frustration as she continued: 'I am sick, sick, of hearing him say "I can't face" –

or "daren't risk" – etc. etc. I am sick of hearing him talk of his "roots" – as if roots were always healthy, as if they didn't bind and strangle.' But then her tone changed once again. 'Is he very frightened of Mary? I think he is ... And he can't bear failure in anything – and now he feels he must simply go to earth & write poetry about it ... Oh Laurie ... I do understand what he feels about her & the boys – I understand almost everything really.'[4]

She was certainly sufficiently understanding to be willing to take him back, on the same terms as before. In a letter to Rupert Hart-Davis, urging him to intervene with Day-Lewis, she wrote: 'He will make wonderful poetry out of his self-torture & my torture – but he will never be a whole human being now – if he does this. I cannot lose him to this criminal course – he will say he's got to murder someone, & he's decided it's to be me, & he can't help himself ... He tells me he is "stretching his arms to me from the further bank, longing to help & comfort me, powerless". Tell him he must find the power in himself to cross to the other bank before it's too late & I'm gone.'[5]

Despite her dismay about his continuing inability to leave Mary – 'they are like two wheels of a bicycle propelling the stark frame of their life together', she told Lee[6] – Lehmann retained her fundamental belief in romantic love. She and Day-Lewis had found that rare thing, the love of equals, she told Kenneth Clark, and therefore it was worth preserving at all costs.[7]

Guaranteed a warm welcome at The Manor House, Day-Lewis set aside any doubts he still harboured about returning to Lehmann during a weekend at Brimclose with Rex Warner. Warner had been briefed by Lehmann in advance and was himself in the process of leaving his wife Frances for Barbara Rothschild.

By the end of July Day-Lewis had spent '4 very happy days' at Little Wittenham, Lehmann reported to Lee, and both were determined to live only for the present. 'It is more wonderful than words can say to be with Cecil again ... As for the future, I mustn't brood about it. Some doors must be closed & locked, for ever, & maybe it's for the best.'[8]

Mary was informed by her husband of the latest turn of events by letter. As she reflected alone on the future of her marriage, she noticed Billie Currall out and about in Musbury with her new baby. During his darkest moments of despair over Mary and Rosamond, Day-Lewis had once more renewed his friendship with Currall. He had even given her a ring that had once belonged to his mother. Whereas 'On the Sea Wall' had shown Day-Lewis looking on at Currall from afar in 1945/6 (though she later contradicted this), 'Meeting', written at an unnamed date between 1943 and 1947, is both more immediately passionate and more tentative, describing their sexual reunion as half reality, half dream, perhaps a tactic to avoid a rebuke from a cuckolded Lehmann.

Did I meet you again?
Did I meet you again in the flesh we have come to know,
That evening of chorusing colours a week ago?
Or was it delusion wrung from a faulted brain

When we seemed enveloped in love like naked dunes
Effaced by a seventh wave's onrush and undertow?
Did I meet you again?

'Meeting': *Poems 1943–1947* (1948)

In 1947 Currall gave birth to a son, John. He was named after his father and no questions were raised over his parentage, but Mary noted a striking resemblance between John Currall junior and her own husband, and more particularly between John and her second son, Nicholas. She wondered out loud in later life to her other son Sean if John was in fact Day-Lewis's child.[9] At the end of her life, Billie, never an entirely reliable witness, told Sean that John had indeed been 'Po's son'.[10] If he was, it seems Currall never informed either Day-Lewis or John himself.

With her husband once again spending much of his time with Lehmann, Mary ruefully anticipated in her diary for May 1948 the anniversary of his attempt to leave her. 'It is nearly a year since Cecil decided not to go, he has gone most of the way.'[11] When she wrote this he was away in Italy with Lehmann at Villa I Tatti, the spectacular home at Settignano outside Florence of the Renaissance art historian, Bernard Berenson.[12] A friendship had developed between Berenson and Lehmann after he wrote her a fan letter following the publication of *The Ballad and The Source*.

At first Day-Lewis had been reluctant to accompany Lehmann to Italy. 'If BB is as painted by Maurice [Bowra]', he had written to her on April 14, 'seven days with him would be as intolerable as ten.'[13] Berenson, for his part, may have viewed the visit with similarly mixed feelings. Now in his eighties, he liked the company of beautiful women but was less interested in their husbands and partners. He preferred to be the presiding male at his court. John Lehmann wrote that Berenson favoured being treated as 'a mixture of the Oracle of Delphi and God the Father'.[14]

Rosamond, though, would not be deterred from her plans. She wanted Day-Lewis at her side. She had sent out in advance to Berenson copies of *Word Over All* and *The Poetic Image*, 'which seems to many others besides myself to go further into the nature and the springs of poetry than anything other ..., I was going to say since Coleridge'.[15]

By all accounts Lehmann and Berenson got on famously. He responded to her beauty and intelligence and she flattered and flirted. Day-Lewis stayed in the background, emerging from their shadows only occasionally to read some of his poems or to perform the Tom Moore songs learnt as a child at Monart. 'I enjoyed you both,' Berenson wrote after the couple had returned to England, 'Cecil no less than yourself, in so far as possible for one who, like me, is so exquisitely aware of sex in women & so little in men.'[16]

Before arriving at I Tatti, Day-Lewis and Lehmann spent a happy few days in first Rome then Siena and finally Florence, visiting galleries and enjoying each other's company away, briefly, from the troubles that cast a shadow over their lives back in England. It was Day-Lewis's first visit to Italy and he was enchanted on this 'voyage of discovery' by the Tuscan landscape.[17] He was inspired to begin writing poetry again in earnest. The rest of 1948 and into 1949 were taken up with what became *An Italian Visit*. It contains 'Elegy Before Death: At Settignano', one of his most revealing works about Lehmann, written in the form of an elegy for their lost love, while she was still planning their future together. The short distance between love and death was already familiar in Day-Lewis's work – notably in the playful 'Is it far to go?' – but here it was explored more lyrically.

The opening stanza places the lovers of the poem in Berenson's villa at sunset, looking out over Florence in the distance.

> *Come to the orangery. Sit down awhile.*
> *The sun is setting: the veranda frames*
> *An illuminated leaf of Italy.*
> *Gold and green and blue, stroke upon stroke,*
> *Seem to tell what nature and man could make of it*
> *If only their marriage were made in heaven. But see,*
> *Even as we hold the picture,*
> *The colours are fading already, the lines collapsing*
> *Fainting into the dream they will soon be.*

Quickly though, the transience of love emerges as the dominant theme.

> *. . . Could we compel*
> *One grain of one vanishing moment to deliver*
> *Its golden ghost, loss would be gain*
> *And Love step naked from illusion's shell.*
> *Did we but dare to see it,*
> *All things to us, you and I to each other,*
> *Stand in this naked potency of farewell.*

Lehmann is simultaneously the object of Day-Lewis's love, and his nemesis.

> *Her orbit clasped and enhanced in its diadem*
> *All creatures. Once on a living night*
> *When cypresses jetted like fountains of wine-warm air*
> *Bubbling with fireflies, we going outside*
> *In the palpitating dark to admire them,*
> *One of the fireflies pinned itself to her hair;*
> *And its throbbings, I thought, had a tenderer light*
> *As if some glimmering of love inspired them,*
> *As if her luminous heart was beating there.*

Yet a few lines further on, he writes of her:

> *My vision's ara coeli, my lust's familiar,*
> *All hours, moods, shapes, desires that yield, elude, disarm –*
>
> *All woman she was. Brutalizing, humanizing,*
> *Pure flame, lewd earth was she, imperative as air*
> *And weak as water, yes all women to me.*

The use of the past tense echoes the description of his lover elsewhere as 'ghost' and 'shade'. It emphasizes the sense that Day-Lewis, in this moment of to-getherness and celebration, is actually leaving her behind, adored, revered but no longer bearable in his life. In the terms of the poem, she was dead.

> *I imagine you really gone for ever. Clocks stop.*
> *Clouds bleed. Flames numb. My world shrunk to an echoing*
> *Memorial skull.*

He had long ago realized that all that bound him to Mary was the past and his guilt – about leaving her alone when she still clung to him, and about their sons. Now, he was admitting to himself that he also wanted to be free of Lehmann, however much he still loved her. It was not a conclusion he had articulated to another person. Indeed he had grown more and more reluctant to confide in any of his close friends about the problems he was grappling with as his indecision had dragged on. In letters to Stephen Spender from the period, for example, he restricted himself to talking about poetry save for a single throwaway line – 'I've been in a state' – to explain why he had taken so long to reply to Spender's last letter.[18] Here he was, though, finally sorting out his confusion and paralysis over his emotional future by confiding in a poem. He wrote, he once remarked, 'not to be understood but to understand'.[19] Now he understood that it was no longer a question of choosing between Rosamond and Mary, but of disentangling himself from both of them.

When Lehmann eventually read a draft of 'Elegy Before Death', she was disconcerted, but saw, as lovers are prone to do, only what she wanted to see. 'I never thought at the time that it was more than a beautiful, romantic farewell to an idyll,' she later recalled, 'though with hindsight it does seem strange, as if he was already denying us a future together.'[20]

The Italian trip came as his relationship with Lehmann, though recently restored and still yielding moments of great joy and togetherness, was des-cending into a more general tetchiness. 'I shall have to confine my letters to facts,' he wrote to her in 1948, 'if tiny little jokes [about schoolgirls which Lehmann had taken as wounding to her daughter, Sally] reach your end swollen in to great aggressions'.[21]

Natasha Spender reinforced the image of Day-Lewis increasingly tiring of Lehmann's demands and 'tendency to be self-dramatising'. She recalled having dinner with him in Edinburgh. 'Both of them could give the impression that they were playing out some intense literary drama. I remember in the late 1940s being at the Edinburgh Festival with him. We went to see a performance of *Medea*. Afterwards he exploded like a volcano about women with such passion that I could only assume he was referring to Rosamond.'[22]

Whatever his feelings about Lehmann, however, their professional lives remained intertwined. In May 1948, he wrote an introduction to a Jonathan Cape edition of the *Collected Poems* of their mutual friend, Lilian Bowes-Lyon, a first cousin of Queen Elizabeth. Bowes-Lyon, a diabetic, had had to have both legs amputated because of gangrene. She died the following year.

And later the same year, he provided a foreword to a new edition of the 1862 sonnet-sequence *Modern Love* by George Meredith,[23] also much admired by Lehmann. She had taken the title of her first novel *Dusty Answer* from a line in a Meredith poem. Introduced to Meredith by Lehmann, Day-Lewis felt a particular connection with Meredith's candid – and at the time of its publication, scandalous and critically reviled – psychological account of the failure of his first marriage because of the adultery of both partners.

> *In tragic life, God wot,*
> *No villain need be! Passions spin the plot;*
> *We are betrayed by what is false within.*

Modern Love: George Meredith

Exploring the 'false within' was to become one of the distinguishing qualities of Day-Lewis's verse. It was not, as has been suggested, imitation of Meredith, but a case of Day-Lewis reacting to a quality in another poet's writing which then revealed or gave voice to something inside him which had hitherto been buried.

In September, he returned to writing fiction for children for the first time since *Dick Willoughby* in 1933. *The Otterbury Incident* became a minor children's classic, remaining in print for nearly half a century. Dedicated to his two godsons – Jonathan Fenby, son of Charles, and Richard Osborne, son of Eileen 'Jinnie' Hedges and her second husband, Tony – it tells how Ted, Toppy and Nick, schoolboy detectives all, catch a counterfeiting gang headed by Johnny Sharp and 'The Wart' that has so far alluded the police. The illustrations were by Edward Ardizzone[24] and the overall approach of this fast-moving adventure story (geared for boys of roughly the same age as Day-Lewis's second son, Nicholas) owed a good deal to Richmal Crompton's[25] William stories. Children outwit adults by cunning and resorting to what their parents and teachers would certainly not regard as model behaviour. At the end of *The Otterbury Incident*, the local policeman, Inspector Brook, summarizes only half in jest the criminal offences for which Ted, Toppy *et al.* might be prosecuted, as 'carrying lethal weapons with intent to wound, breaking and entering, intimidation, assault and battery, shooting at certain fellow citizens and discharging rockets at same'.

The following month saw publication of Day-Lewis's new collection of poems, all written during a deeply troubled period in his personal life and sombrely entitled simply *Poems 1943–1947*. Day-Lewis's own mental and emotional disarray was reflected by there being no connecting theme as in previous collections and no overall image to tie the various poems together. Lacking too is the single longer poem around which Day-Lewis had previously built volumes. The careful ordering that was usually a Day-Lewis hallmark is missing with poems on similar subjects scattered throughout the collection.

It contains very little material that touches on the broadly political sphere and in its heavy concentration on the poet's private life, both current conflicts and past experiences, there is little hope offered. Instead a congenial pessimism dominates. Of the two epigraphs Day-Lewis chooses, one from Hardy and one from Valéry, (his translations of 'The Graveyard By The Sea' and another poem,

'The Footsteps', are included), it is the grim fatalism of Hardy's 'I seem but a dead man held on end/To sink down soon' rather than the emphatic determination to live for the moment in Valéry's '*Le vent se lève!* . . . *il faut tenter de vivre!*' that seems most apt.

So 'Buzzards over Castle Hill' are likened to 'earth-souls doomed', lovers kiss 'over an opening grave' in 'Heart and Mind', and the poet is exposed by a receding tide as nothing more than 'listless sediment of sparkling days' in 'All Gone'. Rather than look forward, or even confine himself to the present, Day-Lewis reaches back into his own past to find the explanations for his present predicament. So where *Word Over All* began exuberantly with poems about his new found love for Lehmann, now he reflects more on his collapsing marriage. It is Mary rather than Rosamond who is invoked most, though both Lehmann (in 'The House-Warming') and Billie Currall (in 'Meeting' and 'On the Sea Wall') do figure.

'The Revenant' must have made especially painful reading for Mary. Orpheus's parting from Eurydice as she enters the mouth of the underworld becomes, obliquely, a metaphor for the Day-Lewises' marriage. He has to part from Mary if he is to escape death and be reborn. But he adapts the story so that Orpheus does not so much abandon her as Eurydice banishes herself. Unable to act himself to break the impasse, Day-Lewis wanted Mary to send him away.

> *He felt the cord parting,*
> *The death-wound smarting:*
> *He turned his head but to glimpse the ghost of her.*

Day-Lewis was trying to make sense of his own anguish through his poetry. In the 1950s, in a lecture, he spoke of a poet's 'need to communicate' coming from two sources: 'to create an object in words and to explore reality and make sense of his own experience'.[26] Yet in *Poems 1943–1947* he was struggling with one of the consequences of that personal focus. 'The poem,' he said in his lecture, 'must stand up after the poet has got out from underneath it; it must apply beyond the individual experience out of which it arose, and carry meaning beyond the poet's own time and social environment.'[27] Some critics judged that *Poems 1943–1947* did not manage such a feat as successfully as had *Word Over All*. The collection, they felt, was too personal. Day-Lewis's remarks in his 1951 lecture may have been a tacit acknowledgement that they were right.

The collection was also publicly exposing those around him to a greater extent than ever before. He did not use names – save for the 'Quick, Rose, and kiss me' at the end of 'Is it far to go?' – but to anyone who knew the various people concerned, the autobiographical thrust of the poetry and characters involved would have been all too obvious. Mary, in particular, who went to such great lengths to protect her children from knowing anything about the troubles in their parents' marriage, would have preferred greater discretion. Instead, she was given a voice to express her point of view – or what Day-Lewis took to be her point of view – in both 'Married Dialogue' and the poem that follows it, 'The Woman Alone'.

One distinctive theme in *Poems 1943–1947* was Day-Lewis's concern with the creative process itself. Among several poems on the subject is 'A Failure', using a ruined field of wheat to evoke the writer's block that had afflicted him often in the previous four years and which had caused him to scrap one long poem after months of work.

> Some galloping blight
>
> From earth's metabolism must have sprung
>   To ruin all;
> Or perhaps his own high hopes had made
>   The wizened look tall.

His use of varying line lengths gives the poem a music all of its own, but the extent of the failure he is describing goes deep. While on one level referring to his own tearing up of an unsatisfactory piece of work, Day-Lewis also alludes to his own death as a kind of release (a theme he returns to more explicitly later in the collection in 'The Neurotic').

> But it's useless to argue the why and the wherefore.
>   When a crop is so thin,
> There's nothing to do but to set the teeth
>   And plough it in.

'A Failure' is followed by 'The Unwanted'. It likens writing a poem to lovers conceiving a baby but in its last stanza again broadens out and contains a hint of a reflection by his natural father on the birth of William Currall.

> Sun locked up for winter;
>   Earth an empty rind:
> Two strangers harshly flung together
>   As by a flail of wind.
> Oh was it not a furtive thing,
> A loveless, damned, abortive thing –
> This flurry of groaning dust, and what it left behind!
>
> Sure, from such warped beginnings
>   Nothing debonair
> Can come? But neither shame nor panic,
>   Drugs nor sharp despair
> Could uproot that untoward thing,
>   That all too fierce and froward thing:
> Willy-nilly born it was, divinely formed and fair.

The other distinctive group of poems in the collection is a series of tributes to other poets. There are 'Lines for Edmund Blunden on his Fiftieth Birthday', 'Who Goes There', dedicated to Walter de la Mare on his 75th birthday, 'Emily Brontë',[28] and 'Birthday Poem for Thomas Hardy'.

> Great brow, frail frame – gone. Yet you abide
> In the shadow and sheen,

All the mellowing traits of a countryside
That nursed your tragic-comical scene;
And in us, warmer-hearted and brisker-eyed
Since you have been.

It was a signpost, if signpost were needed, of the influence of Hardy on Day-Lewis at the time. Critics questioned whether he was too influenced and not enough his own man. Overall, *Poems 1943–1947* generated less critical acclaim than its predecessor. Day-Lewis was particularly affected, Lehmann told Dadie Rylands, by a negative review from a fellow poet. 'Cecil is sweating, though in an ironic way, over a piece of feline nastiness from the pen of Miss Kathleen Raine[29] in *Britain Today*.'[30]

Since the end of 1947, Lehmann had started spending more time in London with Day-Lewis, clinging ever closer as if sensing that he was secretly entertaining thoughts of escape. They had rented a house in Redington Road in Hampstead and continued to grace literary occasions, seeming to casual observers a golden couple. In March 1949, Jonathan Cape published *The Beautiful Visit* by Elizabeth Jane Howard, a 26-year-old first time novelist. As a result she was invited to a drinks party by her publisher at his offices at 30 Bedford Square. 'Jonathan led me up the room to a piano at which were standing Cyril Connolly, Rosamond Lehmann and Cecil Day-Lewis. Cyril looked at my satin shirt with buttons and said "do all those buttons undo". Rosamond never liked younger women. And Cecil just smiled kindly. That was it. He was wonderful to look at – elegant, craggy and irresistibly attractive, I would have thought, to any woman he chose to mark out. He had this slightly mannered Anglo-Irish accent. Sometimes it was more marked than at other times, but it was very attractive.'[31]

Despite the indifferent reviews for *Poems 1943–1947*, Day-Lewis's reputation as a writer had never been higher. It was reinforced in the spring of 1949 with a major commission, worth £1,200, from the BBC to translate Virgil's *Aeneid*, and by the publication by the Hogarth Press of another edition of *Collected Poems 1929–1936*. When early in the year, there were concerns for the health of the Poet Laureate, 71-year-old John Masefield,[32] after 'flu had turned to pneumonia and was then followed by appendicitis, there was discussion in some of the press about a suitable successor. Day-Lewis's name was amongst those mentioned, though Edmund Blunden was the favourite.

Four years earlier, Dylan Thomas and John Davenport had written a satirical novel, *The Death of the King's Canary* (only published in 1976 long after their deaths), in which they parodied and poked fun at a list of candidates for an imagined vacancy for a Poet Laureate. Day-Lewis is eventually chosen by the Prime Minister from a field that includes Auden, Spender, Edith Sitwell, T. S. Eliot and Louis MacNeice, but this fictional victory could hardly have been counted as a compliment. Meanwhile in the real world Masefield eventually recovered and talk of a vacancy evaporated. Had he succumbed, though, Day-Lewis's recent links with communism may well have counted against him with any appointments' committee as the world moved towards the Cold War.

Day-Lewis was above such calculation, however, and was happy, in June of 1949, to attend with Rex Warner a dinner at the Dorchester in London organized by the Society for Cultural Relations with the USSR. The Soviet chargé d'affaires was on hand to celebrate the 150th anniversary of the birth of Pushkin.[33] Day-Lewis's own links with the Communist Party had been broken several years earlier, but he bore it no ill will.

MI5 was on hand at the Dorchester checking those attending and added a note to the Day-Lewis file, dormant since 1944. It was to be the penultimate entry before the file was closed, the last note in 1952 simply reporting that he had not 'come to notice' in recent years.[34]

In September, Day-Lewis set off for Italy once more – this time without Lehmann. He was heading for Venice for an international gathering of the writers' organization, PEN. Also attending were Stephen Spender and W. H. Auden. While Spender remained close to both Day-Lewis and Auden, spending the greater part of the years between 1947 and 1949 in the States where Auden had now taken citizenship, the link between Day-Lewis and Auden had grown distant.

Geography was one factor. Differing stances on faith was another. Auden had embraced Christianity. 'On his mantelpiece [in New York] a crucifix denoted the change in his beliefs', Spender wrote of him. Moreover, Spender added, Auden 'had shed all preoccupation with politics. He explained that his politics in the 1930s had been based on the conviction that the anti-Fascists could really stop the war. When he realized that this view was mistaken, he dropped the ideas that went with it.'[35]

Day-Lewis, by contrast, had refined his position of the 1930s into a broader support for the public role of poetry, but he never disowned his writing from that decade. Auden, as Spender noted, 'produced at the end of the war a volume of *Collected Poems* in which the poems were arranged according to the alphabetical order of the first letter of the first line of each poem. In this way all trace of development from poem to poem was suppressed'.[36]

So their reunion in Venice was not entirely without its tensions. As the three sat outside a café in Piazza San Marco, Natasha Spender took a photograph, the only surviving pictorial record of the three 1930s poets together. Auden is holding forth, as didactic as ever. A tanned Spender grins but looks at the ground. The bow-tied Day-Lewis looks the least at ease, his hands clasped anxiously in his lap and his broad smile creasing his face, but more polite than real.

Yet the schoolboyish camaraderie that had been at the core of their 'movement' remained. When Spender revealed his plans to write an autobiography, Auden was shocked. 'Did you know?', he asked Day-Lewis. 'I did', he replied. 'Well, why didn't you stop him?' 'How would I stop him?' 'You know perfectly well, Cecil, that no poet should ever write an autobiography.' 'Oh.' 'Has he got it here?' 'Probably.' 'Then we'll go and burn it.'[37]

Chapter 24

In a Dream

There was no precise point at which to say
'I am on the wrong road'. So well he knew
Where he wanted to go, he had walked in a dream
Never dreaming he could lose his way.
'The Wrong Road': *Pegasus and other poems* (1957)

The actress Jill Balcon was sure that Day-Lewis had hardly noticed her when they had shared a studio for BBC's *Time for Verse* in January 1948, but she was mistaken. Day-Lewis had been impressed enough by her performance that evening – and on radio programmes he had heard – to request shortly afterwards that she join him on stage for a poetry recital in Salisbury. Balcon, though, was much in demand. The previous year she had made an eye-catching screen debut as Madeleine Bray alongside Sybil Thorndike and Stanley Holloway in an adaptation of *Nicholas Nickleby,* and she had just committed to a season with the Bristol Old Vic theatre company.

She was already packing her trunk at her flat in Clarendon Street in Pimlico when the telephone call about the recital in Salisbury came through. She was pleased by the professional compliment, but sent her apologies. 'I had to say no, but regretted it for the whole time I was in Bristol,' she remembered. Day-Lewis had made a lasting impression on her. 'He had charm – in the original sense of the word – a kind of magical magnetism.'[1]

The attraction was mutual. With her pale skin, thick blue-black hair, large dark eyes and slight figure, Balcon was striking, Natasha Spender recalled. 'She looked like the sort of beautiful woman you only see on a Greek vase.'[2] Of eastern European Jewish descent, she was the only daughter of Sir Michael Balcon,[3] head of Ealing Studios (who had disapproved of her choice of career), and his wife, Aileen. She had first glimpsed Day-Lewis when a 12-year-old schoolgirl at Roedean. She had just been promoted to the senior school and was at the back of the assembly hall in 1937 when 33-year-old Day-Lewis came to judge the annual verse-speaking competition. She had wanted to take part, but was told she was too young by her teachers. Instead she sat watching, captivated by the distinguished guest. Poetry, as she put it, 'had been my passion since the age dot'.[4]

When she returned from Bristol to London in the summer, she was contacted by L. A. G. Strong with whom she was friendly. He invited her to give what was described as a 'demonstration recital' at the English Festival of Spoken Poetry at the Institut Français in London. She agreed. This request from one of Day-Lewis's oldest friends may not have been entirely innocent, for Day-Lewis was on the judging panel at the festival.

Balcon performed Robert Frost and Thomas Hardy in her recital. Afterwards she sat next to Day-Lewis at dinner. 'We talked about the poets we liked and found that, as well as Frost and Hardy, we also had Emily Dickinson[5] in common,' she recalled. 'We got on well but I was not aware of any element of flirtation.'[6]

Day-Lewis, though, responded to a light-hearted postcard she sent from the south of France while on a summer holiday with her mother with an invitation to dinner when she got back. They went to the Maison Basque in Dover Street in Mayfair and afterwards walked around St James's Park. She was flattered by his attentions, but knowing of the complications in Day-Lewis's life from their mutual friends did not believe there could be any future in a relationship with him. Indeed weeks later, while she was helping out between acting jobs on the publisher André Deutsch's stand at the *Sunday Times'* Books Fair at Grosvenor House in London, she saw Day-Lewis and Lehmann very much together as honoured guests at the event.

Balcon had mentioned casually when he ambled over to the Deutsch stand that she had been sitting for the sculptor, Jacob Epstein,[7] who had approached her one evening in the Caprice Restaurant asking to make a bronze of her head. Day-Lewis decided he wanted to see the final result and so a dinner and viewing was arranged for Balcon, Epstein and Day-Lewis.

When Day-Lewis casually mentioned the planned gathering, it was the first time Lehmann had registered Balcon's name. 'Didn't you say you were living with me and that we didn't ever go out without each other?' she demanded of Day-Lewis, wanting to know why she hadn't been invited too. When he returned home late after the dinner, Lehmann remembered challenging him: ' "Miss Balcon's after you", and he said "Oh, nonsense." "Of course she is!" "You know I could never think of anybody but you." So it faded away.'[8]

For Lehmann perhaps. The couple's life continued in its usual round of social and literary functions. There was a visit to the novelist Somerset Maugham's[9] villa at Saint-Jean-Cap-Ferrat in the south of France, where Day-Lewis continued working on *An Italian Visit*. Back home in England Lehmann began to court the now adult Sean Day-Lewis, who at eighteen was awaiting call-up to the RAF. She was eagerly anticipating the arrival of the time when both of Mary's children were sufficiently old no longer to be an obstacle to their father's departure from Musbury.

The tensions in the relationship between Day-Lewis and Lehmann were, however, all too evident to those close to them. At a dinner party at the home of Hester Chapman, the writer Elizabeth Jenkins witnessed a particularly public falling out. The couple arrived late 'and Cecil Day-Lewis was looking absolutely green − it was more than pallor − and he'd hardly taken up his soup spoon when Rosamond said "We've just been arguing about how much men *lie* to women". Cecil just put his spoon down and said "My *God*, I thought we'd gone through all that".'[10]

Day-Lewis spent Christmas 1949 at Musbury, sending Lehmann a brief, business-like letter. But he had posted Balcon as a present *The Way to Poetry*, an anthology of English verse from Chaucer to Sydney Keyes, compiled by E. Ellerington Herron with a foreword by Day-Lewis himself. Over the Christmas holiday he heard Balcon performing on the radio and wrote at once to her. 'What I am really taking up the pen about is your Ottima [in a production of Robert Browning's *Pippa Passes*] the other night. I was shaken to the depths by it and am still in a flutter whenever it returns to my mind as it keeps on doing in a haunting way. Until now I had thought of you as one of the two best women readers of poetry in the country [Peggy Ashcroft was the other] but this was something a bit more, such passion, diversity of mood, power and attack. Oh dear, oh dear. I went off to bed feeling as if I had just been stampeded over by a herd of wild horses. Pray don't do this too often on the air or you'll be responsible for the collapse of the elderly party. This is the first fan letter I have ever written to an actress, believe it or not, but Ottima was great acting or something uncomfortably near it.'[11]

He concluded his fan letter with another invitation to dinner at the Maison Basque on January 12. Two days after he posted it there was a low-key celebration at Brimclose of the Day-Lewises' 21st wedding anniversary. He arrived back at Little Wittenham in time to see in the New Year. Laurens van der Post[12] and his wife were Lehmann's guests and watched as, on the stroke of midnight, she took her lover's arm and said 'isn't it wonderful to be together at this moment'. Van der Post clearly saw Day-Lewis flinch.[13]

He had already admitted to himself, while writing 'Elegy Before Death', that he wanted to leave Lehmann. So far it had been an abstract wish. Now in Balcon, 21 years his junior, he had met someone who might give that real impetus. After their second dinner at the Maison Basque, he walked Balcon home past what had once been George Eliot's[14] house in Chelsea's Cheyne Walk. They carved their initials in the tree outside. That night they became lovers.

Balcon, though, did not expect any commitment from Day-Lewis given his already complicated domestic arrangements. And, whatever he may have been contemplating, he offered none. Five days later Lehmann had planned a grand 16th birthday for her daughter, Sally. Day-Lewis, Peggy Ashcroft and the pianist Angus Morrison were to give an Apollo Society performance at The Manor House. The day before his dinner with Balcon he had written to Lehmann trying to soothe her concerns, expressed in another tense telephone conversation, that something was amiss between them and that it might spoil Sally's big day.

'I promise you I'll do my very best to sustain you through Sunday's ordeal, & up to it – be just as loving as I know how, not irritable / why should I be irritable? I'm depressed and nervous before these things but surely not necessarily irritable, not cold; & I'll do my best not to be abstracted. I'm so sensitive to your moods that the least indifference or preoccupation on your part, such as I felt last weekend, is apt to inflate itself into a lofty barrier which I see no way round or over. If I was different, I should knock it down, which is what you want me to do. And, oh how often I wish I *was* different.'[15]

He continued by answering a charge she had made in their telephone conversation: 'If I'd thought you were arranging the party as a framework for myself, I should have said No to it long ago: but I don't really think this was your idea, so you shouldn't dart it at me ... you cruel girl. I'm sure we shall both do much better if we forget all about – or at least don't recur to the lamentable scenes before the last recital ... I'm just like you: I need to be given confidence & the feeling of being loved: and one way to give confidence to each other is not to remind of past failures and warn against their repetition ... I shall read & sing for you alone, remove your headache beforehand, fill you with love, dislodge the poisoned dart, & all will be well. Yours C.'[16]

The party was a success with Day-Lewis playing his part with conviction, guests reported, though Lehmann later claimed to know all the way through that something was wrong. It took place on a Sunday. The next day Day-Lewis set off for London for Chatto & Windus. From there he sent Lehmann a letter telling her that he had fallen in love with Jill Balcon and that he was leaving her.

Resorting to a letter was a cowardly way to behave, but was also an indication of how paralysed Day-Lewis had become when faced with a determined Lehmann. He had a lifelong dread of confrontation that dated back to witnessing his father rebuking Knos over household expenses, and he feared that in a face-to-face conversation with Lehmann his courage might desert him altogether as it had when he tried to leave Mary.

If he had hoped Lehmann would allow him to go, he was mistaken. She received his letter, by her own account, with astonishment and anger and threw it in the fire.[17] She wrote back at once demanding that he come and explain himself. He arrived at Little Wittenham the next day showing what Lehmann described as 'diabolical indifference', and was unbending about his plans.[18]

Lehmann was convinced that he was infatuated with Balcon and that a kind of madness had overtaken him. 'He looked like a murderer. It was exactly as if you'd seen someone you'd liked and trusted split apart and a stranger emerging. Even the eyes, the colour of them, black, dark.'[19] Years later she wrote on the back of his letter of January 11 'sent six days before he left me' as if she still couldn't believe that he could have written such words of love when he knew he was about to end their relationship.[20] They were, indeed, misleading, but Day-Lewis always chose his words with great care. There was nothing in the letter that promised her a future together.

Lehmann made one request of Day-Lewis before he left – that he agree not to see Balcon for three months so as to test whether he was truly as in love with her as he believed. She was sure that he would quickly tire of her. Seeing how shaken Lehmann was, Day-Lewis weakly agreed but he had already telephoned Balcon to ask her to spend the rest of her life with him. Completely taken aback given how recent was their relationship and her few expectations of a man already with a wife and a lover, Balcon nevertheless had said yes at once. Together, they had resolved to face down all the problems ahead. Lehmann's demand for a three-month cooling off period was the first obstacle to overcome.

Day-Lewis's next task was to tell Mary. Travelling down on the train to

Musbury, his mind, however, was wholly occupied by Balcon: 'Coming down here on the train I thought of you for three hours and 50 minutes continuously, with Chekov's short stories lying unread on my lap. Anything that can distract me from Chekov is a miracle ... To get your letters and know that you feel as I do, that it wasn't a dream, that we were one in the sight of George Eliot, darling it makes me absolutely light-headed.' He likened meeting her to 'a landfall, having a whole new country to explore; wonderful for me to think that I have so much more of you still to find out. I'm so excited that I can't think about my entanglements, my weakness and cowardice but only of the future ... The way you have accepted these things and let me find my way to you through them in spite of them without any conditions and complaints, you've no idea how I love you for that ... I still can't believe its me you love ... All the peace and gentleness you felt coming from me was reflected back from you. I found it and gave it back to you.'[21]

Mary met him off the train at Axminster station on January 31. His determination to confront her with the facts once again briefly deserted him. It took him three days to summon up the courage to tell her the truth by which time she had already been forewarned by a letter from Lehmann.

Mary's reaction to the news was much the same as Lehmann's, as Day-Lewis told Balcon in a letter the next day. She 'thinks (as others will) that it can only be the sort of infatuation for a girl that a middle aged man often falls victim to. I told her as kindly but plainly as I could that it is nothing of the sort, and said I wanted to divorce her. She is dead against this at present, but I think if I am kind and patient with her, she may come round. I said that whether she divorced me or not, I intended to go and live with you.'[22]

The conversation with his wife, Day-Lewis reported to Balcon, had been 'a terrible ordeal for me ... and terrible for M – the trouble is that she loves me still (heaven knows why), while I have great affection and respect for her, and nothing more. But she has never done me any harm, which makes it so much more difficult to do this to her. One thing I'm sure of – bloody as these three months will be, they can prove to me, better even than being with you, how firm and real and overpowering my love for you is.'[23] In her diary Mary wrote simply: 'Jill Balcon comes into the picture. Everything has the feeling of nightmare, I broke down.'[24]

True to his word to Lehmann, Day-Lewis occupied himself in London and Devon as he sat out the three months. His only link with Balcon was via letter. Travelling down to Brimclose he complained to her 'how slow the time is going. If I hadn't this old *Aeneid* to occupy me I think I should go mad ... ' Later, in the same letter, he turned to what would have been a familiar theme to Lehmann, but in writing to Balcon his essential pessimism about the endurance of love was invested with new hope. 'This happiness business – well of course it must be transient. The great thing is not to be intimidated by the knowledge that it is so, not to clamp it down under a microscope, or tear off its wings by trying to keep it when the time comes for it to fly off again ... Why shouldn't we go on making new kinds of happiness possible for each other, long, long after this first paradise of being together?'[25]

As their frustration at being forced apart grew, Balcon arranged for an intermediary, her great friend the novelist, Elizabeth Jane Howard, to have lunch with Day-Lewis in London at Antoine's. 'I knew,' she remembered, 'that the whole idea of the separation was wrong. It was like throwing fire on the oil. Lovers thrive on those things. I think he only agreed to it because he felt so guilty. He'd have agreed to anything. He was in the most awful position. Mary wanted Cecil as the father of her children and Rosamond was absolutely determined to marry him. He had done all the chasing with Jill. Not the other way round. She was bowled over by him. Especially with her intense reverence for poetry, his attention was overwhelming for her. And he had clearly fallen very much in love with Jill and felt he had to make this move.'[26]

While Day-Lewis and Balcon were enduring the separation, Rosamond and Mary met at a Mayfair hotel in February. It was a curious meeting for the two very different women who had loved and tried to keep Day-Lewis for themselves over the past decade. Mary had long experience of his habit of embarking on relationships and then tiring of them. She wanted to see Balcon as merely the latest in a long line that included both Lehmann and herself. Rosamond, by contrast, was struggling with wounded pride. The only possible explanation she could see for Day-Lewis's behaviour was mental illness. She persuaded a reluctant Mary to agree that together they should insist that he saw a psychiatrist.

Day-Lewis again agreed to this second demand from Lehmann and saw a consultant in Wimpole Street. The result was, however, helpful from his point of view. Since the psychiatrist reported back that he was clearly of sound mind, Lehmann backed down on her demand for a three-month separation and summoned him to Little Wittenham on March 20. He assumed it was to collect his few belongings, but found Lehmann in a vengeful mood. It was a painful parting after nine years for both parties. Lehmann's incredulity had turned to anger and bitterness. She accused Day-Lewis of 'smirking' at her distress.

At her tiny flat in Pimlico Balcon paced about waiting anxiously for Day-Lewis's return. When he finally arrived, it was the early hours of the morning and he had come all the way by taxi, having missed the last train back to London after walking the five miles from The Manor House to Didcot station. He looked, Balcon said, 'as if he had been tortured'.[27]

He had brought nothing with him. Later Lehmann dispatched the Lawrence Gowing portrait she had commissioned of Day-Lewis to Brimclose. Mary did not want it and passed it on to her son, Sean, who in turn agreed that it could remain with his father until he had a home of his own in which to display it.

Lehmann was left devastated. She forbade Day-Lewis to publish *An Italian Visit*, the collection he had been working on since their visit to Bernard Berenson's villa two years earlier. In her anguish she shared widely with mutual friends details of what she presented as Day-Lewis's appalling betrayal. In April, she wrote to Norah Smallwood: 'I am temporarily *hors de combat* – have had a complete physical or nervous breakdown & been put to bed for I don't quite know how long. I expect you know I've been in sad trouble. Cecil went off in January with a young woman he scarcely knew. I tried to stop him but he wouldn't stop, and I think it's a terrible disaster all round, but he insists – although he doesn't seem to understand this sudden explosion any more than any of his friends do. It is very hard to believe in after nine years of mutual love and devotion sustained with so much trust and sense of responsibility on both sides – up to the last moment. It is very hard to bear or to surmount – but I must. It wasn't my fault! I suppose he hasn't a heart in the sense I understand heart.'[28]

To Dadie Rylands she reported that her daughter Sally, who had seen Day-Lewis as a second father, was taking it very hard, but that her son Hugo was being very supportive. 'It seems possible that there will be at least one man in my life who won't turn out a hysteric or a neurotic. I am still incredulous, Dadie . . . considering the grotesque circumstances of C's great bid for happiness, how could I not believe that it was a brainstorm from which, given pause for reflection, he would recover? But now, even supposing he should bitterly regret it, as he half feels that he may [a suggestion for which there is no other evidence], I know that I would never attempt to resume our relationship. This hasn't been, in any way, a decent human being, but a thing rising up from some hideous underworld in him that I never suspected.'[29]

Lehmann's accounts of Day-Lewis's behaviour did cause tensions in some of his oldest friendships. He refused to answer the charges she laid against him, or match her often-embellished accounts by revealing how wretched she had made him latterly. If people were curious, the details were all there in his poems such as 'The Neurotic'. Some took his silence as an admission of guilt and never forgave him. Rex Warner's second wife, Barbara, for instance, took Lehmann's side so staunchly that the bond between the two men which dated back to Oxford days was damaged for ever.

With his own family, Day-Lewis was forced to answer questions. Aunt Knos, on hearing of what he had done, was sure of the cause of his troubles. 'It was a fatal thing,' she wrote from Ireland, 'when [you] gave up Church worship . . . [you] have a very fine character but it would have been more fine if [you] regularly got sacramental strength to resist temptation.'[30]

Sean and Nicholas Day-Lewis were kept in the dark until long after the three month separation had been abandoned. They gathered with their parents at Brimclose at Easter 1950 to celebrate the award of a CBE to Day-Lewis in the King's Birthday Honours' List. Day-Lewis was pleased and amused, given his not so distant communist past. 'Commander of Broken English' was how he referred to his CBE in reply to letters of congratulation.

Neither of their parents gave the two sons any sign that anything was wrong. In July Mary and Nicholas joined Day-Lewis at Buckingham Palace to receive his decoration from the King. It was only in August 1950, when Mary had reluctantly agreed to divorce him, that Day-Lewis took sixteen-year-old Nicholas to lunch in London. 'The announcement, finally made once we had reached his office, was a tremendous embarrassment all around – very painful to him, obviously, and leaving me utterly disbelieving. In fact, for months I had the feeling the whole thing was a dreadful mistake.'[31]

Sean, away on RAF duty, was informed by letter on Chatto notepaper. Describing how he and Sean's mother had grown apart 'for about ten years now', Day-Lewis emphasized 'the fault was entirely mine'. He mentioned his involvement with Lehmann and now Balcon and how Mary was going to divorce him. 'This is a very hard thing for Mummy, I know: but I do badly need someone I can love, and who shares my interests. And, though I don't approve of people divorcing lightly, I think it is dishonest and in the end disastrous to go on living with somebody when your heart and mind are with somebody else.'[32] On Monday September 11, Day-Lewis left Brimclose for the last time. He booked a taxi to drive him to Axminster Station, leaving Mary to be comforted by her old friend from Sherborne, Diana Jordan. This time there would be no turning back.

In the letter telling her he was leaving, which she had burnt, Lehmann remembered Day-Lewis speaking of his desire to be with Balcon in terms of renewal. This was happening on several levels. At its most obvious it was renewing for a man coming up to his 46th birthday to find a reciprocal love with a beautiful and successful young woman of 25. The power of the attraction allowed him to set aside his usual inhibitions and indecision and make a bold grab for a new life. But it went deeper. Balcon's love of poetry, her knowledge of poets and her skill as a performer of verse led Day-Lewis to believe, as he told his son Sean, that they were akin to soul-mates in a way that he had never been with Mary. With Lehmann, he had come closer, but her involvement in his work and her remorseless promotion of it in the end threatened to overwhelm him.

That urge to renew was intimately linked to his poetry. Living a divided life had produced some of his most distinctive and best poetry in *Word Over All* but *Poems 1943–1947* had been almost too inward looking, too pessimistic and therefore less successful. Falling in love with Balcon held out to him both the chance of something fresh and positive in his personal life and therefore renewal as a writer by giving him a new range of feelings and experiences to examine in his poetry.

It was not so cynical as embarking on a new relationship in order to find new material. He was, friends remember from the time, genuinely and profoundly in love with Balcon. Her appreciation of and pre-existing dedication to his work only increased his sense of being hugely fortunate. But he was also able to see in their love a break with the past and a way forward from a place in his life that had become in every way sterile. 'Cecil had to be in a romantic clinch,' said Elizabeth Jane Howard (who was to work closely with him at Chatto in the decade ahead). 'That drove him to write his best poetry. The rest was marking time or practising. And when the romance was under attack – from Rosamond, from their friends, from Jill's family – in one way he thrived. Like many poets he thrived on anxiety of one kind or another.'[33]

Balcon was acutely conscious of the danger that for Day-Lewis 'I represented what John Betjeman calls in his poem "Pot Pourri from a Surrey Garden" "the slippery third path", that I offered an escape route from Rosamond and Mary'.[34] In this scenario, he was unable to leave both of them until there was another woman to go to – a need, psychologists might suggest, prompted by the early loss of his mother. But for the time being, though they were shunned by family and some friends, the new couple was simply overwhelmingly happy. In the cramped conditions of Balcon's flat in Pimlico, Day-Lewis would sit working at a small gate-legged kitchen table while Balcon attempted to master making the puddings and cakes that satisfied his sweet tooth. Her first effort at pancakes, she remembered, turned out so tough that they 'resembled Keats' death mask'.[35]

In August Day-Lewis ended a letter to her with the optimistic quotation from Paul Valéry that had introduced *Poems 1943–1947* but scarcely been reflected in the collection: '*Le vent se lève*'.

PART FOUR

A Kind of Peace

Chapter 25

The Estate of Simple Being

Fleeing from love and hate,
Pursuing change, consumed by motion,
Such arrivistes, unseeing,
Forfeit through endless self-evasion
The estate of simple being.
'The Tourists': *Pegasus and Other Poems* (1957)

In 1951, Day-Lewis became the second living writer to be featured in 'The Penguin Poets' paperbacks. Only T. S. Eliot had been honoured before in a popular series which drew a broad, non-specialist audience. It was an indication of Day-Lewis's standing as a poet in the early 1950s.

In his introduction to the selection, Day-Lewis wrote: 'Looking back over my verse of the last 20 years, I was struck by its lack of development – in the sense of one poetic phase emerging recognizably from the previous one and leading inevitably to the next: it would all be much tidier and more in accordance with critical specifications, were this not so. But my verse seems to me a series of fresh beginnings rather than a continuous line.'[1]

There had been clear and dramatic changes, most notably when he turned his back on the communist-inspired propaganda of the 1930s. Yet he was also being disingenuous about the overall lack of shape to his journey. While his path had not been straight, a route can be traced from those early Georgian works, through the political engagement and self-consciously modern imagery of the 1930s, and on to his poems about the divided self of the 1940s. His dedicated craftsmanship remained a constant. The self was always and unashamedly at the core of his poems, while his preoccupation with nature was a key component of his imagery, even when he was also writing about railroads and pit-heads. Most of all there was his determination that poems had to be about something, had to broaden beyond their form and his own experiences, to engage a wide public.

What may have been behind this denial of any element of continuity in his poetry was Day-Lewis's anxiety to escape what had already become his tag – 'poet of the thirties'. He saw himself as moving forward professionally, mirroring the renewal in his private life, and therefore wanted to travel unencumbered by the baggage of his past. 'Change I can see,' he conceded, 'change but I hope not decay ... This is partly because my interests have changed and my sympathies perhaps widened.'[2]

The Penguin selection appeared as Day-Lewis had reached another crossroads. He was questioning his future direction as a poet. The staples of the past no longer seemed as urgent or as compelling as subjects. He had left party politics behind at the end of the 1930s, though he remained engaged in his writing by issues confronting society. By resolving the conflicts in his private life when he committed his life to Jill Balcon, he had effectively removed much of the emotional tension that had made for such distinctive poetry in the 1940s. 'I have known great happiness and great unhappiness in my life,' he told Balcon soon after they fell in love, 'but I have never known such peace.'[3]

Yet peace and contentment are not usually the subjects of memorable poetry. Instead Day-Lewis was drawn in this mature period to the everyday, whether witnessed or remembered. There remained in his poetry the essential lyricism that had been there from the start but, without the impetus of trauma in his life, it took on a more sober, occasionally dry and ironic, often detached tone. A conversational, narrative element was increasingly apparent in verse that remained intensely personal but which more and more saw Day-Lewis acting as the seasoned observer, holding himself and his actions at arms' length.

The influence of Hardy was still central, though *Poems 1943–1947* may be judged to have marked its high point. Indeed, influence can be a misleading word for it suggests that Day-Lewis was simply imitating a poet he had so admired from undergraduate days. Another way of seeing it was that, like Hardy, Day-Lewis was one of the heirs to an English tradition that stretches back to William Wordsworth and beyond of writing of the ordinary, commonplace things and investing them with a sense of wonder.

There were parallels between his own career and that of Wordsworth, as Day-Lewis recognized in an article for the *New York Times* written in 1950 to mark the centenary of the Lakeland poet's death. Both had been swept up as young men by revolution and its promises of a new dawn – in Wordsworth's case by the French Revolution of 1789 – but both had grown disillusioned as they saw revolutionary ideals betrayed.

Within such a tradition, Day-Lewis grew steadily more assured and even experimental, for example shaping dialogue into verse. He became markedly less reactive to the poetic fashions of the moment in his writing, if not in his publishing career, even to the point of seeming old-fashioned.

The relationship between the poet and tradition was one of the subjects that Day-Lewis addressed publicly following his election in February 1951 as Professor of Poetry at Oxford University. The previous incumbent had been Maurice – now Sir Maurice – Bowra, his old tutor. Tenure was for five years. The salary was £250 a year for which Day-Lewis would be expected to deliver three lectures annually and carry out various ceremonial and judging roles at the university.

The post of Professor of Poetry was one of only two – the other being the Lady Margaret Chair of Divinity – for which all those who held a Master of Arts degree from the University (roughly 30,000 alumni) were entitled to vote. Such popular academic suffrage could fuel intrigue amongst the university's dons. In a letter to his American colleague, Wallace Notestein, the historian Hugh

Trevor-Roper[4] described the machinations at Oxford surrounding the 1951 Professor of Poetry election as 'one of those important and all-absorbing saturnalia in English life'.[5]

The chair had a long connection with Magdalen College, dating back to Matthew Arnold's[6] decade-long tenure in the 1850s. Bowra's obscure predecessor, The Revd Adam Fox, had managed to secure election in 1938 over the much better qualified David Cecil only after a concerted campaign by his colleagues, the Magdalen dons, to get their past pupils to turn up and vote. Having failed in 1946 to find anyone prepared to stand against Bowra, the same dons were now strongly backing the claims of C. S. Lewis, English tutor and Fellow of the college, well-known outside the university for his popular books on Christianity.

The combination of Lewis's Magdalen background and his religious beliefs, however, led academics at other colleges to cast around for a candidate with sufficient prestige to defeat him. They decided what was needed was a practising poet. C. S. Lewis did write verse, but only as a sideline. One of his leading detractors, Enid Starkie, a Fellow of Somerville College – and according to Trevor-Roper 'the Joan of Arc of the Resistance'[7] – had met Day-Lewis in 1944 at a dinner party given by Bowra and had subsequently become a contributor to the short-lived Orion. She contacted Day-Lewis and persuaded him to allow her to put his name forward as a stop C. S. Lewis candidate. His platform, she decided, would be that he was dissimilar to Lewis in everything but name. Where the Magdalen don was to be painted in this scenario as the representative of old, academic values, Day-Lewis, with his communist past, agnosticism and daily life as a poet, was to be promoted as the torchbearer of the future. As the Observer noted: 'Day-Lewis, though by now an established, almost venerable figure in English poetry, still represented something dangerous and new to many of the older graduates of Oxford.'[8]

As was the tradition with all candidates, Day-Lewis left the campaigning to Starkie and her circle. Such were the politics at the university, however, that another anti-C. S. Lewis grouping, led by the Provost of Worcester College, had nominated Edmund Blunden, eight years older than Day-Lewis and a poet for whom he had the greatest respect. With the opposition camp split between two candidates, it had been assumed that C. S. Lewis would triumph when votes were cast on February 8. However, at the last minute Blunden pulled out (and subsequently left his sick bed to vote for Day-Lewis). 'I feel very distressed,' Day-Lewis wrote to him, 'that I didn't get my withdrawal in first – it's another case of Gresham's Law, I fear – if that is the law by which the higher is driven out by the lower ... I am awfully touched by your generosity'.[9]

Day-Lewis won by a narrow majority – 194 to 173. It was the one occasion, he suggested, when the confusion around whether or not to use a hyphen in his surname had served him well. 'I attribute my narrow victory over CS Lewis to a handful of aged voters who, though determined to support the eminent Magdalen candidate, through failing sight or powers of concentration confused CS and CD Lewis on their voting papers.'[10]

For his first lecture – on June 1 – he took as his theme 'The Poet's Task'. It was recorded and broadcast by the BBC on its Third Programme. In a profile of Day-Lewis in the *News Chronicle*, reporter Kaye Webb described the scene: 'I had been expecting a few earnest undergraduates. Instead the biggest hall in Schools [the Examination Schools where finals are taken] was crowded ... people sat on the floor and clung to the window sills. Everybody gazed at him with adoration. It was more like a film star's appearance. I felt like asking him for an autograph myself. If Day-Lewis becomes the next Poet Laureate – and he would be a strong candidate for the post if he is interested – he will be the most popular since Tennyson.'[11]

The enthusiasm generated by that inaugural address was sustained through-out his tenure. In November 1951 Day-Lewis wrote to Balcon of his second lecture: '[it] was a success, I think. At any rate there was not a seat unoccupied in the Examination Schools and the Clerk of the Schools said that it was the biggest audience they had had since Arnold Toynbee lectured there.'[12] He seemed more pleased, however, by having had dinner afterwards with Bowra and Howard Florey,[13] Nobel Prize winner for his work on penicillin.

His lectures as Professor of Poetry were, Day-Lewis privately believed, a tri-umph of style over content. It was his performance that drew the crowds. He felt that he had little that was new to add to what he had first articulated at Cambridge in his Clark Lectures. Although a couple of his Oxford texts came out as pamphlets, in response to popular demand, he refused all offers to gather them as a book, as he had with the Clark addresses.

There was a more intimate tone to the Oxford lectures compared to Cam-bridge. This time Day-Lewis spoke more of his own approach to poetry. In his first lecture, he described it as nothing more or less than a habit. 'More and more, that is to say, the person who writes verses will find that he is dependent upon it, not only for pleasure ... He is now, for better or worse, committed to poetry as a way of life.'[14] He could not, he said, match the academic scholarship and knowledge of his predecessor, Bowra. Instead he offered reports back from his own particular coalface. 'Throughout that long series of love-affairs with Words which is the poet's working life, and wherein Thought must play the delicate dual role of chaperone and pandar, he is as selfish and egotistic as any other lover: he is concerned with the love-affairs of his colleagues only in so far as they may advance his own: he is out for what he can get out of them.'[15]

In such a spirit, he did, in the course of the lectures that followed, offer detailed assessments of Emily Dickinson and Edward Thomas. He also articu-lated some key beliefs, rejecting once again the F. R. Leavis school of criticism, this time by summoning Wordsworth as a witness. 'In "A Poet's Epitaph", [he] said the truest thing about one's attitude to poetry: it should be hanging, in very large print and a golden frame, above every critic's desk:

He is retired as noontide dew,
Or fountain in a noon-day grove;
And you must love him, ere to you
He will seem worthy of your love.

We must love the poet, in his work, before we find critical reasons for approving that work. Yes, the only way to knowledge about poetry is through love of poetry.'[16]

Those early Oxford lectures, as well as his ongoing translation of the twelve books of the *Aeneid* for the BBC, were written in Day-Lewis's new home, a studio at 73a Bedford Gardens in Campden Hill, west London. Balcon's bachelor girl Pimlico pied-à-terre had proved just too small. In May 1950 the couple had been the only witnesses to the marriage at Kensington Register Office of Laurie and Kathy Lee. It was a simple affair. 'Afterwards,' Balcon recalled, 'we went to a pub at the bottom of Kensington Church Street. There were a lot of dustmen in there and they raised a toast to Laurie and Kathy – "here's to a long life with plenty of trimmings".'[17] Opposite the pub was an estate agents'. Day-Lewis and Balcon looked in the window and saw Bedford Gardens advertised.

They had few possessions between them to bring to their new home. From Brimclose Day-Lewis had brought only two low armchairs, a green mat, his books and the narrow Pembroke table with two flaps and elegant, thin legs on which he liked to write. He preferred it – and the chair that went with it – to a conventional desk.

The flat was one of three studios in the building. They slept in a gallery and Balcon cooked in a tiny kitchen at the back below the bedroom area. The whole place was lit by a huge main window and was heated by a small stove. While Day-Lewis worked at his table on the days he wasn't at Chatto's, Balcon would learn her lines by practising them out loud in the tiny bathroom with the door shut so as not to disturb him.

Next door to them was the studio of the sculptor Franta Belsky[18] who befriended the couple and went on to make a bronze of Day-Lewis that is now in the National Portrait Gallery. Another neighbour was Ronald Searle,[19] the artist and creator of St Trinian's, the anarchic fictional boarding school.

Elizabeth Jane Howard visited the Day-Lewises soon after they had moved in. 'The best thing about the evening as far as I was concerned was finding that Cecil laughed at the same things, and not only that, but that he was just as good at being convulsed to the point of tears as Jilly had always been.'[20]

All who came into contact with the couple heard the laughter. Even Sean Day-Lewis, though distressed by the break-up of his parents' marriage, wrote: 'When I encountered them for the first time after they had set up house together, the release of all inhibitions was palpable. Their continuous endearments and physical touchings, their constant proximity to one another, suggested that they could hardly believe their luck.'[21]

Though Musbury was now out of bounds, Day-Lewis quickly introduced Balcon to his beloved Dorset. In October 1950, a friend recommended the New Inn, a pub with rooms above in the village of Piddletrenthide in the heart of the Dorset countryside in the Piddle Valley. In a small public sitting room, Day-Lewis could work in the mornings, while Balcon sat with him reading. Then they would set off, with a picnic supplied by the pub, to explore Hardy country, guided by an old book of sepia photographs which identified the real life settings of some of his novels.

Here in this niche on the face of the May morning,
Fast between vale and sky, growth and decay,
Dream with the clouds, my love, throb to the awakened
Earth who has quickened a paradise from clay,
Sweet air and clay.

Now is a chink between two deaths, two eternities.
Seed here, root here, perennially cling!
Love me today and I shall live today always!
Blossom, my goldenmost, at-long-last spring,
My long, last spring!

'On A Dorset Upland': *Pegasus and Other Poems* (1957)

They even entertained the idea of finding a home in Dorset far away from London. One property in particular, a small Georgian house in the coastal village of Burton Bradstock, came up for sale three times. Each time they viewed it and talked about buying it, but finances would not permit. And, they decided, it was too far from London to enable them to carry on with their work.

In August 1950, Day-Lewis had come to a financial agreement with Mary when she finally consented reluctantly to divorce him. He was to give her Brimclose, pay for Nicholas's school fees at Sherborne until he left in 1952, and provide Mary with an income of £1,000 a year. It would leave him with around £2,000 a year to live on. It was, he believed, a fair settlement (and one he augmented with substantial cheques at Christmas and on Mary's birthday) but meant that for Day-Lewis and Balcon, without a home that they owned, money would always be tight and a continual source of worry. When in August 1951 they were invited to join the Spenders for a holiday at an inn on Lake Garda in Italy, they had to sell a pair of silver coffee-pots, given to them as a present, to pay the fare.

More pressing initially, however, was the fear that the courts would not grant Mary's petition for divorce on the grounds of her husband's adultery because she would be judged already to have condoned such behaviour during his long and public relationship with Rosamond Lehmann. Such an obstacle to Day-Lewis remarrying threatened to deepen the difficulties Balcon had already encountered in convincing her parents of the wisdom of her choice of an older, already married partner. Indeed Sir Michael and Lady Balcon had gone so far as to contact Mary in an effort to persuade her to go back on her decision to divorce. They hoped that if the prospect of marrying Day-Lewis was removed, their daughter might be talked into breaking it off with him.

'Of course if a divorce is refused by the courts,' Day-Lewis wrote to Balcon after a meeting with Mary, 'and the lawyers say that M cannot bring an action because of condonation, then we will all have to think again. I could at least get a legal separation and you change your name by deed poll, but we needn't yet worry about this alternative.'[22] He went on to reflect upon Lady Balcon's decision to join her husband in outright opposition to Day-Lewis, having initially remained neutral about him: 'About your parents, dear love, it seems to me that horrible as it is for you at the time, your mother's change of front is the best thing that can have happened. It means that she and your father are reconciled, are not at loggerheads about us, and therefore that you need feel no more of the guilt you felt for creating this between them. Your trouble now is a single, simple one, though bad enough: their combined attitude to you. This must surely alter when I make an honest woman of you. They must surely come round when I make an honest woman of you, mustn't they? I shall never forgive them myself for treating you like this but that's another matter. For God sake, my own beloved Jill don't give in to any emotional blackmail on their part. I know how desperately hard it must be for you to harden your heart against them, but a time comes when one has to fight hard and piteously for one's own life and love and what is most real to one.'[23]

On March 5, 1951 the *Daily Telegraph* headlined a report from Southampton 'Decree For Wife of C Day-Lewis: Actress Cited'. The undefended action for divorce had been granted on the grounds of Day-Lewis's adultery with 'Jill Balcon, the actress ... the daughter of Sir Michael Balcon, the film chief'. A similar report appeared prominently in both the *Sunday Times* and the *Evening Standard*, further antagonizing Balcon's parents. Sir Michael went so far at one stage as to threaten to kill Day-Lewis. Sean was another to be upset. He resented the fact that it had been his mother who was forced to attend court in Southampton – 'silly, dull, sordid' were the words she used to describe the experience in her diary[24] – when it had been his father who had destroyed their marriage.[25]

Divorce law demanded that adultery be proved. This gave Day-Lewis two options. The first was to arrange to be 'caught' in a hotel room with an anonymous woman, hired for the purpose and then part of the divorce petition. This would have spared Balcon's reputation but there was the ever-present fear that Rosamond Lehmann, furious at Day-Lewis's betrayal, might have then intervened in court proceedings to detail his adultery with her and so threaten the smooth passage of Mary's petition.

Reluctantly Day-Lewis had to fall back on the second option of allowing Balcon to be named in court. 'It involved,' she recalled, 'a stage version of a country detective from Winchester coming up to town and visiting us "unexpectedly" at our flat in Bedford Gardens. It was a farce. When he rang the bell, I was making dinner in my apron but Cecil was out having a drink with Nick Roughead. It was obvious the flat only had one bed, but the detective insisted that was not enough. "No, I have to find you both together," he said. So he came back later when Cecil, Nick and I were having dinner. That, evidently, was proof enough for the courts.'[26]

The couple were now free to get married. On April 27, 1951, Day-Lewis's 47th birthday, they returned to Kensington Register Office. Balcon wore a coral coloured dress, with a Victorian neck-line, with a pale pink short jacket, bronze sandals and a coral hat with pale pink veil. Her bouquet was freesias and she had on the eighteenth-century aquamarine ear-rings and necklace Day-Lewis had given her. The groom was in a dark suit and his trademark bow tie.

Their witnesses were Balcon's cleaning lady from her Pimlico flat, Mrs Pizzey, and Lady Balcon. There was a small lunch afterwards in the upstairs room at the Ivy restaurant near Seven Dials, paid for by Sir Michael. He had telephoned his daughter before the wedding but refused to attend. Balcon's only contact with her parents had been clandestine meetings with her mother in her parked car in Hyde Park.

Other guests at the lunch included Charles Fenby and Charles Tennyson, a grandson of the poet and an old family friend of the Balcons who had tried unsuccessfully to persuade Sir Michael to attend. Standing *in loco parentis*, the elderly Tennyson made a speech in which he quoted approvingly from *Noah And The Waters*, unaware that Day-Lewis had been trying to forget his attempt at a morality play since its critical drubbing in 1936. Before the meal Sir Michael was persuaded by one of his colleagues to come to the entrance hall of the Ivy for a few minutes, but his disapproval of the marriage remained unaltered.

After the celebration the couple returned home to find Ronald Searle had left them a cartoon propped up in one of Day-Lewis's armchairs as a wedding present. It showed the headmistress of St Trinian's introducing a new girl to three hardened inmates who held their instruments of torture behind their backs. 'Prudence is new to St Trinian's', the caption read. 'I want you to take care of her, girls.' On the back Searle had added: 'For Prudence, read Jill'.

The weekend after their wedding was spent at the Tennysons' cottage in Walberswick on the Suffolk coast. Ivy Tennyson had packed a hamper and Balcon's brother Jonathan lent his car as transport. On their return, the couple's professional lives continued as before. Balcon remained sought-after as an actress. At the Old Vic she played Zenocrate to Donald Wolfit's Tamburlaine in Christopher Marlowe's play of the same name. It was the first production in 300 years. Directed by Tyrone Guthrie, it was part of a Guthrie season which also saw her play Titania in *A Midsummer Night's Dream*. After a lengthy British tour, there was an invitation to join the company for performances in South Africa, but Balcon decided to stay in London with her new husband.

Day-Lewis was busy completing his translation of the *Aeneid*. The two of them had also begun, at Bristol Old Vic in October 1950, performing together as readers of poetry. 'Cecil was a natural. He read not as an actor but as a poet,' remembered Hallam Tennyson, son of Charles and a BBC producer who worked with both of them. 'Jill was the professional. Her trained voice was rich and multi-toned and, when it was appropriate, heart-wrenching. They were both enormously glamorous and made a perfect pairing on stage.'[27] It was a verdict shared by Elizabeth Bowen who wrote to Balcon, after seeing the two of them perform: 'there can be a touch of genius and certainly you and Cecil have it. I do thank you both, with love, for letting me share it.'[28]

In life, too, Day-Lewis and Balcon were opposites who together, friends believed, made a whole. 'There was a warm, emotionally open side to Jill,' Tennyson said, 'whereas Cecil was always welcoming, full of interest in you, but in a way detached, almost repressed about his own emotional life. I always felt that she gave him confidence to realize himself emotionally as a poet and as a person, to continue to develop and explore at an age when many men settle back.'[29]

In June 1951 Day-Lewis's line-for-line translation of the Latin of Virgil's *Aeneid* into loose English hexameters began to be broadcast on the BBC as part of the Festival of Britain, staged by the government to celebrate the country's post-war progress. Virgil's work was thought to contain the right mixture of the epic and the nationalistic to contribute to the Festival's other purpose – boosting British morale at a time when some rationing was still in force.

Its combination of the heroic and the patriotic was also part of its attraction for Day-Lewis. His translation of the *Georgics* in 1940 had helped him rediscover his love for his country after the disillusionment of his communist period, while his taste for heroes dated back to childhood. Moreover, the strong narrative in the *Aeneid* and its passages of lyrical verse played to his already established strengths as a poet.

Day-Lewis had, though, originally planned to play a role in the Festival by another route. He had been part of the committee set up to adjudicate a competition for poetry to be included in the celebration, but had resigned when he decided he wanted his still unpublished *An Italian Visit* to be entered in the competition. Lehmann was still withholding her permission for sections of it to be made public. However, because other parts of it had been broadcast already on the Third Programme, it was eventually barred from the competition. *The Aeneid of Virgil* proved a more effective and acceptable contribution.

It was widely praised by critics both at the time of its broadcast and following its publication the following year. The *Observer* hailed Day-Lewis's translation as 'richly rewarding ... for some tens of thousands of listeners a rediscovery of the father of Western civilization'.[30] An unsigned piece in the *Times* complained that some of the contemporary phrases Day-Lewis had used would eventually become dated, making the translation 'largely a period piece', but concluded: 'on the whole it is in the urgent and resourcefully varied metre that Professor Day-Lewis's translation achieves its highest success. There is no question of the vigour and animation with which he has proceeded through so long and exacting a labour.'

It was precisely Day-Lewis's success in rendering the first-century BC tale of Aeneas, a Trojan who travelled Italy and played his part in the foundation of Rome, in language relevant to and resonant of 1950s Britain, that made the translation such a success. He had been given considerable help in the task by W. F. Jackson Knight, a classical scholar from Exeter University – 'a tubby, twinkling little man,' he reported to Balcon, 'with a voice like a castrated seagull'.[31]

Amongst admirers of the work was Patric Dickinson, the BBC poetry producer who had first brought Day-Lewis and Balcon together. 'A translator,' he later wrote, 'must translate for the times he lives in. The problem he sets himself is almost impossible to solve, for he has to feel the style and rhythm of the original and translate both style and rhythm into an idiom his own times will accept, as poetry in itself, without doing damage to the master.'[32]

Another element that had drawn Day-Lewis to the *Aeneid* was the echo he found of his own circumstances as he worked on his translation. The task was undertaken during the period that saw the breakdown of his marriage and the ending of his relationship with Lehmann. In the early books, in particular, Virgil describes agonized scenes between a guilty Aeneas and an outraged Queen Dido as he struggles to abandon her and what he regards as a doomed love affair. Whatever the parallels between Dido and Lehmann, however, Day-Lewis claimed that he had always had Balcon's voice in mind as he wrote the queen's lines. The BBC producer, Basil Taylor, cast her instead as Venus, the goddess of love, arguably a more appropriate role since it is Venus who rescues Aeneas from those who would destroy him because of his betrayal of Dido.

The success of his translation of the *Aeneid* brought with it a fresh wave of publicity for Day-Lewis. The *Sunday Times* featured him in its 'Portrait Gallery', captured on camera smoking his pipe. Listing his endeavours that included writing, translating and reading verse, serving as Professor of Poetry at Oxford, and penning 'dazzling detective novels', the paper concluded: 'how unfair that accomplishments enough to satisfy the pride of six men should be united in Mr Day-Lewis'.[33]

Chapter 26

Find our Balance

Now is a chance to count the change,
To check the income against the outgoings, and find our balance
'The Homeward Prospect': *An Italian Visit* (1953)

In the spring of 1952 Day-Lewis gave a series of lectures in Italy at the invitation of the British Council. The tour started in Palermo, Sicily, and ended in Venice. He described it as 'living in the grand manner' in a letter home to Balcon, who had stayed behind because she was touring with the Old Vic, but he quickly tired of the round of dinners and drinks parties that accompanied his talks and poetry readings. 'I dine at the embassy [in Rome] after the lecture on Monday,' he reported to her, 'a rather formidable programme of other social engagements are planned for me with writers . . . and the usual Roman culture-loving princesses. I wish it was all over. I'm so exhausted in between the efforts to be sociable and communicative with all these people.'[1]

Despite the outward appearance he always gave of being charming, interested and at his ease at such events, Day-Lewis never really enjoyed standing around with a glass in his hand making small talk. 'Our friend Ralph Vaughan Williams[2] used to call them perpendicular parties,' Balcon remembered. 'As we stepped up to the front door and heard the buzz of voices and laughter, he would go pale with horror.'[3] And, though he was an accomplished and sought-after performer, he was not one who for ever craved the limelight. He saw taking to a platform as part of the public duty of a poet – again investing his craft with a kind of displaced religious significance. While he enjoyed the endorsement of an audience and was aware of his own capacity to hold their attention with his voice, looks and manner, there was always a slight reluctance about him in public, accentuated by a natural modesty, that only increased his appeal.

For all his horror of 'Roman culture-loving princesses', Day-Lewis was once again inspired on the British Council trip by the Italian landscape. Belatedly he had developed a taste for travel and Italy had become a favourite destination with its 'lineaments of gratified desire' which seemed to him to have been 'laid out for the lust of the eye'. The lines are taken from *An Italian Visit*, the collection he had written in a rush in the immediate aftermath of his visit with Rosamond Lehmann to Bernard Berenson's villa near Florence. After he left her, Lehmann had asked that it should not be published as a collection, and he had acceded to her request, although the delay brought with it more financial hardship. Finally she relented in January 1953.

255

An Italian Visit sees Day-Lewis return to his early 1930s style of writing a sequence of poems – though this time with titles. There is, though, none of the evangelizing spirit of old, as he stresses when he amusedly looks back on his younger self at the start of Part Three.

We who 'flowered' in the Thirties
Were an odd lot: sceptical yet susceptible,
Dour though enthusiastic, horizon-addicts
And future-fans, terribly apt to ask what
Our all-very-fine sensations were in aid of.
We did not, you will remember, come to coo.
Still there is hope for us. Rome has absorbed
Other barbarians: yes, and there's nobody quite so
Sensuously rich and reckless as the reformed
Puritan . . .

'A Letter from Rome'

Overall this travel book in verse combines Day-Lewis's love of what he saw while in Italy – from great works of art to everyday fountains and street scenes celebrated in often elaborately colloquial terms – with a series of ambitious poems carefully crafted in the style of poets he loved. It was these that constituted the most discussed section of the collection when *An Italian Visit* was published.

In the autumn of 1952 Day-Lewis had returned to Italy again, this time with Balcon, and retraced part of the journey he had made with Lehmann to see works of art in Florence. He describes these in Part Five. As the artists involved had been inspired by others, he, as a poet, was acknowledging his own debts. Each was clearly acknowledged with initials at the start of the poem. There is Luca Della Robbia's 'Singing Children' in the manner of Thomas Hardy, Donatello's 'Judith and Holofernes' (W. B. Yeats), Leonardo's 'Annunciation' (Robert Frost), Piero di Cosimo's 'Perseus Rescuing Andromeda' (W. H. Auden) and Verrocchio's 'Boy With Dolphin' (Dylan Thomas). This last is perhaps the most surprising inclusion, Thomas having had little obvious or elsewhere acknowledged influence on Day-Lewis, though his distinctive style was inviting of pastiche.

All critics were impressed by Day-Lewis's skill in adopting with wit but not malice his colleagues' voices but some went on to ask was Day-Lewis also revealing how imitative he was, how devoid of his own voice. 'There should be no need to insist upon Mr Day-Lewis's technical accomplishment,' his friend Raymond Mortimer wrote in a long review in the *Sunday Times*, 'it is so conspicuous . . . History shows that in Europe men have continually felt impelled to innovate in all the arts. Once in a way an individual artist refuses to march with the times, because the new methods do not suit his genius.' Mortimer's view that Day-Lewis was not an innovator seemed to be confirmed by his detailing at some length what he saw as the influence of Robert Browning on *An Italian Visit*. He then concluded: 'a good artist might be defined as a man who puts to good use the inventions made by other good artists'.[4]

256

The charge that he lacked his own voice because he was so drawn to the voices of others was one that Day-Lewis had already tackled in the preface to the Penguin Poets selection. There he had written: 'If, like myself, he [the poet] is a writer still much more open to the influence of other poets, he will often find that he has more or less consciously used some other poet to mediate between his material and his imagination.' Freely acknowledging his influences – listed as Yeats, Frost, Auden and Hardy, all featured in Part Five of *An Italian Visit* – Day-Lewis went on: 'they suggested to me ways of saying what I had to say. Any poem thus influenced is not secondhand: I think it possible that a reader with a sensitive ear, a dispassionate point of view, and a thorough knowledge of the poetry of Hardy, say, would find as much difference as similarity between a poem of mine, influenced by him, and one of Hardy's own'.[5]

The other distinctive and unusual section in *An Italian Visit* is the playful opening section, 'Dialogue at the Airport', where Day-Lewis experiments with form to show three travellers, Tom, Dick and Harry, all representing aspects of the poet, in a conversation shaped into hexameters. Tom is a hedonist who cares only for the present and the opportunities it offers. Dick is more angst-ridden, a Romantic and a scholar, looking to the past, hungry to achieve again the perfection made manifest in great works of art. And Harry is a social philosopher who broods on the future and the destiny of man. Each contains elements of Day-Lewis's own divided self. What unites them, though, is the anticipation that the act of setting out on a journey will reveal to them new meaning. As Dick puts it:

> *If I could find that place where nymph and shepherd meet*
> *And distance melts into deity, I would unearth my buried*
> *Heirlooms, my sealed orders. Genius of the place, remarry*
>   *These sundered elements, make one circle at last complete!*

As ever, though, Day-Lewis is aware that investing such hopes in a journey will lead to inevitable disappointment.

> *A driven heart, a raven-shadowing mind*
> *Loom above all my pastorals, impend*
>   *My traveller's joy with fears*
>   *That travelling has no end.*
>
>   'Bus To Florence': Part Four

It is a theme that helps build up to the climax of the whole sequence, 'Elegy Before Death', which, as seen already, both anticipates Day-Lewis's break with Lehmann, and revisits one of his constant themes – namely that nothing endures, everything contains within it the seeds of its own destruction, and only living for the moment makes any sense.

> *Our sun is setting. Terrestrial planes shift*
> *And slide towards dissolution, the terraced gardens*
> *Quaver like waves, and in the garden urn*
> *Geraniums go ashen. Now we are tempted, each*

To yearn that his struggling counterpoint, carried away
Drowned by the flood's finale, shall return
To silence. Why do we trouble
A master theme with cadenzas
That ring out, fade out over its fathomless unconcern?

The final section of *An Italian Visit*, 'The Homeward Prospect', sees Day-Lewis try, only partially successfully, to lift the gloom that he has drawn down over the beautiful Italian landscape. He has Tom, Dick and Harry reprise their earlier conversation, now looking back over what they have learnt on their journey. Tom goes home 'enriched', Dick 'sobered' and Harry 'lightened of one illusion, and therefore one truth the richer'. In the closing lines of the collection, spoken by Harry, Day-Lewis offers a note of thanks to Lehmann.

For one immeasurable moment the world's hands stood still
And the worm that ticks at the heart of the golden hoard was silent.
Losing my heart to this alien land, I renewed my true love:
Lending my love to death, I gained this grain of vision.
I took my pen. What I wrote is thanks to her and to Italy.

It reads like an epitaph to his life with Lehmann and potentially offers another insight into how he viewed the course of their relationship. Their love renewed his true love – for poetry – but she was sacrificed to that love, having served her purpose and given him the grain of vision that inspired him to take up once again his pen.

If it was indeed a final farewell, then seeing it in print could only have added to Lehmann's pain at what she continued to regard as Day-Lewis's bewildering betrayal. There had been no contact between them after he left her except for the brief exchange of notes in late 1952 that cleared the way for *An Italian Visit* to be published. By a curious irony it was Mary Day-Lewis with whom Lehmann continued to correspond. She had sold The Manor House soon after Day-Lewis left and had moved back to London. Their paths would occasionally cross, despite Day-Lewis's best efforts to avoid it. At a centenary reception given by Chatto's in 1954, he had absented himself from the receiving line for guests in case his former lover, a sometime Chatto author, should arrive and make a scene. All was well until a malicious journalist came up to Day-Lewis, standing with Balcon, and told him that Lehmann, who had been carefully guided into another room, wanted to speak to him. When he approached her she told him he was mistaken and launched a stinging and public attack on his conduct towards her. He withdrew and left the party at once, his face the colour of parchment.

For years afterwards Lehmann would tell anyone who listened about how shamefully he had treated her. Almost two decades after their break up the diarist Frances Partridge recorded a conversation with Lehmann while on a trip to Italy. Lehmann told her, Partridge wrote, that Day-Lewis's 'desertion was a complete surprise and shock and she still cannot get over it, or recognize it as genuine. It's a measure of her innocent vanity that she still thinks of it as "wrong and mistaken".[6]

After Day-Lewis's departure, Lehmann completed only two more novels, the second, *A Sea-Grape Tree*, published in the 1970s and widely seen as inferior in stature to her earlier works. *The Echoing Grove* of 1953 was, however, a more substantial work, later filmed, and has been taken by some as her revenge on Day-Lewis. The title, with references to William Blake's[7] description of female love as 'the infernal grove', also recalls both Day-Lewis's earlier anthology *The Echoing Green* and the line in 'Elegy Before Death' where love is betrayed in 'this ilex grove where shades are lost in shade'.

The connection between the novel and Day-Lewis could have been made all the more powerfully if Lehmann had followed her original intention to call it *Buried Day* – a quotation from the same Meredith stanza in 'Modern Love' that had given her the title for *Dusty Answer* 26 years earlier. Her publishers, however, advised her against such a choice, fearful that if she did the novel would only be read as her account of her relationship with Day-Lewis (though it was published in France as *Le Jour Enseveli*).

Such an outcome would have done Lehmann a great disservice as a writer for the book is much more than a *roman à clef*, but it does contain parallels with her own recent experiences, worked into the narrative, reshaped and rearranged. When Dinah asks Madeleine, late in the novel, if she now has a lover, her middle-aged sister replies: 'A lover? No. Nor want. It's all over, it won't happen any more. I like company and I've got a few friends. I don't miss having an emotional life.'

With his translation of the *Aeneid* and *An Italian Visit* now completed, Day-Lewis began urgently exploring new projects. One driving force was the need to earn money. Balcon was pregnant and expecting their first child in September. Day-Lewis provided the voice of Leonardo da Vinci in a Basil Wright documentary for television, *The Drawings of Leonardo da Vinci*. He was a late recruit to the project, stepping in at the last minute when Dylan Thomas withdrew. There was a new Nicholas Blake in the spring of 1953. *The Dreadful Hollow* was set in Dorset in Piddletrenthide, renamed Prior's Umborne. Day-Lewis also renewed his interest in writing drama. It started with an approach from J. B. Priestley who suggested that Day-Lewis might rewrite his new play in verse. Though he was flattered, especially since Priestley had previously questioned his war record, Day-Lewis decided against. 'I doubt if it's a good proposition', he told his son, Sean.[8] Instead he embarked on his own stage play, a Cold War drama called *The Exiles*, but was disappointed when the finished product failed to excite any interest.

Its political preoccupations reflected Day-Lewis's alarm at the growing antagonism between East and West. He still believed passionately in the poet's role to animate public debate and so agreed to support the Authors' World Peace Appeal (AWPA), a left-leaning organization set up in the early 1950s to warn of the danger of nuclear proliferation between the superpowers and to promote dialogue between the protagonists. Dylan Thomas, L. A. G. Strong,

Naomi Mitchison and Doris Lessing[9] were other names drawn to a well intentioned but largely ineffective venture.

Stephen Spender was distressed to see Day-Lewis involved and wrote to chastise him after reading newspaper reports of a statement his old friend had written for an AWPA conference. It provoked another of their characteristically frank exchanges. 'Dear Stephen,' Day-Lewis began, 'I am much too fond of you to reply in kind except to say that bits of your letters seem to me peevish, supercilious, insulting.' If he had read the full text of his statement, rather than the newspaper report, he continued, Spender would have had less cause for alarm. 'You would have seen that I was concentrating on two main points. First, that it is my belief that it is better to try to maintain some contact with individuals "on the other side" and to try to make them realise that there is a will for peace on this side, than to throw up one's hands in despair. Second I was warning the members of the AWPA not to let their movement get in the hands of communists and be used as a political weapon. I am well aware of the danger of the latter: but I am prepared to risk playing into the hands of the CP (which we are not in yet); to be frightened of any peace activity by this danger is play into the hands of fear itself.'[10]

The temporary awkwardness with Spender, whose magazine *Encounter* was later shown to have received CIA-funding without his knowledge, was quickly resolved. Day-Lewis was not one to harbour grudges. If he felt he was being misrepresented, however, he could be waspish. In early 1953, the young, highly-rated (by Day-Lewis among others) poet, John Heath-Stubbs[11] penned a satirical article in the literary quarterly, *Nine*, describing Day-Lewis as a 'knave' who had trampled over the better qualified C. S. Lewis to become Professor of Poetry at Oxford because he was greedy for the money it brought him. The charge was, Day-Lewis was advised, actionable, but he restricted himself to sending a letter pointing out that his 'salary' as professor was only £250 a year. The magazine's unrepentant editor, Peter Russell, replied that people in Day-Lewis's position should 'accept public criticism without resentment', prompting a second letter from Day-Lewis, detailing his own distrust of the motives of people who wrote satire. 'Personal satire, such as [Roy] Campbell's, seems to me nowadays nearly always a parade or a bolstering-up of the writer's own ego.'[12]

There was more conflict, this time of a less public kind, when Nicholas Day-Lewis, by now an undergraduate at his father's old Oxford college, Wadham, became engaged to what he quickly saw was a totally unsuitable girl. 'Having finally realised my stupidity,' he recalled, 'I tried to break it off. The girl's mother wrote to Cecil demanding that I marry her. I had previously managed to get the girl pregnant, and her mother had obtained an abortion for her, but as a result felt I was duty bound to stay with her. Cecil, who was quite within his parental rights to castigate me for my behaviour, was not in the least judgemental but took my side and wrote back to the girl's mother telling her it was my decision and she should "butt out".'[13]

The mother had threatened to go to the newspapers, hoping Day-Lewis's public standing would make his son's actions into headlines. However, Nicholas said, his father was not prepared to sacrifice his son to protect his own good name, remained 'very supportive' throughout, and eventually faced down the mother's accusation of breach of promise.[14]

Such discord was put to one side when, on September 17, Balcon presented Day-Lewis with his first daughter. Lydia Tamasin was born at Queen Charlotte's Hospital, London, almost a fortnight early. The couple had chosen Lydia, Day-Lewis told a newspaper, because of its classical allusions, and Tamasin after Thomas Hardy's Thomasin Yeobright in *The Return of the Native* and Tamasin, a character in Ivy Compton-Burnett's[15] 1947 novel *Manservant and Maidservant*.

The impending arrival of Tamasin, as she was always known, had prompted her parents to look for a new home. Their studio flat would not accommodate a baby and the nanny, Minnie Phyllis Bowler, they had employed to look after her using a small allowance that Balcon agreed to accept from her estranged father. He had once again exploded when Day-Lewis failed to mention Balcon's maiden name in a birth announcement in the *Times*, but by the time Tamasin was three months old Lady Balcon had arranged for her granddaughter and nanny to be collected by her husband's chauffeur and driven over for a visit. Sir Michael was soon doting on Tamasin.

Just before Tamasin was born the Day-Lewises had found a small, terraced Regency house just round the corner from their studio at 96 Campden Hill Road. The short lease at £250 a year was affordable. It had a basement kitchen and tiny dining room, giving on to a small rear paved garden with a cherry tree. At the front was a shed that could house Tamasin's pram. Her bedroom, the day nursery and the nanny's room, all compact, were squeezed on to the top floor. At street level was a drawing room and the first floor housed the couple's bedroom at the front and Day-Lewis's study at the back. Scouring local antique shops and auctions, they managed to augment their few possessions and furnish it. One purchase was a fender for the fire, recorded in his poem 'Lot 96'. Another find was a round rent table, with a Regency top and a Victorian base. It cost just £30 because of this mismatch and became Day-Lewis's desk.

Sitting at it, he began, as an exercise when he had no other 'inspiration', to describe the view. It developed into a poem dedicated to Kenneth Clark.

From where I am sitting, my windowframe
Offers a slate roof, four chimneypots,
One aerial, half of a leafless tree,
And sky the colour of dejection.
          'View from An Upper Window': *The Gate and Other Poems* (1962)

From such superficially unpromising material, he crafted a wider meditation.

Perhaps I should think about the need for frames.
At least they can lend us a certain ability
For seeing a fragment as a kind of whole
Without spilling over into imbecility.

Day-Lewis's life, as he told Balcon in a note attached to her Christmas present in 1953, had never been happier. 'Darling, this has been such a wonderful year, my happiest year, with you and the divine Tamasin you presented me with that it demands a special present to commemorate it. I adore you, sweet Jill.'[16] But, as he had written so many times in his poetry, such happiness seldom lasts long unchallenged. Day-Lewis's attention had been drawn to her closest friend.

Chapter 27

Self-Betrayal

Betrayal is always a self-betrayal
Where love is concerned. The beautiful place,
Mortgaged by our ancestral sin,
Grows more untenable and more unreal
Each time, however needfully, we sell
Some share of it
'George Meredith 1861': *Pegasus and Other Poems* (1957)

To assist Day-Lewis with his work as their Reader, Chatto & Windus employed a series of assistants, many young English graduates fresh out of university, happy to write reports on unsolicited manuscripts for very little money. Elizabeth Jane Howard was an exception in that she was already a published novelist when she was taken on, at Day-Lewis's own suggestion, to help him out around the start of 1954.

Howard had been a close friend of Balcon's since their days together at the BBC during the Second World War. Since Balcon's marriage to Day-Lewis she had also come to know him well and had sought his 'avuncular advice' on her writing career and her unhappy personal life.[1] It was a mark of how close she was to both the Day-Lewises that they asked her to be one of Tamasin's god-mothers and later invited her to accompany them on one of their jaunts to Piddletrenthide in Dorset. Balcon believed she had every reason to trust the friend she had asked to be a go-between with Day-Lewis in the early, troubled days of their relationship.

Just turned 30 and with striking good looks that had seen her model for *Vogue*, Howard also possessed a vulnerability and neediness that had attracted a string of well-known male admirers. An early, ill-fated marriage at 19 to the naturalist Peter Scott, son of the polar explorer and 14 years her senior, had collapsed following her affair with his half-brother. When she left Scott, she relinquished the care of their daughter, Nicola, and had only limited access to her as she grew up. Her subsequent affairs had ended unhappily, most recently a liaison with old Etonian, Paul Bowman.

Howard had worked first as an actress in repertory, then with her deep, sensual voice as a broadcaster, but had latterly turned to writing fiction. Her first book, *The Beautiful Visit*, a coming-of-age story, had won the John Llewellyn Rhys Prize for young novelists in 1951 and had attracted great acclaim. Antonia White[2] had hailed her as a 'tremendous talent', but Howard's publisher,

Jonathan Cape, had paid her little for the work, instead chasing her round his office trying to force his attentions on her. Short of money, she was struggling to complete what became her 1956 novel, *The Long View*, one of her most critically admired works, a study of a marriage told backwards in time.

Over dinner with the Day-Lewises, she revealed that she needed part-time work to pay the rent. Cecil snapped her up as his assistant at Chatto's. For much of her time there, she would be in on the alternate weeks when he was writing at home. He had now switched to working one week on and one week off. Often, though, they would overlap, especially when it was time to write the jacket blurbs for books. They shared his office at the top of the building. 'It was very small and very dusty,' Howard remembered. 'Everything was covered in a kind of greasy soot. There would be pigeons outside the window on the parapet and Cecil was forever eating bath buns and then feeding the crumbs to them.'[3] Soon Day-Lewis had a pet name for Howard – Lizbie – taken from a Hardy poem 'To Lizbie Brown'. While Balcon was away for the night at a party to mark the tenth anniversary of the Bristol Old Vic, they took a trip together to Dedham Vale on the borders of Essex and Suffolk to pay homage to John Constable. Day-Lewis recorded it in a poem. 'Dedham Vale, Easter 1954', is dedicated to EJH.

She had, she claimed, no suspicion that he might be falling in love with her until the day he declared himself. 'I tried but I didn't have the strength to resist him. I would defy any woman to resist him. He was an exceptionally beautiful man. His was a very lived-in face and the more handsome for it. He dressed to suit his persona – he was more than debonair, he was glamorous. He had one trick that was unique to him: he could purr continuously, like a cat.'[4]

At the time she was, she recalled, lonely, low and longing to be in love and therefore both inviting of and receptive to Day-Lewis's advances. The three-month affair was intense but short-lived.

It was Howard's guilt about betraying her friend, Balcon, that prompted her suddenly and without warning to end the affair. 'I knew that if it went on much further, I was going to be completely overwhelmed by him and would want to spend my life with him. I couldn't do that because of Jill. So I told him it had to stop.'[5] In her autobiography, *Slipstream*, Howard later described her betrayal of Balcon as 'one of the worst things I ever did'.[6]

It was the first time that a woman had left Day-Lewis rather than the other way round and his male ego took it very hard. He tried at first to persuade Howard to change her mind. When this failed, his attitude changed. He became angry and abusive and sent her a copy of a new poem, 'Moods of Love'. This sonnet sequence begins with a celebration of love.

> *Together on the gentle dunes, they know*
> *A world more lucid for lust's afterglow*

Quickly, though, it turns bitter as Day-Lewis launches an attack on womankind that is uncharacteristic of his writing in general but echoes the sentiment he had expressed in 'Elegy Before Death' when he had realized that he had to leave Lehmann.

The dance, the plumage, all that flaunting day
Of blood's clairvoyance and enchanter's wit
Making trite things unique – you reckon it
Tells more than brute necessity at play?

Unwise. Another tedious, piteous woman
Was Helen, got by heart. Can you adore
The human animal's ecstasy, yet ignore
The ground and primitive logic of being human?

The penultimate sonnet unleashes a fury and a scorn that Howard was convinced was directed specifically at her.

Better a brutal twitching of the reins
And off, than this devouring pious whore
Who in soft regret will twine you fast
Where thigh-bones mope along the tainted shore
'Moods of Love': *Pegasus and Other Poems* (1957)

Reading the manuscript Day-Lewis had sent her, Howard decided that she had to leave Chatto. 'At the time,' she reflected, 'I thought ending it had ruined my life.'[7] Thereafter, they continued to meet occasionally at the instigation of Balcon who did not suspect their affair. Day-Lewis's hurt at his rejection was slow to heal. In his 1962 collection, *The Gate and Other Poems*, 'A Loss' was prompted by a remark made by Howard to Day-Lewis during a meeting with her and her second husband, James Douglas-Henry.

'You are nice' – and she touched his arm with a fleeting
Impulsive gesture: the arm that had held her close
And naked a year ago. She was not cheating,
But it falsified their balance of profit and loss.

Her gesture saluted a magnanimity shown
When he asked if she was happy with her new
Lover. That cool touch scalded him to the bone:
The ingenuous words made all words ring untrue.

Though Balcon only learnt of the affair later, Day-Lewis had risked ruining his second marriage after just three years and at a time when he had a new daughter and a beautiful young wife whom he was telling had made him happier than ever before in his life. When he had been married to Mary, one clear cause of his infidelity had been the lack of sexual and intellectual compatibility which led him first to the earthy Billie Currall and then to the cultured, well-read and passionate Rosamond Lehmann. Now in Balcon, though, he had found someone who shared his love of poetry and with whom he had a fulfilling physical relationship. Within weeks of Tamasin's birth Balcon had been pregnant again, but the couple decided the strain on her of a second baby so soon after the first would be too great and so ended the pregnancy.

Why then did he stray? There was opportunity. Balcon was distracted with their new baby, her work and trying to run their home. If she noticed that her husband was distant, if she was disturbed by the attack on women that she read in 'Moods of Love' which appeared in a collection dedicated to her, she decided to overlook it. The freedom from scrutiny she gave Day-Lewis became part of their relationship. Having seen the strain inflicted on him by Lehmann when she constantly made scenes – he once told Balcon that he was 'more scened against than scene-ing'[8] – Balcon had resolved from the very start of their time together to try to avoid jealousy, insecurity and confrontation.

Her discretion, though, could be taken by her husband as licence. Howard believed that Day-Lewis was fundamentally an opportunist who saw being open to new experience, regardless of the hurt it might cause to those around him, as part of being a poet. 'He told me that all practising artists have to be like chocolates with hard centres. I think that was true of him. There was a very hard, selfish core to Cecil that was very much concealed behind the charm.'[9] It was something Day-Lewis himself touched on in a later interview. 'I'm sure,' he said of poets in general, 'that one has to have a sort of splinter of ice in the heart.'[10]

Some of those closest to Day-Lewis were completely unaware of this 'other side' to his personality. His Chatto colleague (and later his literary executor), Peter Cochrane, remembered an occasion at a publishing dinner soon after Howard had departed the firm when someone made a remark alluding to Day-Lewis's infidelity. 'I rounded on the man and said "that's absolute balls" but Norah Smallwood stopped me taking it any further by telling me the truth. I never raised it with Cecil. He didn't invite that sort of intimacy. But I never quite managed to reconcile it with the man I knew. I assumed he and Jill were as happily married as I was to my wife. Which they were, but there was this curious other side. Clearly there was something in Cecil's make-up that demanded new experiences.'[11]

Day-Lewis was not a man who liked to talk difficult issues over with those concerned or with close male friends like Cochrane. Instead he reflected on them in his writing. Aside from 'Moods of Love', his other significant written response to Howard's rejection came in his 1957 Nicholas Blake book, *End of the Chapter*. Set in a publishing house whose premises bore a close resemblance to the Chatto offices, it was the story of the gruesome murder of a highly strung, smothering romantic novelist, Millicent Miles, who had a history of using and discarding men at whim and who had also handed her child over to others' care.

If the killing of Miles was an attempt to purge Howard from his system, Day-Lewis may also have left a clue in the detective novel to his own wider motivations in the character of Stephen Protheroe, presiding literary arbiter of taste at the fictional publishing house and a poet. He had written one outstanding collection, *Fire and Ash*, inspired by a collapsed love affair and its bitter fall out, but since had found that a comfortable life had inspired in him only mediocre verse. Reflecting on Protheroe's writer's block, Blake's detective, Nigel Strangeways, remarks: 'poets are very tough inside, you know. They don't give up the ghost because of anyone else's sufferings.'

Aside from the latest Blake novel, Day-Lewis had also since *An Italian Visit* published a series of lectures he had given at Queen's University, Kingston,

Ontario in Canada in 1954 on Emily Brontë, George Meredith and W. B. Yeats under the title *Notable Images of Virtue*. The trip had been his first to North America. At Christmas 1954, he made a rare appearance in T. S. Eliot's imprint, Faber and Faber, in the 'Ariel Poets' series. His domestic poem 'Christmas Eve', with illustrations by Edward Ardizzone, was produced as a four-page pamphlet. It dismisses the idea that Christmas is a 'time-worn, tinsel routine' and instead Day-Lewis, a new father all over again, concentrates on how a child's sense of wonder can inspire surrounding and hitherto 'numb' adults.

> you lose your self in his yearning, and borrow
> IIis eyes to behold
> Your own young world again. Love's mystery is revealed
> When the father becomes the child.

As an alternative for Christmas present buyers that year, Cape joined forces with the Hogarth Press to bring out Day-Lewis's *Collected Poems*. It contained almost everything he had written from *Transitional Poem* to *An Italian Visit*. *Beechen Vigil* and *Country Comets* were omitted, along with the final section of *A Time To Dance* and all but two choruses of *Noah and The Waters*. In his introduction Day-Lewis admitted he had been tempted to exclude more of his work from the 1930s – as some of his contemporaries had in their recent collections – but had resisted. 'Reading over my verse written during the last 25 years,' he reflected, 'I have felt both surprise and regret: regret that so much energy should so often have run to waste; surprise, to hear a buried self speaking, now and then, with such urgency.' He could not, however, bring himself to rewrite and improve these earlier works, he said, because 'the selves who wrote those poems are strangers to me'. Instead he preferred to look forward, he concluded, belatedly accepting some threads of continuity, and therefore 'write another poem, feeling my way along the same themes with the self I am now'.[12]

Reviewers were respectful rather than enthusiastic. George Fraser in the *New Statesman* compared him unfavourably with Stephen Spender who had his own *Collected Poems* out at the same time. 'As a verse craftsman, he [Day-Lewis] has a more consistent and various dexterity ... but perhaps a less unified poetic personality and, because of the many skilfully absorbed influences, a less individual tone of voice'.

Despite this critical downgrading Day-Lewis continued to be honoured and in demand. He co-edited *The Chatto Book of Modern Poetry* with John Lehmann, published in 1956. Lehmann's view was that Day-Lewis's break with his sister should not end their personal and professional relationship. Of the five Day-Lewis poems Lehmann chose to include in the anthology one was 'The Album'.

Day-Lewis had been invited in 1954 to join the council of the Royal Society of Literature. It required his unpaid attendance at eight meetings a year, a distraction from writing and one that Day-Lewis could ill afford but took on in a spirit of public service.

Music was another of the enthusiasms he shared with Balcon. Her first present to him had been a recording of Verdi's Requiem, 20 sides of 78s which they had to take round to Elizabeth Jane Howard's home to play because they did not have a gramophone. In the summer of 1954 they had attended a Promenade Concert at the Royal Albert Hall in London to hear the performance of *A Song of Welcome*, a new piece for soprano and bass soloists, chorus and orchestra, with music by Sir Arthur Bliss,[13] Master of the Queen's Music, and words by Day-Lewis. It marked the return of the young Queen, Elizabeth II, from her first tour of the Commonwealth.

Bliss recognized in Day-Lewis a poet with both a love and a technical understanding of music. In September of the same year they collaborated on 'Elegiac Sonnet', a Day-Lewis poem set to music by Bliss and performed at London's Wigmore Hall in memory of the pianist Noel Mewton-Wood. And in 1956 they worked together again on an idea for an opera based on the legend of two elderly sisters and a Roman fountain that Day-Lewis had come across while in Italy. However, Bliss judged Day-Lewis's first draft as 'too like *La Bohème*' and the project was shelved.[14]

At home the young Tamasin was growing, and early in 1957 Balcon discovered she was pregnant again. Day-Lewis's older children were taking their first steps in their professional careers, Nicholas as an engineer and Sean as a journalist who after 1960 became a mainstay of the *Daily Telegraph*. In the same year Sean married Anna Mott at Hampstead Register Office. At Oxford, Nicholas had met his future wife, Josephine Pike. Soon after marrying in London in 1958 they went to live in South Africa where Pike's British parents had settled in the apartheid era. Day-Lewis liked the bride, he wrote to Sean, but added: 'I fear the parents must be rather the Stockbroker-Tudor type: this enormous wedding and pretentious reception [at the Dorchester] they plan fills me with some foreboding.'[15]

The impending wedding of their son prompted Mary and Day-Lewis to meet beforehand in London for the first time since he had left her. It was a civilized affair, the start of regular encounters over lunch in the years to come, but left Day-Lewis in reflective mood.

> *It is grief that the pureness and plenitude of*
> *Their love's long-flowering day*
> *Could, like baser, flimsier stuff,*
> *Corrupt or melt away.*
>
> *Nothing left of the cells they stored*
> *With joy, trust, charity*
> *For years? ... Nature, it seems, can afford*
> *Such wastefulness: not we.*

'A Meeting': *The Gate and Other Poems* (1962)

There was shocking news in 1957 for Day-Lewis when he learnt that Sally, Rosamond Lehmann's daughter to whom he had once been almost a second father, had died suddenly at the age of 23 in Java where she was living with her husband, the poet and critic, P. J. Kavanagh.[16] She had caught poliomyelitis. Day-Lewis had bumped into her in a street market shortly before she set off for

Indonesia. It was, he felt, an 'affectionate conversation'.[17] Lehmann, though, recorded another version of the meeting. 'She [Sally] told me of his distress and embarrassment ... "I wish you could see him Mummy. You would feel better. He's not the person we knew and loved any more. He looks so changed, so awful". But I was very glad for her. After that he was at least exorcised.'[18]

The generation above Day-Lewis was thinning out. Since his father's death he had dutifully visited his stepmother Mamie in Bournemouth where she had retired to a large house she renamed Edwinstowe to be cared for by an Irish maid. It was on the route to Dorset but he found it an oppressive place when he called in with its hunting pictures and constant smell of boiled vegetables. He would escape for walks by the sea, reporting back to Balcon with amusement at the existence of a 'Lower Pleasure Gardens' as 'the only thing to recommend Bournemouth'.[19] His anger with Mamie had long abated and, though he never acceded to her desire to be called Mother, he admired the quiet courage with which she fought the cancer that finally killed her in January 1955.

She left £146,000 in her will, a fortune by the standards of the time. It was distributed between a cats' home, the Anglican diocese of Southwell in which her husband had served, and an RAF Benevolent Home. There was £1,000 each for Sean, Nicholas and Tamasin and another £1,000 for Day-Lewis with which he was able to buy a Hillman, his first decent car since setting up home with Balcon. She was bequeathed Mamie's furs. Publication of the will spurred Sir Michael Balcon, speaking through his wife (who remained the link between him and his daughter), to express his outrage that Day-Lewis hadn't been left a larger share of a valuable estate. 'But Cecil believed Mamie's distribution of money was entirely fair,' Balcon recalled. 'He worked out that she was giving to his children roughly what his father had brought to the marriage. The rest had been hers all along.'[20]

In the same month, Uncle Willie, Canon William Squires, also died, breaking another link with Ireland. Only Knos now remained, but as his physical ties with Ireland became more tenuous than ever, Day-Lewis began to examine his emotional attachment to the land of his birth with a greater intensity than ever before. In his new collection, *Pegasus and Other Poems*, published in June 1957, was one of the first fruits of that labour, 'The House Where I Was Born', his account of the framed photograph of Ballintubbert House that had been hidden in dark corners of Frank Day-Lewis's vicarages.

The poem comes in Part Three of the carefully ordered *Pegasus*, where Day-Lewis looks backwards and forwards to reflect on his relationships with the family around him. It is followed by 'Father to Sons', a *mea culpa* directed towards his grown-up sons for his failings as a father, perhaps now more apparent as he was going through the experience all over again.

How often did words of mine, words out of season,
Leave smouldering chagrin like fag-ends to char
Your fresh-painted sill of life! my unreason
Or too much reason chill the air
For your tendril career!

After asking their forgiveness, he seeks also to forgive himself for his treatment of his own father in 'Son and Father'.

> *Ungenerous to him no more, but unregenerate,*
> *Still on frozen earth I stumble after*
> *Each glimmer of God, although it lights up my lack,*
> *And lifts my maimed creations to beg rebirth.*

Part Two of the collection, containing poems written as far back as 1949, sees him still picking over his culpability in the collapse of his relationships with Rosamond Lehmann and Mary Day-Lewis in 'The Wrong Road' and 'Love and Pity'. He is wryly self-critical in 'Almost Human', contrasting his public image with his private behaviour.

> *The man you know, assured and kind,*
> *Wearing fame like an old tweed suit –*
> *You would not think he has an incurable*
> *Sickness upon his mind.*
>
> *Finely that tongue, for listening people,*
> *Articulates love, enlivens clay;*
> *While under his valued skin there crawls*
> *An outlaw and a cripple.*

The most ambitious part of *Pegasus*, however, is its opening section where Day-Lewis, inspired by his success with his translation of the *Aeneid*, takes four epic classical narratives and reshapes them so as to allow their mythological themes to frame – as he put it in 'View from An Upper Window' – his own divided thoughts about love. More subtle and – because of their classical roots – more detached than the angry 'Moods of Love' which comes almost at the end of the collection, these poems in Part One allow Day-Lewis obliquely to handle volatile autobiographical themes which might otherwise have proved too painful for those around him.

The opening poem, 'Pegasus', reworks from Homer's *Iliad* the tale of Bellerophon's pursuit of the winged horse Pegasus to cast light on the creative process and how the poet is forever chasing allusive inspiration.

> *A young man*
> *Challenging, coaxing, pursuing, always pursuing*
> *The dream of those dewfall hooves: a horse which ran*
> *Quicksilver from his touch, sliding and slewing*
> *Away, then immobile a moment, derisively tame,*
> *Almost as if it entered into a game.*

Day-Lewis extends the metaphor to embrace the pursuit of love. It is a theme he then addresses more directly in 'Psyche' in which he retells Apuleius's second-century AD fable from *The Golden Ass* as an ultimately bleak parable about shortcomings of erotic love. Psyche is so anxious for love that she breaks Eros's rule that they can only be together under cloak of darkness, but in the process destroys what they had.

> And the light became a clear, impassable window
> Through which her love could gaze but never go.

By contrast in 'Baucis and Philemon', Day-Lewis retells the legend of a couple who grow together like a pair of trees with intertwining roots. In his reworking of these characters from Ovid's *Metamorphoses*, he produces a narrative about the sort of enduring and exclusive love that he aspired to with Balcon, but which he had already betrayed.

> They climbed that hill each evening of their lives
> Until, one day, their clasped hands uttered leaves
> And the tired feet were taken underground.
> 'Goodbye, dear wife', he called as the bark closed around,
> And his branches upheld the cry in a carol of birds.
> She yearned to his oaken heart, with her last words
> Sweet as lime blossom whispering on the air –
> 'It's not goodbye.'
>   We found them growing there
> And built the wall around them; not that they need
> A ring to show their love, or ever did.

He was laying bare his own contradictions. He wanted simultaneously both the eternal oneness of Baucis and Philemon and the erotic consummation, however short-lived, of Psyche. He concludes Part One with an attempt at some sort of synthesis of his conflicting ideas on commitment and desire in the form of a dramatic monologue based on another myth, 'Ariadne on Naxos'. He examines the betrayal by Ariadne of her father, King Minos of Crete, after her passion for Thesus has led her to connive with him to kill her half-brother, the monster Minotaur. Day-Lewis's monologue – a popular recital piece for Balcon – takes up the story when Ariadne in her turn has been betrayed by Thesus and abandoned on Naxos, not knowing if she will be rescued and forgiven. She is full of self-recrimination, but issues a plea for forgiveness for her failings that may allow her some sort of redemption and a happy conclusion.

> Listen! What is this word
> The bushes are whispering to the offshore breeze?
> 'Forget'? No. Tell me again. 'Forgive.' A soft word.
> I'll try it on my tongue. Forgive. Forgive ...
> How strangely it lightens a bedevilled heart!

The extensive use of classical references in *Pegasus* highlighted the gap that was opening up between Day-Lewis's poetic interests and those of a new generation of young poets emerging in the mid-1950s. The Movement poets, a term coined by J. D. Scott, the editor of *The Spectator*, to link Philip Larkin,[21] Kingsley Amis,[22] D. J. Enright,[23] Robert Conquest,[24] Donald Davie[25] and Thom Gunn,[26] were joined by, among other things, their dislike of classical allusions and anything too self-consciously poetic. They preferred plain, straightforward and often sardonic language and regarded the Day-Lewis/Auden/Spender generation with 'derision' as Davie wrote in 'Remembering the Thirties'.

Just as *New Signatures* had identified Auden, Spender and Day-Lewis as a youthful, exciting new wave in the early 1930s, so the 1956 collection *New Lines* signalled the arrival of the Movement poets. In reality, they were – like the 1930s poets – a diverse group. Despite Davie's scorn, some of their number knew and liked Day-Lewis. With Larkin, in particular, he shared a friendship based in part on a shared love of Thomas Hardy's poetry. Kingsley Amis later recalled 'I had bought *Word Over All* as soon as it came out – a convincing tribute from one on a second lieutenant's pay. I also (which does not necessarily follow) read it, and re-read it, and liked it.'[27] But in this second half of the 1950s, he had little time for what he saw as Day-Lewis's dated approach, concerns and language. The poetic momentum was moving away from Day-Lewis and his generation.

Chapter 28

Change of Address

Such desirableness
Of place or person is chiefly a glamour cast by
Your unsuccess
In growing your self. Rebirth needs more than a change of
Flesh or address
'Ideal Home': *The Gate and Other Poems* (1962)

At the close of 1957, the Day-Lewises moved once again, to 6 Crooms Hill in Greenwich. This tall, elegant, well-ordered early eighteenth-century house, with its wood-panelled rooms and stately lime tree in the back garden, stood in the shadow of an impressive array of historic buildings – the Royal Naval College, Inigo Jones's Queen's House and the Old Royal Observatory. There were views over Greenwich Park, the masts of the nineteenth-century clipper, the *Cutty Sark*, and beyond it the Thames. It seemed to many who visited the Day-Lewises there an entirely fitting home for a poet who had become, as Cyril Connolly affectionately put it, 'a founder member of the literary establishment'.[1]

It was the house in which Day-Lewis came closest to that sense of peace and rootedness that part of him had long yearned for, but it did not resolve his eternal ambiguities.

Never would there be lives enough for all
The comely places –
Glimpsed from a car, a train, or loitered past –
That lift their faces
To be admired, murmuring 'Live with me'.
'Ideal Home': *The Gate and Other Poems* (1962)

He worked in his study next to the front door. It was lined from floor to ceiling with books, broken up by drawings, including a sketch of his hero, Thomas Hardy, and, after 1963, an original manuscript of Wilfred Owen's poem, 'Strange Meeting', scored through and scribbled over. It was given to him by the poet's brother, Harold, in recognition of Day-Lewis's sensitivity when editing and introducing an edition of Owen's *Collected Poems* for Chatto.[2]

The round table where Day-Lewis wrote was usually neat and orderly. On it stood a sculpture of a nymph in printers' lead by Franta Belsky, his old neighbour, which had been a present from Balcon.[3] He kept a small book in which he would jot down phrases and words that had made an impact on him.

His poems were written, amended and rewritten in longhand, sometimes in pencil, in cheap notebooks, often competing for space alongside parts of the latest Nicholas Blake he was working on.[4]

On the weeks when he wasn't working at Chatto, he would settle into the study for the morning, emerging for a simple lunch of cheese and digestive biscuits, an apple and a Penguin bar. After an afternoon walk, sometimes through the Thames foot-tunnel to the Isle of Dogs from where he could look back, as Canaletto once had, on the Greenwich skyline, he would return to work, fortified by his customary bun. For distraction he had a telescope, another present from Balcon, with which he could 'bring closer to me the great cargo-liners rounding the Isle of Dogs, the tugs and their strings of lighters, the wharves, warehouses, power stations, the skyline restless with cranes, the blue diamond lights of welding and the indigo smoke from tall chimneys – all the river life which, here at Greenwich, overlooked by the palace and the park, enlivens their elegance with a workaday reality'.[5]

When at home, the domestic routine revolved around Day-Lewis and his need for quiet. In the evenings, though, Balcon would occasionally accompany Day-Lewis on the piano as he revisited the Tom Moore songs of his youth. Balcon carried on working as an actress, sharing the household costs equally with her husband. Increasingly she eschewed the theatre and work which would necessitate long periods away from home, preferring instead roles in television drama where shooting schedules could be fitted around her responsibilities at home: in the kitchen behind Day-Lewis's study, as hostess in the first floor drawing room, and as mother on the nursery floor.[6]

The main impetus for the move to Greenwich had come with the arrival on April 29, 1957, two days after Day-Lewis's 53rd birthday, of Daniel Michael Blake Day-Lewis. Daniel was chosen because it combined the provenances of both his parents. Day-Lewis admired the nineteenth-century Irish politician Daniel O'Connell who forced the British to grant Catholic emancipation in 1829. And the biblical Daniel reflected Balcon's Jewish roots. Michael was an olive branch to her father who remained unhappy at his daughter's choice of husband but took delight in his grandchildren. Blake was one of Day-Lewis's mother's names that he used in his crime fiction alter ego.

Nanny Bowler, who came with them to the new house, remarked on first seeing her new charge that he looked like a cross between Norman Wisdom, the comedian, and a bishop.[7] Day-Lewis was more starry-eyed as he celebrated Daniel's arrival with a poem about renewal.

> Welcome to earth, my child!
> Joybells of blossom swing,
> Lambs and lovers have their fling,
> The streets ran wild
> With April airs and rumours of the sun.
> We time-worn folk renew
> Ourselves at your enchanted spring,
> As though mankind's begun

Again in you.
This is your birthday and our thanksgiving.

'The Newborn': *The Gate and Other Poems* (1962)

In a subsequent lecture Day-Lewis recalled writing the poem and gave an insight into his working method. 'Filled with euphoria, I dashed off a poem about this event, a poem in four-line rhyming stanzas. I had not gone far when the poem stalled. I raised the hood and examined the engine: it had seized up – yes, obviously; but what should I do next? I decided to start again, with – so to speak – a new engine. Perhaps I could distance myself from my still raw emotions by employing a more complex stanza form. So for the four-line stanza I substituted one of ten lines, rhyming abbacdbcdb. There were still several misadventures on the way, but the poem "The Newborn" got to its destination.'[8]

Daniel had been born at home at Campden Hill Road. The Day-Lewises had hung a red bandanna handkerchief on the balcony outside their bedroom window to alert their good friends among the neighbours. One day, to head off any jealousy Tamasin might have felt towards the new baby, her parents took her by river boat to Greenwich Park for a picnic. They walked past the row of Georgian houses in Crooms Hill and admired them. A few weeks later they spotted in a newspaper an advertisement for one of them, but were too late. The young writers, Nicholas and Claire Tomalin, had already offered the asking price. Day-Lewis, though, had liked a part of London, where, he later wrote, 'old and new can be focussed together in a historic present'.[9] When soon afterwards another house came up for sale on the corner of Crooms Hill, he was first in the queue. Its owner, a doctor's widow (his old surgery was attached at the back), was keen it should go to a family. A deal was agreed for the asking price, £5,990.

It was a large sum when they had no capital and an already overstretched income. Because of the age of the property, Day-Lewis and Balcon could not raise a mortgage on it from a building society.[10] Eventually, however, he managed to obtain one on his life, while Balcon cashed three life insurance policies, taken out by her father when she was a child, to provide the deposit. They moved in during a cold winter. They were to shiver until they could afford to install central heating in 1964.

It may have been anxiety about money that prompted Day-Lewis to agree to write his autobiography, thereby setting aside Auden's dictate, delivered with his usual certainty to Spender at Venice in 1949, that poets should avoid such undertakings at all costs. Certainly money was scarce in those early years at Crooms Hill. In a correspondence with the collector, Alan Hancox, Day-Lewis was negotiating prices for the sale of what original manuscripts of his poems he had retained.[11] There was a developing market for such material in America. In the late 1950s the University of Texas had paid £2,800 in a charity auction for a hand-written version of *The Waste Land* by T. S. Eliot. Day-Lewis had always been casual about such documents, often turning them over and letting them be used as scrap paper for his children's drawings. Some had been given as presents to friends and lovers. Many others had simply disappeared.

His original plan with the autobiography was to base it on his poems and add a little mortar around them to explain the circumstances in which they had been written. He discussed the idea with his journalist son, Sean. 'But he quickly realised that it would mean having to spell out things in them best not spelt out.'[12] So instead he wrote a straight prose account about his life up to 1940. The cut-off point had several advantages. It focused on the 1930s, the period with which Day-Lewis remained most closely associated. It allowed him to spare Mary in a way that he had failed to with his poems of the 1940s. And it ruled out any named reference to the still angry Rosamond Lehmann.

There was a brief postscript about Balcon and their children. 'Yesterday was the eighth anniversary of my second marriage,' he writes. 'I shall play my luck while it lasts. At last I am learning to live with myself, to view in some kind of focus and in some degree to reconcile the contradictory elements that make up the man of whom this book is a portrait.' He reflects of advancing years: 'One sits more easily to life as one grows older, the self-torture of youth far behind now, still distant the pains and physical ignominy of old age. Since I am no longer sodden with guilt for things done and left undone, I can accept other people for what they are, not needing to turn them into mirrors, props, blue-prints or Aunt Sallies.'[13]

As a title, he had chosen the Meredith phrase which Lehmann had earlier toyed with before being persuaded to call her 1953 novel *The Echoing Grove*. *The Buried Day* was dedicated to Knos and was published in May 1960. Elegantly written, witty, entertaining, its habit of glossing over some of the conflicts Day-Lewis felt in his youth and in the 1930s was noted by Cyril Connolly in the *Sunday Times*. '*The Buried Day* is, I feel, not wholly successful in its own right so much as an accompaniment to the poetry to which the author is constantly referring us back. He is poet first and autobiographer second.'[14] The *Times*'s reviewer noted the pastoral tone of Day-Lewis's prose to match that found in his poetry. 'In describing spring, Mr Day-Lewis has chosen an autumnal note, when the full felicity of the reader demands the expansion of summer.'

Despite the care Day-Lewis had taken to avoid giving offence, *The Buried Day* did briefly sour one long-standing friendship. Charles Fenby, his old housemate from Oxford, was by now staunchly pro-American and pro nuclear deterrent in his outlook and, when the two occasionally met up with their families, the subject of politics was studiously avoided. However, Day-Lewis's innocent reference in the book to Fenby's career at Westminster Press as having been helped by a family connection was taken as a slight on his reputation. A long silence resulted.[15] Day-Lewis's friend, the Irish poet Patrick Kavanagh,[16] was more vocal about his disappointment with the book. 'Ah Cecil,' he said, 'you should have torn your heart out and left it bleeding on the page.'[17]

There was much about Ireland in *The Buried Day*. Day-Lewis had been delighted in 1958 when five of his poems were included in Donagh McDonagh and Lennox Robinson's *Oxford Book of Irish Verse*. His interest in Ireland continued to grow. His friend Peter Cochrane even noted a slight change in Day-Lewis's pronunciation. 'He started using the Irish pronunciation more than he had before. So where he would once have said film, he now said fil-um.'[18]

Aside from what Day-Lewis described at the Foyle's lunch at the Dorchester to mark the publication of *The Buried Day* as the 'great self-indulgence' of venturing into writing his memoirs, he continued working in more familiar territory with four Nicholas Blakes in the first five years at Greenwich. His 1958 *A Penknife in My Heart* was accused by some reviewers of lifting its plot from Patricia Highsmith's 1950 thriller, *Strangers on A Train*, (filmed by Alfred Hitchcock in 1951), but Day-Lewis responded by pointing out that 'to my consternation' he had not read the American author's book.[19]

In a letter to the young poet Elizabeth Jennings, whom he admired, befriended and promoted, Day-Lewis recounted a lunch he had once had with T. S. Eliot. Day-Lewis had just been away at a school presenting the annual prizes. 'He gave me a considering look and said "do you do it very often?" I replied that this was the first time. He pondered for a few moments and then said "If I were you, I would not do it too often – perhaps once a year".'[20]

As the 1950s turned into the 1960s, Day-Lewis increasingly ignored such advice. His willingness to accept invitations to speak did not come from any great vanity. There was still plenty of interest in him and his work – he was a guest on BBC Radio's *Desert Island Discs* in 1960 – even if he was no longer quite as fashionable and critically acclaimed as once he had been. And he rarely received any money for his efforts, despite his straitened circumstances. His motivation was his continuing belief that the poet had a public, civic role, that the delights and power of poetry needed to be extolled to each generation. 'There was no ambition in him,' recalled Hallam Tennyson, the BBC producer Day-Lewis worked with often. 'He was genuinely very modest, but he had this highly developed sense of civic duty. He genuinely wanted to do good for fellow human beings not for himself.'[21]

Day-Lewis feared that poetry itself was under threat. 'Its narrative function has been taken over by the novel,' he warned in a lecture on 'Poetry for the Public' that he often gave on his travels round the country, 'epic has been taken over by the cinema, prose has become the accepted medium for the theatre, the song lyric is crowded out by the pop record. What ground is left for poetry to stand on?' He compared what he saw as a growing English indifference to poetry and poets with his observations of other countries. 'When I last visited Italy, a lift boy, on discovering that I was an English poet, bowed to me with extreme reverence. I could walk any London street with Mr Eliot, Mr Robert Frost or Professor Robert Graves – indeed I have done so – and hardly a head would be turned, even if they were preceded by a loudspeaker announcing their names. This is probably all to the good for the poet himself; like the secret agent, he pursues his mission best in anonymity. But, so far as it reflects public apathy towards poetry, we must deplore it.'[22]

He went into battle on several fronts. He was active, for instance, on the committee which decided who should receive the Queen's Gold Medal for Poetry. With the chair of the committee, the Poet Laureate, John Masefield, now in his eighties and housebound, Day-Lewis feared that the new generation was being marginalized in terms of such civic recognition. Despite his differences of approach with the Movement poets, he championed their cause vociferously in correspondence with Masefield. Elizabeth Jennings, Thom Gunn, Philip Larkin and Ted Hughes[23] were all names he put forward in preference to what he saw as the unimaginative step of giving the medal in 1960 to his own contemporary, John Betjeman. 'I cannot see how so successful a poet could be considered for an award,' Day-Lewis argued, 'which, I had understood, if it went to an older poet, went to one whose work had not achieved the success we felt it deserved.'[24] In the end a compromise was reached and the award went to Frances Cornford.[25]

In December 1961 he further added to his burden of unpaid 'good works' by agreeing to chair the Poetry Panel of the Arts Council. It had a meagre annual budget of £3,000 to distribute, but met four times a year to make its decisions. With the chair came a seat on the main Arts Council and required attendance at between twelve and fifteen meetings a year. Day-Lewis also actively supported public campaigns to save the BBC's Third Programme, under threat from budget cuts, joining, with Balcon, the cast of well-known names who performed at the Royal Court Theatre in a 'Third Programme Entertainment'.

He was involved too in more overtly political campaigning. In September of 1959 he had written a poem, 'The Unexploded Bomb', to be performed at the Campaign for Nuclear Disarmament's fund-raising Midnight Star Matinée at the Royal Festival Hall. And in October 1960, he had a cameo in one of the most celebrated of court-room dramas, the attempted prosecution of Penguin Books under the new Obscene Publications Act for, 32 years after it was first banned, allowing D. H. Lawrence's *Lady Chatterley's Lover* into bookshops.

Day-Lewis was called by the defence as one of a series of expert witnesses from the literary establishment. Gerald Gardiner QC, a future Labour Lord Chancellor, led for the defence but Day-Lewis was questioned on the fourth day of the trial by Gardiner's junior, Jeremy Hutchinson, a friend who was then married to the actress Peggy Ashcroft. Day-Lewis began his evidence by confirming that he was also Nicholas Blake, the writer, a fact unknown to those in the public gallery where there was an audible intake of breath. He was then asked by Hutchinson if Lady Chatterley was, in his opinion, immoral. 'She does certain things,' he replied, 'which one can call acts of weakness; but, as a whole, taking her character as a whole, I think there is more good than bad in her.' He went on to deny that the book promoted vice. 'I find it is recommending a right and full relationship between a man and a woman.'[26]

Hutchinson had assured him there would be no cross-examination, so Day-Lewis was taken aback when Mervyn Griffith-Jones QC, leading for the prosecution, rose to challenge him on the last point. How, he asked, could a relationship be described as 'right and full' when the two hardly spoke to each other, except about 'copulation'? Day-Lewis was unable, under pressure from Griffith-Jones, to name other sections of the novel where Lawrence's characters talked about more mundane matters. Though visibly shaken, he did, however, stick to his guns. 'After their first meetings,' he asserted, 'they do in fact copulate on each occasion. They are lovers and it seems perfectly natural they should.' 'Perfectly natural?' 'Yes.'[27]

The prosecution, Hutchinson recalled, 'had got punch drunk. After so many witnesses defending the book, Mervyn Griffith-Jones hadn't been able to think of anything new to say to them. We had therefore assumed he wouldn't cross-examine Cecil, but suddenly he leapt up and started on him. In one way it was flattering that he thought Cecil worth it after letting so many big names go unchallenged. He was a criminal barrister and treated all witnesses as criminals. Cecil was certainly pretty white by the time he had finished with him.'[28] Never one who relished a confrontation, Day-Lewis described his ordeal in the witness box to Christine Caldwell, an old friend of Balcon's: 'I don't remember ever being so aware of such hostility directed towards me.'[29]

In the early 1960s Day-Lewis tried once more to widen his range from writing detective stories into drama, this time for television. He completed the script of a thriller, *Wanted – Bearded Man*, based on an advertisement he had spotted in the Personal Columns of the *Times*. However, it was not taken up by any producer and the original is now lost. That interest in placing characters in stories and giving them a voice – seen already in his retelling of classical myths in *Pegasus* – did bear fruit, however, in the two long poems around which his next published collection was grouped. *The Gate and Other Poems* appeared in May 1962, almost five years after *Pegasus*. Its centre pieces are 'The Disabused' and 'Not Proven'. Both concern fatal tragedies of the sort that might have embroiled Nigel Strangeways.

'The Disabused', a dramatic monologue first performed by Day-Lewis on BBC Radio, is a father recalling for his daughter his failure, 40 years earlier, to save his brother from drowning and the on-going consequences of his self-disgust.

> This happens
> So quickly, and yet your dying seems to go on
> For ever. You struggle silently, your eyes
> Howling for help. And I, a feeble swimmer,
> Must let you drown or flounder out and let you
> Drag me under.

'The Disabused' has particularly harsh words for those who indulge in self-deception. Day-Lewis was one who recognized the pain caused by his own contradictions. The poem was based on an imagined incident, but 'Not Proven' sees Day-Lewis revisiting the celebrated trial for murder, in Edinburgh in 1857, of Madeleine Hamilton-Smith. She had been accused of poisoning her former lover after he had threatened to show her old love letters to her disapproving father. In court the letters were read out, causing as great a storm in Victorian Britain as *Lady Chatterley's Lover* was later to do. The jury found the charges against Hamilton-Smith 'not proven', an unusual verdict, allowing for another trial if new evidence emerged. Smith lived to be 92, but refused all offers to tell her story. In his monologue, Day-Lewis imagines what she may have said if she had broken her silence. He also uses her example to question whether there can ever be truth where the human heart is concerned.

But so long ago it happened, how
Can I be sure? Their busy arguments
Hummed in my ears like echoes from a dream,
Making unreal all that had passed between us.

Both poems once again show a mastery of the narrative form in verse that dates back to the 1930s and 'The Nabara', but they also see Day-Lewis, as he had in parts of *An Italian Visit* marrying a conversational tone with highly structured poetic verse. And both, as had his retelling of classical tales in *Pegasus*, allow Day-Lewis under the cloak of writing about others to explore the contradictions about love and loyalty that he continued to experience himself.

These issues are more directly addressed in other poems in *The Gate*. 'Fisherman and/or Fish' sees him looking back with hindsight and a certain amusement at his emotional entanglements of the past.

The river's veteran, I
Shall flick my rod, my fin,
Where nothing can drag me in
Nor land me high and dry.

Yet there are also celebrations of domestic life in poems such as 'Getting Warm – Getting Cold', an account of Tamasin seeking out a hidden present, and of his marriage to Balcon in 'An Upland Field', recalling another of their visits to Dorset and the discovery of heartsease in a ploughed field near Plush.

No marvel that she, who gives me peace
Wherein my shortening days redouble
Their yield, could magically produce
From all that harshness of flint and stubble
Whole acres of heartsease.

Such episodes of apparent contentment rub shoulders with evidence of Day-Lewis's still active desire to explore. 'An Upland Field' comes in the collection just two poems after 'A Loss', recalling his affair with Elizabeth Jane Howard. 'Travelling Light', inspired in part by the experience of watching his stepmother slowly dying in a house so crammed full of possessions that she was afraid to leave it for fear of thieves, suggests a desire to abandon all worldly responsibilities.

Think of streamlined whales and hulls
Accumulating barnacles
By moving long enough immersed
In their own element.

These were, by now, familiar themes, as was commitment to political engagement and the building of a good society in 'Requiem for the Living'. This sequence uses the order of the sung prayers in mass, learnt by Day-Lewis in childhood, to offer an agnostic vision of the fate of humanity in a nuclear age. Religious imagery and phrases are more present in *The Gate* than previously.

While he remained unwavering in his rejection of Christianity's claims, there was, he remarked, 'a churchy agnostic' in him who delighted in the sound of bells, singing hymns, in rituals and in the language of the faith of his upbringing.

He sent 'Requiem for the Living' to his friend Benjamin Britten[30] in the hope that he might set it to music. Britten, though, was in the midst of *War Requiem*, based on Wilfred Owen, and declined. Another composer, Donald Swann,[31] did, however, subsequently take on the task and the work was given its first performance in September 1969 at the Church of the Ascension in Blackheath, close to Crooms Hill.[32]

Two other poems in *The Gate* stand out as of particular significance. The first 'Sheepdog Trials in Hyde Park' is dedicated to Robert Frost and recalls a visit the New England poet made to the Day-Lewises in London in 1957. They had gone to Hyde Park to see sheepdog trials. Written in the style of Frost, it concludes by using the sheepdogs' labours as a metaphor for the composition of a poem.

> *To lift, to fetch, to drive, to shed, to pen*
> *Are acts I recognize, with all they mean*
> *Of shepherding the unruly, for a kind of*
> *Controlled wool gathering is my work too.*

For some such pastiche of Frost was further evidence that Day-Lewis lacked a distinctive voice. 'No-one,' wrote John Bayley, Warton Professor of English at Oxford, 'has as it were "got" Frost more exactly than Day-Lewis ... It is a nice point whether the upshot is not to diminish the Frost poem rather than to elevate the Day-Lewis; but in any case the contact is so persuasive that a new and fascinating sort of effect is ... added to the sum total of poetic reality.'[33]

'Sheepdog Trials in Hyde Park' has often been included in anthologies – including Philip Larkin's 1973 *Oxford Book of Twentieth-Century English Verse* – but its enduring reputation is as nothing compared to the popularity of 'Walking Away', Day-Lewis's reflection, many years after the event, on waving his son Sean off at school.

> *It is eighteen years ago, almost to the day –*
> *A sunny day with leaves just turning,*
> *The touch-lines new-ruled – since I watched you play*
> *Your first game of football, then, like a satellite*
> *Wrenched from its orbit, go drifting away*
>
> *Behind a scatter of boys. I can see*
> *You walking away from me towards the school*
> *With the pathos of a half-fledged thing set free*
> *Into a wilderness, the gait of one*
> *Who finds no path where the path should be.*
>
> *That hesitant figure, eddying away*
> *Like a winged seed loosened from its parent stem,*
> *Has something I never quite grasp to convey*
> *About nature's give-and-take – the small, the scorching*
> *Ordeals which fire one's irresolute clay.*

I have had worse partings, but none that so
Gnaws at my mind still. Perhaps it is roughly
Saying what God alone could perfectly show –
How selfhood begins with a walking away,
And love is proved in the letting go.

It captures perfectly an emotion most parents will have felt, when instinct has to be restrained. 'Walking Away' grew in popularity only slowly, however. For *The Gate* did not attract the attention that Day-Lewis had grown accustomed to when his new collection of poems came out. It was no longer the event it had once been. Reviews became scarcer, shorter and more mixed, while his reputation, especially with a younger generation of readers and writers, was coming to rest less on the strength of his verse than on his public role as one of the great and good on various influential committees, helping writers, and promoting literature and the arts in general.

Chapter 29

Easing Away

A man begins his absence
From a loved one, easing
Away as if he peeled
Gently a cling-close dressing
From a wound unhealed –
A wound as yet scarce felt.

'Days before a Journey': *The Room and Other Poems* (1965)

Day-Lewis's reputation as a grand old man of letters was confirmed in early 1964 when he was appointed by the Royal Society of Literature as a Companion of Literature, a new honour limited to only ten living writers. His old friend the Anglo-Irish novelist Elizabeth Bowen was named at the same time. They joined John Masefield, Edmund Blunden, Winston Churchill, E. M. Forster, Edith Sitwell and Evelyn Waugh.

Day-Lewis was not alone in feeling neglected by a new generation of critics and writers. 'I've been meaning to write [to] you about your *Selected Poems*,' Auden told him in a letter from Vienna in July of 1963, 'to tell you how delighted I was to find your later poetry so much finer than your earlier. The critics, of course, think all our lot stopped writing 25 years ago. How silly they are going to look presently.'[1]

Day-Lewis took a generally benign view of such marginalization but did, occasionally, send up the currently fashionable names – and himself.

When Willie Yeats was in his prime,
Said the old codger,
Heroic frenzy fired his verse:
He scorned a poet who did not write
As if he kept a sword upstairs.

Nowadays what do we find,
Said the old codger,
In every bardlet's upper room?
– Ash in the grate, a chill-proof vest
And a metronome.

'Said the Old Codger': *The Gate and Other Poems* (1962)

He continued, such barbs to one side, to work hard to encourage young, aspiring poets. One hopeful later recalled that 'Cecil wrote the nicest rejection letters I ever received'.[2] Day-Lewis championed the unknown Hebridean,

283

George Mackay Brown[3] whose collection *Loaves and Fishes* was published in 1959 in the Hogarth Press imprint, now part of Chatto & Windus. Three years later he provoked Mackay Brown's fury by rejecting his next collection as 'badly flawed by outcrops of dead metaphor'. The young poet accepted Day-Lewis's verdict, he wrote back, 'in the spirit of a man found guilty by the jury who knows, nevertheless, that he was nowhere near the place at the time'. Later, though, Mackay Brown was to express his gratitude to Day-Lewis for pushing him in the right direction when his subsequent 1964 collection, *The Year of the Whale*, was published by Hogarth Press to widespread acclaim.[4]

In his own work, there was a sense that Day-Lewis was covering old ground. There were more Nicholas Blakes. *The Sad Variety* was set in a wintry Dorset, based on his experience over New Year of 1963 of being snowed in at the Old Rectory, Litton Cheney. It was the home of the engraver, Reynolds Stone,[5] and his wife, Janet, who had become friends in the late 1950s after being introduced to the Day-Lewises by Kenneth Clark. Janet Stone played the role of hostess, gathering writers and artists under their roof and photographing them. The couple was, another visitor Iris Murdoch[6] wrote, 'perfect hosts, and their beautiful house and huge wild garden provided a place of rest and inspiration for their friends, many of whom came to stay there in the tradition of the "reading party".'[7] It was the Stones's young daughter, Phillida, who inspired the Day-Lewis poem 'This Young Girl' in *The Gate*.

1963 had seen the publication of a further Day-Lewis translation from Virgil, this time of the *Eclogues*. These ten short poems, Virgil's first major work, are also known as the *Bucolics* and their setting is rural and their concerns those of the countryside. Virgil's heavy use of mythology and his moulding into verse of conversations between shepherds and goatherds had an obvious technical and intellectual appeal to Day-Lewis, but overall, as he admitted, in a letter to a New Zealand friend, Elaine Hamilton, he had quickly lost interest in them. 'The *Eclogues* had very good notices over here, which surprised me a bit as they are not poems I find altogether inspiring as a translator.'[8]

If Day-Lewis was in something of a rut professionally, his domestic life with his second family afforded him great pleasure. 'That image Cecil and Jill gave of being so united when they were on stage at a recital was how they were in private too,' remembered their friend Christine Caldwell with whom they often stayed when performing in the south-west. 'There was always a happy banter going on between them.'[9] His love for Balcon is evident, albeit with the distancing effect of writing in the more formal third person, in a short poem he penned while she was in hospital for a minor operation.

The knife, whose freezing shadow had unsteeled
His loved one's heart, moved in at last to shear
Impassive flesh: she was no longer there –
Only a surface to be botched or healed.

While this went through, he felt the critical blade
Cut from his own heart all the encrustation

Of years and usage: bleeding with compassion,
He found his love laid bare, a love new-made.

'An Operation': *The Room and Other Poems* (1965)

Phillida Stone also recalled how Day-Lewis, though outwardly venerable and rather remote, revealed on his visits to Litton Cheney an unexpected knack for getting on with children. 'In my experience, he was never condescending like most adults who'd simply ask you how you were doing at school and then not wait for the answer. He didn't ignore you like a lot of grown ups.' One favourite trick she and others described was his 'King Edward potato face', when he would simultaneously squint, stick out his tongue and blow out his cheeks.[10] Another involved pulling his red and white spotted bandanna handkerchief from his pocket, furling it up, holding it to the side of his nose and winding it as if cranking up an old fashioned gramophone, all the time uttering a shrill 'kkkkkkkk' noise until he went bright red in the face and looked as if he was going to explode.

With the children of his first marriage Day-Lewis had often been a distant figure as his career was blossoming in the 1930s and his marriage failing in the 1940s. He had also been acutely aware of the need to avoid indulging in the excesses of 'smother love' that his own father had shown him. Second time around, though, he was relaxed and self-confident, if not exactly hands-on, as Tamasin Day-Lewis recalled. 'He would guide rather than lay down the law. He didn't want to interfere too much in daily discipline. He felt like the last post in that he hated confrontation. We always went on long walks with him and he somehow made us desperate for his approval in the best sense of the word. We wanted him to think we had done something to make him proud of us, usually writing, drawing or some childhood project. He always showed he loved us, and a brief coldness of tone or show of disapproval had more effect if we were being diabolical than a major outburst. He had that effect.'

'There was an easy-goingness about him,' she remembered, 'and that was part of our life as a family. But there was another side too. Unlike my mother, my father was essentially solitary. You always had the sense about him that he had another life going on in his head and he could tune out, leave us behind, even when he was in the room. He would seem to leave the conversation as though some poetic abstraction, thought or line was playing in his head and had to be attended to, and we knew then not to interrupt. We had to knock on the door before we entered his study, knowing from an early age that the Muse might flee if we barged in when Papa was writing, breaking the invisible line from head to pen.'[11]

Their father would usually emerge in the early evening to read stories to them before bedtime. With Daniel there would be occasional trips to the Round Pond in Kensington Gardens, Day-Lewis's own childhood haunt. But as a father he would often distance himself from family life. One reason was his age. Unlike the parents of many of Tamasin and Daniel's friends, he was too old for rough and tumble and games of soccer in the park. Or at least that is what he told them.[12] It went deeper, however. He belonged to an earlier generation with different ideas about parenting. Moreover he had no role model, in his own father, for being a successful parent. And the tension that he felt between the draw of domesticity and the instinct to escape and explore remained strong in him.

So the chance of a well-paid professorship at Harvard had an immediate appeal. Spending six months in the States, as it entailed, free from the usual pressures to earn his living and support his family, potentially offered Day-Lewis another moment of renewal in his life, coming soon after he had celebrated his 60th birthday.

The Charles Eliot Norton Chair in Poetry at Harvard was set up in 1925 in memory of the American university's first professor of fine arts. It was well-endowed, offering a salary of £8,000 a year, and had therefore been able to cast its net wide around the world in choosing the most distinguished candidates for the one-year post. Some of the leading poets of the twentieth century – including T. S. Eliot and e. e. cummings[13] – had in the past been appointed to deliver the statutory six lectures. Musicians and artists had also been selected.

Day-Lewis had been invited to take it up from September 1964. 'I hastily accepted it before they could have time to write again and say they really meant CS Lewis,' he wrote to a friend.[14] The appointment was both a mark of his standing in the States – where he had a record of critical and commercial success stretching from *The Magnetic Mountain* through to his classical translations – and a ringing endorsement of his whole body of work.

The boost to the always strained family finances would be substantial. It paid for the purchase of a second-hand Mercedes, the sort of car the otherwise unmaterialistic Day-Lewis had long desired. To maximize that financial benefit, Day-Lewis suggested to Balcon that he should go to Harvard alone. It would also, he explained, avoid disrupting their children's schooling.

Balcon was unhappy, though, about being left behind. Her disquiet owed something to her discovery that her husband's attention had been attracted by other women. Among the authors that he had been nurturing at Chatto was an Indian writer, Attia Hosain,[15] the wife of an Indian diplomat living in London with her two children. In 1953 she had published a well-regarded volume of short stories, *Phoenix Fled*. Eight years later she submitted to Chatto a novel, *Sunlight on a Broken Column*, set against the backdrop of the partition of India into separate Hindu and Moslem countries at the time of independence. It was the first time a woman writer from the Asian subcontinent had tackled such a theme and it was much admired within the publishing house. But the manuscript was judged too long. It was Day-Lewis who worked closely with Hosain to cut it back.

She was, by her own account, delighted to have him as her editor. 'I couldn't have dreamt of such a thing happening,' she said later. 'I, who had read his poems and been that girl in my school reading all these people and wanting so much to meet poets and writers.'[16] Her son, the film director Waris Hussein later recalled 'my mother was in awe of Cecil. He'd come to our flat in Chelsea for tea and they'd talk about books and literature. She felt it a privilege to sit and listen to him talk.'[17] Later at her request he put into verse her literal translations of Urdu texts for a film documentary her daughter, Shama Habibullah, was making.

Beautiful and scholarly, Hosain was in her late forties. Her husband was largely absent, spending most of his time in India. She was free to enjoy more of Day-Lewis's time than many other Chatto authors. Accounts of precisely what happened between them, however, differ.

When Day-Lewis's son Sean published his book about his father in 1980 and hinted at a sexual relationship between the two of them – though without naming Hosain – she denied it. 'My mother was very conservative in her attitude to sex,' according to Waris Hussein. 'She disapproved thoroughly of infidelity. She would not have had an affair.'[18] Sean Day-Lewis, despite yielding to her demand and rewriting the offending section in the paperback edition, believed that Hosain and his father had been seen together in what appeared at the time to be a compromising position when he had lent his father his flat in London's Chancery Lane.[19]

Balcon's suspicions were aroused when a theatrical friend told her that her husband had been visiting Hosain in her dressing room at the Savoy Theatre, where in 1962 she was appearing on the West End stage as the wife of the governor of Kashmir alongside Gladys Cooper in *A Bird In Time*. A chance remark at the end of another dinner by an acquaintance of Day-Lewis's about having seen him out and about with Hosain also put her on her guard.[20]

Balcon though remained wary of confrontation with Day-Lewis. Instead of challenging her husband she decided to keep quiet, hoping, as Mary Day-Lewis had in the past, that the infatuation would pass. 'The only question I can remember asking him, one day as he was sitting in an armchair in our bedroom at Crooms Hill, was what he believed marriage to be. He replied "it's a habit, a very good habit".'[21]

By contrast, his attitude to relationships with women outside marriage was later stated crudely and with a cold detachment in a letter to a friend as offering 'a sort of consummation, as when two bodies (not in the legal sense but in the sense of for the first time working perfectly together) reach a point which can never be excelled, only echoed. And then again it is also true that poets do tend to fall in love with a woman (sometimes consciously even) in order to beget a poem upon her; and when that's done, gradually withdraw.'[22]

However, given Hosain's vocal protests at Sean Day-Lewis's account, it may be that the flirtation between the two of them never went further than that. Day-Lewis was attracted to clever as well as beautiful women. An affair was not simply a question of sexual fulfilment for him.

His own version of what happened can only be surmised from his published writings. In his 1965 collection, *The Room*, 'Seven Steps in Love' initially presents love as an angel who will 'hand you a bunch of roses/And lay you on the rack'. He writes about wanting to escape love's clutches but being unable.

But when her naked eye selects you,
Better lie down, lie down.

287

But in section three, love becomes something – or someone – different.

> ... *the dark Unknown*
> *Which makes him an explorer. Gales and spices*
> *For him alone*
> *Breathe in her singing words, her silences*
> *Are silver mines, her frown*
> *Ripples with lynx and cobra ... It is the strangeness*
> *That lures him on.*

The reference is opaque but plausibly carries an echo of Hosain, said those who knew her.[23]

Publication in America of Day-Lewis's collections had fallen out of step with *Pegasus* which only appeared on the other side of the Atlantic a year after it came out in England and included several poems that had to wait at home until *The Gate*. In 1964 the later poems from *The Gate* plus the earlier ones from Day-Lewis's 1965 British collection *The Room* came out in the States as *Requiem for the Living* and included an expanded and reordered version of 'Seven Steps in Love', entitled 'A Course in Love'. In it, the angel is absent and a man is embarking on a love affair as he contemplates the start of the autumn of his years.

> *His season of life marched so with hers. The two*
> *Converged. Their weather was right for a late flowering.*
> *Love, that had filled or failed them often enough, came out*
> *Ingratiating, devouring.*

Again it cannot be established if this stanza, missing from the British version, was inspired by Hosain. Or, indeed, if it was omitted at home to cover his tracks with Balcon. Stephen Spender liked to claim that Day-Lewis would kill off women he had once been in love with in his Nicholas Blake thrillers.[24] Mary and Jane look-alikes had already been murdered and, in *The Deadly Joker* in 1963, there is a hint of Hosain in the character of Vera Paston, chatelaine of the local big house who meets a brutal end.

Day-Lewis left for Harvard at the end of September, flying out from Dublin after spending a last weekend there with Balcon. Almost at once he was pining for her. On arrival he wrote to her: 'I've been very much depressed all this week, realising how much I shall miss you – not only as bed-mate and house-keeper, whatever you may say.'[25] His lodgings were in Lowell House, one of the twelve undergraduate residential houses at Harvard. He recorded the scene that greeted him.

> *The crimson berry tree navelled upon this court*
> *Twinkles a coded message, a wind-sun tingling chord,*
> *Curious round her foot saunters one blue jay:*
> *Fallen leaves swarm and scurry – a game of running away*
> *Slides from play to panic.*
> *Young men pull the berries*
> *To pelt one another, or go their way to seminars*
> *On art and the organic.*
>
> 'Madrigal for Lowell House': *The Room and Other Poems* (1965)

A young assistant professor from New Orleans, Albert Gelpi, and another aspiring academic Barbara Charlesworth, became Day-Lewis's closest friends at Harvard. Gelpi and Charlesworth were to marry in June 1965 and Day-Lewis regarded himself as a kind of guardian angel who had presided over their romance. Gelpi was a resident tutor at Lowell House and had met Day-Lewis at the airport when he arrived. Their friendship took root from the first dinner they had together that night. 'The differences in age and culture and experience,' Gelpi wrote, 'somehow worked to kindle the regard and friendship we instantly felt for each other and found in each other. I was beginning to study the American poetic tradition, and it was daunting and thrilling that he came to my lectures on American poets whenever he could.'[26]

Gelpi took Day-Lewis on a New England autumn pilgrimage to Emily Dickinson's house and grave at Amherst. Spending time with young people as an equal, not a father or literary mentor, gave Day-Lewis his first real chance to experience what the 1960s social and sexual revolution was all about. As well as more formal teaching situations, there would be pre-dinner drinks most nights at Lowell in different studies where Gelpi and his young colleagues would talk without embarrassment about their lives. Gelpi confided in Day-Lewis about his worries about marriage and commitment.[27] There were playful moments – as when Day-Lewis got them all to try out his pet notion that red wine and chocolate in the mouth at the same time produced the taste of strawberries, or later when he was taken to the annual ritual of the Harvard-Yale football game. Gelpi and Charlesworth introduced Day-Lewis to the music and lyrics of Bob Dylan and Joan Baez. And one lunchtime at Lowell, Day-Lewis met Allen Ginsberg, hero of the beatnik generation. 'Cecil would have avoided Ginsberg,' Gelpi recalled, 'but Allen sought him out. And Cecil was surprised and delighted by Ginsberg's engagement with poetic technique.'[28]

With his lectures already written and his other workload light, Day-Lewis was able to reflect on all these new influences in a burst of creativity. 'The poems are going well,' he reported back to Balcon in October. 'I've written no less than five since the beginning of the month, one of which is the best I've done for a long time: some undergraduates here who run a hand press are going to print it as a broad sheet.'[29]

The poem in question was 'On Not Saying Everything'. It begins with the Elm tree outside his Harvard window (which becomes a Linden in the poem).

Even if its branches grew to span
The continent; for nature's plan
Insists that infinite extension
Shall create no new dimension.
From the first snuggling of the seed
In earth, a branchy form's decreed.

The limitations of the tree lead him on to the limitations of a poem.

A poem, settling to its form,
Finds there's no jailer, but a norm

289

Of conduct, and a fitting sphere
Which stops it wandering everywhere.

And from the limitations of the poem, he moves on to the limitations of human love, that central tension between staying and exploring that had informed much of his poetry since 'O Dreams, O Destinations'. On the other side of an ocean from Balcon, he feels free to celebrate their love.

Play out then, as it should be played,
The sweet illusion that has made
An eldorado of your hair
And our love an everywhere.

But he ends with a plea about how they should try to behave when he eventually returns to London.

But when we cease to play explorers
And become settlers, clear before us
Lies the next need – to re-define
The boundary between yours and mine;
Else, one stays prisoner, one goes free.
Each to his own identity
Grown back, shall prove our love's expression
Purer for this limitation.
Love's essence, like a poem's, shall spring
From the not saying everything.

'I believe so strongly,' he said later of the poem, 'in the doctrine of limitations that it speaks for – that everything, a tree, a poem, a human relationship lives and thrives by the limits imposed upon it.'[30] He was explaining to Balcon the contradictions within him and addressing the hurt his infidelities had caused her.

The doctrine of limitations was also one of the central messages of his Norton lectures. 'On the platform,' Gelpi recalled, 'the first batch of lectures were beautifully delivered and enthusiastically received.'[31] In some Day-Lewis sang as well as spoke. He later published his lectures as *The Lyric Impulse* and was keen throughout to show the close connection between poetry and song. In one lecture, he was given a standing ovation when he demonstrated his new-found knowledge of 1960s culture with a rendition of Pete Seeger's 'Where Have All The Flowers Gone?' 'Initially Cecil had been put off by Bob Dylan's gravely voice when I played him an LP in my rooms at Lowell,' recalled Al Gelpi. 'It was so different from the mellifluous tenor quality of Tom Moore, but Cecil came to recognize the genuine "lyric impulse" in Dylan's songs.'[32]

In his lecture on 'The Golden Bridle' (after the restraint Bellerophon tried to place on Pegasus), Day-Lewis coupled his belief in an unconscious source of poetic inspiration, already described in 'Pegasus', with the doctrine of limitations as set out in 'On Not Saying Everything'. 'Paul Valéry wrote somewhere,' he told his audience, ' "Why do I use strict form? To prevent the poem from saying everything". That is an extremely profound remark. A poetic form ... provides the poet with a system of checks and balances external to memories, thoughts and images, which an incipient poem catches, and which – if not controlled – may run away with it. The form is a discipline which helps to select from an incoherent mass of material those data that are relevant to the poem's still undecided purpose. But the form is not always merely selective and disciplinary: many poets must have observed in their own work, as Valéry did, that the need for a rhyme in a certain place, or the exigency of a metre, has thrown up a revealing phrase, a creative idea, which might well not have come into existence without the prompting of the formal agency. Form, in a word, not only restrains but stimulates.'[33]

Day-Lewis's concern for craftsmanship and his rejection of free verse were already well-recorded. Here, though, he was acknowledging what he had not said before – that the poem itself has limits. He also addressed the American critical establishment, as he had already done with their British equivalent at first Cambridge and then Oxford, on the pitfalls of the prevailing current of Modernism. He was all in favour, he said, of 'innovation in language', 'violent juxtapositions' and 'deliberate discords' to achieve greater 'complexity, intellectual toughness and irony' – all aspirations of the poetry he had written while working closely with Auden and Spender – but he rejected the breaking of form in poems advocated by Modernism as potentially alienating readers.[34]

'We cannot be pleased with a state of affairs where poetry is nothing but a closed circuit', he said. Some modernist poets, he claimed, 'are secretly happy to write for other poets alone'. His passionately held conviction that poetry was for a broad audience and had to engage in their concerns was reiterated forcibly. 'We are so inured nowadays to accepting poetry as an art for the minority that it is difficult to put ourselves in the minds of the people who knew it as a popular art.'[35]

Taken as a whole his lectures insisted, unfashionably for the time, that poetry had to rediscover its 'source' in simplicity, sincerity, purity and 'complete truth to feeling'. The poet, he urged, must 'submit to the lyric impulse, when it comes his way – the impulse to grieve or to rejoice single-mindedly, to discover images and rhythms which convey the elemental states of mind a man shares with all other living men and has in common with his remotest ancestors'.[36]

Day-Lewis returned home for Christmas 1964. It was a happy reunion in Greenwich but on Boxing Day he woke with a nose bleed. 'He started,' Balcon recounted to Gelpi in a letter, 'a very violent & terrifying haemorrhage from the nose at 4am & for 36 hours it went on intermittently & getting worse each time.'[37] Day-Lewis refused to allow Balcon to call a doctor, insisting it would clear up, but, when his trust in his own fundamental good health evaporated and he relented, it was discovered that he had alarmingly high blood pressure. Had it not been revealed by the nose bleed, he was told, it could have caused a fatal stroke. He was taken to hospital where an ear, nose and throat surgeon tried to cauterize his nose but failed. 'Stemming the flow of blood,' Balcon told Gelpi, 'was (according to the surgeon) the most difficult task he'd ever had of its kind.'[38]

Eventually it was possible and slowly Day-Lewis recovered. His return to Harvard was delayed until early February while he rested in bed, with Balcon reading him Jane Austen's *Sense and Sensibility*. 'Just now, I'm having a glorious time,' Day-Lewis wrote to Gelpi, 'can't think why anyone wants to get up.'[39]

His good humour, however, disguised a sobering realization. After 60 years of robust good health – 'I've previously had the constitution of an ox' he told Gelpi[40] – he was suddenly frail. As he rested in his bedroom at Crooms Hill, he reflected on just how close he had come to death.

> *Slowly he turned his head. By gust-flung snatches*
> *A shower announced itself on the windowpane:*
> *He saw unquestioning, not even astonished,*
> *Handfuls of diamonds sprung from a dazzling chain.*
>
> *Gently at last the angels settled back now*
> *Into mere ornaments, the unearthly sheen*
> *And spill of diamond into familiar raindrops,*
> *It was enough. He'd seen what he had seen.*
>
> 'A Privileged Moment': *The Whispering Roots* (1970)

He was now dependent on pills to stay alive. His blood pressure problems had left him often impotent. That 'still distant ... ignominy of old age' that he had written about at the end of *The Buried Day* was suddenly upon him.

Chapter 30

Haunted by Darkness

The child's eye,
Unpuzzled, saw plain facts: I catch a glint from
The darkness they're haunted by.
'Fishguard to Rosslare': *The Room and Other Poems* (1965)

Day-Lewis and Balcon were in a lift at the BBC's Broadcasting House in central London in 1963 when they bumped into one of her acquaintances from the theatre, the actor Sebastian Shaw. She introduced the actor to her husband. 'I'm very interested to meet you,' Shaw said to Day-Lewis. 'I own the house where you were born.'[1] In the ensuing conversation Shaw invited them to visit Ballintubbert House the next time they were in Ireland.

They went in the autumn of 1963, one of many trips to Ireland that they made, sometimes with their children, sometimes without, in the years immediately before and after Day-Lewis's tenure at Harvard. The pull exerted by the land of his birth and childhood holidays grew ever stronger as the years of his exile increased.

At Ballintubbert House, they were joined by Sean Day-Lewis, already in Ireland for his newspaper. The property was empty. An elderly caretaker showed them round. The old rectory had seen better days, the front lawn kept in check only by donkeys. 'Wandering about the empty rooms,' Sean recalled, 'no memories could be awakened, but Cecil grew pensive with the weight of the past. "You should never come back", he said . . .'[2]

And he never did again – to Ballintubbert. But the following summer just before his departure for America, the family holiday was taken on the coast of first Co. Galway and then Co. Mayo at the Old Head Hotel in Louisburgh. In the shadow of Croagh Patrick and overlooking Clew Bay, Old Head made such an impression on the Day-Lewises that they returned each year thereafter (and Tamasin, as an adult, was to buy a holiday home there). 'We found the people there congenial,' remembered Balcon. 'The hotel was owned by Alec Wallace who was also a philosopher and mathematician. It was shabby, smelt of dogs and we felt utterly at home.'[3]

Day-Lewis and Balcon were in Dublin again in March 1966 braving the crowds to mark the 50th anniversary of the Easter Rising which had precipitated the end of British rule and hastened the marginalization of the Anglo-Irish within Ireland. In Harvard, Day-Lewis had been introduced by a Celtic expert at Lowell House, John Kelleher, to a theory that would give him deeper roots in

Ireland than membership of the now defunct Protestant overlord class. Kelleher had planted in Day-Lewis's head the idea that his forebears may have been the O Deaghaidhs of Co. Clare. It appealed to Day-Lewis and he liked to quote it, but gave it no real credence.

The Dublin trip also included a last, sad meeting with Knos where she was drifting, her memory all but gone, towards the end which finally came at the age of 92 in December 1966. 'My Mother's Sister', Day-Lewis's tribute to her, was one of several 'Irish' poems in *The Room and Other Poems*, the collection he published in the autumn after his return from Harvard. It ends:

> ... Now, sunk in one small room of a Rathmines
> Old people's home, helpless, beyond speech
> Or movement, yearly deeper she declines
> To imbecility – my last link with childhood.

> The battery's almost done: yet if I press
> The button hard – some private joke in boyhood
> I teased her with – there comes upon her face
> A glowing of the old, enchanted smile.

> So, still alive, she rots. A heart of granite
> Would melt at this unmeaning sequel. Lord,
> How can this be justified, how can it
> Be justified?

When he would read the poem at recitals, Day-Lewis's voice in the final stanza was full of rage and incomprehension.[4] How could the God in whom Knos had placed her trust throughout her life have rewarded her selflessness and devotion to others by allowing her such a long, lingering, undignified death? Religious phrases and imagery crept more and more into his later verse. They reflected a spiritual yearning in him as he entered old age and found himself one step away from death. And they came too as part of his renewed focus on his childhood in which the rituals, words and sounds of organized religion had played such a part. However, equivocal though he was on many matters, on the subject of faith, Day-Lewis remained steadfast. He did not stray beyond his 'churchy agnosticism', tempting though it might have been.

The Room reaches back into his own store of memories of youthful trips to Ireland with 'Fishguard to Rosslare'. The idea of dedicating a whole collection to his origins was already forming in Day-Lewis's mind. *The Room*, however, had many other threads to collect together. There were the poems written during his creative burst at Harvard – 'On Not Saying Everything', 'Days Before a Journey', 'Madrigal for Lowell House' and 'Saint Anthony's Shirt', a meditation on the by now familiar theme of the rootedness *and* rootlessness of identity, inspired by a remark of Keats that the self is like a religious relic, patched and repatched by monks until nothing is left of the original. Day-Lewis takes as his metaphor the nine houses he had lived in during his lifetime.

> I walk these many rooms, wishing to trace
> My frayed identity. In each, a ghost

Looks up and claims me for his long-lost brother –
Each unfamiliar, though he wears my face.
A draught of memory whispers I was most
Purely myself when I became another:

Tending a sick child, groping my way into
A woman's heart, lost in a poem, a cause,
I touched the marrow of my being, unbarred
Through self-oblivion. Nothing remains so true
As the outgoingness. This moving house
Is home, and my home, only when it's shared.

There are also in *The Room* poems about love and lovers ('Seven Steps in Love' and 'The Fox'), observations of nature ('Grey Squirrel: Greenwich Park'), observations of himself ('A Passion for Diving', inspired by a cruise of the Greek islands he and Balcon had taken in 1962 on a boat charted by his Chatto colleague, Peter Calvocoressi), a translation of Baudelaire's 'The Voyage', and tributes to friends. 'For Rex Warner On His Sixtieth Birthday' was prompted by their meeting while he was in America. Warner was now teaching at the University of Connecticut. 'Few, if any, nicer things have come to me in my life', Warner wrote when he received the poem. He added a postscript. 'You showed an unusual degree of restraint in not bringing in communism, fascism or lechery.'[5]

'Elegy for a Woman Unknown' sees Day-Lewis returning to another poetic form in which he had previously excelled. He had been handed at Chatto some poems written by Fiona Peters who had died of cancer. They had been delivered by her pathologist husband, Michael. His wife, he explained, had been an admirer of Day-Lewis's poetry. She had recorded in verse her feelings during her three-year battle for survival. Much as he had wanted to feel they were suitable for publication, given the background story, Day-Lewis judged they fell short of the mark. So, instead, his empathy led him to write the poem Peters had found beyond her. He found the inspiration, he had told one of his Harvard audiences, on the Greek island of Delos during a sightseeing trip on the cruise with the Calvocoressis.

Sitting next to the celebrated Lions of Delos, a monument to endurance, he described how he had 'heard – almost as if the lions had spoken it out of the island's holy hush, "Not the silence after music, but the silence of no more music". To me, those words had an extraordinary momentousness. I connected them at once with the dead woman; and the elegy began to get written ..."[6]

And silence – not the silence after music,
But the silence of no more music. A breeze twitches
The grass like a whisper of snakes; and swallows there are,
Cicadas, frogs in the cistern. But elusive
Their chorusing – thin threads of utterance, vanishing stitches
Upon the gape of silence, whose deep core
Is the stone lions' soundless roar.

In an interview with the *Guardian*, published to coincide with the appearance of *The Room*, Day-Lewis acknowledged that in some of the poems in the collection his style had become less lyrical, more conversational. 'What we call the poets of the 'fifties,' he said, 'have influenced me, I think, in the sense that they've rather encouraged me to get dryer myself.'[7]

While other reviewers expressed enthusiasm for the collection, the *Times Literary Supplement*'s anonymous critic damned *The Room* as consisting merely of 'placebos and plastic blooms'. It picked out two poems as 'positively embarrassing' – 'Pietà', inspired by the assassination of American President, John F. Kennedy, in 1963, and 'Who Goes Home?' a three-part tribute to Winston Churchill written quickly for the BBC as the wartime Prime Minister lay dying and when Day-Lewis himself was still recovering from his own brush with mortality. Even Auden sent a message to his old friend via his son Sean, whom he met for tea in Edinburgh, that 'Who Goes Home?' was an example of the sort of writing his father shouldn't be doing because 'he obviously doesn't believe in what he is saying'.[8]

There is a hint, however, that Day-Lewis had been expecting a critical drubbings. Included in *The Room* is 'A Relativist'.

> He raged at critic, moralist – all
> That gang who with almightiest gall
> Lay claim to the decisive vote
> In separating sheep from goat.
>
> So on the last day, when he's got
> His breath back again, it will not
> Be goats or sheep that rouse his dudgeon
> But the absurdity of judging.

The Room lacks Day-Lewis's usual clear focus. Its poems are grouped under two headings – 'Fables and Confessions' and 'Others', without any obvious pattern. The charge was occasionally made – by admirers as well as critics – that Day-Lewis published too much. As someone who tried to make a living from being a poet, there was a direct economic pressure on him to publish regularly. On his return from Harvard, moreover, he was keen to see the poems written there in print and so may have filled out the collection with some material that he might otherwise have put to one side.

Among the younger generation of poets he continued to encourage as a publisher was John Horder, whose second collection, *A Sense of Being*, he accepted for Chatto. However, he was horrified when Horder took part in a demonstration in October 1967 against Arts Council policies that culminated in a book-burning in London's St James's Square. The protest was against grants made to individual writers by the Council's Literature Panel, chaired by Day-Lewis. Horder and his colleagues claimed that such awards were being mis-directed by the establishment figures on the panel towards already established names at the expense of promising young writers. 'This is demonstrably untrue,' Day-Lewis told Horder in a letter deploring his participation in the 'Nazi-thug'

protest. 'Like many others I have spent a great deal of time which I can ill afford
... in caring for poetry and trying to help poets – old or young, *avant garde*,
derrière garde, or any other *garde* – so long as I believed the individual poet was a
good or promising one.'[9]

He renewed his membership of the Arts Council for a second term when he
came back from Harvard, impressed by the new enthusiasm and new resources
being pumped in by the Labour government elected in 1964 and in particular by
its high profile Minister for the Arts, Jennie Lee. The funds now available to
Day-Lewis's Poetry Panel – whose brief had been widened to encouraging literature in general – had grown considerably from a few thousand pounds to
£66,000.

More money, though, meant more expectations, more choices to be made and
more controversy over decisions. Day-Lewis tried to keep out of the wider
machinations of the Arts Council under its flamboyant leader, Lord Goodman,
attending meetings but restricting his remarks to his own field of literature. Yet
he found himself caught in a national spotlight after the book-burning protest. If
Horder and his fellow demonstrators directed their anger at the choice of writers
to be supported, the *Times Literary Supplement* launched a very personal attack
on Day-Lewis himself. As chairman of the selection panel he was, the paper
wrote, 'scoutmasterly' in his language while making 'easy assumption of some
kind of absolute wisdom, not just in matters of literary discrimination, but also
in life itself'. This second assault in quick succession on him by the paper made
Day-Lewis begin to suspect that the *TLS* and its editor, Arthur Crook, were
indulging in a vendetta.

Another writer taken under Day-Lewis's wing at Chatto was A. S. Byatt.[10] In
1964, Chatto published this 28-year-old's first novel, *The Shadow of the Sun*, the
story of a young girl growing up in the shadow of a dominant father. Day-Lewis
was her editor. He was attracted to clever, young women novelists. With Byatt –
whom he called Tony – there was a shared love of poetry and of Emily Dickinson in particular.

Day-Lewis's admiration for Byatt's mind and work, and his efforts in the
editing process to bring out the best in her manuscript, spilt over into a more
personal attachment as it had with Attia Hosain. Byatt, an English graduate from
Cambridge who was teaching in the extra-mural department of the University of
London, was at the time married but she responded to Day-Lewis's advances,
though the relationship was not, she later said, consummated.[11]

He had continued to write to her when he was in the States. The Day-Lewises
were on holiday at Louisburgh in the summer of 1965 when Balcon went up to
their hotel room to fetch some cigarettes for her husband from his jacket pocket
when she stumbled across a letter from Byatt. It spoke of romantic afternoons
spent together in Bloomsbury.[12]

Balcon's patience with her husband's wanderings snapped. This time she did
not bury her anger as she had Attia Hosain. Indeed, her suppressed anguish over
that earlier betrayal may have explained why she was so distraught by her latest
discovery. She walked out on the family and spent the next two days sitting in a

cave on a nearby beach, contemplating the future of her marriage, returning to the hotel only occasionally to eat and sleep.

When Day-Lewis tried to explain his actions to her, she remembered, 'he described himself as an "old lag", someone who kept returning to bad habits in spite of himself'.[13] It was something to do with being a poet, he had suggested in one of his Harvard lectures. 'To write a good lyric of love today, the poet must have surrendered to the feeling of love and been possessed by it.'[14] Domestic life with two small children could not be described in such romantic terms of surrender and possession.

'He was apologetic. He said he had never intended to hurt me,' Balcon recalled.[15] But, whatever his intention, he had. She decided, finally and after seeking the advice of Norah Smallwood, her friend and Day-Lewis's colleague at Chatto, that she would not leave him – for the sake of their children and because she still loved Day-Lewis and needed him. Her silence up to now on his infidelity may have made him think she didn't mind about it. She did, very much, and she now insisted that he break off all contact with Byatt.

A relieved Day-Lewis described their making peace in 'Sailing from Cleggan', an account of a perilous sailing trip in choppy waters on the Galway hooker of the poet, Richard Murphy.

> Never will I forget it –
> Beating out through Cleggan Bay
> Towards Inishbofin, how
> The shadow lay between us,
> An invisible shadow
> All but severing us lay
> Athwart the Galway hooker.

It concludes:

> Miracle sun, dispelling
> That worst shadow! Salt and sun,
> Our wounds cautery! And how,
> Havened, healed, oh lightened of
> The shadow, we stepped ashore
> On to our recaptured love –
> Never could I forget it.

'Sailing from Cleggan': *The Whispering Roots* (1970)

Their love may, for him, have been renewed on that day but Balcon had in reality never stopped loving the husband she had admired as a schoolgirl. She was, though, now on her guard, suspicious of occasions when Day-Lewis appeared to want to attend an event on his own in case a young woman, especially another clever, young author, might catch his eye. Even days working at Chatto & Windus with another new writer, she feared, might pose a threat.[16]

Balcon had met Elizabeth Jane Howard for lunch at the Charing Cross Hotel soon after returning from Ireland. She had, in the years since Day-Lewis's affair with Howard, come to realize that something had gone on between them, but again had held her peace. When she mentioned her discovery of Byatt's letter, Howard took it as a cue to discuss her relationship with Balcon's husband, and made plain that it was she – not Day-Lewis – who had ended it.

It all contributed to Balcon's struggle to trust him again. Her unhappiness culminated in an episode late in 1967 when Day-Lewis had just been appointed as the first visiting Compton Lecturer in Poetry at Hull University. The Vice Chancellor had asked for either Day-Lewis or John Betjeman. The university's librarian, Philip Larkin, approached Day-Lewis.

Flattered by the invitation, Day-Lewis initially doubted he had anything left to say.'I have already lectured about everything I have the least acquaintance with', he told his American friend, Al Gelpi.[17] But he still accepted. 'I am particularly gratified,' Day-Lewis wrote back to Larkin, 'because it comes from you.'[18]

When it came to his inauguration and first teaching sessions, however, he announced he was going to travel to Hull alone. He told Balcon that she hadn't been invited and – unaccountably to her mind – that he has failed to ask for her to be included. She was silent and furious as she dropped him at the railway station for the journey. Knowing her distress, he wrote to her from Hull. 'I have not told you about my doings and meetings here because Hull is a sore subject with you.'[19]

He ended with an affirmation that reveals some of the issues that had come between them since she had stumbled on Byatt's letter. 'I value you and love you. I'm often bad at showing this and I know I should try harder and take more trouble about doing so. But now, I must say this. I feel you often *show* very little affection for me. I *know* how much love you have to give, but what I *get* is blame ... sometimes well justified blame, but not always. We are both difficult to live with – I do recognise how difficult I am.' He asked for her forgiveness for 'failures of understanding, of sympathy, failures to show outward & visible signs of the deep love I feel for you. We both must know that patience & tenderness are what keeps a marriage – all that *can* keep it when one partner has failed the other physically. You are an outspoken character, I am not, but I will try to *show* patience and tenderness more clearly. You do the same too, *please*.'[20]

The increasing problems with impotence that he referred to effectively ended the instinct he had described so often in his poems to run after love. It was never, though, only about sex and in these years he maintained a flirtatious correspondence with a young New Zealand woman, Elaine Hamilton, 30 years his junior, who had first sent him a fan letter in August 1962. In October 1967, he confided in her: 'it's a bloody humiliating thing to have the spirit so willing and the flesh so weak.' He went on: 'Thank God I'm too old now to face or stand the strain of two-way loving: it always ends in tears: which is not to say that it isn't worth it. I don't approve of the moral desperado inside of me (I've had seven mistresses – statistic, not boast), and try to prevent him getting out, with only moderate success so far.'[21] Balcon was aware of six – Alison Morris, Billie Currall, Rosamond Lehmann, Elizabeth Jane Howard, Attia Hosain and A. S. Byatt (though in the cases of the final two the word mistress may not be appropriate).[22] That left one missing name. It could have been Margaret

Marshall, when he was a young man. Or, since their relationship had begun when he was married to Mary and living with Rosamond, he might have meant Balcon, although she went on to become his second wife.

Neither the strains at home nor his 'dust-up' at the Arts Council, as he described it, deflected Day-Lewis from continuing to take on unpaid roles to promote poetry, literature and other good causes. He supported in 1967 the Library Association in its campaign to get funding from government for a Public Lending Right to reward financially authors whose books were borrowed from libraries. He became a Vice-President of the London Library and he enthusiastically backed a British Museum initiative to build up its collection of poetry manuscripts, launched with an exhibition, *Poetry in The Making* in April 1967.

Increasingly Day-Lewis was agreeing to take part in events in place of John Masefield, the Poet Laureate, as an unofficial deputy. So in April 1964, for example, it had been Day-Lewis in the pulpit of Westminster Abbey preaching the sermon at a celebration to mark the 400th anniversary of Shakespeare's birth. In ill health and his late eighties, Masefield had been in office since 1930. He had never been especially active in the role – posting the occasional poem to the *Times* for inclusion at great moments in the life of the nation, but always including a stamped addressed envelope in case they didn't want it. He had now, however, all but abdicated. To one Oxford friend who suggested coming over to see him in the early 1960s, Masefield had written back simply 'Better Not'.

The spread of gangrene into his foot and leg and his refusal to undergo amputation lead to Masefield's death on May 12, 1967. His body was cremated. He had asked that his ashes be scattered in the open air but instead they were deposited in Poets' Corner in Westminster Abbey.[23] Almost at once speculation broke out as to his successor – and the future of an office that many had forgotten existed during Masefield's low-key tenure.

Some felt that such a royal appointment with its stipend of £70 a year plus a £27 grant in lieu of the traditional 140-gallon butt of sack (Spanish wine), was anachronistic and urged abolition. The *Times* sat on the fence. 'It does no harm and may, who knows, do some good.' For the majority who wanted it to continue, albeit modernized, the leading candidate was Robert Graves, invited to travel from his home in Spain to give the memorial address for Masefield as he was interred in the Abbey. It seemed like a very public placing of the mantle on his shoulders and Graves indicated that he was willing to accept the offer when it came.

John Betjeman, a popular broadcaster and conservationist as well as poet, was also in the frame along with Edmund Blunden, now, finally, Professor of Poetry at Oxford, but in ill health and soon to relinquish that post early. Day-Lewis was the other leading candidate, two years older than Betjeman, and nine years younger than Graves. Question marks, though, were raised publicly and privately about his communist past and about his current standing as a poet after his recent bad reviews. How would a younger generation of writers react to the office going to someone who had, in his writings, so charted a course against the prevailing fashion?

Set against such drawbacks, however, were his freely acknowledged left-wing leanings, stronger than in the other two principal candidates. He was a paid-up member of the Labour Party and it was the Labour Prime Minister, Harold Wilson, who would advise the Queen on which of the names produced by the patronage secretary to select. His recent willing service as Masefield's deputy was seen as another plus. Moreover Day-Lewis's particular popularity with a poetry-loving public counted for him, the result of the many lecture tours and recitals he had given free-of-charge in church halls, schools, libraries and colleges as well as theatres and universities. And his lifelong commitment to championing poetry and poetry's public role made him an ideal fit for the vacancy.

He was inevitably asked during the interregnum by newspaper interviewers whether he wanted the job. 'I wouldn't be able to write Court poetry,' he admitted candidly. 'I'm not disloyal to the Royal family but I couldn't write that sort of thing.'[24] As he had already found out, he might have added. Day-Lewis also urged that the post should go to the best British poet and that, in his opinion, was Robert Graves. At Bedales, where she was now a boarder, 14-year-old Tamasin and her classmate Tomas Graves, son of Robert, fought mock duels on the playing field to decide whose father should emerge victorious.

On December 14, an official letter from 10 Downing Street arrived at Crooms Hill. Balcon left it with her husband when he returned home from Chatto's. She was hurrying off to the Royal Society of Literature to give a recital of Larkin poems. When she got back she found her husband still sitting in the same armchair in his study where she had left him. He was looking pleased and slightly incredulous. Though the news had to be kept secret until the New Year, he had been offered the post of Poet Laureate.

Chapter 31

Second Childhood

Roots are for holding on, and holding dear.
Mine, like a child's milk teeth, came away gently
From Ireland at the close of my second year.
Is it second childhood now – that I overhear
Them whisper across a lifetime as if from yesterday?
'The Whispering Roots': *The Whispering Roots* (1970)

When news of the appointment of C Day-Lewis as Poet Laureate was made public on New Year's Eve, 1967, the national and international media descended on Crooms Hill. It was still 'pandemonium', Day-Lewis wrote to his friend, Noel Annan, ten days later.[1] There were 400 letters wishing him well and 60 telegrams, including messages of congratulation from Robert Graves and John Betjeman. Even Day-Lewis's bank manager was moved to put pen to paper. 'The whole Midland is rejoicing with you', he assured him, although he may have been imagining that the annual royal stipend would amount to a little more than £70.[2]

There had been an official Poet Laureate since the reign of Charles II when he named John Dryden[3] to the post, but the tradition of having versifiers at the royal court was of longer vintage. Geoffrey Chaucer[4] had served Edward III in the fourteenth century and Edmund Spenser[5] Elizabeth I until his death in 1599. Since Dryden, the office, part of the Royal Household, had been through illustrious and threadbare periods.

Between them, Wordsworth and Tennyson had given it renewed significance for much of the second half of the nineteenth century. Both had been duty bound to produce verse for royal occasions. By the time of Day-Lewis's appointment, however, such stipulations had been quietly dropped, although they still dominated the popular estimation of his job description. In reality he could draw up his own to include as much or as little as he chose. As Auden wrote to him at the time: 'Now you are Poet Laureate. I rejoice for your sake in the honour, but I cannot say I envy you, because I haven't the faintest idea what, in these days, the function of the Poet Laureate is supposed to be. Have you?'[6]

Part of the wave of interest in the appointment was generated by the novelty of it all. There hadn't been a new Laureate since 1930. Contrasting the Labour-voting, twice-married Day-Lewis, with his attractive actress wife and young children, with the elderly Masefield, the *London Evening News* declared him the 'swinging laureate' for the swinging 1960s. 'What is so welcome about the appointment of C Day-Lewis is that for all his 63 years,' agreed the *Daily Mail*, 'he is nonetheless a modern poet, speaking in contemporary images, writing of the problems of today.'

His first task was to produce a poem to support the *Mail*'s 'I'm Backing Britain' campaign. It made the front page on January 5. Summoning up the Blitz spirit, 'Then and Now' concluded:

> *To work then, islanders, as men and women*
> *Members one of another, looking beyond*
> *Mean rules and rivalries towards the dream you could*
> *Make real, of glory, common wealth, and home.*

It was given a warm reception by readers, but failed to impress the critics and commentators. Bernard Levin, in his account of 1960s Britain, *The Pendulum Years*, recalled Day-Lewis 'celebrating' his appointment with 'Then and Now' which 'almost immediately . . . made many regret their impulsive rejoicing at the death of his predecessor'.[7] Whether the poem was good or bad – and Day-Lewis chose not to include it (unlike other 'official' compositions) in his next collection – he seemed already to be experiencing the negative side of being Laureate. Because of the antagonism such an ancient office generated, particularly among those who felt the Royal Family was an anachronism, his efforts simply offered another opportunity for attacking the establishment.

Among other questions that Day-Lewis addressed in that first rush of interviews, all accompanied by domestic pictures of him at home with Balcon, 14-year-old Tamasin and 11-year-old Daniel, were his Irish background and his 1930s communism. Both, it was suggested, made him an unusual choice for the job. The latter had been, he told one journalist, 'a case of the blind leading the short-sighted'.[8] He joked that what had concerned him and Auden much more of late was their competition about whose wrinkles were coming on best. 'Although Auden now looks like a tortoise, I've got the advantage because some of my wrinkles run diagonally across my forehead.'[9]

He took a more genuine pride in being, as he put it, 'the first expatriate son of Ireland' to hold the post (though he was overlooking the claim of the eighteenth-century Laureate, Nahum Tate,[10] also the London-based son of a Church of Ireland clergyman).'We Irish like feathers in our cap,' he explained to one television interviewer, when asked why he had taken on a post that had such a reputation for ruining poetic reputations. In more sober mood, he told another friend that he had accepted it 'for my children'. Despite his earlier advocacy of Graves as the best candidate because he was the best living poet, he refused to see his own appointment as conferring similar status on himself. When Mary, his ex-wife, heard the news, she wrote to congratulate him, saying he must feel as he did when receiving the verse prize all those years ago at Sherborne School. 'No,' he replied, 'in those days the news was merely confirmation that I was, or at least would be, a Great Poet: no such illusion possesses me today!'[11]

What did inspire him, however, was the laureateship's potential, unrealized by

Masefield or indeed by his predecessor, Robert Bridges,[12] who did not write a single 'official' poem during his 25 years in office. As he told Susan Barnes in the *Sun*: 'if one is going to make anything of this job, one doesn't want to waste time trying to influence the top people. Their minds are already made up anyway – like rocks most of them.'[13] He saw the laureateship instead as the ultimate platform to promote his belief that poetry had once more to connect with a mass audience by addressing its concerns in a manner it could understand.

He was still deciding precisely how to do this when he returned to Hull on January 17 to give one of his Compton lectures. The Laureate, he pointed out, was now stripped of his traditional functions – as an entertainer, he had been superseded; as moralizer he would not be listened to. 'To many people he looks like a man desperately and unintelligibly semaphoring from a sandcastle crumbling at the tide's encroachment.' Yet there was, he insisted, valuable work to be done. A first priority was 'to purify the language of the tribe, to ensure that our English language shall be kept clean, resourceful, adventurous, alive'. Broadening his remit, he said he hoped also to reawaken the country to the role of poetry at a time of social change, unrest and left-wing agitation, especially on university campuses like Hull. 'First there is a certain consoling and reassuring rootedness about poetry. It was noticeable how during the last war the sales of poetry were greatly increased. The generation who lived in crisis – and we are still living there – do seem to need something more stable, less ephemeral than the common run of books: something nearer the bedrock of humankind. Poetry, reminding us of the past, puts us in touch with countless dead generations.'[14]

With such a lofty ambition, it helped that Day-Lewis was the first Laureate who was a consummate performer on both radio and television. His plans, however, were not always assisted by the nature of the requests that came his way and by his habit, at least initially, of saying yes to invitations that, with hindsight, he might have done better to decline. With the creation of a new county borough of Teesside in 1968, he was asked to produce a poem by the regional paper, the *Evening Gazette* in Middlesbrough. The result was, he later agreed, 'about as memorable as leading articles in newspapers', but added by way of justification: 'The important thing is to keep the idea of poetry before the public eye.'[15]

Thereafter, he did manage to choose his occasions with more discernment. In May 1968, he wrote something to mark the Old Vic Theatre's 150th anniversary. The following year he offered a poem in support of National Library Week in May and another in October for the premiere of a film about the Battle of Britain. There were occasional royal poems, including one for the investiture of the Prince of Wales on July 1, 1969, which appeared in the *Guardian*, though the heir to the throne was said later to have preferred John Betjeman's tribute in the *Times*.

Lyric poets, like Day-Lewis, tend to write their best verse when they can summon up strong personal feelings, often taking months, years or even decades for a subject to emerge onto paper. Writing to order in a hurry about matters and institutions about which he had mixed or indifferent feelings was a challenge for Day-Lewis. In one regard, however, he was well equipped. He had plenty of experience of making political points in his poetry.

His 'Feed My Little One' was written to mark Oxfam's silver jubilee and was read by Dame Sybil Thorndike at the Royal Festival Hall. 'Keep Faith with Nature' was an appeal for environmental awareness long before it had arrived on the national agenda.

> Now more than ever we need
> True science, lest mankind
> Lording it over nature's
> Territories, by greed
> Or thoughtlessness made blind,
> To doom shall have consigned
> Itself and all earth's creatures.

And that same willingness to highlight subjects that many politicians would as yet rather ignore was there too in 'Epitaph to a Drug Addict'.

> Mourn this young girl. Weep for society
> Which gave her little to esteem but kicks.
> Impatient of its code, cant, cruelty,
> Indifferent, she kicked against all pricks
> But the dream-loaded hypodermic's. She
> Has now obtained an everlasting fix.

'Epitaph to a Drug Addict': The Whispering Roots (1970)

One perk of the job was being invited occasionally to Buckingham Palace. His first lunch with the Queen began, he liked to recall, with him putting his feet on one of the royal corgis, imagining it was a stool. His faux pas did not prevent him being asked back.

His principal connection with the Royal Household, however, was to chair the committee which recommended names of recipients for the Queen's Gold Medal for Poetry. He used his appointment as an excuse to disband the old committee, privately being tired of its compromises, muddled brief and habit of overlooking those he saw as the best candidates. He gathered round him instead Philip Larkin, Charles Causley[16] and William Plomer. Over a good lunch at L'Epicure, they agreed to honour those with an outstanding body of work to their name. Day-Lewis asked the monarch if she would consent to award the medal in person – something she had not done previously – and was delighted when she agreed.

Their first such recipient was Robert Graves. He came over from his home in Majorca to stay at Crooms Hill and went with Day-Lewis to the Palace on 6 December 1968 to receive his award. BBC cameras were there, filming the first ever close-up television portrait of the Windsors, The Royal Family. They recorded Graves being presented with his medal and then Day-Lewis, to his surprise, being given his insignia of office, a badge and chain which had not hitherto been mentioned to him. 'I shall wear it on my pyjamas,' he told Graves before bidding him farewell.[17] Graves left by a back door, fearing, he said, that his creditors would catch up with him. Day-Lewis went to the Chatto offices where he was telephoned by Balcon. Buckingham Palace had called, she told him, to say that Her Majesty had made a mistake. The badge and chain he had been given belonged to the Chancellor of the Order of St Michael and St George who – in the form of Viscount De L'Isle – was waiting at the Palace to receive it. A royal emissary was dispatched at once to William IV Street.

Four months after his appointment, Day-Lewis published his most auto-biographical Nicholas Blake. In his notebooks, where he had written it in long hand on the right-hand pages, with clues cross-referenced to notes on the facing page, he had called it *Take Her Up Tenderly*. It was published in April as *The Private Wound*, taken from a Shakespeare line in *The Two Gentlemen of Verona* – 'the private wound is deepest'.

'It is time I told this story,' it begins. 'I do not know if I shall ever bring myself to publish it.' Set in the west of Ireland in 1939 against the backdrop of a looming war in Europe, it is about a young novelist, Dominic Eyre, influenced by Christopher Isherwood, who leaves his fiancée behind in England while he rents a cottage on a run-down Irish estate to concentrate on his writing. A self-deprecating, detached figure – 'you got [a feeling] from him that now and then he had moved miles away from you into some desert of his own' – he also has many parallels with Day-Lewis but unlike him is also to go on to be a distinguished soldier.

In Ireland, Eyre is seduced by his landlord's wife, Harriet Leeson. It is her death that gives the book the veneer of a crime thriller, but there is no Nigel Strangeways. Instead Blake largely concentrates on the triangular relationship between Dominic, Harriet and her older, ruined, acquiescent husband, Flurry. If Flurry suggests John Currall, Harriet is unambiguously modelled on Billie Currall. The picture of her on page one of *The Private Wound* echoes Day-Lewis's description of Currall in 'On the Sea Wall'. The book is his confession to their affair.

In a fictional epilogue, written by the now dead Eyre's literary executor, the young writer is described as having been 'haunted' ever after by what happened in Ireland. 'I have often wondered,' the executor writes, 'whether this novel was prompted by some intuition of his approaching death.' For Day-Lewis, too, there may have been a sense, after his collapse in 1964, that this was one part of his life he needed to address before it was too late. As a *mea culpa* for his treatment of Currall, her husband and Mary, it is powerful, yet is no hint of the son – or even sons – that resulted from the affair.

A new crime novel by the new Poet Laureate – especially one with so romantic and tragic a tale to tell – was news, and extracts were printed in the *Daily Express*, with the silhouette of a naked woman juxtaposed with a picture of Day-Lewis. John Currall, Billie's long-suffering husband, was one who read it. 'He may think I don't know what his story is about,' he told Mary Day-Lewis as he walked past Brimclose a few days later, 'but I do, damn his eyes.'[18]

After the initial burst of interest in his appointment Day-Lewis had settled comfortably into office and was glad at some of the perks. He was able, for instance, to use his office to generate headlines for the efforts of the Greenwich Society to stop their area's historic centre being scarred by new road-building plans. He was more amused than anything when on an official trip to Malta, he was piped aboard a boat like a member of the Royal Family. However, he quickly came to realize that he was labouring under twin disadvantages as Poet Laureate. The first was that the honour had come too late. His peak of popularity – especially among other poets – had passed. Had he succeeded Masefield in 1949, as at one stage seemed possible, he might have been able to carry more of the younger generation with him in updating the office and making a wider impact. Instead, many tended to see his appointment as yet more evidence that he was an older, establishment figure out of touch with them and their work.

The second was that, though he had three reasonable years of health after his collapse at Christmas 1964, thereafter he had a series of illnesses that sapped his energy. His first summer as Laureate saw him bed-ridden with glandular fever – unusual in a 64-year-old – and then in pain with severe dental problems throughout the autumn. In March of the following year, while in Malta, stones in his gall bladder caused him to be hurried home for hospital treatment. Later there were also painful bladder stones. On June 11 he was at home with Balcon when he suffered a heart attack. It turned out to have been a mild coronary thrombosis, however, and after a short stay in hospital he was cleared by doctors to lead the annual family pilgrimage to Co. Mayo. He left a happy picture for his children of the chatter in the car on the way to Louisburgh.

> I heard you last summer, crossing Ireland by road,
> Ask the mother to re-tell episodes out of your past.
> You gave them the rapt attention
> A ballad-maker's audience owed
> To fact caught up in fable.

'Children Leaving Home': Posthumous Poems (1979)

There was, the Day-Lewis children remembered, a greater freedom when they were in Ireland compared to the more traditional routine at home where they had their own floor of the house and sometimes only saw their father at mealtimes or for bed-time stories. In Ireland he was both more available – no need to knock on his study door – and seemed younger and more able to join in their games. 'Going to Ireland,' Tamasin said, 'was the highlight of our child-hood. Every year they would ask us where we wanted to go and there would be no question that it was Ireland. It was a magical place. We were allowed to run a bit wild. We never wanted to come back.'[19]

For her parents, there were trips and excursions – to Yeats's Thoor Ballylee and, on another occasion, to his grave in Co. Sligo in the shadow of Benbulben. Day-Lewis wrote in 1967 to Elaine Hamilton of 'a super month in Ireland – Dan caught his first trout, Tamasin came in second in a very tough horse race (the other competitors all being villainous horse-dealers and farmers), and I plunged into the Atlantic every day.'[20]

Tamasin had won a scholarship to Bedales, a progressive boarding school in

Hampshire. Her godmother, Elizabeth Jane Howard, agreed to make a contribution to the fees. Having started his education at the local state primary, Daniel was sent at 11 to Sevenoaks, a more traditional public school in Kent, but found the change a difficult one to navigate. After he ran away, escaping to Bedales to join his sister, there was a difficult interview with the Sevenoaks headteacher. It was decided to move him to Bedales at the end of the year if he passed the entrance exam which he duly did. 'I remember afterwards Cecil saying to Dan "I have complete faith in you",' Balcon said later.[21]

Tamasin was old enough now during school holidays to meet her father for lunch at his office. 'He'd take me out to his favourite restaurants. There was such a closeness between us that I never thought what the lack of things were with him. I guess he gave what he could give.[22] He did have an aura that could appear off-putting, distant, detached, but his incredible sense of humour, his twinkle and subversive wicked side defused it, as when he would drive, guiding the steering wheel with his knees, and say "look, no hands!". When I was at Bedales I began to talk to him about Hardy or anyone else I was studying and started to feel our relationship transform. His letters to school answering any questions I had were always succinct and beautifully and economically written. And very funny.'

There were, both children recalled, times of tension at home between their parents, arguments they overheard from the floors below them. With Day-Lewis's many Laureate duties, more of the domestic burden than ever had fallen on Balcon's shoulders. His failing health too changed the balance in their relationship.

Yet advancing age, declining health and the greater sense of ease that undoubtedly came (despite his denials) with the worldly recognition of being Poet Laureate, had also helped soothe some of the conflicts that had arisen in the Day-Lewises's marriage since Balcon had discovered his relationship with A. S. Byatt. There was a brief flare-up when she discovered – because an *Evening Standard* journalist rang and let it slip – that a week after his appointment as Laureate, Day-Lewis had been seen taking Byatt to lunch in L'Epicure, but it was a brief lapse. Balcon even managed to laugh with her husband at the knitting that Elaine Hamilton would send him from New Zealand at Christmas. She did not smile, however, when she found in the bathroom a note from Hamilton which ended with a lipstick kiss on the sheet of paper and the accompanying gift of a pink satin bra strap.

The subject that Day-Lewis returned to most often in his poetry in these years was Ireland and in March 1970 he published *The Whispering Roots*. The first half of the new collection is made up of poems about Ireland and Day-Lewis's Irish roots. It reprises some of his earlier works – 'My Mother's Sister', 'Fishguard to Rosslare' and 'The House Where I Was Born'. This last is paired with an account of his 1964 return there.

I walk through the unremembered house,
Note on the walls each stain
Of damp; then up the spacious stair

As if I would now retrace
My self to the room where it began.
Dust on fine furnishings,
A scent of wood ash – the whole house sings
With an elegiac air.

Its owner is not at home – nor I
Who have no title to it
And no drowned memories to chime
Through its hush. Can piety
Or a long-lost innocence explain it? –
By what prodigious spell,
Sad elegant house, you have made me feel
A ghost before my time?

'Ballintubbert House, Co. Laois'

That 'elegiac air' is maintained in much of *The Whispering Roots*. Past and present are drawn upon to help Day-Lewis face a future of ageing and death. If there is an acknowledged sentimentality in 'Golden Age, Monart, Co. Wexford', his account of his childhood summers, and in 'Avoca, Co. Wicklow', where he recalls Knos singing Tom Moore songs, there is also a directness and lack of sentimentality in his thoughts on death in 'Ass in Retirement'.

Put out to grass, given a yard more rope
each week, he takes time off from what's under his nose
Only to bray at rain-clouds over the distant bog;
relishes asinine freedom – having to bear
no topple of hay, nor cleeves crammed with turf;
ignorant that he'll come in time

to the longest tether's end,
then strangle or accept
that stake. Either way
on the endless
grass one day
he'll drop
dead.

In 'All Soul's Night' Day-Lewis, 65 at the time of publication, seems to anticipate that he will be joining the dead soon.

Existences, consoling lies, or phantom
Dolls of tradition, enter into me.
Welcome invisibles! We have this in common –
Whatever you are, I presently shall be.

If there is any sort of immortality, he suggests, it lies in this life. There is the prospect of being remembered by your descendants, highlighted in 'Goldsmith outside Trinity', an account of visiting the statue of his ancestor in central Dublin. Or you may be recalled by a grateful public. 'Remembering Con Markievicz' was inspired by a visit to Lissadell House in Co. Sligo, home of this friend of Yeats and one-time heroine of the Irish uprising against British rule. 'Lament for Michael Collins', one of the leaders of a newly free Ireland when he was murdered in 1922, suggests that legacies can be betrayed – 'dare a nation/ Forget the genius who rode through storm on storm'. And 'Kilmainham Jail: Easter Sunday 1966', written after he had visited Dublin to celebrate the 50th anniversary of the insurrection, ends:

> They are gone as a tale that is told,
> The fourteen men. Let them be more than a legend:
> Ghost-voices of Kilmainham, claim your due –
> *This is not yet the Ireland we fought for.*
> *You living, make our Easter dreams come true.*

The best the unrepentant agnostic Day-Lewis can say of immortality comes in 'Harebells over Mannin Bay' where flowers stand against the azure sky and sea.

> *Harebells, keep your arresting*
> *Pose by the strand. I like*
> *These gestures of the ephemeral*
> *Against the everlasting.*

There is often a downward inflection in the last lines of many of the poems in the collection – though not in all. 'A Tuscan Villa' in the second half, made up of a variety of poems not linked to Ireland, sees Day-Lewis celebrating once again the Italian landscape he had first been attracted to when with Lehmann in 1948. This time he was reflecting on a trip to the Italian home of friends Johannes Schwarzenberg, the current Austrian ambassador to the Vatican, and his sculptor wife, Kathleen, who had modelled Day-Lewis's head in clay. And the joyful 'A Marriage Song' was written for his Harvard friends, Al Gelpi and Barbara Charlesworth, when they tied the knot in June 1965.

> *Midsummer, time of golden views and hazes,*
> *Advance in genial air,*
> *Bring out your best for this charmed pair –*
> *Let fly a flamingo dawn, throw open all your roses,*
> *Crimson the day for them and start the dancing.*

P. J. Kavanagh in a *Guardian* review suggested an overall unevenness of tone. 'One poem rings false, then hard on its heels one that is nearer the hurting nerve of indecisiveness'. Reading Day-Lewis, he remarked, was 'like having the spiritual insides of a man's life laid out for inspection'. Others were more full of praise. C. B. Cox in the *Sunday Telegraph* wrote that Day-Lewis's poems 'appear ordinary, plain and simple, but hide a subtle elegance', giving the small things a 'delicate rhetorical grace'.

It was a review in the *Times Literary Supplement* which most needled Day-Lewis. It waited seven months from the publication of *The Whispering Roots* before publishing a piece whose anonymous author was quickly identified as an old adversary of Day-Lewis, Geoffrey Grigson. He was also reviewing a new paperback edition of *Collected Poems*, and a pamphlet that contained Day-

Lewis's Jackson Knight Memorial Lecture of March 1969 at Exeter University 'On Translating Poetry'. Grigson used the opportunity to damn Day-Lewis's complete oeuvre. 'Frigidities predominate,' he wrote. 'Seldom does anything in a poem seem a paradigm of reality or truth. Everything gets itself spoken like speech in public assembly, in which words or images do no more than illustrate in the common manner.' Dismissing the new collection in just three sentences, he wrote that he was not even sure that roots could whisper.[23]

In the gap between publication and the review appearing, Day-Lewis had once again been in hospital – to have his gall stones finally removed. He was growing frailer and so Balcon, alerted to the review by friends, tried to hide the *TLS*, but Day-Lewis had seen it. He had been trying to keep it from her. Some who read Grigson's piece regarded it, in the words of Samuel Hynes, as 'not so much a review ... as a literary mugging'.[24] All Grigson's old resentment of Day-Lewis had been restated, prompted perhaps by the sight of a man he had tried so hard to write off as talentless in the 1930s rising to be Poet Laureate.

Day-Lewis's own attitude to reviewers had long been to ignore them, or to send them up, before and after the event. This attack, however, hit home when he was at a low ebb. Arthur Crook, the *TLS* editor, was showing great reluctance to publish any of the letters from academics and Day-Lewis admirers disputing Grigson's conclusions. Day-Lewis, therefore, wrote to Roy Fuller,[25] now installed as Oxford Professor of Poetry, seeking his intervention so that a contrary voice might at least be heard in the *TLS* correspondence columns. Fuller advised him that, though he did not share Grigson's views, he felt it better to remain silent. 'What we have is not the judgement of some representative of a new generation, but a re-hash of long-held views, scarcely likely to make converts; annoying but not lethal.'[26] Day-Lewis noted in his reply that he had foolishly thought his old detractor had long ago extinguished his old 'lets-set-fire-to-Lewis torch'. He concluded: 'I shall start a campaign for the disestablishment of Crook.'[27]

Chapter 32

Old Captain Death

Old Captain Death, it's time to go we're sick
Of this place. Weigh anchor! Set the course and steer!
Maybe the sky and sea are inky black.
But in our hearts – you know them – all is clear.
'The Voyage': The Room and Other Poems (1970)

In March 1971 Day-Lewis was admitted to Guy's Hospital, suffering from jaundice. He had recently returned exhausted from Rome where he had, as Poet Laureate, laid a wreath of laurel leaves on Keats's grave in the Protestant Cemetery to mark the 150th anniversary of his death. Tests revealed that Day-Lewis had an inoperable cancer on his pancreas. The surgeon's diagnosis was delivered to Balcon on the telephone. She was advised, as was often the practice at the time, not to tell her husband the truth. He had, the medics estimated, around a year to live, but it was better, Balcon was counselled, if he lived in hope. It was her first experience in facing the death of anyone close to her. Her parents were still alive. Not knowing any better, she went along with the approach the doctors prescribed.

If he suspected that the diagnosis was worse than he was being told, Day-Lewis said nothing. As he was discharged, he seemed to accept the doctors' reassurance that there had simply been more problems with his gall bladder. Balcon shared the burden of the awful news with Sean Day-Lewis, but kept her own younger children in the dark.

Back home in Greenwich, Day-Lewis appeared to have lost none of his appetite for life. There was a happy celebration of his 67th birthday and the couple's 20th wedding anniversary on April 27, but two days later he collapsed with dehydration. He was returned to hospital where diabetes was now also diagnosed, but again he was told that drugs could sort it all out. He was worried by his own slow recovery, as he indicated in a letter to Al Gelpi. 'My own health is pretty shaky again – my pancreas has forgotten the art of digesting fat, so I am a sort of Belsen figure of skin and bone, who has to crawl around like a non-agenarian. However, by dint of swallowing myriads of assorted pills per day, I am supposed to be getting this slowly straightened out.'[1]

When he had been in hospital he had been contacted out of the blue by Billie Currall. News that he was seriously ill had reached her via someone in Musbury who had been talking to Mary Day-Lewis. She, in turn, had been kept informed of the situation by her sons. Impulsively Currall had called Guy's where Day-

Lewis had to be helped to the telephone. He agreed to meet her when he was feeling better.

Once he was home they began exchanging letters. Currall's husband John had died in 1969 of cancer. She proposed marriage to Day-Lewis four times in a single missive. He sent her by way of reply a copy of *The Private Wound*. 'When you are in London you must have lunch with me. June or July. Pick me up at Chatto's. You're very welcome to stay the night at Greenwich – Jill, my wife, would like to meet you, but you may not be able to or want to.' By August, conscious that the hoped-for recovery was still not happening, he wrote again to Currall. 'Do come to London – I don't know how long I have to live and it would be nice to see you before I am trundled off to the tomb.' Finally they met in November. 'Seeing her,' he wrote to Currall afterwards, 'quite bucked me up'.[2]

Despite the restrictions on his diet, his weight loss and the side effects on his digestive system and energy levels of the drugs he was taking – all of which he turned into jokes against himself – Day-Lewis returned to work at Chatto in the spring of 1971. If he believed he was mortally ill, he did not mention it to anyone and was determined to carry on as usual with his Poet Laureate functions – in June, for example, going to 10 Downing Street with Balcon to attend an official dinner with the Italian Prime Minister.

In August the family went to Ireland for their summer holiday. At the Old Head Hotel Day-Lewis rested, giving up his Atlantic swims but seeming in good spirits. His increasingly gaunt appearance had, however, alerted his old friends that something was amiss. They began to ask questions. Stephen and Natasha Spender were among those sufficiently concerned to speak to Balcon. She confirmed Day-Lewis had terminal cancer.

In October when Auden stayed with the Spenders on his way through London en route for America, they took him to Crooms Hill for the last chapter of a friendship that stretched back over 40 years. 'Wystan would have been so upset not to have seen Cecil,' Natasha Spender recalled, 'but we were worried about how he would behave if we told him Cecil was dying. He was given to delivering lectures to the dying on how they had to face up to death. He must have realised at once when he saw Cecil, but it was a happy visit. We talked of the here and now, of public figures. There were jokes, friendly gossip. In the car on the way home, though, Wystan was very quiet.' "I'll never see Cecil again," he said. Wystan was profoundly distressed.'[3]

Another who learnt through the Spenders that Day-Lewis was gravely ill was Rosamond Lehmann. After years of hostility towards him, she wrote him a friendly letter from her flat in Eaton Square, suggesting lunch. If Day-Lewis detected any hint in her change of heart that she feared he was dying, he ignored it when he replied. 'I was very glad to get your letter. At present I'm at a very low ebb and haven't been out of the house for three weeks – but the doctor thinks there are signs of improvement. When it comes and I'm a bit mobile, it would be nice to see you.'[4]

As his strength ebbed, there were occasional moments when Day-Lewis came close to raising the subject of death. One afternoon when he was resting in their bedroom at Crooms Hill, Balcon sat reading to him from Turgenev's *Torrents of Spring*. Picking up on something from the text, Day-Lewis asked, almost casually, 'do you think I'm getting better? I think I'm getting worse'. A short silence followed as Balcon tried to formulate a response. 'Still,' he said, 'we mustn't brood.'[5]

He went slowly downhill with dignity and great courage, displaying to all comers his customary love of life and keeping any morbid thoughts to himself, sharing them, if at all, only in his poetry, albeit in the detached third person, notably in 'Recurring Dream', published after his death.

> He'd sensed, during his lone
> Climb, others doing the course. Quite solitary
> The new ordeal – no chambermaid, waiter, guest
> To show him the way out. Frantic he raced
> From end to end of the floor. A deep staircase
> Appeared at last, pointing the right direction,
> Down which he flew; but has no recollection
> Where or indeed whether one egressed.

'Recurring Dream': *Posthumous Poems* (1979)

In December 1967 he was at Bedales to see Daniel on stage as Florizel in a school production of *The Winter's Tale*. Tamasin had just learnt that she had passed the entrance examination for King's College, Cambridge, one of its first intake of 35 female undergraduates.

Knowing of Day-Lewis's skill as a performer, but unaware of the nature of his illness, Norman Swallow, head of BBC television arts features, had contacted him in August 1971 about presenting a series of programmes on BBC1 on the subject of poetry, a first for the channel. The challenge was, as Swallow put it, to 'use the latest means of communication to put over the oldest of the arts'.[6] It was not one that Day-Lewis, even in his weakened state, could resist.

The series was to be called *A Lasting Joy*. Balcon kept the truth about Day-Lewis's diagnosis from the BBC team as she and her husband worked to select the poems they were going to read for the programmes, with help from John Gielgud and Marius Goring, around six broad themes: childhood, human heroism, satire and hatred, love and friendship, times and seasons, and death and immortality. The choice of poets gives a clue to the abiding passions of Day-Lewis's life: Emily Brontë, Robert Browning, Emily Dickinson, Thomas Hardy, Gerard Manley Hopkins, Wilfred Owen, William Wordsworth and W. B. Yeats. Two of his own were also included: 'For Rex Warner on His Sixtieth Birthday' in the programme on 'love and friendship', and 'In The Shelter', from *Poems 1943– 1947*, based on a war-time recollection, included as part of 'human heroism'.

Filming was due to start in January 1972 by which time Day-Lewis was judged too ill to travel to the BBC Television Centre in west London. Instead crew and performers gathered in the Day-Lewises' sitting room – along with emergency generators because a miners' strike was threatening power cuts. One evening, after filming, when the lights had gone off again, Balcon was making a fire in Day-Lewis's study. As he sat watching her, he remarked, as if recalling his youth in Edwinstowe, 'I'm always on the side of the miners.'[7]

Day-Lewis's mouth was permanently dry because of the drugs he was taking, but he was determined to continue with the filming. After each session, he retired to his room to rest, but with the filming spread out over a month he was able to complete the task to his own satisfaction.

Between each reading of the poems he had selected, Day-Lewis addressed a few words of guidance to his audience. Introducing Shakespeare's sonnet 'Shall I compare thee to a summer's day?', which concluded the programme on 'death and immortality', Day-Lewis remarked: 'Shakespeare held out no conventional religious hope of immortality'. But in a few of his sonnets, he does convey a sort of humanist message; he says that a man may live on after death through the eternal lines of poetry.'[8] It was a sentiment that summed up Day-Lewis's own unwavering attitude to death and after-life.

In March, Nicholas Day-Lewis flew in from South Africa to say his farewells to his father. Later that month Elizabeth Jane Howard came to interview Day-Lewis for *Queen* magazine. She had maintained contact since the days of their affair, but it had been sporadic and she knew nothing of the seriousness of his illness or the strain it was placing on Balcon.

'I knew he'd been in hospital but I didn't know why. I was so appalled by his appearance. He looked so ill sitting in an armchair in his study with a rug wrapped round his legs. He'd lost a lot of weight and was almost skeletal. His face was grey. He insisted on going through with the interview. It wasn't very good because I was so confounded by his state of health. Afterwards Jill didn't want to discuss how he was except in general terms. She didn't use the term cancer.'[9]

Balcon did mention, however, that she was due to start filming a television series, *The Strauss Family*, at Elstree Studios in Hertfordshire but was worried about leaving Day-Lewis alone during the day. Howard was now married to the writer Kingsley Amis and living in a large late-Georgian house on Hadley Common, outside Barnet in north London. Her brother Colin – known always as Monkey – lived with them, along with a painter friend, Sargy Mann. Howard's mother had been staying too, recovering from a broken hip in a ground floor bedroom, with its own bathroom, attended to by a nurse, but was now on the road to recovery.

Howard offered Balcon the use of that room for the duration of the filming. The house was very close to Elstree so Balcon would be only fifteen minutes away if Day-Lewis needed her urgently. There would be plenty of company from the others in the house to cheer him up and the nurse would be available if he needed her. It was a generous offer to make, and an unusual one, given what had happened between them in the past. 'Perhaps it was guilt,' Howard conceded subsequently, 'but I felt an absolute need for Cecil to be as comfortable as possible. I had got long past minding about spending my life with him or not. It wasn't to do with that anymore. I didn't want him to die in hospital or without Jill in the house in Greenwich.'[10]

An exhausted Balcon, who had not had an uninterrupted night's sleep for several weeks, discussed the offer with her husband. Together they decided to accept. She told Howard of the true diagnosis and the doctors' advice to keep it from Day-Lewis. Howard began making preparations. Concerned that the Day-Lewises' habitual worries about money were playing on their minds, she wrote to some of their friends, suggesting a fund to tide Cecil over his critical illness. Peggy Ashcroft, A. D. Peters, Iris Murdoch and Jeremy Hutchinson were among those who contributed.

On April 6, 1972, Balcon drove her husband and children up to Hadley Common. The initial plan was that he would stay for a week. Monkey Howard installed a record player in the ground floor bedroom so Day-Lewis could listen to music. A plentiful supply of books was provided.

'Nobody was better at getting the utmost pleasure from the simplest things as Cecil,' Howard later wrote. 'A bunch of flowers, a toasted bun, a gramophone record (we left our catalogue with him so that he could order his records each evening for the following day), a piece of cherry cake, a new thriller that he'd not read before, various ice creams that Monkey kept in a deep freeze, the bird table outside his window, a chocolate, a piece of sweet-smelling soap, a herb pillow, being read to – Jill excelled at that, but if she was working or cooking him something he sometimes fell back on me.'[11]

After a week it was suggested the stay should be extended. All agreed it was a good idea. On fine days Day-Lewis would sit in the sheltered courtyard at the back of the house, watching spring arrive. He even took a trip round the garden in an electric wheelchair that belonged to Howard's mother. Old friends came to see him, forewarned that it was farewell. Hallam Tennyson recalled his visit. 'Cecil knew he was dying, but he didn't mention it. He was brave and stoical. He didn't want to distress anyone around him which was how he had always been. It was part of his modesty. We talked about the Victorian poets and he talked a lot about Auden. Any sense of competition he had ever felt with him had long gone.'[12]

In his second week at Lemmons, Day-Lewis asked Balcon to get him a notebook. Slowly he wrote a poem as a gift for his hosts.

Above my table three magnolia flowers
Utter their silent requiems.
Through the window I see your elms
In labour with the racking storm
Giving it shape in April's shifty airs.

Up there sky boils from a brew of cloud
To blue gleam, sunblast, then darkens again.
No respite is allowed
The watching eye, the natural agony.

Below is the calm a loved house breeds
Where four have come together to dwell
* – Two write, one paints, the fourth invents –*

Each pursuing a natural bent
But less through nature's formative travail
Than each in his own humour finding the self he needs.

Round me all is amenity, a bloom of
Magnolia uttering its requiems,
A climate of acceptance. Very well
I accept my weakness with my friends'
Good natures sweetening each day my sick room.

'At Lemmons': *Posthumous Poems* (1979)

He confided in a poem with the mention of requiems what he did not say to anyone else. Though Balcon had now told her children that their father had cancer, she was still reluctant to go against the doctors' advice and broach the subject with him. On one occasion, he did mention his stepmother. 'She was brave and she had cancer,' he remarked, without adding the word 'too'.[13]

Kingsley Amis wrote later: 'At no time did Cecil mention death. My own strong feeling is that he came to draw his own conclusions from his physical decline and increasingly severe – though happily intermittent – bouts of pain, but, out of kindness and abnegation of self, chose not to discuss the matter.'[14]

He celebrated his 68th birthday on April 27. Each present he was given was greeted with delight. 'But these are the most magnificent slippers I have ever seen' he said as he undid one parcel. It was more than politeness, Amis suggested. 'It came directly from his inner nature. That nature not only saw every new thing as a potential source of delight, it also saw the familiar, even the commonplace, as worth a second and a third look.'[15]

With Balcon he continued to make plans, especially for their annual summer holiday in Ireland. He had been given a new pair of binoculars and felt that, although he wouldn't be able to go on walks, he could sit on a bench and watch the wildlife. Officially he was simply resting at Lemmons until he felt fully recovered. It was the story that appeared in the papers. 'Poet Laureate Recuperates at the Amis' Home', the London *Evening Standard* reported on May 9.

On the weekend of May 20 and 21, as Day-Lewis was slipping in and out of consciousness, Ursula Vaughan-Williams, widow of the composer Ralph, came to Lemmons to give her support to her friend Balcon. Sean Day-Lewis was there and Tamasin, on her gap year, and Daniel, at Bedales, were summoned. They gathered round the death bed, Daniel holding the right hand of his father's wasted body.

Day-Lewis had said once that it was not so much death that he feared but the act of dying. In the end it came peacefully, on the morning of Monday May 22, with his loved ones around him.

There were many tributes in the newspapers, including a piece by Auden which concluded: 'Thank you, Cecil. It was a great privilege to have been permitted to know you.'[16] Day-Lewis's friend, the poet Charles Causley, remembered him in verse.

318

Birds from sharp branches of the luckless may
Their glittering warnings to the woods relay.
A man must speak when he has words to say.
The poet wrote until his dying day

For fifty years, across the changing bay
He sailed his patient, scribbled boats away
From a strong tower of breath and country clay.
The poet wrote until his dying day

His words, like fine leaves, whisper on the spray;
The seasons halt, and do not have their way
Till sifting time tells what will go, will stay
To burn this momentary death away.
The poet wrote until his dying day

Day-Lewis was buried on May 26 at the thirteenth-century St Michael's Parish Church, Stinsford, close to the grave of Thomas Hardy who had called the village Mellstock in *Under The Greenwood Tree*. Day-Lewis had given no instructions as to his wishes but he had been baptized and confirmed an Anglican and to bury him with Hardy seemed appropriate. In one of the last notebooks that he had used, almost his final jotting was to write the name of the Stinsford church[17]: as Laureate he had helped raise £5,000 for it to be repaired.

A family friend, Tamasin's godfather and the vicar of St Martin-in-the-Fields, the Revd Austen Williams, arranged the burial and came to Dorset to conduct the service. Julian Bream played three movements from Bach's lute suites. Balcon placed a wreath of laurel in the grave. His memorial service, at Williams's central London church on October 25 and including Fauré's *Requiem*, was broadcast live on BBC radio. The final instalment of *A Lasting Joy*, on death and immortality, was aired as a tribute on BBC 2 the day after his death, with the remainder being broadcast in July and August on BBC 1.

Several years earlier, at a dinner, Day-Lewis had been asked what he would like his last words to be. 'I see there's a lot to be said for the other side,' he joked.[18] The wording for his gravestone, designed by Michael Harvey, prompted a final unhappy correspondence. In all but his earliest publications, Day-Lewis had used his initial not his Christian name. However, the chancellor of Salisbury diocese, under whose jurisdiction the Stinsford church fell, insisted that only his full name could be used. So he was Cecil Day-Lewis.

At Sean Day-Lewis's suggestion the inscription was taken from 'Is it far to go?'

Shall I be gone long?
For ever and a day.
To whom there belong?
Ask the stone to say,
Ask my song.

Epilogue

... what shall I have to bequeath?
A sick world we could not change, a sack of genes
I did not choose, some verse
Long out of fashion, a laurel wreath
Wilted ...
'Children Leaving Home': *Posthumous Poems* (1979)

The car is coming slowly and cautiously down the steep hill from the Iron Age fort into Musbury on a sunny winter's morning. The narrow lane is lined with high green hedges which direct the eyes forward to the Axe valley, spread out before us, and beyond it the blue of the sea. Sean Day-Lewis, retired newspaperman, is at the wheel, pointing out the landmarks of his father's – and his own – life.

We stop on a bend. Just ahead of us is the house his parents called Brimclose when they bought it in 1938. Soon after his father died, Sean's mother, Mary, sold up, finally knowing that there was no longer even the remotest chance of her ex-husband coming home to her. The new owners renamed it Woodhayes and have since extended it and painted it sky blue and white, remodelling over the years the garden Mary spent 35 years tending.

The details have changed but the landscape that so inspired Day-Lewis has not. To our right Sean points out a wooden bench, concreted in position and with a plaque recording Mary Day-Lewis's life and death, from cancer, in 1975. To our left is the wood that lay between Brimclose and Bullmoor Farm, where his father and Billie Currall would meet in those heady pre-war days.

Of his departure from this spot in 1950, Day-Lewis later wrote: 'Self-exiled, I left what seems in retrospect a little Paradise. But, as Proust so wonderfully showed, for certain temperaments the only Paradise is Paradise Lost.'[1] He had lived, Day-Lewis wrote in 1965 in 'St Anthony's Shirt', in nine houses. As a poet Day-Lewis had a great capacity to respond to new places and new landscapes – Ireland, Dorset, Tuscany all inspired him. And to human beauty. Some of the women he fell in love with were famed for their good looks. But he never truly settled, physically or emotionally, however much part of him yearned for it. Each paradise was always, as he admitted, lost, often through his own actions. One side of him remained forever the traveller of his poems.

There is not, then, a single landscape where you have the sense of walking in his footsteps. In Musbury that day, with his eldest son at my side, he felt as close as he ever would as Sean mapped out the minutiae of their sparse domestic life in the early 1940s in a cottage that is now comfortably refurbished. I could almost hear the cricket ball being whacked around the weedy tennis court as Day-Lewis and Rex Warner fought it out. But later, when I returned without Sean to the cottage to recapture once again that connection with my subject, Day-Lewis was gone.

The obvious place to look for him is in his poetry. And there, warts and all, he most certainly is. Day-Lewis was among the most autobiographical of poets. As I have included stanzas in the preceding chapters to reflect his state of mind at the various crossroads in his life, I have been acutely aware that making such a direct link would be dangerous and impossible with most writers. With Day-Lewis it feels the natural and right thing to do. There is, of course, a degree of licence – there were, for example, more than nine houses. And on some matters, such as his relationships with Attia Hosain and A. S. Byatt, the poems offer little clarity. But, more often, they do demonstrate an almost painful honesty about the important things.

Yet even as he opens his heart in poetry, seeks to understand not to be understood as he put it himself, confides as he did nowhere else, he is also simultaneously holding himself apart, observing, suspecting, judging himself and his readers. Poems, he told BBC viewers in episode five of *A Lasting Joy*, 'can be written from not knowing the answers. Perhaps they always are.' It was only in the 1930s, out of idealism and in imitation of Auden's tone of certainty, that Day-Lewis offered answers in his poetry. With hindsight they were shown to be hollow.

While writing this biography I chanced upon a magazine interview with an American folk singer. 'Losing my mother early,' she told the journalist, 'has made me distant with people. I don't do intimacy.' Surely it can't be that straightforward, I said aloud to myself, noting at once the parallels with Day-Lewis. And anyway he had Knos, not a mother but someone who loved him, as 'My Mother's Sister' so poignantly makes clear, to the very end.

That ability in Day-Lewis to be and do two things at once did, however, start very early. And persisted. Even when he was with his second wife, who studiedly avoided smothering him in the way that both his father and Rosamond Lehmann had, he continued to opt out – away from her in Harvard and Hull, away from her with other women. Balcon gave him a good deal of freedom at significant emotional cost to herself, but never broke his habit of keeping something of himself separate. As he lay dying, she had to write to Elaine Hamilton, with whom he had been conducting a flirtatious correspondence from his Chatto office, to ask her to stop sending him intimate letters. The tension between being there and being elsewhere, repeated many times in his poetry, was never satisfactorily resolved and affected all his relationships.

It left him a contradictory character, a man of great charm who inspired and returned loyalty in his friends but who could simultaneously wound the women he loved; a poet who wrote epic narrative verse about the heroism of others but who did not want to fight himself; a private man who preached that 'we must consume our own smoke' but who then shared the intimate secrets of himself and those around him in his poems; a man of such self-abnegation that he didn't break the taboo around mentioning he was dying, but whose poetry can often border on the self-obsessed. It is not, as some critics have said, that he had no voice of his own. Rather that he had too many.

When asked about enduring literary fame, Day-Lewis was characteristically modest. Roger Woodis, another of the long list of young poets whom he had encouraged while at Chatto, recalled that he once asked Day-Lewis how you could discern if a writer was one of the greats. 'The only way to tell is to rise from the grave 100 years from now – and even then you can't be sure', he replied.[2] That same wry common sense was in evidence in a newspaper interview he gave in 1968. 'Such immortality as I ever want is for a few people to read my poems for a few years after I am dead.'[3]

There were two he picked out in particular – 'O Dreams, O Destinations' and 'On Not Saying Everything'. Both contained many of the elements of conflict that he continuously examined in his lifetime and therefore are fitting monuments to his work. To their number, in various anthologies of twentieth-century verse, have been added 'The Album', 'Where Are the War Poets', 'Sheep Dog Trials in Hyde Park', 'My Mother's Sister', among others. All have a place in the canon while his translation of Virgil's *Aeneid* is still widely used and held by many, including scholars, to be peerless. A new audio recording of it was made in 2003 with Paul Scofield, Toby Stephens and Jill Balcon.

What may have surprised Day-Lewis is the popularity of one of his domestic poems, those everyday observations from life which feature heavily in his mature work. 'Walking Away' was a 1962 reflection on waving his son off at school. Its last line – 'Love is proved in the letting go' – was used in 2006 on the publicity posters for *The Ballad of Jack and Rose*, a film starring Day-Lewis's son, the Oscar-winning actor, Daniel, and written and directed by his wife, Rebecca Miller. Given Daniel's acclaim, some of those who are so drawn to 'Walking Away' as a summing up of the central dilemma of parenthood may have Daniel's face in mind as they read or listen to the words. It was, however, inspired by my guide in Musbury, his older half-brother, Sean.

If poets are often popularly remembered for a single poem, their 'best bet at remembrance' as Robert Frost put it, then 'Walking Away' has become Day-Lewis's legacy. In a 2000 poll in the *Radio Times*, the public placed it in their top ten poems of childhood. As an introduction to his work, a glimpse of his capacity to move from the personal to the universal, it serves admirably. But it is best regarded as an invitation to explore further Day-Lewis's work.

That, however, has largely failed to happen since his death in 1972. A volume of *Posthumous Poems* was published in 1979, a *Complete* volume in 1992 and compilations in 1977 (selected by Ian Parsons, his long-time colleague at Chatto & Windus) and in 2004 (chosen by his widow to mark his centenary). There have been periodic upsurges in public interest – such as that which accompanied the 'Young Writers of the Thirties' exhibition at the National Portrait Gallery in 1976, with its shared spotlight on Day-Lewis, W. H. Auden, Stephen Spender, Christopher Isherwood and Louis MacNeice.

However, overall his work has suffered a neglect since his death. The claim by the critic G. M. Young, trumpeted on the jacket of subsequent editions of his 1938 collection *Overtures to Death and Other Poems*, that 'I should like to have it on the record that in 1938 someone had the wit to foresee that in 2038 Day-Lewis's "Nabara" would be numbered among the great English poems' now sounds a little off-the-mark.

So why is the Day-Lewis that lies beyond 'Walking Away' and the laurels of the laureateship overlooked? Part of the reason may simply be because the very art of poetry today is suffering from the sort of widespread public indifference that he recognized, warned of and tried to counter.

There is also that natural cycle of interest in a writer's work, the necessary lull that often comes after his or her death before a truer, dispassionate evaluation can be reached once distanced from the literary fashion and the distracting headlines of what in Day-Lewis's case was a very public life. It often happens with writers that when they die they disappear in more senses than one, leaving only the question of whether their reputation will be born again.

Some modern critics are today so severe in their judgements of Day-Lewis that any resurrection seems out of the question. The Irish poet Eaven Boland, for example, writing in *PN Review* in 1998, accused him of writing 'cool, dejected, rose-water poems, with their flowery symbols of transience'.[4] Even Spender, who outlived his old friend by many years, was doubtful in reviewing the *Complete* volume of poems in 1992, accusing Day-Lewis of 'writing more for the beautiful speaking voice than out of the inward voice, the hidden persona which is the touchstone of poetry'.[5]

The most public sign of this questioning of Day-Lewis's enduring worth as a poet has been the refusal so far to allot him in a space in Poets' Corner in Westminster Abbey. He had in his lifetime assumed – often out loud – that being Poet Laureate would be sufficient qualification. He was asked, he liked to recall, in 1970 to write a guide to Poets' Corner by the Abbey authorities. So one lunchtime he slipped away from Chatto's to do his research but in the Abbey he was denied access by an officious verger. 'But I am the Poet Laureate,' Day-Lewis told him, 'and I want to get into Poets' Corner before I die.'

The final decision on posthumous admission rests with the Dean of the Abbey and his advisers, and they seem at present unconvinced. Despite a 50-strong letter of petition in 2001 from the Royal Society of Literature, signed by, among others, the Nobel Laureate and Day-Lewis admirer Seamus Heaney, the Dean has so far refused to budge.

The factors that seem to count against Day-Lewis in this and, more generally in critical debate, have all been addressed in this biography – the echoes of others in his work, the accusation that he published too much, the formality of his writing, his rejection of Modernism, and his struggle adequately to escape the tag of poet of the 1930s.

Yet there has always remained a staunch body of opinion in literary and academic circles that fights against the tendency to sideline Day-Lewis. In 1998 his friend from Harvard, Al Gelpi, now Professor of American Literature at Stanford University, published *Living In Time*, a critical study of Day-Lewis's verse which argues trenchantly that he remains 'one of the great and important poets of the [twentieth] century'. John Bayley, Warton Professor of English at Oxford, is another who has defended Day-Lewis publicly, especially against the charge that he was simply Auden's best-known camp follower. 'Because he threw himself into whatever appealed at the time, Day-Lewis's poetry travelled in the end further than Auden's, however unexpectedly,' Bayley has written. 'Auden, for all his different interests, was stuck with his inescapable persona: his admiring disciple was free to derive a poetic voice from anywhere else he chose – from Italy to the English past, other voices and other rooms.'[6]

And in a lecture at Day-Lewis's old Oxford college, Wadham, to mark the centenary of his birth in 2004, the poet and academic Bernard O'Donoghue concluded, after reviewing his work, 'there are many reasons to believe with Auden that his [Day-Lewis's] hour will come again, even if "the critics" do not yet quite look silly for believing that "our lot" stopped writing in the thirties. Poems like "The Nabara" have a power and a relevance to our times which have not been recognised. But that too is a victim of the aesthetic fashions of an age which is resistant to the long poem.'[7]

A final factor that I believe has militated against continuing wider interest in him in the years since his death has been the absence of a biography. As its title suggests, *The Buried Day* is less than revealing. *C Day-Lewis: An English Literary Life*, Sean Day-Lewis's 1980 book about his father, began the task of revealing the man behind the public persona, but was not considered by its author to tell the whole story. Yet Day-Lewis was, as already pointed out, unusually auto-biographical in his verse, and so to understand the particular references and context of his writing is, I hope, a spur to read more of it.

If proof were needed that reacquaintance with Day-Lewis is fruitful, it came in a review of the centenary edition of his poems in the *Times Literary Supplement*, the paper that at the end of his life was forever attacking Day-Lewis. The critic, William Wootten, begins by rehearsing all the familiar arguments about why Day-Lewis is deservedly neglected. 'In a world where talent in poetry gets few rewards,' he adds for good measure, 'this poet was lucky enough [in his lifetime] to receive too many.'[8] The curse of the Poet Laureateship again.

Yet as the article continues, and Wootten rereads some of Day-Lewis's work, he is forced to reconsider. G.M. Young would be delighted to see that Wootten is particularly drawn to 'The Nabara'. It is, he finds, 'a stirring narrative poem'. As he progresses to the 1940s, Wootten gets still more enthusiastic. 'The war poems . . . remain some of the best of the Home Front. The poems of private life hold up even better.' And even if in the 1960s, when Wootten complains that Day-Lewis published 'too many poems that are slight, occasional or about such subjects as Christmas', he continues to find 'unexpected pleasures', highlighting 'The Disabused' as 'chillingly compelling'.

The review ends up reading like something that might have been written in the 1930s when Day-Lewis was at the height of his critical acclaim. The cycle of praise and neglect can turn again. Too many biographies of poets (and artists in general) begin or end with the authors offering superlatives about their subjects. Given Day-Lewis's own modesty, such claims would be out of place here. Instead, there is only a plea. Like Wootten, delve into Day-Lewis's poetry one more time. In particular read collections such as *Word Over All* in the light of his life and see if you agree with John Betjeman's verdict on him, written in the year Day-Lewis died: 'I am absolutely sure his poetry is underrated. He persists in the mind. I just rattle on the ears.'[9]

Notes

There is no single collection of Day-Lewis's papers. He was casual with them in his lifetime, often turning letters and manuscripts over and using them as scrap paper. Since his death his widow, Jill Day-Lewis, has carefully preserved those papers which he had kept. His son, Sean Day-Lewis, has also cared for the papers his mother had at Brimclose, as well as adding his own material about his father, much of it collected while researching his book about him.

I am grateful to both Jill and Sean Day-Lewis for their permission to quote from the materials they hold, and particularly to Jill Day-Lewis for permission to include so many of Day-Lewis's poems in my text.

Day-Lewis rarely dated letters. I have made my best efforts throughout to work out when they were written. Similarly every effort has been made to clear permissions for any material included in this biography. My thanks for their co-operation in this regard to Edward Mendelson on behalf of the Auden estate; to Lady Spender on behalf of the Spender estate; to Patricia Maguire at King's College, Cambridge, home to the Rosamond Lehmann archive; to The Society of Authors as the literary representative of the estate of Rosamond Lehmann; to Scott Taylor and Nicholas Sheetz in regard to the Elizabeth Jennings papers in the Special Collections Division of Georgetown University Library; to Gayle Richardson and her colleagues at the Huntingdon Library in California; and to Faber & Faber. If, however, there are omissions, the publishers will be happy to rectify them in subsequent editions. The following abbreviations have been used:

AG – Professor Al Gelpi
CDL – C Day-Lewis
JDL – Jill Day-Lewis
KCC – King's College, Cambridge
NS – Natasha Spender
RL – Rosamond Lehmann
SDL – Sean Day-Lewis
SS – Stephen Spender
TBD – *The Buried Day* (1960)
WHA – W. H. Auden

Prologue
1. Letter from CDL to Al and Barbara Gelpi 1/1/1968.
2. Penelope Betjeman: *Sunday Express* 14/5/1967.
3. WHA's Letter of Introduction to *C Day-Lewis: The Poet Laureate – A Bibliography* (Chicago and London, 1968).
4. SS in a review of *The Complete Poems of C Day-Lewis* in the *Independent* 23/5/1992.

One
1. All poems quoted at the start of the chapters are by C Day-Lewis.
2. Daisy, Countess of Fingall: *Seventy Years Young* (London, 1937).
3. Later a colleague at Harvard was to suggest that Day-Lewis's ancestors were the O'Deaghaidhs of Co. Clare, but there is no evidence for this.
4. W. B. Yeats (1865–1939).
5. Oliver Goldsmith (1728–74).
6. In conversation with SDL.
7. W. H. Auden (1907–73).
8. TBD.
9. Ibid.
10. Sir George Gilbert Scott (1811–78).
11. The story is recounted on the website of the Church of Ireland diocese of Meath and Kildare.
12. TBD.
13. In conversation with SDL.
14. TBD.
15. Thomas Hodgkin (1978–1866).
16. TBD.

Two
1. Rupert Hart-Davis (1907–99).
2. Damaged during heavy Second World War bombing of the area, Christ Church was finally closed as a place of worship in 1977 when it became structurally unsound and today only its spire survives, incorporated in a housing development.
3. TBD.
4. Ibid.
5. Ibid.
6. Ibid.
7. Ibid.
8. In a 1971 interview with Mark Featherstone-Witty for the Durham University student newspaper.
9. TBD.
10. Ibid.
11. Photograph in the collection of JDL.
12. TBD.
13. Ibid.
14. Ibid.
15. A phrase he often used with JDL when talking about his childhood.
16. TBD.
17. Ibid.
18. Ibid

Three
1. TBD.
2. Ibid.
3. In the poem 'Golden Age, Monart, Co. Wexford' (*The Whispering Roots*, 1970).
4. Ibid.
5. TBD.
6. Ibid.
7. Ibid.
8. Ibid.
9. Tom Moore (1779–1825).

10. TBD.
11. Ibid.
12. (Helen) Beatrix Potter (1866–1943).
13. J. M. Barrie (1860–1937).
14. TBD.
15. Ibid.
16. Ibid.
17. Quoted in *Max Beerbohm: A Kind of Life* by N. John Hall (Yale University Press, New Haven and London, 2002).
18. TBD.
19. Ibid.
20. Ibid.
21. Robert Southey (1774–1823). Poet Laureate 1813–23.
22. In *Poetry For You* by CDL (Basil Blackwell, Oxford, 1944).
23. TBD.
24. Ibid.

Four
1. TBD.
2. Alec Waugh (1898–1981).
3. In a new preface to *The Loom of Youth* (The Richards Press, 1955).
4. Ibid.
5. Arthur Waugh (1866–1943).
6. Evelyn Waugh (1903–66).
7. TBD.
8. Ibid.
9. Ibid.
10. *The Shirburnian*, February 1922.
11. TBD.
12. Ibid.
13. William Wordsworth (1770–1850). Poet Laureate from 1843.
14. Alfred Tennyson (1809–92). Poet Laureate from 1850.
15. John Cowper Powys (1872–1963) from *Autobiography* (1934).
16. Now in collection of SDL.
17. *The Shirburnian*, June 1922.
18. TBD.
19. Ibid.
20. Thomas Hardy (1840–1928).
21. William Barnes (1801–66).
22. In correspondence with the author.
23. TBD.
24. From written recollection of C Day-Lewis in Sherborne School archives.
25. TBD.
26. *The Shirburnian*, November 1919.
27. (Cecil) Maurice Bowra (1898–1971)

Five
1. From written recollection by the Revd T. C. Teape-Fugard of C Day-Lewis in Sherborne School archives.
2. From a dissertation by Elizabeth Mary Sadler, 'The Sale of NCB and Local Authority Houses in Edwinstowe', University of Manchester, 1989.
3. Ibid.
4. TBD.
5. Recollections of Edwinstowe residents collected in 2005 for the author by Dennis Wood.
6. Ibid.
7. TBD.
8. Ibid.
9. Ibid.
10. Ibid.
11. Ibid.

12. Ibid.
13. Recollections of Edwinstowe residents collected in 2005 for the author by Dennis Wood.
14. Now in the National Portrait Gallery collection in London.
15. Recollections of Edwinstowe residents collected in 2005 for the author by Dennis Wood.
16. The law at the time stated that a man could not marry his dead wife's sister.
17. Recollections of Edwinstowe residents collected in 2005 for the author by Dennis Wood.
18. TBD.
19. Ibid.
20. Recalled by JDL.
21. Recollections of Edwinstowe residents collected in 2005 for the author by Dennis Wood.
22. TBD.
23. Recalled by JDL.
24. TBD.
25. Ibid.
26. Ibid.
27. A phrase he used recalled by both JDL and RL.
28. TBD.
29. Ibid.

Six

1. Harold Acton (1904–94).
2. TBD.
3. Evelyn Waugh, *Decline and Fall* (London, 1928).
4. To JDL.
5. John Betjeman (1906–84).
6. From essay by Betjeman in *My Oxford* (London, 1977).
7. TBD.
8. Robert Graves (1895–1985).
9. TBD.
10. Charles Fenby (1905–74).
11. Obituary for CDL by Fenby in Wadham College Gazette (summer 1972).
12. In conversation with the author.
13. Rex Warner (1905–86).
14. TBD.
15. Ibid.
16. Hugh Gaitskell (1906–63). Quote from Philip Williams *Hugh Gaitskell* (London, 1979).
17. In correspondence with SDL.
18. Elizabeth Harman, Countess of Longford (1906–2002).
19. Evelyn Waugh, *A Little Learning* (London, 1964).
20. Tom Driberg (1905–76).
21. Quoted in Francis Wheen's *Tom Driberg* (London, 1990).
22. TBD.
23. Ibid.
24. Mary Day-Lewis's diaries were destroyed by her brother in accordance with her wishes after her death. He did allow SDL access to them before destroying them and all quotes from them are taken from SDL's archive.
25. TBD.
26. See Note 24.
27. Ibid.
28. From 'Golden Age, Monart, Co. Wexford' in *The Whispering Roots* (London, 1970).
29. CDL to Rex Warner July 1924, quoted by SDL.
30. See Note 24.
31. Ibid.
32. Ibid.
33. TBD.
34. Lord David Cecil, literary critic, teacher and biographer (1902–86).
35. Anthony Powell (1905–2000).
36. From *Infants of the Spring: Memoirs of Anthony Powell*, volume 1 (London, 1976).
37. T. S. Eliot (1888–1965) published *The Waste Land* in 1922.
38. TBD.

39. In an interview with Elizabeth Jane Howard for *Queen* magazine in 1971.
40. TBD.
41. In JDL's archive.
42. See Note 24.
43. TBD.
44. Quoted by SDL.
45. TBD.
46. Ibid.
47. Ibid.
48. Emile Coue (1857–1926), French psychologist and pharmacist.
49. TBD.
50. Ibid.
51. WHA to his brother, John 11/4/32, quoted in *Auden* by Richard Davenport-Hines (London, 1995).
52. To JDL.

Seven

1. C Day-Lewis, *Starting Point* (London, 1938).
2. TBD.
3. Frederick Lindemann, Viscount Cherwell (1886–1957).
4. Harold Acton *Memoirs of An Aesthete* (London, 1948), Peter Quennell (1905–93).
5. CDL to Rex Warner, summer 1924 in SDL's archive.
6. CDL's correspondence with Fortune and Merriman (21 letters) is held in the Huntingdon Library in California.
7. Rupert Brooke (1887–1915).
8. Edward Marsh (1872–1953).
9. John Masefield (1878–1967). Poet Laureate from 1930.
10. Quoted in ed. James Reeves, *The Penguin Poets: Georgian Poetry* (London, 1962).
11. D. H. Lawrence (1885–1936).
12. A. E. Housman (1859–1936).
13. Robert Frost (1874–1963). Born San Francisco.
14. Ezra Pound (1885–1972). Born Idaho.
15. Walter de la Mare (1873–1956).
16. Edward Thomas (1878–1917).
17. Andrew Young (1885–1971).
18. Siegfried Sassoon (1886–1967).
19. Edmund Blunden (1896–1974).
20. Harold Acton, *Memoirs of An Aesthete* (London, 1948).
21. Tom Hopkinson, *Of This Time: A Journalist's Story 1905–1950* (London, 1982).
22. TBD.
23. Ibid.
24. L. A. G. Strong (1896–1958).
25. Humbert Wolfe (1885–1940).
26. TBD.
27. Ibid.
28. Lady Ottoline Morrell (1873–1938).
29. TBD.
30. Henry Yorke Green (1905–73).
31. Quoted in Stephen Tabahnick, *Fiercer Than Tigers: The Life and Works of Rex Warner* (Michigan, 2002).
32. In SDL's archive.
33. TBD.
34. Ibid.
35. Ibid.

Eight

1. In JDL's archive.
2. TBD.
3. See Richard Davenport-Hines, *Auden* (London, 1995).
4. TBD.

5. Ibid.
6. WHA, *The Age of Anxiety* (London, 1948).
7. In particular Geoffrey Grigson (1905–85).
8. TBD.
9. Nevill Coghill (1899–1980).
10. See Note 3.
11. TBD.
12. In an interview with Elizabeth Jane Howard for *Queen* magazine in 1971.
13. Published in the American magazine *Shenandoah*, December 1967.
14. SS, *World Within World* (London, 1951).
15. From ed. Peter Salus and Paul Taylor, *For WH Auden* (New York, 1972).
16. Christopher Isherwood (1904–86).
17. WHA, *For The Time Being* (London, 1944).
18. See Peter Parker, *Christopher Isherwood* (London, 2004).
19. Christopher Isherwood, *Christopher and His Kind* (London, 1976).
20. WHA's wedding poem for CDL and MDL – first published in SDL, *C Day-Lewis: An English Literary Life* (London, 1980).
21. (Frederick) Louis MacNeice (1907–63).
22. Louis MacNeice, *The Strings Are False* (London, 1965).
23. Edward Upward (1903–).
24. Edward Upward, *Remembering The Earlier Auden* (London, 1998).
25. See Note 3.
26. TBD.
27. CDL, *A Hope for Poetry* (Oxford, 1934).
28. Ibid.
29. William Carlos Williams (1883–1963).
30. *The Cantos of Ezra Pound* (New York, 1970).
31. Virginia Woolf (1882–1941).
32. James Joyce (1882–1941).
33. See Note 3.
34. In JDL's archive.
35. WHA's Letter of Introduction to *C Day-Lewis: The Poet Laureate – A Bibliography* (Chicago and London, 1968).
36. Pound worked as Yeats's secretary.
37. SS, *World Within World* (London, 1951).
38. TBD.
39. Ed. WHA and CDL, *Oxford Poetry 1927* (Oxford, 1927).
40. TBD.
41. Ibid.

Nine
1. TBD.
2. SDL in conversation with the author.
3. TBD.
4. Ibid.
5. Ibid.
6. Undated letter from CDL on Wadham College notepaper in the collection of the Huntingdon Library, California.
7. WHA's wedding poem for CDL and MDL – first published in SDL, *C Day-Lewis: An English Literary Life* (London, 1980).
8. TBD.
9. Letter from Fortune and Merriman to CDL 2/9/24 in the collection of the Huntingdon Library, California.
10. TBD.
11. Ibid.
12. Ibid.
13. *Approach March: a venture in autobiography*, by Julian Amery (London, 1973).
14. TBD.
15. Nigel Nicolson (1917–2004).
16. Vita Sackville-West (1892–1962).

17. In JDL's archive.
18. WHA, *Paid On Both Sides: A Charade* (1928 – not published separately) – in JDL's archive.
19. See Note 17.

Ten

1. TBD.
2. Referred to by CDL when lecturing on 'The Pure Style' as Professor of Poetry at Oxford – text in JDL's archive.
3. SDL's archive.
4. Quoted in SDL, *C Day-Lewis: An English Literary Life* (London, 1980).
5. CDL to Elaine Hamilton 24/4/70 in SDL's archive.
6. In JDL's archive.
7. WHA's wedding poem for CDL and MDL – first published in SDL, *C Day-Lewis: An English Literary Life* (London, 1980).
8. TBD.
9. John Logie Baird (1888–1946).
10. James Frazer (1854–1941).
11. TBD.
12. WHA to John Auden 20/11/1931.
13. CDL to L. A. G. Strong quoted in SDL, *C Day-Lewis: An English Literary Life* (London, 1980).
14. Leonard Woolf (1880–1969).
15. Vanessa Bell (1879–1961).
16. Undated letter in JDL's archive.
17. WHA's Letter of Introduction to *C Day-Lewis: The Poet Laureate – A Bibliography* (Chicago and London, 1968).
18. Quoted in Stephen Tabahnick, *Fiercer Than Tigers: The Life and Works of Rex Warner* (Michigan, 2002).
19. CDL, 'The Lyrical Poetry of Thomas Hardy', The Warton Lecture 1951 in JDL's archive.
20. T. S. Eliot, *After Strange Gods* (London, 1934).
21. See Note 19.
22. Ibid.
23. Rex Warner, *Wild Goose Chase* (London, 1936).
24. In WHA, *The Orators* (London, 1932).
25. WHA, *Poems* (privately printed 1928, reprinted London 1930).
26. Walt Whitman (1819–92).
27. TBD.
28. John Donne (1572–1631), Andrew Marvell (1621–78).
29. Naomi Mitchison (1897–1999).

Eleven

1. TBD.
2. Ibid.
3. Lionel Hedges (1900–33).
4. TBD.
5. Undated letter from CDL to Rex Warner.
6. TBD.
7. Frank Halliday (1893–1967).
8. Frank Halliday, *Indifferent Honest and Other Plays* (London, 1960).
9. Ibid.
10. TBD.
11. WHA 'September 1, 1939'.
12. TBD.
13. Ibid.
14. *News Chronicle* 28/02/1938.
15. T. S. Eliot, *The Waste Land* (London, 1922).
16. TBD.
17. John Lehmann (1907–87).
18. John Lehmann, *The Whispering Gallery* (London, 1956).
19. Ibid.
20. Michael Roberts (1902–48).

21. Undated letter from CDL to Rex Warner.
22. Ibid.
23. In SDL's archive.
24. CDL, *The Friendly Tree* (London, 1936).
25. Ibid.

Twelve

1. Julian Bell (1908–37).
2. Richard Eberhart (1904–2005).
3. William Empson (1906–84).
4. William Plomer (1903–73).
5. A. S. J. Tessimond (1902–62).
6. Ed. J. Howard Woolmer, *A Checklist of the Hogarth Press 1917–1946* (Pennsylvania, 1986).
7. Rosamond Lehmann, (1901–1990).
8. John Lehmann, *The Whispering Gallery* (London, 1956).
9. Ed. Michael Roberts, *New Signatures* (London, 1932).
10. Elizabeth Jennings (1926–2001).
11. CDL to Elizabeth Jennings 20/11/69 in Georgetown University Library.
12. See Note 9.
13. Ibid.
14. TBD.
15. F. R. Leavis (1895–1978).
16. Ed. Quentin Bell, *Essays, Poems and Letters of Julian Bell* (London, 1938).
17. CDL to Rex Warner, undated letter in SDL's archive.
18. CDL to L. A. G. Strong, undated letter in SDL's archive.
19. CDL to Geoffrey Grigson in Poetry Collection, Lockwood Memorial Library, Buffalo, New York.
20. Cyril Connolly (1903–74).
21. Cyril Connolly, *Enemies of Promise* (London, 1938).
22. CDL, *A Hope for Poetry* (London, 1934).
23. Roy Campbell (1901–57).
24. In *The New Statesman* 11/3/39.
25. In a 1971 interview with Mark Featherstone-Witty for the Durham University student newspaper.
26. TBD.
27. WHA's Letter of Introduction to *C Day-Lewis: The Poet Laureate – A Bibliography* (Chicago and London, 1968).
28. CDL to Geoffrey Grigson in Poetry Collection, Lockwood Memorial Library, Buffalo, New York.
29. In his biography of Auden (London 1981) Humphrey Carpenter produced evidence that all three had been in a BBC radio studio for a recording of 'The Modern Muse' on 18/10/38.
30. Quoted with the permission of Lady Spender from her archive.
31. Edith Sitwell (1887–1964).
32. Louis MacNeice, *The Strings Are False* (London, 1965).
33. Ibid.
34. CDL pamphlet *We Are Not Going To Do Nothing* (*The Left Review*, 1936).
35. TBD.
36. WHA to John Auden 16/9/32.
37. Dylan Thomas (1914–53).
38. In special edition of *New Verse* to mark Auden's 30th birthday.
39. Wilfred Owen (1893–1918) in 'Preface'.
40. See Note 30.
41. WHA to John Auden 11/4/32.
42. TBD.
43. In SDL's archive.
44. CDL to Rex Warner in SDL's archive.
45. In conversation with the author.
46. TBD.
47. Ibid.
48. Ibid.

Thirteen

1. Quoted in SDL, *C Day-Lewis: An English Literary Life* (London, 1980).
2. SS *World Within World* (London, 1951).
3. Undated letter from CDL to Geoffrey Grigson in Poetry Collection, Lockwood Memorial Library, Buffalo, New York.
4. See Note 1.
5. Undated letter in JDL's archive.
6. See Note 1.
7. TBD.
8. See Note 2.
9. See Note 3.
10. Edward Upward, *Remembering The Earlier Auden* (London, 1998).
11. Allen Lane (Williams) (1902–70).
12. E. H. W. Meyerstein (1889–1952).
13. CDL to E. H. W. Meyerstein in SDL archive.
14. CDL to Rex Warner in undated letter in SDL's archive.
15. See Note 3.
16. CDL to Naomi Mitchison in SDL's archive.
17. T. E. Lawrence (1888–1935).
18. Ed. Michael Roberts, *New Country* (London, 1933).
19. Ibid.
20. Ibid.
21. CDL to SS in undated letter in NS's archive.
22. John Moore (1907–67).
23. See Note 1.
24. CDL files in Public Records Office.
25. Ibid.
26. CDL to Rex Warner, undated letter in SDL's archive.
27. TBD.
28. CDL to SS 11/10/34 in NS's archive.
29. TBD.
30. In an interview with Elizabeth Jane Howard for *Queen* magazine in 1971.
31. CDL to SS 15/9/34 in NS's archive.
32. Remark reported by JDL to author.
33. WHA *Sunday Times* 4/6/1972.
34. TBD.

Fourteen

1. *PN Review*, January–February 2005.
2. CDL to SS 20/2/34 in NS's archive.
3. Gerard Manley Hopkins (1844–89).
4. Edmund Wilson (1895–1972).
5. CDL to Lady Ottoline Morrell, undated letter in Harry Ransom Center at the University of Texas.
6. Undated letter from CDL to SS in NS's archive.
7. Undated letter in JDL's archive.
8. T. E. Lawrence to CDL 16/11/34 in SDL's archive.
9. Ibid.
10. CDL to Geoffrey Grigson in Poetry Collection, Lockwood Memorial Library, Buffalo, New York.
11. Undated letter from CDL to SS in NS's archive.
12. Al Alvarez (1929–).
13. In conversation with the author.
14. CDL to SS 11/11/34 in NS's archive.
15. E. M. Forster (1879–1970).
16. J. B. Priestley (1894–1984).
17. Rebecca West (1892–1983).
18. C. S. Forester (1899–1966).
19. V. S. Pritchett (1900–1997).
20. TBD.

21. Christopher Caudwell (1907–37).
22. Christopher Marlowe (1564–93).
23. SS to CDL, undated letter in JDL's archive.
24. CDL to SS 21/4/35 in NS's archive.

Fifteen
1. TBD.
2. CDL, *Starting Point* (London, 1937).
3. CDL to SS, 1935 letter in NS's archive.
4. CDL to SS, 1934 letter in NS's archive.
5. CDL to Naomi Mitchison 27/10/35 in SDL's archive.
6. CDL to SS, undated letter in NS's archive.
7. Rupert Doone (1903–66).
8. See Richard Davenport-Hines, *Auden* (London, 1995).
9. Thomas Mann (1875–1955).
10. CDL to L. A. G. Strong, undated letter in SDL's archive.
11. Elizabeth Bowen (1899–1973).
12. Letter in SDL archive.
13. CDL, *Revolution in Writing* (London, 1935).
14. CDL file in Public Record Office.
15. Ed. Quentin Bell, *Essays, Poems and Letters of Julian Bell* (London, 1938).
16. TBD.
17. CDL to SS, undated letter in NS's archive.
18. CDL to SS 21/4/35 in NS's archive.
19. In conversation with the author.
20. SDL, *C Day-Lewis: An English Literary Life* (London, 1980).
21. Ibid.
22. SDL in conversation with the author.
23. CDL to SS 29/2/36 in NS's archive.
24. CDL, *Noah and The Waters* (London, 1936).
25. Ibid.
26. Ibid.
27. Elizabeth Jane Howard (1923–).
28. In conversation with the author.
29. Ed. J Howard Woolmer, *A Checklist of the Hogarth Press 1917–1946* (Pennsylvania, 1986).
30. Edwin Muir (1887–1959).
31. TBD.

Sixteen
1. Virginia Woolf, 'The Leaning Tower', a 1940 lecture published in *The Moment and Other Essays* (London, 1948) .
2. Ibid.
3. CDL to SS, undated letter in NS's archive.
4. Ibid.
5. Julius Lipton, *Poems of Strife* (London, 1936).
6. *Selected Poems of Robert Frost* with introductory essays by CDL, WHA, Paul Engle and Edwin Muir (London, 1936).
7. Ralph Fox (1900–1937).
8. Claud-Chabrol, *Que La Bête Meure* (1969).
9. CDL to SS 29/2/36 in NS's archive.
10. TBD.
11. Letter in collection of David Whiting.
12. TBD.
13. Ibid.
14. CDL to SS, undated letter of 1934 in NS's archive.
15. CDL file in Public Record Office.
16. Goronwy Rees (1909–79).
17. Louis MacNeice, *The Strings Are False* (London, 1965).
18. See Note 11.
19. See Note 15.

20. Letter in JDL's archive.
21. Hugh Walpole (1884–1941).
22. Arnold Bennett (1867–1931).
23. Graham Greene (1904–91).
24. CDL to SS, undated letter in NS's archive.
25. Ibid.
26. SS to CDL 26/10/38 in JDL's archive.
27. Ibid.
28. Ibid.
29. Ibid.
30. TBD.
31. See Note 15.
32. TBD.
33. CDL, *Starting Point* (London, 1937).
34. Aldous Huxley (1894–1963).
35. TBD.
36. See Stephen Tabahnick, *Fiercer Than Tigers: The Life and Works of Rex Warner* (Michigan, 2002).
37. TBD.
38. See Richard Davenport-Hines, *Auden* (London, 1995).
39. CDL, *A Hope for Poetry* (new edition, London, 1936).
40. George Barker (1913–91).
41. Clifford Dyment (1914–71).
42. David Gascoyne (1916–2002).
43. See Note 39.
44. Edward Sackville-West (1901–65).
45. In JDL's archive.
46. Ibid.
47. CDL to L. A. G. Strong, undated letter in SDL's archive.
48. TBD.
49. Ibid.
50. Ibid.

Seventeen
1. TBD.
2. In SDL's archive.
3. In correspondence with SDL, now in his archive.
4. In conversation with the author.
5. Ibid.
6. In SDL's archive.
7. CDL to SS, undated letter in NS's archive.
8. TBD.
9. In CDL's file in the Public Records Office.
10. TBD.
11. See Jeremy Treglown, *VS Pritchett: A Working Life* (London, 2004).
12. TBD.
13. See Note 9.
14. WHA, 'In Memory of WB Yeats' in *Another Time* (London, 1940).
15. Ed. J. Howard Woolmer, *A Checklist of the Hogarth Press 1917–1946* (Pennsylvania, 1986).
16. In JDL's archive.
17. Nicholas Blake, *The Private Wound* (London, 1968).
18. See Note 3.
19. See Note 4.
20. In correspondence with SDL now in his archive.
21. TBD.
22. Clifford Bax (1886–1962).
23. MDL diaries in SDL's archive.

Eighteen.
1. TBD.
2. CDL to SS, undated letter in NS's archive.

3. In JDL's archive.
4. In correspondence with the author.
5. TBD.
6. In conversation with the author.
7. CDL, 'On Translating Poetry' delivered at Exeter University 6/11/70.
8. Ibid.
9. In SDL's archive.
10. CDL file in Public Records Office.
11. Quoted in SDL, *C Day-Lewis: An English Literary Life* (London, 1980).
12. TBD.
13. Ibid.
14. CDL to SS, undated letter in NS's archive.
15. SDL in conversation with the author.
16. CDL to SS, undated letter in NS's archive.
17. Rebecca West, *Sunday Telegraph* 23/3/80.
18. John Piper (1903–92).
19. TBD.
20. In JDL's archive

Nineteen

1. Beatrix Lehmann (1903–79).
2. Wogan Philipps (1902–93).
3. SS, *World Within World* (London, 1951).
4. Selina Hastings, *Rosamond Lehmann* (London, 2002).
5. Rebecca West, *Sunday Telegraph* 23/3/80.
6. RL in conversation with Selina Hastings quoted in Selina Hastings, *Rosamond Lehmann* (London, 2002).
7. See Note 6.
8. In SDL's archive.
9. CDL file in Public Records Office.
10. Quoted in SDL, *C Day-Lewis: An English Literary Life* (London, 1980).
11. See Note 6.
12. CDL to RL, undated letter in KCC.
13. RL to Dadie Rylands 4/2/42 in KCC.
14. See Note 6.
15. E. M. Forster to Christopher Isherwood 25/7/42 in the Huntingdon Library.
16. James Richards, *Memoirs of An Unjust Fella* (London, 1980).
17. Osbert Lancaster (1908–86).
18. Kenneth Clark (1903–83).
19. See Jeremy Treglown, *VS Pritchett: A Working Life* (London, 2004).
20. See Note 16.
21. Ibid.
22. CDL to RL, undated letter in KCC.
23. See Note 6.
24. CDL to RL, undated letter in KCC.
25. Ibid.
26. Ibid.
27. Ibid.
28. Ibid.
29. Ibid.
30. Ibid.
31. Quoted in SDL, *C Day-Lewis: An English Literary Life* (London, 1980).
32. James Lees-Milne (1908–97).
33. James Lees-Milne, *Midway on the Waves* (London, 1985).
34. In conversation with the author.
35. Laurie Lee (1914–97).
36. See Valerie Grove, *Laurie Lee: The Well-Loved Stranger* (London, 1999).
37. Ibid.

Twenty

1. In the late 1950s it was only after pressure from Hugh Gaitskell, the Labour leader, that Day-Lewis was granted a repeat visa by US immigration authorities.
2. CDL to Dadie Rylands 23/2/49 in KCC.
3. Ed. Richard Crossman, *The God That Failed* (London, 1949).
4. CDL file in Public Records Office.
5. Arthur Koestler (1905–83).
6. Peggy Ashcroft (1907–91).
7. Edith Evans (1888–1976).
8. John Laurie (1897–1980).
9. In a promotional leaflet for the Apollo Society.
10. Laurie Lee to RL 26/11/43 in KCC.
11. CDL to RL, undated letter in KCC.
12. Ibid.
13. Ibid.
14. In SDL, *C Day-Lewis: An English Literary Life* (London 1980).
15. In conversation with the author.
16. Copy in SDL's archive.
17. See Note 11.
18. Ibid.
19. MDL diaries in SDL's archive.
20. TBD.
21. Appeared in 1936, the first of T. S. Eliot's *Four Quartets* (London, 1945).
22. W. B. Yeats in *The Wild Swans at Coole* (London, 1919).
23. The question was asked in a letter he was answering on his death bed.

Twenty-one

1. In conversation with the author.
2. CDL to RL, undated letter in KCC.
3. See Valerie Grove, *Laurie Lee: The Well-Loved Stranger* (London, 1999).
4. RL in conversation with Selina Hastings quoted in Selina Hastings, *Rosamond Lehmann* (London, 2002).
5. CDL to RL, undated letter in KCC.
6. See Selina Hastings, *Rosamond Lehmann* (London, 2002).
7. See Note 3.
8. CDL to RL, undated letter in KCC.
9. See Note 3.
10. Ibid.
11. See Note 4.
12. Sibyl Colefax (1874–1950).
13. See Note 6.
14. Ibid.
15. In conversation with SDL.
16. In JDL's archive.
17. CDL, *Poetry For You* (London, 1944).
18. CDL to RL, undated letter in KCC.
19. See Note 6.
20. Paul Valéry (1871–1945).
21. CDL, 'On Translating Poetry' delivered at Exeter University 6/11/70.
22. Ibid.
23. In SDL, *C Day-Lewis: An English Literary Life* (London, 1980).
24. CDL to RL, undated letter in KCC.
25. MDL diaries in SDL's archive.
26. In correspondence with SDL.
27. Quoted in Adrian Wright, *John Lehmann: A Pagan Adventure* (London, 1998).
28. CDL to RL, undated letter in KCC.
29. CDL to Elaine Hamilton 29/4/66 in SDL's archive.
30. Gillian Tindall, *Rosamond Lehmann* (London, 1985).
31. Ibid.

32. See Note 3.
33. See Note 25.

Twenty-two

1. See Valerie Grove, *Laurie Lee: The Well-Loved Stranger* (London, 1999).
2. Ibid.
3. See Selina Hastings, *Rosamond Lehmann* (London, 2002).
4. Wife of King George VI.
5. See Note 3.
6. C. S. Lewis (1898–1963).
7. CDL in his introduction to *The Poetic Image* (London, 1947).
8. CDL, *The Colloquial Element in English Poetry* (Newcastle, 1947).
9. Anthony Thwaite (1930–).
10. In SDL's archive.
11. CDL to RL, undated letter in KCC.
12. RL in conversation with Selina Hastings quoted in Selina Hastings, *Rosamond Lehmann* (London, 2002).
13. See Note 3.
14. John Lehmann, *The Whispering Gallery* (London, 1956).
15. Peter Calvocoressi, *Threading My Way* (London, 1994).
16. In conversation with the author.
17. Lytton Strachey (1880–1932).
18. Mark Twain (Samuel Langhorne Clemens) (1835–1910).
19. Compton Mackenzie (1883–1972).
20. Sylvia Townsend Warner (1893–1978).
21. In conversation with the author.
22. In SDL, *C Day-Lewis: An English Literary Life* (London, 1980).
23. Ibid.
24. MDL diaries in SDL's archive.
25. See Note 3.
26. In SDL's archive.
27. William Sansom (1912–76).
28. See Note 24.
29. Ibid.
30. See Note 1.

Twenty-three

1. In conversation with the author.
2. MDL diaries in SDL's archive.
3. See Selina Hastings, *Rosamond Lehmann* (London, 2002).
4. Ibid.
5. Ibid.
6. Ibid.
7. Ibid.
8. Ibid.
9. SDL in conversation with the author.
10. In correspondence with SDL.
11. See Note 2.
12. Bernard Berenson (1865–1959).
13. CDL to RL 14/4/48 in KCC.
14. John Lehmann, *The Whispering Gallery* (London, 1956).
15. See Note 3.
16. Bernard Berenson to RL undated 1948 letter in KCC.
17. CDL, *An Italian Visit* (London, 1953).
18. CDL to SS, undated letter in NS's archive.
19. TBD.
20. In conversation with SDL.
21. CDL to RL, undated 1948 letter in KCC.
22. In conversation with the author.
23. George Meredith (1828–1909).

24. Edward Ardizzone (1900–1979).
25. Richmal Crompton (Lamburn) (1890–1969).
26. CDL's unpublished Oxford Lectures 1951–56 in JDL's archive.
27. Ibid.
28. Emily Brontë (1818–48).
29. Kathleen Raine (1908–2003).
30. RL to Dadie Rylands 14/4/48 in KCC.
31. In conversation with the author.
32. John Masefield (1878–1967).
33. CDL file in National Archives.
34. Ibid.
35. SS, *World Within World* (London, 1951).
36. Ibid.
37. TBD.

Twenty-four

1. In conversation with the author.
2. Ibid.
3. Michael Balcon (1896–1977).
4. See Note 1.
5. Emily Dickinson (1830–86).
6. See Note 1.
7. Jacob Epstein (1880–1959).
8. RL in conversation with Selina Hastings quoted in Selina Hastings, *Rosamond Lehmann* (London, 2002).
9. Somerset Maugham (1874–1965).
10. See Selina Hastings, *Rosamond Lehmann* (London, 2002).
11. In JDL's archive.
12. Laurens van der Post (1906–96).
13. See Note 10.
14. George Eliot (1819–80).
15. CDL to RL 11/1/50 in KCC.
16. Ibid.
17. See Note 8.
18. Ibid.
19. Ibid.
20. See Note 15.
21. In JDL's archive.
22. Ibid.
23. Ibid.
24. MDL diaries in SDL's archive.
25. In JDL's archive.
26. In conversation with the author.
27. Ibid.
28. RL to Norah Smallwood 20/4/50 in KCC.
29. RL to Dadie Rylands 3/4/50 in KCC.
30. In SDL's archive.
31. In SDL, *C Day-Lewis: An English Literary Life* (London, 1980).
32. In SDL's archive.
33. In conversation with the author.
34. Ibid.
35. Ibid.

Twenty-five

1. CDL, *Selected Poems* in The Penguin Poets series (London, 1951).
2. Ibid.
3. Undated letter from CDL to JDL in JDL's archive.
4. Hugh Trevor-Roper (1914–2003).
5. Hugh Trevor-Roper to Wallace Notestein 28/1/51 in ed. Richard Davenport-Hines, *Letters from Oxford* (London, 2006).

6. Matthew Arnold (1822–88).
7. See Note 5.
8. *Observer* 24/10/51.
9. Copy in SDL's archive.
10. TBD.
11. *News Chronicle* 3/7/52.
12. See Note 3.
13. Howard Florey (1898–1968).
14. Texts in JDL's archive.
15. Ibid.
16. Ibid.
17. In conversation with the author.
18. Franta Belsky (1921–72).
19. Ronald Searle (1920–).
20. In conversation with the author.
21. SDL, *C Day-Lewis: An English Literary Life* (London, 1980).
22. See Note 3.
23. Ibid.
24. MDL diaries in SDL's archive.
25. In conversation with the author.
26. Ibid.
27. Ibid.
28. Letter in JDL's archive.
29. In conversation with the author.
30. *Observer* 24/10/51.
31. See Note 3.
32. Patric Dickinson, *C Day-Lewis: Selections from His Poetry* (London, 1967).
33. *Sunday Times* 2/9/51

Twenty-six
1. Undated letter from CDL to JDL in JDL's archive.
2. Ralph Vaughan Williams (1872–1958).
3. In conversation with the author.
4. *Sunday Times* 22/2/53.
5. CDL, *Selected Poems* in The Penguin Poets series (London, 1951).
6. Frances Partridge, *Diaries 1939–1972* (London, 2000).
7. William Blake (1757–1827).
8. SDL, *C Day-Lewis: An English Literary Life* (London, 1980).
9. Doris Lessing (1919–).
10. CDL to SS 10/12/54 in NS's archive.
11. John Heath-Stubbs (1918–2006). In his autobiography, *Hindsights* (London, 1993), Heath-Stubbs expressed his regret for this 'satirical squib', paying tribute to Day-Lewis as 'kind and courteous'.
12. Copies in SDL's archive.
13. In correspondence with the author.
14. Ibid.
15. Ivy Compton-Burnett (1884–1969).
16. See Note 1.

Twenty-seven
1. In conversation with the author.
2. Antonia White (1899–1980).
3. In conversation with the author.
4. Ibid.
5. Ibid.
6. Elizabeth Jane Howard, *Slipstream: A Memoir* (London, 2002).
7. In conversation with the author.
8. Recalled by JDL in conversation with the author.
9. In conversation with the author.
10. In an interview with Elizabeth Jane Howard for *Queen* magazine in 1971.

11. In conversation with the author.
12. CDL, *Collected Poems* (London, 1954).
13. Arthur Bliss (1891–1975).
14. In SDL's archive.
15. Ibid.
16. P. J. Kavanagh (1931–).
17. CDL to RL, undated letter in KCC archive.
18. RL note in KCC archive.
19. Recalled by JDL in conversation with the author.
20. Ibid.
21. Philip Larkin (1922–85).
22. Kingsley Amis (1922–95).
23. D. J. Enright (1920–2002).
24. Robert Conquest (1917–).
25. Donald Davie (1922–95).
26. Thom Gunn (1929–2004).
27. *Observer* 28/5/72.

Twenty-eight

1. *Sunday Times* 15/5/60.
2. CDL ed. *The Collected Poems of Wilfred Owen* (London, 1963).
3. When Balcon had asked Day-Lewis what he wanted as a birthday present he had requested 'a nymph on a plinth'.
4. In JDL's archive.
5. TBD.
6. There was also an attic floor where they housed a lodger.
7. Recalled by JDL in conversation with the author.
8. CDL, *The Lyric Impulse* (London, 1965).
9. TBD.
10. Building societies were then reluctant to lend on pre-1919 houses.
11. Correspondence held at Washington University, St Louis.
12. In conversation with the author.
13. TBD.
14. See Note 1.
15. Jonathan Fenby in conversation with the author.
16. Patrick Kavanagh (1904–67).
17. See Note 7.
18. In conversation with the author.
19. *Daily Mail* 25/2/58.
20. CDL to Elizabeth Jennings 20/11/69 in Georgetown University Library.
21. In conversation with the author.
22. In JDL's archive.
23. Ted Hughes (1930–98).
24. In SDL's archive.
25. Frances Cornford (1886–1960).
26. Ed. C. H. Rolph, *The Trial of Lady Chatterley* (Reading, 1961).
27. Ibid.
28. In conversation with the author.
29. Ibid.
30. Benjamin Britten (1913–76).
31. Donald Swann (1923–94).
32. Later performed in Guildford Cathedral.
33. In *The New York Review of Books* (1993).

Twenty-nine

1. In JDL's archive.
2. In a letter about CDL's death in JDL's archive.
3. George Mackay Brown (1921–96).
4. See Maggie Fergusson, *George Mackay Brown* (London, 2006).
5. Reynolds Stone (1909–1979).

6. Iris Murdoch (1919–99).
7. In her preface to *Thinking Faces: Photographs 1953–1979* by Janet Stone (London, 1988).
8. In SDL's archive.
9. In conversation with the author.
10. Ibid.
11. Ibid.
12. Ibid.
13. e. e. cummings (1894–1962).
14. Elaine Hamilton in SDL's archive.
15. Attia Hosain (1913–98).
16. Interview reproduced on Hosain website – www.harappa.com.
17. In conversation with the author.
18. Ibid.
19. See SDL, *C Day-Lewis: An English Literary Life* (London, 1980).
20. JDL in conversation with the author.
21. Ibid.
22. Quoted in SDL, *C Day-Lewis: An English Literary Life* (London 1980).
23. In conversation with the author.
24. NS in conversation with the author.
25. Undated letter in JDL's archive.
26. AG, *Living In Time: The Poetry of C Day-Lewis* (New York and Oxford, 1998).
27. AG in conversation with the author.
28. Ibid.
29. See Note 25.
30. CDL, *The Lyric Impulse* (London, 1965).
31. In conversation with the author.
32. Ibid.
33. See Note 30.
34. Ibid.
35. Ibid.
36. Ibid.
37. JDL to AG 29/12/64 in AG's archive.
38. Ibid.
39. CDL to AG 11/1/65 in AG's archive.
40. Ibid.

Thirty

1. Recalled by JDL in conversation with the author.
2. Quoted in SDL, *C Day-Lewis: An English Literary Life* (London, 1980).
3. See Note 1.
4. See *C Day-Lewis Reads C Day-Lewis*, audio recording from 1967 issued in 1974.
5. In JDL's archive.
6. CDL, *The Lyric Impulse* (London, 1965).
7. *Guardian* 25/10/65.
8. See Note 2.
9. Ibid.
10. Antonia Byatt (1936–).
11. Dame Antonia Byatt decided not to speak to the author about her close friendship with Day-Lewis. 'My only comment,' she wrote, 'is that I might have been part of his list of mistresses in his mind, but I was not his mistress.'
12. See Note 1.
13. Ibid.
14. See Note 6.
15. See Note 1.
16. Ibid.
17. CDL to AG 25/12/69 in AG's archive.
18. In SDL's archive.
19. Undated letter from CDL to JDL in JDL's archive.
20. Ibid.
21. In SDL's archive.

22. See Note 11.
23. See Constance Babington-Smith, *John Masefield: A Life* (Oxford, 1978).
24. *Sunday Express* 14/5/67

Thirty-one
1. CDL to Noel Annan 11/1/68 in KCC archive.
2. Recalled by JDL in conversation with the author.
3. John Dryden (1631–1700).
4. Geoffrey Chaucer (c.1343–1400).
5. Edmund Spenser (c.1552–99).
6. WHA in Letter of Introduction to *C Day-Lewis: The Poet Laureate – A Bibliography* (Chicago and London, 1968).
7. Bernard Levin, *The Pendulum Years* (London, 1970).
8. *Evening News* 2/1/68.
9. *Sun* 15/1/68.
10. Nahum Tate (1652–1715). Poet Laureate from 1692.
11. In SDL's archive.
12. Robert Bridges (1844–1930). Poet Laureate from 1913.
13. See Note 9.
14. *Times* 18/1/68.
15. *Guardian* 21/11/68.
16. Charles Causley (1917–2003).
17. Recalled by JDL in conversation with the author.
18. SDL, *C Day-Lewis: An English Literary Life* (London, 1980).
19. In conversation with the author.
20. In SDL's archive.
21. In conversation with the author.
22. Ibid.
23. *Times Literary Supplement* 6/11/70.
24. Samuel Hynes, *The Auden Generation* (London, 1976).
25. Roy Fuller (1912–91).
26. Roy Fuller to CDL 12/11/70 in John Fuller's archive.
27. Ibid.

Thirty-two
1. CDL to AG 9/1/72 in AG's archive.
2. In SDL's archive.
3. In conversation with the author.
4. CDL to RL 25/3/72 in KCC archive.
5. Recalled by JDL in conversation with the author.
6. CDL, *A Lasting Joy* (London, 1973).
7. See Note 5.
8. See Note 6.
9. In conversation with the author.
10. Ibid.
11. Elizabeth Jane Howard, *Slipstream: A Memoir* (London, 2002).
12. In conversation with the author.
13. See Note 5.
14. *Observer* 28/5/72.
15. Ibid.
16. *Sunday Times* 2/6/72.
17. In JDL's archive.
18. See Note 5

Epilogue
1. TBD.
2. *New Statesman* 25/9/72.
3. *Sun* 15/1/68.
4. *PN Review* May–June 1998.
5. *Independent* 23/5/92.

6. In *The New York Review of Books* (1993).
7. *PN Review* January–February 2005.
8. *Times Literary Supplement* 3/6/05.
9. John Betjeman to Elizabeth Jane Howard 9/11/72 among her papers in the Huntingdon Library.

Bibliography

BY C DAY-LEWIS

Poetry Collections by C Day-Lewis
Beechen Vigil (1925)
Country Comets (1928)
Transitional Poem (1929)
From Feathers to Iron (1931)
The Magnetic Mountain (1933)
Collected Poems 1929–1933 (1935)
A Time To Dance (1935)
Noah and The Waters (1936)
Overtures to Death (1938)
Poems in Wartime (1940)
Selected Poems (1940)
Word Over All (1943)
Poems 1943–1947 (1948)
Collected Poems 1929–1936 (1949)
Selected Poems (1951)
An Italian Visit (1953)
Collected Poems (1954)
Pegasus and Other Poems (1957)
The Gate and Other Poems (1962)
Requiem for the Living (US only 1964)
The Room and Other Poems (1965)
The Whispering Roots (1970)

Fiction
Dick Willoughby (1933)
The Friendly Tree (1936)
Starting Point (1937)
Child of Misfortune (1939)
The Otterbury Incident (1948)

Non-Fiction
A Hope for Poetry (1934)
Revolution in Writing (1935)
We're Not Going To Do Nothing (1936)
Poetry For You (1944)
The Poetic Image (1947)

The Buried Day (1960)
The Lyric Impulse (1965)

Translations
The Georgics of Virgil (1940)
The Graveyard by the Sea (1945)
The Aeneid of Virgil (1952)
The Eclogues of Virgil (1963)

Anthologies
Oxford Poetry 1927 (with W. H. Auden) (1927)
The Echoing Green (1937)
Anatomy of Oxford (with Charles Fenby) (1938)
A New Anthology of Modern Verse (with L. A. G. Strong) (1941)
The Chatto Book of Modern Poetry (with John Lehmann) (1956)
A Book of English Lyrics (1961)
A Lasting Joy (1973)

Crime Fiction as Nicholas Blake
A Question of Proof (1935)
Thou Shell of Death (1936)
There's Trouble Brewing (1937)
The Beast Must Die (1938)
The Smiler with the Knife (1939)
Malice in Wonderland (1940)
The Case of the Abominable Snowman (1941)
Minute for Murder (1947)
Head of a Traveller (1949)
The Dreadful Hollow (1953)
The Whisper in the Gloom (1954)
A Tangled Web (1956)
End of Chapter (1957)
A Penknife in My Heart (1958)
The Widow's Cruise (1959)
The Worm of Death (1961)
The Deadly Joker (1963)
The Sad Variety (1964)
The Morning After Death (1966)
The Private Wound (1968)

Posthumous Collections
Selected Poems (ed. Ian Parsons) (1977)
Posthumous Poems (ed. Jill Balcon) (1979)
Complete Poems (ed. Jill Balcon) (1992)
Selected Poems (ed. Jill Balcon) (2004)

About Day-Lewis
Clifford Dyment, C Day-Lewis (1955)
Ed. Patric Dickinson, C Day-Lewis: Selections from His Poetry (1967)
Compiled Geoffrey Handley-Taylor and Timothy d'Arch Smith, C Day-Lewis: The Poet
    Laureate – A Bibliography (1968)
Sean Day-Lewis, C Day-Lewis: An English Literary Life (1980)
Albert Gelpi, Living in Time: The Poetry of C Day-Lewis (1998)

Other reading
Peter Alexander, *William Plomer* (1989)
Al Alvarez, *Where Did It All Go Right* (1999)
Humphrey Carpenter, *W.H. Auden: A Biography* (1981)
David Daiches, *Poetry and the Modern World: A Study of Poetry in England Between 1900 and 1939* (1940)
Richard Davenport-Hines, *Auden* (1995)
Valerie Grove, *Laurie Lee: The Well-Loved Stranger* (1999)
Selina Hastings, *Rosamond Lehmann* (2002)
Rosamond Lehmann's Album (1985)
Peter Parker, *Isherwood: A Life Revealed* (2005)
Miranda Seymour, *Robert Graves: Life on The Edge* (1995)
Ed. Robin Skelton, *Poetry of The Thirties* (1964)
Jon Stallworthy, *Louis MacNeice* (1995)
John Sutherland, *Stephen Spender: The Authorized Biography* (2004)
Stephen Tabahnick, *Fiercer Than Tigers: The Life and Works of Rex Warner* (2002)
Adrian Wright, *John Lehmann: A Pagan Adventure* (1998)
Philip Ziegler, *Rupert Hart-Davis: Man of Letters* (2004)

Acknowledgements

This book was born of a chance encounter in a BBC radio studio in early 2004 with C Day-Lewis's widow, the actress Jill Balcon. We were both talking on air about the effects of the death of one's parents. After the broadcast, we carried on talking, but now of her late husband's poetry which I had long admired. From that first chance meeting, others followed and eventually this book.

Since the death of C Day-Lewis, Jill Balcon has worked tirelessly as editor, literary executor and performer to ensure his work remains widely available and heard. She brings a unique insight to the task. No one else can match her knowledge and enduring feel for the poetry. She was often the first person to see the hand-written drafts of some of his best remembered poems.

Her support, encouragement, assistance and hospitality during the researching and writing of this book have greatly improved the finished result, though the book's conclusions (and mistakes) are all my own work. Should Jill have been tempted to try to impose her views, her late husband provided in his poem 'The Widow Interviewed' (*The Room*, 1965) such an amusing but unattractive portrait (said to be inspired in part by Edwin Muir's widow, Willa, and partly by Edward Thomas's, Helen) that she would surely have thought better of it.

> 'The Poet' (well, that's the way her generation
> Talked) 'the Poet wrote these for me when first –'
> (She said, touching the yellowed manuscripts
> Like a blind girl gentling a young man's hair)
> – 'When first we were betrothed. I have kept them:
> The rest I had to sell'.

Other members of the Day-Lewis family – Cecil's sons Sean, Nicholas and Daniel and his daughter Tamasin – have all been generous with their time and help. Sean in particular allowed me to look through various papers and transcripts of interviews conducted while writing his 1980 book about his father with people now beyond the reach of a tape recorder. He also helped me retrace his father's footsteps on the Devon–Dorset border.

Professor Al Gelpi and his wife Barbara have generously shared their considerable knowledge and memories of C Day-Lewis. So to have Christine Caldwell, Peter Calvocoressi, Peter and Louise Cochrane, Jonathan Fenby,

351

Phillida Gili, Elizabeth Jane Howard, Lord Hutchinson QC, Viscount St Vincent, Lady Spender and the late Hallam Tennyson. Richard Davenport-Hines, biographer of W. H. Auden, has been especially generous with his time and expertise.

I am grateful too for the assistance given by Al Alvarez, Michael Arditti, Ronald Blythe, Stephen Bristow, Jane Bown, Kay Dunbar, Orna Ellickson, Dr Simon Eliot and his staff at Sherborne School, Jane Ferguson, John Fuller, Kerry Gill Pryde, Valerie Grove, Shama Habibullah, Waris Hussein Habibullah, Diana Hall, Michael Harvey, Selina Hastings, Matthew Hickman, Fergus Hoban, Liz Hunt, James Huntington-Whiteley, Graham Johnson, Anthony Lejeune, Carolyn Losseff, Frank Manning, Jerome Monahan, Anita Money, Andrew Motion, Sara Scott, Stephen Stuart-Smith, Stephen Tabahnick, Andrew Tuck, Salley Vickers and David Whiting.

Particular mention must go to Dennis Wood of Edwinstowe who tirelessly tracked down those amongst his fellow parishioners who had memories of the days when the Revd Frank Day-Lewis was their vicar.

As ever my agent, Derek Johns, has been a calm, constant and resourceful guide, along with his assistant Anjali Pratap. Carolyn Armitage, Andrew Walby and Robin Baird-Smith at Continuum have shown great faith in the book through all its stages.

I am particularly grateful to the Society of Authors for awarding me an Elizabeth Longford Grant to support the research and writing of this biography. The Elizabeth Longford Grants are sponsored in affectionate memory of the noted and much-missed biographer by her grand-daughter, Flora Fraser, and Flora's husband, Peter Soros.

And to my family. My children Kit and Orla have lived and breathed C Day-Lewis for almost three years now without complaining. He's as much part of their lives as Dr Who. And my wife, Siobhan, has lovingly counselled, encouraged and – as my first reader, working her way through the emerging manuscript – said much which has made me think afresh, in greater depth and more clearly, a gift which she brings to everything about our life together.

Index

The abbreviation CDL stands for C Day-Lewis; NB stands for Nicholas Blake, the pen-name under which Day-Lewis wrote his crime fiction.